Formerly Associate Editor of the L[...]
magazine, Nick Foulkes writes reg[...]
Country Life, High Life and the Mai[...]
and Day'. He is also a contributing editor at GQ.

'Nobody with the slightest empathy for [this] period and its values and aspirations should fail to read this book. Foulkes's complete understanding of d'Orsay's various contexts, social and historical, his own stylistic dash and polish and the flawless pace of his high-stepping narrative make this as perfect a memorial to the incomparable Count as d'Orsay could possibly have desired' *Literary Review*

'Foulkes has done well to reveal the character of d'Orsay and his lost age, and gives us many insights into the mindset of a louche, generous, arrogant but above all genuine gentleman. His interest in the era is infectious, his writing is easily read and carries with it a clarity of which the Count would surely have approved. Bravo' *Erotic Review*

'His judgements – and in particular his assessment of d'Orsay as a dandy and an artist – are acute' *Country Life*

'This witty, well-researched book is written with bounce and due elegance. You can almost whiff the great dandy's favourite cologne' *The Field*

'Foulkes tells this strange story with admirable *élan* and confidently handles an impressive cast' *Daily Telegraph*

'Wickedly entertaining and highly recommended' *Gay Times*

'Exhilarating and thoroughly entertaining reading' *Daily Mail*

SCANDALOUS SOCIETY

*Passion and Celebrity
in the
Nineteenth Century*

NICK FOULKES

An *Abacus* Book

First published as *The Last of the Dandies* in Great Britain
in 2003 by Little, Brown

This edition published by Abacus in 2004

Copyright © Nick Foulkes 2003

The moral right of the author has been asserted.

A CIP catalogue record for this book
is available from the British Library.

ISBN 0 349 11547 8

Typeset in Fournier by M Rules
Printed and bound in Great Britain by
Bookmarque Ltd, Croydon, Surrey

To Alexandra, Max and Freddie

CONTENTS

PREFACE

I CAME ACROSS COUNT D'ORSAY QUITE BY ACCIDENT IN 1997. I
had been sent a copy of Colin McDowell's entertaining book, *Man of
Fashion*, to review and amongst a diverse array of male icons, including Buffalo Bill and Basil Rathbone, McDowell gave a charming pen
portrait of the enigmatic charismatic Count d'Orsay.

D'Orsay dominated fashion during the 1830s and 1840s, scandal-
ising the part of polite society that he did not charm. A number of
elements fascinated me about him. His dress sense aside, he painted,
he sculpted, he gambled, he shot, he rode, he involved himself in the
literary and political life of the day. It is fair to assume that he had
affairs with his patron, the free-spending Earl of Blessington, and the
earl's wife, prominent hostess Lady Blessington. He also married
Lord Blessington's daughter.

D'Orsay lived at a fascinating time in European and particularly
English history, an interstitial phase slotted in between the elegant
brutality of the Regency and the high principles of the Victorian era.
Moreover, in many ways he was the first modern celebrity; despite his
many accomplishments, he was primarily famous for being famous
and his reputation was inflated by the nascent popular, gossipy press
of the day.

And yet beneath the reputation; the numerous daily changes of
scented gloves; the story of a solid-gold dressing case that could only

be carried by two men; the roll call of famous friends; and the avalanche of debt that finally engulfed him, there is d'Orsay the man – as kind, generous and intelligent as he was vain, self-centred and profligate.

I very much enjoyed learning about him, his contemporaries and his way of life. I must also confess to a little bit of what might be called method-writing: inspired by d'Orsay's example of scented gloves I have taken to dabbing my watchstraps with Caron's Coup de Fouet and I've even purchased a white buckskin greatcoat, of which I am sure the count would have approved.

D'Orsay has been the subject of three biographies in English. The first, written by Teignmouth Shore in the early twentieth century, is an evocative, lively read in which it is possible to sense the author's frustration at being tantalisingly close in time to his subject. The second, written by Michael Sadleir, is really a joint account of the lives of Lady Blessington and Count d'Orsay, in which Lady Blessington's less than spotless reputation is rehabilitated at the expense of Count d'Orsay. The third, published in 1952 by Willard Connely, is a painstaking account of the count's life a century after he died. My research has been illuminated by all three of these books.

I would also like to thank a trio of researchers for helping me to assemble a mountain of d'Orsay-related ephemera, some of which has until now remained unpublished. Two of them, Andrea Wulf and Emma Gieben Gamal, have been so put off research that they have since embarked on careers as authors. So far the third member of my research team, Sophie Robinson, has been able to resist a career as an author and as well as helping with research has acted as an Argus-eyed proofreader.

At Little, Brown I would like to thank my editor, Alan Samson, for his enthusiasm, his erudition and his guidance; Catherine Hill for her patience; Linda Silverman for her picture research; and Peter James for his excellent copyediting skills.

Without my agent, Luigi Bonomi, this book would never have been written. Luigi is a very gifted man, but if you do not enjoy this book as much as you hoped you should take it up with him – he is essentially the one to blame for nudging me in the direction of historical biography.

I would like to thank those of my friends and family who have taken the time to wade through early drafts of the book and offer their comments: in particular I am grateful to Jean Pierre Martel for his insight and historical knowledge of the decorative arts, and Count Franz Larosée for reading an early draft of this book and supplying the Breitling chronograph used for timekeeping during its writing.

When the life of this intriguing nineteenth-century dandy became too stifling, I would seek out Edward Sahakian of Davidoff of London and enjoy a cigar and a coffee there, or go and visit Andrea Riva at his eponymous restaurant. Thank you both for your patience and for refraining to ask exactly when I might finish this book.

Many libraries, county record offices, institutions and individuals have been very helpful with material and I hope that they are all properly acknowledged in the notes and bibliography. I am particularly grateful to Edwina Ehrman, and to Leslie du Cane for being so generous with his quite remarkable archive relating to Notting Hill and its short-lived racecourse.

Others I would like to thank for their support and help include the Hon. Christopher Gilmour; Dr Simon Thurley; the staff of the London Library; the staff of the British Library; the Marquess of Londonderry; the Duke of Wellington; the Duke of Beaufort; Comte Armand-Ghislain de Maigret; Hubert de Bodard at the Association d'Entraide de la Noblesse Française; Terry Haste of Huntsman; Anne-Marie Colban of Charvet; Philippe Louineau of the Mairie de Chambourcy; John Ceriale; and Oliver Peyton.

I should add that, as far as I know, the d'Orsay who is the subject of this book has nothing to do with the Musée d'Orsay in Paris. The

Musée d'Orsay was a railway station built on the site of the Palais d'Orsay, which was named after the Quai d'Orsay, construction of which commenced in the early eighteenth century. It was completed by Napoleon and was named after Charles Boucher, Seigneur d'Orsay, who had been Provost of the Merchants when the first part of the Quai was built.

Finally, while I have tried to make this book as accurate as possible, I hope that you will forgive any mistakes I have made and most importantly that you will find it a good read. It is an excellent story, and I hope I have done it justice.

CHAPTER ONE

A Child of Empire

'ALL HIS SYMPATHIES DURING THE WHOLE OF HIS LIFE WERE with the Bonaparte family,' wrote one of the Count d'Orsay's closest friends.

> The ardent enthusiasm inspired in his boyish mind by Napoleon (whose page he was to have been), kept possession of his mind in after years. So far was the feeling carried, that at the entrance of the Bourbons into Paris, though but a mere boy, he betook himself to a retired part of the house, that he might not see or hear the rejoicings that were made for the downfall of Napoleon and his Empire, and gave vent to his feelings in tears and strong expressions of repugance to the new regime.[1]

Napoleon and his personal mythology had a prolonged and powerful impact on the mind of the precocious Parisian youth Alfred d'Orsay. To the end of his life he remained at heart a Bonapartist. It was no coincidence that in the intervening decades d'Orsay's path was crossed in various European cities by some of the greatest names in the Napoleonic firmament: Ney, Walewski, Borghese, Beauharnais, Madame Mère, Joseph, Jérôme, Léon. It could be said that his defining characteristic – his role as the last of the dandies – owed much to the Empire Style.

The date most widely accepted for the birth of Alfred d'Orsay is 4 September 1801. However, perhaps because his sister Ida would have had to be conceived almost immediately after his birth and, even then, her birthdate of 19 June 1802 would make her premature, one of d'Orsay's biographers gives the date of Alfred's birth as 4 February.[2] February would seem to be correct, given that Disraeli's letters of the 1830s would point to d'Orsay himself celebrating his birthday on this day.[3] Moreover, 4 February is the birthdate carved on his tombstone. His tomb, in the cemetery of the small suburban town of Chambourcy outside Paris, raises another question about his birth: while most sources state that he was born in 1801, the year carved in the pale marble of his memorial is 1800.

If he was indeed born in February 1800, he would have been only a few months short of his fifth birthday at the time of Napoleon's coronation as emperor in Notre Dame, on 2 December 1804. At that age this event, no mere royal pageant, but an imperial spectacle, would have made a lasting impression. For almost two hours Napoleon and Josephine, propped up on white velvet cushions, drove around Paris in a gilded coach pulled by four pairs of horses in red harness. At midday, Napoleon, in purple robes embroidered with the letter N surrounded by laurels, advanced along the nave of Notre Dame with Josephine at his side and a total of eight train-bearers behind them. The ensuing three-hour ceremony, with its quasi-medieval rituals, the choir chanting in Latin and the cabal of extravagantly clad Napoleonic henchmen clustered around the altar, was a skilful piece of propaganda intended to dazzle and impress his subjects.

Rather like the setpiece Nuremberg rallies of Hitler in the

Cathedral of Light created by Albert Speer in the 1930s, this was a theatrical masterpiece, the sumptuous nature and scale of which is best captured by David's painting of the event. It was an act of *de haut en bas* bonding with his people, with Napoleon borrowing symbols from the imperial past of Rome and the chivalric past of France to impress a congregation of thousands drawn from all parts of the nation. Even those who were not among the crowds inside the cathedral or lining the streets of Paris during the day and then gathering to marvel at the brightly illuminated Tuileries Palace in the evening, soon got to hear about it.

From a Corsican nonentity, an obscure artillery officer, Napoleon Bonaparte had, at the age of thirty-five, become the most powerful man in Europe. Ingres, in his overblown 1806 portrait of Napoleon I seated on his imperial throne, depicts him as little short of a god, with sceptre, hand of justice, Charlemagne's sword, fur-trimmed robes and imperial laurels. As Alfred d'Orsay was growing up, Napoleon was creating a new world order. He established an imperium that made the efforts of two great empire-builders of the eighteenth century, Catherine the Great of Russia and Frederick the Great of Prussia, seem like the work of fumbling amateurs. Even in the following century neither Stalin nor Hitler would rival the achievements of Napoleon; both were in their forties when they became leaders of their respective countries (Napoleon was just thirty when he became first consul).

What was more, this empire had risen with astonishing speed out of the chaos and destruction of the French Revolution. With the storming of the Bastille in 1789, France had embarked on a bloody period of political experiment, administrative upheaval and civil strife, to which (from 1792) was added a series of expensive foreign wars against coalitions of neighbouring countries. In 1793 the king and queen, Louis XVI and Marie Antoinette were executed, and a new organ of revolutionary government calling itself the Committee of

Public Safety unleashed its Terror on the French people, with ferocious resort to the guillotine. Disintegration and famine ensued, from which France was rescued in 1795 by the more stable regime instituted by the Directory. It was against the Directors that Napoleon launched his *coup d'état* four years later, before embarking on the creation of his empire.

Europe had not seen anything like it since the Romans. By the second decade of the nineteenth century, Napoleon effectively ran Europe from the Baltic to the Mediterranean and from the Atlantic to the River Vistula. He incarcerated Pope Pius VII and switched his prisoner around between Florence, Grenoble, Avignon, Nice, Savona and Fontainebleau. He considered moving the Vatican to Paris. He installed his brothers on the thrones of Naples and the Two Sicilies, Spain and Holland. He made his generals into marshals and then gave them grand titles and great estates. He created federations, kingdoms and principalities around Europe as he wished. His eponymous Code Napoléon was the rulebook by which this enormous heterogeneous empire was run. His power seemed absolute, his Grande Armée invincible. And in September 1812 he entered the suburbs of Moscow. A sergeant of the Old Guard recorded the moment thus:

> The sun was reflected on all the domes, spires and gilded palaces. Many capitals have I seen, such as Paris, Berlin, Warsaw, Vienna and Madrid; they only produced an ordinary impression on me. But this was quite different: the effect was to me – in fact, to everyone – magical. At that sight troubles, dangers, fatigues, privations were all forgotten, and the pleasure of entering Moscow absorbed all our minds.[4]

Alfred d'Orsay grew up amid the glamour of Napoleon's Paris. He was enrolled at the Pension Hix, a famous if austere academy on the Rue Matignon, where pupils followed the curriculum of the Lycée

Bonaparte. Among his schoolfriends was the young Alfred Victor, Count de Vigny. Vigny would later achieve fame, if not happiness, as the author of the romantic drama *Chatterton*, which described the tragic fate of the young British poet who poisoned himself with arsenic. Such a melancholic theme was typical of Vigny, who suffered many setbacks in life – domestic misery and a failure to enter Parliament are just two of them – but his school experiences seem to have been the first and most bitter of his disappointments. Vigny's disgust at the black bread and stagnant water served through railings by a miserable, malicious porter would stay with him until his death.

But according to Vigny's biographer of 1910, Ernest Dupuy, the biggest unhappiness came with the discovery that his fellow schoolboys were hateful, envious, iniquitous, tyrannical and cruel, much in the way that the majority of mankind would later appear to him. He had hitherto enjoyed a protected childhood in a household of intellectual and aristocratic refinement. The Academy of M. Hix was quasi-military in character and imperial in style, its charges were the sons of senators, generals and princes of the Confederation of the Rhine. It seems to have been something of a melting pot of the Empire and doubtless, had the Napoleonic regime prospered, establishments such as the Pension Hix would have been expected to churn out generation after generation of imperial administrators and soldiers, much in the way that the English public school system functioned on behalf of the British Empire.

'Are you noble?' children would ask him, and when he answered that he was, they chased him. Vigny records perpetual fights with pupils 'weaker than him in spirit, yet stronger in body and older'. Moreover he was tormented by the realisation that 'I was forced to hide what I knew and lower myself in the opinion of my masters to live in a friendly fashion with the pupils.'[5] He was later to write that attempting to replace the family environment with a school, which he stigmatised as 'evil and the source of incalculable vice and depravity', was a monstrous abuse.[6] He found some solace, however, in the company of an extraordinarily good-looking boy four years his junior: the young Count d'Orsay. His looks were already apparently breathtaking, and, when writing about his schoolfriend many years later in 1852, Vigny's lyrical description has something of the love letter about it.

'In my classes I catch glimpses of and am acquainted with a tall, willowy boy who does little or no work. His hair is a mass of ringlets, he resembles Alban's lovers and those whom Girodet painted at the breast, shoulders and on the knees of Venus, Galatea and the Danaides. This is Alfred d'Orsay.

His sister is less feminine and delicate in her bearing than the young boy Alfred. His untouched rosebud lips, which he should preserve as such forever, glow like those of a young English girl when she parts them and lets you glimpse her pearl white teeth and small tongue, which enunciates *th*.'[7]

There is much more in this vein: how d'Orsay enjoyed sketching clothes; how his family were happy to see in the young count and his sister Ida the living image of the then new and fashionable painting by Gérard, *Amour et Psyche*; how elegant he was; how Grecian his body; how delicate his profile. Vigny's account ascribes a sensuality to the young man that, particularly in his depiction of the mouth and the image of the young Englishwoman's tongue, borders on the erotic. He captures a sexual ambiguity and a feminine quality that were to stay with d'Orsay throughout his life. Indeed a painting of the sixteen-year-old count shows a pretty, soft-skinned, curly-haired cherub, the sort of epicene youth who might have appealed to Caravaggio.

D'Orsay and Vigny were to maintain a friendship that was to last throughout their adult lives. In d'Orsay Vigny had found someone who shared nobility, an aristocratic bearing and most importantly a multitude of interests and precocious tastes that ranged far beyond the gloomy, gated schoolyard.

While nominally educated *chez* Hix, d'Orsay's real schooling took place amid the glamour and cosmopolitan sparkle of his grand-mother's house, the Hôtel Craufurd. It was here for example that he met and dazzled Gronow, a young officer in Wellington's army of occupation. On first meeting the chestnut-haired teenaged count, Gronow was struck by his 'remarkable beauty and pleasing manners', adding that 'when I first knew him, he might have served as a model for a statuary'. According to Gronow the young count really did have the body of a Greek god, as 'beautiful as the Apollo Belvedere in his outward form'.

The Hôtel Craufurd provided a unique environment in which the gifted young count's talent and charisma could flower. D'Orsay's grandmother, the daughter of a tailor from Lucca, had begun her adult life as an attractive and sexually magnetic dancer called Anne Franchi who toured Europe with a theatrical company at a time when the term 'actress' was almost synonymous with prostitute. An eighteenth-century adventuress, she had married a member of her acting troupe, but by 1768 this liaison was behind her. The 1770s saw her set up by the Duke of Württemberg. After bearing two of his children, one of whom was d'Orsay's mother, she left him, moved to Koblenz and took up with the Chevalier d'Aigremont. She followed him to Paris, only to drop him in favour of a rich Irishman called Sullivan, a leading figure in the East India Company. Sullivan whisked her off to India, whence she returned with the immensely wealthy Quintin Craufurd, who had gone to the East in his teens, and spent twenty years accumulating a fortune, which he returned to Europe to spend. Something of *un homme sérieux manqué* while in the East, Craufurd spent his time and money after the East India Company travelling around Europe, assembling works of art and writing improving books such as a history of the Hindus and another of the Bastille.

He had been a frequent visitor to the court of Louis XVI and Marie Antoinette. As well as achieving success as scholar, author and courtier, he also managed what the actor, the German ruler, the French chevalier and the Irish merchant prince had not: he kept his Italian mistress Anne Franchi interested, in spite of the repeated attentions of former admirers. However, Craufurd's involvement in a plot to smuggle the king and queen out of Revolutionary France resulted in his exile from Paris, first to Brussels and then to Vienna. Eventually the couple legitimised their relationship of almost twenty years. Given his Protestant faith, her Catholicism and possibly her reputation as a bolter, their marriage was solemnised no fewer than three times: once at the British Embassy, next at the English Church and lastly by a Catholic priest at Saint-Germain-en-Laye.

Now legally Madame Craufurd, the former Anne Franchi set about establishing a serious salon, of which Alfred and his sister Ida were a chief attraction. Her theatrical past was of use when it came to stage-managing the appearance of the young count and countess.

It was the life of a child star in the salons of early-nineteenth-century Paris that began to shape the character and tastes of the Count d'Orsay. Moreover it was a life formed by the company of women. With his father Albert, a general in Napoleon's conquering armies, off on the campaign trail, a distant figure, his grandfather locked in his library, working on one or other of his historical treatises, it fell to his grandmother and mother to mould the young prodigy. Both were strong and ambitious women – d'Orsay's mother is spoken of as *dame d'honneur* to Napoleon's nymphomaniac sister Pauline Borghese.[8] There was a tradition in Paris of powerful women leading influential lives: women like the ravishing Madame Récamier, the seductive Madame Tallien and the exotic Creole *femme fatale* Josephine Beauharnais.

Life in the upper echelons of imperial Paris was certainly sumptuous. Modelled on Rome and stuffed with art treasures looted from numerous campaigns around Europe, Napoleon's Paris was intended, like Hitler's Berlin remodelled by Albert Speer, as the warlord's ultimate trophy — indeed as the capital city of the world. It was a city of architectural *grandes gestes*. Napoleon cut through the warren-like jumble of alleys and streets with the splendid avenue that is the Rue de Rivoli, and also laid down the Rue Castiglione, which turns into the Rue de la Paix. He introduced gas lighting. He produced the stone embankments or *quais* along the Seine. He put three bridges across the river. And of course he commissioned the Arc de Triomphe.

His rule also saw the reintroduction into domestic décor of gold, ormolu and giltwood, an addition that must have been especially noticeable in a country grown shabby through years of revolution. Every clock, vase, console table, day bed, cheval glass, commode, cupboard, armchair and sofa that could take it, and several that really could not, were embellished with gold or gilt-bronze mounts. It was in effect Napoleon who re-established state patronage of the decorative arts in a way that had not been seen in France since the days of Louis XVI.

In his biography of the Emperor of the French, Vincent Cronin makes the point that 'Napoleon encouraged rich decoration as a way of helping manufacturers: one of his reasons for restoring the court, he said, was to provide a market for France's many luxury craftsmen.'[9] Certainly Napoleon, the greatest warrior of the time, was not averse to a little bit of conspicuous consumption: in one year alone, 1810, he ordered 162 bottles of a neroli-based eau de cologne from Chardin, the parfumier.[10] Why wear a dressing-gown of wool when one could be swathed in one of swansdown? Why use a razor with a steel or bone handle when there is mother of pearl to be had? After all, personal effects had to be in keeping with the sense of classical grandeur and imperial permanence imparted by ever more solid, massive furnishings decorated with a profusion of classical motifs. Lyres, laurels, arrows, fasces, wreaths, anthemia, amphorae, palms and of course eagles found their way on to everything from embroidered fabrics to chests of drawers.

Not content with ransacking mythology for forms with which

they could decorate their wares, the furniture makers and goldsmiths of the age invented new pieces based on artefacts that had been excavated from archaeological sites. Typical of such stylistic neologisms was the athénienne, a multi-purpose item that might be a washstand, incense burner or, in the case of the most celebrated athénienne of all, a baptismal font for Napoleon's son, the King of Rome. Despite its distinctly Grecian nomenclature, the King of Rome's athénienne was a copy of a tripod discovered during excavations at Pompeii. No matter, such cross-cultural borrowings were all part of the heady cocktail that would become known as the Empire Style. Furniture took on an anthropomorphic tone: chair legs exploded into elaborate caryatids supporting armrests, table legs appeared as sphinxes resting on leonine paws. Pedestal tables, or guéridons as they were known, often resembled the huge forepart of, say, a griffon, with a marble slab lying across the top. It was in this fantastical world, where the entire bestiary of mythology leaped out from everyday objects such as chairs and tables, that the precocious count's taste was nurtured.

And then within the space of eighteen months the world that had created this gilded fantasy was swept away. Despite the morale-boosting heroics of Marshal Ney, named 'the bravest of the brave' by Napoleon, the retreat from Moscow in the winter of 1812 was a fiasco. The Russian campaign dealt the hitherto all-powerful, battle-hardened Grande Armée a blow from which it would not recover: almost six hundred thousand French troops had died, deserted or been captured. From then on Napoleon would only be able to field an army composed largely of raw, unseasoned troops. The campaign had also cost the lives of two hundred thousand horses, seriously impairing the future effectiveness of the French cavalry.

By the end of 1813, Wellington, once dismissed by Napoleon as a 'sepoy general' – an allusion to the early years of his career in India – had crossed the Pyrenees into France after defeating several French armies during the seven-year Peninsular War. Paris capitulated at the end of March 1814, and Napoleon abdicated on 6 April. A month later Louis XVIII entered Paris as king of France, twenty-one years after his elder brother Louis XVI had been guillotined. If not quite a puppet monarch, he was nevertheless backed by Britain, Russia, Prussia and Austria, the Allies who had defeated Napoleon. The restoration of the Bourbon monarchy was an indication that, with Napoleon on his way to exile on Elba, a return to republicanism was not to be tolerated.

CHAPTER TWO

The Precocious Parisian

HAD THE INCOMING KING BEEN DYNAMIC AND GLAMOROUS, youthful and vigorous, like d'Orsay himself, perhaps the young count might have found the transition from Empire to mere monarchy easier to bear. Sadly Louis XVIII was not an inspiring figure. Almost sixty years old, fat and rather boring, he had difficulty walking. His ideology was as sluggish and uninspiring as he was. He firmly believed in the divine right of kings and, although he agreed to a charter safeguarding many of the freedoms secured during the Revolution and took a firm grasp of the nation's finances, he committed a couple of significant propaganda blunders.

He replaced the national flag, the tricolour, under which France had conquered much of Europe, with a white flag covered with blue fleurs-de-lis. The heraldic lily had appeared on the old French royal coat of arms; and those well versed in heraldry must have been reminded of the reign of Louis VII in the twelfth century, when the national standard was liberally covered with the device. He snubbed veterans of the Napoleonic Wars and further wounded the national pride by retiring many of the officers who had marched under the tri-colour. He went on to add to the insult by reforming various Royalist regiments and installing some six thousand aristocratic émigrés in positions within the army, even though many of them had little or no military experience.

It was a confusing period, during which loyalties were tangled, stretched and divided. The experiences of the d'Orsays must have been typical of many well-connected families of the time. It was indeed true that young Count d'Orsay had grown up a pampered youth, enjoying the benefits of life in imperial Paris, a true child of the Empire; it was all he had known. But although his father had embraced the Napoleonic regime and prospered in its service, this was more from force of circumstance and the pragmatic consideration of having a wife and young family in Paris.

Before the Revolution, d'Orsay's family had enjoyed prosperity and social prominence. From relatively obscure beginnings as a provincial tax collector d'Orsay's great-great-grandfather had risen to be a *fermier-général*, early in the eighteenth century. 'Before the French Revolution, the largest fortunes in France were possessed by the farm-ers of the revenue, or *fermiers-généraux*. Their profits were enormous, and their probity was very doubtful,' in Captain Gronow's view. 'The prodigality, magnificence, and ostentation of these Croesuses were the subject of every play and every satire.'[1]

To be a *fermier-général* was, for those not born into the aristocracy, the apotheosis of life in seventeenth- and eighteenth-century France. For many, like d'Orsay's great-great-grandfather, the foothills in which this epic of social and economic alpinism began were to be found among the ranks of provincial civil servants involved in the col-lecting, receiving or counting of the numerous levies and taxes; a town with a population of twenty thousand could expect to have about twenty such officials.

In the course of a lifetime, a man with ability and ambition, unencumbered by too many scruples, could rise from obscurity to a position of wealth and influence; at least two *fermiers-généraux* started life as valets. But the ascent from small-town tax collector to *fermier-général* was steep. While there might be one financial bureaucrat for every thousand Frenchmen – and by the end of the eighteenth century France was the most populous nation in Europe with 26 million inhabitants – there were only forty *fermiers-généraux* in the entire country. Every six years they pooled their resources and purchased from the state the right to collect the many indirect taxes needed to supplement income from direct taxation.

It is a supreme understatement to describe the taxation system of pre-Revolutionary France as unfair. It was positively medieval in the preference it showed towards the aristocracy: the nobility simply did not pay the main state tax, or taille, the levy raised from the part of the population not engaged in military service. As the population grew the system became more distorted. Every child of an aristocrat enjoyed aristocratic status (unlike in England, where the system of primogeniture prevailed), as did their children, grandchildren and so on. Similarly exempt from taxation were the clergy and many of those in public office.

There also existed a system of indirect taxation, tolls and internal customs, operated by private enterprise. So intrusive were these levies that it was sometimes easier for internal administrative areas to trade with foreign countries than with each other. There were periodic attempts to centralise and modernise the economy, which were of course vigorously thwarted by the *fermiers-généraux*. Tax farming offered the fast track to wealth and power, if not universal popularity. The riches, and unpopularity, of the *fermiers-généraux* reached their peak in the mid-1780s, when the notorious Wall of the Farmers-General, complete with impressive gates, was erected around Paris as a giant customs post.

Like his father, d'Orsay's great-grandfather was also a *fermier-général*. He married the daughter of another *fermier-général*, became extraordinarily rich and had bought a pleasant, moated fifteenth-century castle near Versailles from two old women. However agreeable its views and solid its foundations, it was the exotic panoply of titles accompanying the property that were the real attraction, allowing this fortunate tax collector's son to style himself Count d'Orsay of Autrey and Nogent-le-Retrou, Baron de Rupt, Seigneur of the sovereign principality of Delaine and other places in the Franche-Comté, Seigneur d'Orsay Courtaboeuf, La Plesse and Les Villefeux. The new Count d'Orsay also acquired a genuinely aristocratic wife, his third, who in December 1748 bore him a son, albeit posthumously: Pierre-Gaspard-Marie Grimod, d'Orsay's grandfather.

By the late 1760s, barely out of his teens, this young man had acquired from the Duke de Chaulnes the Grand and Petit Hôtels de Chaulnes built by the fashionable architect Jean Le Blond on the Rue de Varennes on Paris's Left Bank. He also married. His wife was 'an heiress of one of the most ancient houses in the Pays Bas, the Princesse de Cröy', who coincidentally 'brought a noble dowry to her husband, himself a man of princely fortune'.[2] As was only appropriate for a newly married couple of such financial and social prominence, he had his wife's portrait painted by the chief painter to Louis XV and the leading exponent of rococo, the sexagenarian François Boucher. To set off the portrait, he surrounded himself with all the beautiful objects he could afford, shopping on an heroic scale; purchasing works contemporary and antique. His acquisitive zeal slowed down to welcome the birth of a son, Albert, d'Orsay's father, in the summer of 1775 – the happiness of which event was eclipsed by the death of his wife. However, it might be argued that this Count d'Orsay liked to look on the bright side of death. His wife may have gone to her grave but at least he would be able to build a monument suitable to her memory. Even after the ravages of the Revolution, the ruins of the Princess de Croy's tomb at Orsay were a source of wonder.

His wife safely interred, the count returned to his collecting. The *vieux hôtels* of Paris were the equivalent of the vast mansions of the English aristocracy overlooking first Green and later Hyde Parks. With their stately courtyards, gardens, graceful architecture, salons with painted ceilings and even door panels decorated by the leading artists of the day, they were the ultimate status symbol. Their power to impress was increased by the contrast they presented to the way of life outside their walls and beyond their double gates.

Most of Paris's population of half a million were crowded within the medieval boundaries of the city, clusters of its tenements intersected by narrow, rubbish-strewn, sewage-scented, ravine-like streets, which, after heavy rain, turned into fast-flowing rivulets bridged by precariously arranged planks of wood. At night what light there was came from the moon or the occasional guttering lantern. The *hôtels particuliers* were oases of refined living. During the years approaching the Revolution, the Hôtel d'Orsay was, even by the luxurious standards of the day, a remarkable place. It was one of the main attractions of the French capital.

In addition to the lavishly painted ceilings and intricately decorated door panels, the house was stuffed with works of art, including at least four representations of Venus and four Bacchic figures, a larger-than-life wounded gladiator, a similarly proportioned centaur on a plinth, a statue of the Emperor Augustus and so on. Contemporary art was represented by a bronze of Louis XV and, of course, by depictions of the d'Orsay family. In fact everywhere visitors to the Hôtel d'Orsay looked were bronzes, sculptures in white and coloured marble, vases, columns and pedestals. The vast garden where bloomed the rarest exotics[3] boasted many pieces of sculpture, one of the most impressive of which was a gigantic Neptune in the middle of a huge rock. The dining room was decorated with giant marble columns taken from the temple of Nero in Rome.

The Hôtel d'Orsay must have seemed like a museum, and the

young artists of pre-Revolutionary Paris were allowed to come and study the works of art in its salons. However, there can be few museums, either then or since, which boasted the refinement of the state drawing rooms, which had musical folding doors. On the opening of the doors a sophisticated system of pedals was activitated, producing a strain of music, which was picked up and continued by the next set of doors in the suite to be opened. That slippery statesman Talleyrand probably captured the feel of the Hôtel d'Orsay when he said it 'almost realised the notion of a fairy palace'.[4]

Long after its creator had died, the nobility of the *ancien régime* would tell nostalgic tales of the splendour, beauty and innovative luxury of the Hôtel d'Orsay. What made these stories more poignant was that the splendour of the *hôtel* was so short lived. During the Revolution the house was plundered, not by the mob, but by the state. Its major works of art were seized and distributed among various museums and state buildings, with the larger pieces going to the Tuileries, the Luxembourg Gardens and the gardens of Saint-Cloud. By the late 1820s the dining room that had once been decorated with Nero's columns was a stable, the inhabitants of which grazed in the garden.

D'Orsay's grandfather did not want to fall victim to the excesses of the Revolution. In 1787 he had moved to what is today Germany but was at that time one of the many Ruritanian principalities and statelets that had yet to be welded into the Reich. He had married again and his father-in-law was the ruling prince of Bartenstein. He did try to return to France on one occasion, but his vast wealth, the title that his father had bought and the aristocratic connections the family had worked so hard to foster counted against him. He offered to sell his goods and donate half the proceeds to the state as what was euphemistically called a 'patriotic contribution', then he scuttled back to Germany.

The son from his first marriage, d'Orsay's father Albert, had only childhood memories of the Hôtel d'Orsay and of their little castle in the country. From the age of nine or ten he grew up and was educated in the towns of German-speaking Europe. After three years with a tutor in Strasbourg, he studied in Frankfurt and at Heidelberg University. He then lived at Bartenstein, Leipzig, Frankfurt and Strasbourg. By the time he reached the age of eighteen, his father and stepmother were separated and impoverished, and he was just another deracinated penniless aristocrat drifting around Europe, different only in that he was judged to be extraordinarily good looking, so good looking that he earned the soubriquet 'Beau' d'Orsay. The only occupation for a good-looking, well-connected young man in need of a living was the army, and indeed armed service, for various rulers, was to form Beau d'Orsay's career. His first post was as a sub-lieutenant in the Austrian army.

Austria at the end of the eighteenth century was a superpower, born out of the remains of the Holy Roman Empire, with possessions stretching from the Netherlands to northern Italy. At the time it was engaged in a titanic struggle with the armies of Revolutionary France, attempting to stop exportation of its Revolutionary ideals. Young Count Albert d'Orsay served first in the regiment of his step-uncle, Prince Hohenlohe-Bartenstein. It was, most likely, a position achieved through the nepotism of his stepmother, with whom he seems to have remained on good terms, even living under her roof for a while in the 1790s. He then served in the Schwartzenberg Hussars, seeing action in Flanders and Champagne and acquitting himself particularly well at Maubeuge. After the Treaty of Campo Formio in the autumn of 1797, he quit the army with the rank of captain of cavalry and decorated with the Cross of Maria Theresa.

The Treaty of Campo Formio was the controversial peace concluded by a lank-haired, twenty-eight-year-old Corsican-born French general who had made his international debut with a north Italian campaign in 1796–1797. Born Nabulione Buonaparte, Napoleon

Bonaparte and his Army of Italy had cut through the northern Italian states. Fighting in sixty-seven actions, decimating the Austrian army in eighteen pitched battles, the French had taken 150,000 prisoners, seized 170 enemy standards and appropriated countless masterpieces to enrich the art collection of the nascent French republic, augmenting the sort of items taken from émigrés like the d'Orsays.

Europe, doubtless including the young Captain Count d'Orsay of the Schwartzenberg Hussars, was stunned by the military flair of this dazzling Corsican youngster. However, when it came to the negotiating table Napoleon lacked the old-world polish of his opponent in diplomacy, the wily and intriguing Count Ludwig Cobenzl. Cobenzl's delaying tactics infuriated Napoleon to such a degree that he shouted, 'Your emperor is nothing but an old maidservant accustomed to being raped by everyone!'[5] He went on to emphasise his point by smashing a valuable tea service that had been given to Cobenzl by Catherine, Empress of Russia, and telling the aristocratic Austrian that the same thing would happen to his Empire.

This unique style of teapot diplomacy got results. A treaty was signed. Bonapartists construed the Peace of Campo Formio as a towering achievement. Others in France, especially those who saw this twenty-something general (the minimum age for membership of the governing Directory was forty) as a threat to the newly established order, perceived the treaty as an embarrassment for France. The conditions imposed on Austria were believed to be far too lenient given the scale of the French victory.

If the treaty was overly favourable to Austria this was probably due to the subtlety, wiliness and intrigue of Count Cobenzl, assisted by the suave Beau d'Orsay. Indeed in his 1928 book *Le Prince des Dandys: Le Comte d'Orsay*, Maurice Lecomte suggests that Beau d'Orsay earned his rank and his decoration in part at least serving as a secret agent for Cobenzl. As well as a captaincy and the Cross of Maria Theresa, Beau d'Orsay had also found himself a wife, the strikingly beautiful Eléonore, Baroness de Franquemont, the daughter of the King of Württemberg and the exotic actress Anne Franchi. Had the King of the Württemberg been rich and had Eléonore been his legitimate daughter, the match might have augured well for the young count's fortunes. Unfortunately for him, neither was the case.

And soon Beau d'Orsay made his way to Paris, on another mission from Cobenzl. The Paris of the Directory period was corrupt and gaudy. It witnessed the coming together of the *déclassé* dregs of the *ancien régime* and the *nouveaux riches* who had got rich extremely quickly through purchasing confiscated property, profiteering from the war and so on. It is described epigrammatically by the historian Alfred Cobban as a society 'in which the vices of the court met and fused with those of the courtyard'.[6]

After the austerity of the Terror, Parisian society was once again discovering the pleasures of money and its lavish expenditure. It was also a society in which women, the mistresses and wives of political and military figures, wielded considerable power with their salons and dances. In the sexually permissive atmosphere that characterised Paris at that time, Beau d'Orsay's bearing and his looks made him a great success with the women of the Directory, including Napoleon's wife Josephine. Her most consistent lover of this period was a lieutenant in the French army, Hippolyte Charles. Like Beau d'Orsay, Charles was an officer in a regiment of hussars; he was also handsome and paid great attention to his appearance, favouring such extravagant accessories as a silver-embroidered cape trimmed with the fur of a red fox and red leather boots with tassels. Given Josephine's celebrated sexual voracity, it is feasible that she fell for the charm of Beau d'Orsay, and it is tantalising to speculate that perhaps she even found time to slot him into her busy sexual schedule.

However, the return of Napoleon from his Egyptian adventure in October 1799 and the subsequent coup of November, after which he proclaimed himself First Consul, changed the climate again. In

November Beau d'Orsay was arrested. It has been suggested that only the intercession of Josephine saved him from execution and he was instead sent into exile in Mons in Belgium. But wife and husband did keep in close enough touch throughout what were to be more than two years of absence from France to have two children together.

In September 1802 Beau d'Orsay returned to Paris, taking advantage of an amnesty allowing émigrés to go back to France provided they accepted the offer before the 23rd of that month. After the Peace of Amiens, signed the previous March, France was, for the moment, no longer at war with its neighbours.

In reality this period of peace was no more than a breathing space before a resumption of hostilities. Napoleon would have a use for brave and dashing men like Beau d'Orsay and, on 18 August 1804 – or 'le 26 Gendre an 13' of the Revolutionary Calendar, as the military records show it – this former Austrian captain entered the French army as 'Chef de Bataillon au Service de France dans le 112ᵉ Régimt de ligne'.[7] Once he had taken the part of Napoleon, d'Orsay seemed to dedicate himself to the glory of the Empire. His rise was impressive, as was his courage. He received a gunshot wound to his right leg near Odezzo in Italy in May 1809, but made a rapid recovery and was fit enough to serve again in Germany the following month. By 1811 he had made the rank of colonel, in July 1813 near Pamplona he was wounded again, this time in the left knee but soon recovered, and by November he was made a general.

Napoleon seemed well pleased with him and was impressed with his looks. 'It is said that when the Emperor Napoleon first saw him, he observed that he would make an admirable model for a Jupiter, so noble and commanding was the character of his beauty.'[8] There is a mystique that surrounds even the most mundane of objects which have belonged to historical figures (Napoleon's toothbrush is apparently a money-spinning tourist attraction in Cuba to this day), and this is true of even their most banal utterances. Napoleon was celebrated for his mastery of the common touch and it would be easy to dismiss this Jupiter remark as a throwaway compliment intended to swell the breast of its recipient. However it is likely that it was with such comments and stories about his father that the younger d'Orsay concocted a view of his male parent, a distant and gallant warrior, far removed from the gaiety of his grandmother's salon.

It is against the turbulent background of life in continental Europe at the time of the Bourbon restoration in 1814 that Alfred d'Orsay's family situation has to be viewed. Although strands of various European countries were woven into the colourful history of the d'Orsays, their position was by no means atypical of that facing many families. A man who had grown up a spoiled child of pre-Revolutionary France, had become an adolescent in the statelets of the Rhine and had worked variously as an Austrian spy and a French general might be inclined to view the reinstatement of a scion of a dynasty under which his grandfather and father had prospered with at least an open mind. Moreover, if Beau d'Orsay had ever been an idealist, his experiences in the field and the wisdom of passing years would have done something to temper those feelings with a degree of pragmatism.

From having to live on his wits and his family connections in the late eighteenth century Beau d'Orsay had prospered in a society from which he had been deported as an undesirable in the pay of a foreign power. Perhaps the general's instinct for survival guided him to go along with the corpulent king imposed by the victorious powers. The disillusionment aroused in him by the political life of France seems to have been fairly widespread among the French: a disillusionment that would be manipulated during the remainder of the nineteenth century by one or other of four factions: Bonapartists, Republicans, Orleanists and Legitimists. For most of the century there would always be a significant proportion of the population willing to see the demise of one form of government in the hope that its successor might be more to their taste. In a period that would see the country switching frequently between empire, monarchy and republic, a man might have to switch his allegiances rapidly and repeatedly if he wanted to get on or, in the case of Beau d'Orsay and his wife, see their children get on.

Thus, although it may have grated with young Alfred d'Orsay's violent and romantic attraction to the Napoleonic cause, the pragmatism of his father and the social ambition of his mother and grandmother would have propelled him into the midst of such events as the meeting of the Royal Staghounds in the Bois de Boulogne on 27 August 1814.

The fragmented and curious climate of the times is neatly illustrated by the identities of the three most famous men at the meet: the Duke de Berry, Louis XVIII's nephew and a leading figure in Bourbon circles; the Prince de la Moskowa, otherwise known as Marshal Ney, the popular and famously pro-Bonaparte war hero; and the conquering British commander-in-chief, the Duke of Wellington. The sporting and social elite of Paris turned out to watch the two famous generals conversing amicably and riding side by side. It is perhaps one of history's more ironic snapshots: two generals who had been implacable foes, and by the next summer at Waterloo would be again, chatting politely. After Waterloo Ney would be executed by firing squad for treachery, and the Duke de Berry would be killed by an assassin while leaving the opera in 1820.

It was at this meet of the royal hunt that young Count d'Orsay first came to Wellington's notice. 'One youth attracted great attention that day,' remembers Lord William Pitt Lennox, son of the fourth Duke of Richmond, who had recently left Westminster School to join Wellington's staff and was himself only a youth of fifteen or sixteen, 'from his handsome appearance, his gentlemanlike bearing, his faultless dress and the splendid English hunter he was mounted upon. This was the late Alfred d'Orsay, afterwards so well known in London society.'[9] The horse, a Leicestershire hunter, upon which d'Orsay had been mounted had been sent to him from England by the Duke de Grammont, who in a couple of years would marry Ida, d'Orsay's sister. 'The Count was presented to Wellington and his staff, and from that moment he became a constant guest at the Hôtel Borghese [where the British Embassy had been set up].'[10] Pitt Lennox notes with approval that the 'fine shape, simple saddle and bridle' of d'Orsay's mount 'contrasted favourably with the heavy animals, and smart caparisons, then in fashion with the Parisian Nimrods'.[11]

D'Orsay became a regular at meets of the royal hunt, where his considerable style was equalled by his spirited horsemanship. 'Nothing occurred during the day's sport to merit any particular comment,' writes Pitt Lennox of a meet on 9 September:

> Perhaps the most amusing part of it was our 'lark' home across the country, when myself, Fremantle, and other *attachés* of the English embassy, led some half dozen Frenchmen a rather stiff-ish line of stone walls and brooks. Among the latter was d'Orsay, who, albeit unaccustomed to go 'across country,' was always in the 'first flight,' making up by hard riding whatever he may have lacked in judgement; he afterwards lived to be an excellent sportsman and a good rider to hounds.[12]

Rambouillet was the venue of the next meet, where the Duke of Wellington was dressed in French hunting costume of 'cocked hat, gold-laced coat, *couteau de chasse* and leather jack-boots'.[13] When the hunt met at Fontainebleau, the French princes returned the Duke's compliment, mounting themselves for the chase d'Orsay-style on 'English thorough-bred hunters'.[14] D'Orsay's daring Anglophile fashion statement of the meet of 27 August, when the fine shape of his mount and the simplicity of its bridle and saddle had provided such a stark contrast, had quickly become the prevailing equestrian trend.

Indeed it was during this meet that d'Orsay demonstrated another decidedly English attribute, sentimentality towards an animal at bay. 'The stag now gained the lake, and plunged in,' recalled Pitt Lennox, after a descriptive passage worthy of Surtees. 'Anxious to save the noble animal, the Duke and Fremantle whipped off the hounds, while de Grammont, d'Orsay, and myself dashed up to our middles in water attempting, with a lasso formed of stirrup leathers, to secure the "poor sequestered stag."'[15]

Not all the French were on such cosy terms with their conquerors as to go hunting with them. Napoleon, in exile on his little island kingdom of Elba, was not slow to exploit the rumblings of national discontent and in March 1815 launched his last reckless attempt to retake Europe: his 'Hundred Days'. Court complacency at his landing at Fréjus turned to fear when Marshal Ney, despatched to 'bring him back in a cage', actually went over to Napoleon. On the night of 19 March, fat old Louis XVIII waddled off into exile again and Napoleon was back in power.

For once, Alfred's father, General Count d'Orsay, did not perform another of his tactical U-turns; instead of going over to Napoleon as did most Frenchmen, he went into exile with his family in England. The culture shock for the young Count d'Orsay must have been immense. London in 1815 was nothing like as refined as the city in whose salons he had become a social star. Viewed at the distance of a couple of centuries it seems inevitable that two countries that had been at war, or at least mutually hostile, for the better part of twenty years should have developed along very different cultural lines.

While Napoleon had presided over a revival of luxury in France, a former cornet in the 10th Hussars and an intimate of the Prince of Wales, George Bryan Brummell, had subjugated English Society with the unique froideur of his manner. Like Napoleon, Brummell was something of an outsider. While the Corsican Bonaparte smashed one society and created another, Brummell, the grandson of a wine merchant, made the aristocracy his slaves in matters of taste, manners and dress. What Napoleon was on the battlefield, Brummell was in the ballroom. 'He used to stand for a few minutes at the door of the ballroom, glance round, criticize it in a sentence, and disappear,'[16] wrote Jules Barbey d'Aurevilly in his 1844 study *Du Dandysme et de Georges Brummell*. Brummell's 'talk was as mordant as the writing of Hazlitt' and his 'witticisms crucified'.[17] D'Aurevilly also identifies one of the cornerstones of Brummell's dandyism: while he astonished others, he must never display emotion. 'His indolence forbad his being lively, for to be lively is to be excited; to be excited is to care about something, and to care about anything is to shew oneself inferior.'[18]

While much has been made of Brummell's dress sense and the exaggerated, at the time revolutionary, understatement of his clothes, it is his sang-froid, literally cold-bloodedness, that is his greatest legacy to England and the English. It later became an integral part of the caricature of the English gentleman, and a quality on which that Victorian invention the British Empire was built: Brummell would doubtless have approved of the cool understatement of such remarks as 'Dr Livingstone, I presume.' In 1815, a year before Brummell, broken by debt, was forced to flee to Calais, London must have seemed a very strange place.

It would seem even stranger to us today. Despite being the capital of England, the countryside was never very far away; for instance, Brummell's aunt lived in a cottage in Green Park, where she kept and milked cows. Nor was Hyde Park the collection of well-planned lawns, walkways and flowerbeds that it is today. Gronow described the Park at this time:

That extensive district of park land, the entrances of which are in Piccadilly and Oxford Street, was far more rural in appearance in 1815 than at the present day [he was writing in the 1860s].

Under the trees cows and deer were grazing; the paths were fewer, and none told of that perpetual tread of human feet which now destroys all idea of country charms and illusions. As you gazed from an eminence, no rows of monotonous houses reminded you of the vicinity of a large city, and the atmosphere of Hyde Park was then much more like what God had made it than the hazy, gray, coal-darkened, half-twilight of the London of to-day. The company which then congregated daily about five was composed of dandies and women in the best society; the men mounted on such horses as England alone could then produce. The dandy's dress consisted of a blue coat with brass buttons, leather breeches, and top boots; and it was the fashion to wear a deep, stiff white cravat, which prevented you from seeing your boots while standing.[19]

The sight that d'Orsay encountered must indeed have been a curious one. The Park must have seemed like a parade of mummies: their necks encased in yards of starched linen, their hair combed up in an aspect of shock – not unlike the coiffure of punk rockers 160 years later – their breeches or wide-legged trousers ballooning out from under waists pulled in with belts, corsets and stays. An 1818 cartoon by George Cruikshank of 'Dandies Dressing' shows the lengths to which men would go to make themselves appear in the vanguard of fashion. 'D–n it,' says one, his head thrown so far back by his neckcloth as to risk permanent neck injury, 'I really believe I must take off my cravat or I shall never get my trowsers on.' ''Pon honor, Tom you are a charming figure! You'll captivate the girls to a nicety,' says another to his friend, who, his shoulder pads in place, is being laced into a corset by his valet. 'Do you think so, Charles?' comes the reply. 'I shall look more the thing when I get my other calf on.'[20] A glance at his skinny calves reveals that, at present, only one of his false calves has been fixed into place. Doubtless had calf-augmentation surgery been available to these followers of Brummell they would have availed themselves of it. Indeed, so prized was a well-turned leg that some men had breeches made for standing in and others cut from a pattern that enabled them to sit.

Little wonder, then, that the daily fashion parade took place at five. It must have required most of the day for the men to truss themselves up and make their way to the Park to watch their idol. 'All the world watched Brummell to imitate him,' said Gronow, 'and order their clothes of the tradesman who dressed that sublime dandy.'[21] 'All the world' of course meant only persons of quality. 'In those days, "pretty horse-breakers" would not have dared to shew themselves in Hyde Park; nor did you see any of the lower or middle classes of London intruding themselves in regions which, with a sort of tacit understanding, were then given up exclusively to persons of rank and fashion.'[22]

Democracy had yet to invade the parks and those who did present themselves there without proper authority would be treated with a merciless severity, as Gronow recalled:

In London, in bygone days, a worldly man or woman would, without scruple, cut their father or mother did they not belong to the particular set which they considered good society. Mr. S— was once riding in the park many years ago with the Marquis of C—, then one of the kings of the fashionable world, and some other dandies of that day, when they met a respectable looking elderly man, who nodded somewhat familiarly to S—. 'Who's your friend?' drawled Lord C—. 'That?' replied S—, 'oh, a very good sort of a fellow, one of my Cheshire farmers.' It was his own father; a most amiable and excellent man, and who had better blood in his veins, and a larger fortune, than any of the lordlings by whom his unworthy son was surrounded. A celebrated leader of fashion, Lady X—, never asked her own mother, a well-born and well-conducted, but somewhat eccentric person, to any of her parties; she ignored her very existence; and yet she was by nature a kind, well-meaning, and good-natured woman. But the world's canker had eaten into her heart.[23]

As Gronow pointed out, 'In these days of railways and monster parties, the folly of exclusiveness has very much died away; cutting near relatives is out of fashion – it is unnecessary in the whirl and bustle of life.'[24] However, at the time of Napoleon's return from Elba, Stephenson's Rocket was a piece of science fiction and in London 'cutting', 'quizzing', blue coats, brass buttons and boots blacked with the finest vintage champagne consumed the attentions of polite Society.

With Waterloo in June 1815, Napoleon was finally vanquished and the d'Orsay family could once more return to Paris. It was a different city to the one that they had fled. During the first restoration of the Bourbons the Allies had been lenient with the French: in effect it had been Napoleon who had been punished. But Waterloo had been a close call: the Duke of Wellington's verdict on the battle that cemented his reputation was that it had been 'a damned nice thing – the nearest run thing you ever saw in your life'.[25] The Congress of Vienna was not about to let circumstances prevail that might lead to another Waterloo.

Louis XVIII was put back on the throne; his status as a puppet monarch was in no doubt. France was humiliated: restricted to its pre-Revolutionary borders, ordered to return the booty gathered during the Napoleonic era and saddled with a huge reparation bill; moreover, an army of occupation was to stay billeted on the French until it had been paid.

Bizarrely enough, during this period of national shame the Anglophile character of the Count d'Orsay continued to blossom.

One powerful reason for this predilection of the young count was the contrasting conduct of the different nationalities of occupying troops. Having endured French occupation for several years, the Prussians set about exacting revenge. 'They remembered always the former treatment of Prussia,' recalled Wellington, 'and levied large contributions, and sometimes two or even three rations for each man. When I urged to Gneisenau* the importance of husbanding our supplies and not exasperating the people, he answered, *On n'a pas pensé à cela en Prusse*; and when I spoke to him against the double and triple rations, he said, *C'est très bon pour notre estomac*.'[26]

However, Count August von Gneisenau was a model of tact and grace in victory when compared to his superior the maverick Marshal Blücher. Apparently once on a visit to London, when asked how he liked the city, he replied that it was a splendid place, which it would be a pleasure to sack. Blücher 'well understood a field of battle'.[27] It was just peacetime with which he had a problem. Even in Paris with Louis XVIII back on the throne he behaved as if he were still fighting Waterloo. One of his *idées fixes* was a plan to demolish the bridge of Jena, named after one of Napoleon's more spectacular victories against the Prussians. Though Wellington and indeed Blücher's comrades Gneisenau and Müffling were opposed to the notion, Blücher, according to Wellington, was 'violently for it. In spite of all I could do, he did make the attempt, even while I believe my sentinel was standing at one end of the bridge. But the Prussians had no experience in blowing up bridges. We, who had blown up so many in Spain, could have done it in five minutes. The Prussians made a hole in one of the pillars, but their powder blew out instead of up, and I believe hurt some of their own people.'[28]

Unable to destroy the bridge of Jena, Blücher consoled himself gambling and in one night alone was reported to have lost ten

* General Count August von Gneisenau (1760–1831).

thousand pounds[29] (a figure approaching half a million pounds in early-twenty-first-century terms). 'Though a very fine fellow,' Blücher was, according to Gronow, 'a very rough diamond, with the manners of a common soldier.' Indeed his barbarian antics were a source of wonder, and the irascible marshal became something of a tourist attraction:

> On his arrival in Paris, he went every day to the *salon*, and played the highest stakes at *rouge et noir*. The *salon*, during the time that the marshal remained in Paris, was crowded by persons who came to see him play. His manner of playing was anything but gentlemanlike, and when he lost, he used to swear in German at everything that was French, looking daggers at the croupiers. He generally managed to lose all he had about him, also all the money his servant, who was waiting in the ante-chamber, carried. I recollect looking attentively at the manner in which he played; he would put his right hand into his pocket, and bring out several rouleaus of Napoleons, throwing them on the red or the black. If he won the first coup, he would allow it to remain; but when the croupier stated that the table was not responsible for more than ten thousand francs, then Blücher would roar like a lion, and rap out oaths in his native language which would doubtless have met with great success at Billingsgate, if duly translated: fortunately, they were not heeded, as they were not understood by the lookers-on.[30]

Blücher also had his own agenda for reparations. 'The Bank of France was called upon to furnish him with several thousand pounds, which, it was said, were to reimburse him for the money lost at play. This, with many other instances of extortion and tyranny, was the cause of Blücher's removal, and he took his departure by order of the king.'[31] The Prussian soldiers did their best to live up to the standards of vandalism and hooliganism established by the great marshal: assaulting civilians, knocking coachmen off their seats with the butts of their muskets, smashing the windows of shops in the Palais Royal, cutting down the best trees in the Bois de Boulogne, even setting areas of the wood on fire.

The contrast with English troops such as the dandified Gronow and the Duke of Wellington, who was thought by some to be too indulgent to the vanquished French, was marked. It seems that little was done that might have been thought provocative. Thus although French women thought the 'want of culottes' on kilted Highland regiments 'most indecent',[32] on the whole Wellington seems to have communicated a measure of his restraint to the other ranks. He famously described his men as the scum of the earth, who had enlisted with the intention of escaping from bastard children and getting drunk as frequently as possible. He treated them accordingly. He frequently used the gallows to maintain discipline and it was during the Spanish campaign, when English soldiers were hanged for such indiscretions as the unauthorised shooting of pigs, that he established his reputation as a disciplinarian.

Lord Ellesmere recorded one instance when a couple of soldiers were discovered looting and assaulting a woman. 'Having satisfied himself as to the guilt of the soldiers, Wellington turned round to the Provost-Marshal, and in that brief expression which ever characterized him, said, "In ten minutes report to me that these two men have been executed."' When news of this reached Junot, one of Napoleon's commanders in the Peninsular War, he was reported to have been taken aback. 'Ma foi!' he exclaimed. 'La discipline anglaise est bien sévère.'[33]

Instead of vandalising Paris, smart Britons imported their own amusements; four-in-hand or stagecoach racing was quickly established as a pastime among the more fashion-conscious English officers. Crowds would form to watch the teams gather outside the house of the Russian plutocrat Demidoff, which later became the Café de Paris, and set off through the streets and on a course that ended at the then unfinished Arc de Triomphe.

Such glamorous pursuits, combined with the comparatively good behaviour of the occupying British, could be counted on to appeal to d'Orsay. And, in addition to Wellington's benevolent disposition towards the French, family connections brought d'Orsay into contact with the portion of English Society that established itself in Paris after the restoration of the Bourbons. Taking time off from his literary endeavours (his later books included a study of Pericles and a history of ancient and modern India), Quintin Craufurd was able to make himself useful to the incoming English by such services as enabling the purchase of what became the splendid Embassy on the Rue Faubourg Saint-Honoré. Hitherto it had been owned by Napoleon's sister Pauline. Madame Craufurd's salon became a celebrated meeting place for the upper and fashionable echelons of expatriate English Society. And it was at the Hôtel Craufurd that Gronow first met the young d'Orsay.

And there was of course d'Orsay's friendship with Wellingon and his young aide de camp Lord William Pitt Lennox, with whom he got on very well. Wellington kept a box at the Théâtre Français of which d'Orsay and Pitt Lennox made almost constant use, before setting off to tour the city's pleasure spots. The sumptuously decorated Café des Milles Colonnes made a great impression on Pitt Lennox.

Paris during the Bourbon restoration was a lively place. For the majority of the Napoleonic period, continental travel had been out of the question for most English people, so those who could now afford it made for the cafés and restaurants of the French capital. From seven o'clock in the evening, the Palais Royal would be crowded with a mixed throng of curious foreign visitors, continental princes and dukes, kings from the German statelets, as well as English, Russian,

Prussian and Austrian officers. This was the centre of fashionable life, a Parisian riposte to the manly pleasures of St James's and the fashion parade of Hyde Park, all in one location, without the notional propriety that divided the all-male St James's from the unisex decorum of the Park.

Indeed the Palais Royal was an adult theme park, where sex, or the suggestion of it, was omnipresent. At the sides of the jewellers, dressmakers (conveniently placed for men to purchase gifts for their companions) and other shops that filled the ground floor, dirty staircases led to first-floor cafés. These were superintended by more than usually attractive women, *très décolletées* and diamanté-bedecked. Here men would gather, enjoy their ices, sip their cups of mocha and discuss the two important issues of the day: gambling and women. In the Palais Royal, the brothels were located on the floor above the casino and were extremely luxurious. It was not unheard of for an officer to take leave from the army, rent a set of rooms there and never quit the Palais Royal for the duration of his leave. But the atmosphere was not always conducive to an entirely relaxing stay. For instance the Café Foy was a favourite rendezvous of Prussian officers and it was here that French officers would go to pick fights; Gronow mentions one particularly bloody encounter in which fourteen Prussians and ten Frenchmen were either killed or wounded.

With shops, cafés, prostitutes, some of the best-appointed brothels in the world and a casino that was packed from noon with the likes of the irascible Marshal Blücher, the Palais Royal at the time of the Bourbon restoration was, as Gronow would have it, 'the rendezvous of all idlers, and especially of the particular class of ladies who lay out their attractions for the public at large. These were to be seen at all hours in full dress, their bare necks ornamented with mock diamonds and pearls; and thus decked out in all their finery, they paraded up and down, casting their eyes significantly on every side.'[34] In the years immediately following Waterloo, Paris was, in short, the very centre of the fashionable world.

It was at this time that d'Orsay's ties with Bourbon high Society and its English backers were further strengthened. In 1818, his sister Ida married the Duke de Guiche, the man who had supplied the elegant Leicestershire hunter on which d'Orsay had cut such a dash at the meet of the Royal Staghounds in 1814. Heir to the Duke de Grammont, the Duke de Guiche was about as grand as it was possible to be in early-nineteenth-century France. His noble lineage stretched back to ninth-century Spain. One of his antecedents had written a celebrated account of English society at the end of the seventeenth century. Another had been executed during the French Revolution. His parents had followed Louis XVIII into exile and had lived in Scotland, where de Guiche's mother had died in 1803 and been interred in the royal vault of the chapel at Holyrood. In gratitude to the island that had offered his family shelter de Guiche had served in the 10th Hussars in the Peninsular War.

The connections between the royal family of France and the family of the Duke de Grammont were to continue after the restoration. By the end of the 1820s, de Guiche was a highly influential figure in court circles. The hereditary principle prevailed among senior courtiers as much as it did with the ruling family, and de Guiche demonstrated a great degree of tact and insight as well as a loyalty to the regime his family had served for generations.

'It would be fortunate, indeed, for the King of France if he had many such men as the Duke de Guiche around him – men with enlightened minds, who have profited by the lessons of adversity, and kept pace with the rapidly advancing knowledge of the times to which they belong,' noted one observer, adding ominously, 'Painful, indeed, would be the position of this excellent man should any circumstances occur that would place the royal family in jeopardy, for he is too sensible not to be aware of the errors that might lead to such a crisis, and too loyal not to share the perils he could not ward off . . .'[35] But in 1818, when the marriage of Ida d'Orsay and the Duke de Guiche took place, such worries and gloomy portents were at least a decade in the future.

CHAPTER THREE

A Frenchman in London

WHEN THE DUKE DE GRAMMONT WAS DESPATCHED TO REPRESENT Louis XVIII at the coronation of George IV in July 1821, it was decided to make it into a family excursion, with de Grammont accompanied by de Guiche, his beautiful blonde, blue-eyed wife Ida[1] and d'Orsay.

D'Orsay was now around twenty-one and stunningly good-looking; de Guiche too cut a dash, with his dark, faintly hidalgo features, crisp dark curly hair and large eyes. Writing to a friend in 1842, Walter Savage Landor described the pair thus: 'The Duke de Guiche is the handsomest man I ever saw. What poor animals other men seem in the presence of him and d'Orsay.'[2] De Guiche's links with Britain had been forged not only by military service during his time in exile from France, but also by the marriage in 1806 of his sister to Viscount Ossulston.

D'Orsay caused a sensation in London. 'A fortnight after his arrival he had already made himself the centre of a court of fashionables who imitated him to the best of their abilities; at the end of a month, everybody who prided themselves on elegance, swore only by him; he had picked up the sceptre of Brummell.[3]' That is the rather enthusiastic account of d'Orsay's conquest of London as recounted by Jacques Boulenger in his 1907 book *Sous Louis-Philippe: Les Dandys*. Boulenger may be accused of hyperbole, and also of some inaccuracy, in that Brummell and d'Orsay differed on many points, not least in the former's froideur as against d'Orsay's good-natured enthusiasm. Fashionable London of 1821 was not a big place and a newcomer such as d'Orsay would have created a stir, as one of the more exotic visitors present for a major state ceremonial; but the splash that d'Orsay might have made in a section of fashionable Society has to be set in the wider context of the London of the time.

The London of the 1820s was a fast-growing city. Its population had increased by 50 per cent since the turn of the century: 1.5 million people now lived in the metropolis. It left visitors like the precocious young composer Felix Mendelssohn 'struck with awe' at the pace and scale of life. 'To see a harbour as large as Hamburg's treated like a pond', he wrote to his family in 1829, 'makes one's heart rejoice over the great world.' The essayist and MP William Cobbett called it 'the Great Wen'. Thomas Carlyle, the eminent author and moralist, writing to his brother in 1824, agreed:

it is like the heart of all the universe; and the flood of human effort rolls out of it and into it with a violence that almost appals one's every sense. Paris scarcely occupies a quarter of the ground, and does not seem to have the twentieth part of the business . . . No wonder Cobbett calls the place a Wen. It is a monstrous Wen! The thick smoke of it beclouds a space of thirty square miles; and a million of vehicles, from the dog-or-cuddy-barrow to the giant waggon, grind along its streets forever.

Yet even the cerebral Carlyle could not help but find the atmosphere invigorating. 'There is an excitement in all this,' he continued:

> the carman with his huge slouch-hat hanging half-way down his back, consumes his breakfast of bread and tallow or hog's lard, sometimes as he swags along the streets, always in a hurried and precarious fashion, and supplies the deficit by continual pipes, and pots of beer. The fashionable lady rises at three in the afternoon, and begins to live towards midnight. Between these two extremes, the same false and tumultuous manner of existence more or less infests all ranks.

A sensitive and precocious young man such as d'Orsay who had already drunk in the vibrant, sensual and dissipated cocktail of life in the Palais Royal would certainly have responded to the invigorating possibilities of life in London, which was emerging as the world city *par excellence*, capital of a victorious nation, a twenty-four-hour city that dwarfed all other conurbations in Europe. Its energy was omnipresent.

Stimulating though such constant tumult might have been, it occasionally boiled over and proved too effervescent for the resources of the city. London was at times ill equipped to curb the excesses and the appetites of its citizens. The anti-Catholic Gordon riots of 1780 had occurred within living memory. Until the Metropolitan Police Act of 1829, what law and order there was remained in the care of beadles, parish constables and nightwatchmen, the last often spending the time in their watchboxes, asleep, drunk or between the legs of a whore.

In the 1820s a gang of indigenous brigands, often numbering many hundreds, terrorised Bethnal Green, lurking in abandoned brickfields,

from which they would emerge to ambush the huge herds of
cattle being driven along the main highways to Smithfield
Market. The drover would be knocked on the head and the
fiercest beast removed to their lair until night-fall. Then they
would sally out through the unlit darkening streets, shouting
and hallooing and driving the terrified bullock before them.
Noise, confusion and alarm would ensue, and anyone whom
they met would be assaulted and robbed. Within the space of a
single fortnight in 1828 over fifty people were attacked, and one
of the gang had been seen with 'nearly half-a-hat-full of
watches'.[4]

It would have been to St James's and in particular St James's Street
that d'Orsay would have gravitated. Today this is not a street for
idlers or *flâneurs*. Tourists may photograph each other at the side of
the impassive guardsmen outside St James's Palace. From time to
time, a suited figure totters out of one of the clubs. But St James's
Street is not a place to linger. The throng of humanity that shambles
slowly along Piccadilly, sashays down Bond Street or gawps inanely at
Piccadilly Circus and Leicester Square has little time for St James's
Street. Occasionally, though, it is possible to glimpse St James's as it
was during the early years of the nineteenth century. On the wall
behind the cash desk in the venerable premises of the hatter James
Lock there hangs a small hand-coloured engraving; it depicts well-
known 'Bond Street Loungers' of the 1820s. There is the Earl of
Sefton, his powerful hunchbacked frame encased in a greatcoat that
reaches almost to his ankles. The trim Duke of Devonshire clutches
an elegant bamboo cane to his nipped-in waist. A rather gloomy
frock-coated 'Poodle' Byng directs a drooping eye at the portly Lord
Manners, who leads a half-shaved poodle on a leash. And on the far
right of the group is the black-clad Duke of Beaufort, his mutton-
chop whiskers skimming the top of a high white collar. Dressed in

high-crowned black silk top hats with curled brims and wearing gloves of yellow dogskin, these are the type of men who used to populate St James's in its heyday, when it was the most fashionable thoroughfare in the civilised world.

In the absence of prestigious quasi-official institutions, such as the Académie Française in Paris, the grand St James's clubs of White's and Brooks's acted as meeting places for the ruling and landed elite, as well as pleasure zones and places of manly dissipation. No lady who valued her reputation could be seen without a chaperone in St James's. The street itself was broad and agreeable enough, and was busy night and day with the clatter of carriages. However, just off it were the taverns and gambling hells, the notorious gaming houses, of Georgian London. The city had yet to divide itself into areas inhabited by one class or another, so that the very grandest in the country and those who served them often lived in close proximity.

Prostitutes were everywhere. Flora Tristan, an early socialist and feminist, recorded a visit during 1839 to 'the new suburb which lies on either side of the long broad thoroughfare called Waterloo Road at the end of Waterloo Bridge. This neighbourhood is almost entirely inhabited by prostitutes and people who live off prostitution; it is courting danger to go there alone at night. It was a hot summer evening; in every window and doorway women were laughing and joking with their protectors. Half-dressed some of them *naked to the waist*, they were a revolting sight,' she noted before taking a seat on the bridge to watch the rush hour that would develop between 'the hours of eight and nine' as prostitutes streamed into the West End, 'where they ply their trade all through the night and return home between eight and nine in the morning. They infest the promenades and any other place where people gather, such as the approaches to the Stock Exchange, the various public buildings and the theatres, which they invade as soon as entry is reduced to half-price, turning all the corridors and foyers into their receiving-rooms.'[5]

Yet just off St James's Street on King Street were Almack's Assembly Rooms, the primmest and most fashionable meeting place of the early-nineteenth-century elite. 'One can hardly conceive the importance which was attached to getting admission to Almack's, the seventh heaven of the fashionable world,' wrote one habitué of London's West End at the time. 'Of the three hundred officers of the Foot Guards, not more than half a dozen were honoured with vouchers of admission to this exclusive temple of the *beau monde*; the gates of which were guarded by lady patronesses, whose smiles or frowns consigned men and women to happiness or despair.'[6] His enthusiasm was not for the level of entertainment provided at Almack's. Dances were staid. Refreshments were restricted to tea, lemonade and cake (alcohol was forbidden). The dress code was so strict that even the Duke of Wellington was once asked to leave because he was wearing dark trousers rather than knee breeches.

However, Almack's was the most 'exigent marriage market in the world'.[7] It was Smithfield for spouses, an exchange where a man with a title could find a young wife with a fortune. As much as being presented at court, attendance at the weekly Wednesday-night balls at Almack's was the hallmark of a debutante's suitability. Thus as well as marriage market, Almack's functioned as Society's assay office, operating a *de facto* vetting system. The social power of Almack's moved the poet and Society figure Henry Luttrell, the illegitimate son of the second Earl of Carhampton, to write:

> If once to Almack's you belong,
> Like monarchs, you can do no wrong;
> But banished thence on Wednesay night,
> By Jove you can do nothing right.

The Almack's name alone was sufficient to guarantee that a racy *roman à clef* of the same name, published in 1826, became an instant bestseller.

Vouchers for admission to the weekly balls were issued by a council, or committee of 'seven ladies of high rank'. And while they might have demanded the highest standards from those to whom they issued vouchers, in their younger days some had enjoyed affairs with prime ministers and even the prince regent. While not proper, such a liaison was not entirely inappropriate, as St James's Palace was a few steps away.

The Court of St James's was still very much the social hub of the country. And as well as the location of the court, St James's Palace was also where the royal dukes resided, one of whom was to become William IV. And although George IV had instructed Nash to remodel Buckingham House – bought from the Duke of Buckingham by George III in 1762 – as a regal residence, it was not to be finished in his lifetime. Indeed it was not to be lived in by a monarch until Victoria came to the throne in 1837. Thus fashionable Society gathered at St James's Palace.

It was at a royal 'Drawing Room' that debutantes, dressed in white gowns and headdresses of three curled ostrich feathers, were presented to the king. George IV was no longer the dashing regent who had ruled during his father's madness. Instead he was a fat elderly man who walked with a stick and was to die in 1830 at the age of sixty-eight. Nevertheless England, London and especially St James's reflected his love of contemporary architecture and the arts, as well as his dissipation and extravagance. And it was St James's and its environs that formed d'Orsay's playground, where a sponsor of the calibre of de Guiche to introduce him to Society, a couple of pithy remarks at Almack's, a stylish bit of equestrian activity in the Park and an intriguingly cut coat at dinner would be enough to create a reputation as a man of fashion.

D'Orsay's initial success, even if not quite on the scale that Boulenger recounts, was considerable. The prevailing male fashion at that time was a Byronic look, slightly unkempt, pale, quasi-consumptive and lethargic; it was the development of Brummell's disdain into a melancholic romantic pose. Vigorous and well dressed, d'Orsay was the antithesis of this in both spirit and appearance. 'Nothing succeeds in London like insolence,'[8] and according to Chateaubriand, writer, politician and ambassador extraordinary at the English court who arrived the following year, d'Orsay was soon galloping around Hyde Park leaping turnpike gates, gambling, 'tutoying' the dandies and thoroughly enjoying himself. His reputation, his self-confidence and his ducal connections swiftly carried him into fashionable houses and inevitably into the fine, long and richly gilded dining room of Holland House.

Henry Richard, third Lord Holland, nephew of Charles James Fox, the celebrated bon-vivant political titan of the eighteenth century, was a prominent Whig politician. His ancestral seat Holland House, a Dutch-gabled brick-and-stone structure dating from the reign of Elizabeth I, lay just outside London. Set in a pleasant park, part of which still remains as Holland Park, it was a country estate conveniently located for political entertaining. Here it was possible to evoke the ambience of a country-house party almost within sight and earshot of London.

Dinners there were legendary, and from May 1799 Lady Holland kept a diary of the influential guests who sat down at her table. 'Holland's society is very good; you always see someone or other in it worth knowing,' wrote Byron in his journal.[9] Often as many as fifty of the leading literary, political, scientific and military figures of the day would gather around the table to enjoy good society and plentiful food and drink. 'Stuffed myself with sturgeon, and exceeded in champagne and wine in general,' recalled a satisfied Byron of one gathering.[10]

Society at Holland House, especially in its early years as a political meeting place, was predominantly male. This was not so much because the character of the conversation excluded women, but rather because of Lady Holland's reputation. Born in 1771 to Richard Vassal, the owner of extensive estates in Jamaica, she married at the age of sixteen, a south-coast baronet and MP called Sir Godfrey Webster, who was thirty-three years her senior. The marriage was a disaster and, in the hope that a change of location would make life more agreeable, Sir Godfrey and Lady Webster went travelling on the continent for a number of years, settling in Florence in 1794. Here Lady Webster fell in love with Lord Holland, bore him a child and returned with him to London, where after being divorced by her husband she remarried, to become Lady Holland and chatelaine of Holland House.

Her status as a divorcée did not augur well for her smooth entry into Society; that she was snubbed doubtless contributed much to the imperious and domineering manner she would develop. She ran her crowded dinner table like a martinet. A sharp tap of her fan was a signal that she disapproved of the line the conversation might be taking. She gave the impression of running Holland House primarily as a demonstration of her social hegemony rather than for the amusement or comfort of her guests. Byron for instance could not bear the cold, but he felt that he could remove the screen she had placed in front of her fire only after she had left the room. 'When she retired, I watched their looks as I dismissed the screen, and every cheek thawed, and every nose reddened with the anticipated glow.'[11] Even late in life she insisted on dining at 5 p.m., long after the fashion for eating at a later hour had become the norm.

She was a monster, a dragon, the hostess from hell, but by the time carefree Count d'Orsay came to London she had taken two decades to cement her position at the pinnacle of the social pyramid. With her husband acting as Lord Grey's right-hand man at the top of the Whig party and with a new monarch, who as prince regent had been a visitor to Holland House, Lady Holland, no longer the disgraced, wayward wife of a baronet but an indomitable fifty-year-old matriarch, was unassailable.

D'Orsay cannot have been unaware of Lady Holland's status when he accepted an invitation to dine at Holland House, and it was here that in his uniquely mischievous fashion he further embellished the mythology that was already growing up around him. The count enjoyed the dubious privilege of sitting next to his hostess. As he was the latest and prettiest curiosity in London it was natural that Lady Holland would seek to make him her creature; that was her way. But it was also her way to subjugate her guests. To enjoy Lady Holland's patronage one had to submit to her yoke. Whether it meant sitting in an unheated room or arriving for dinner at an unfashionably early hour, she liked to impose her will on people and proceedings alike. A social juggernaut, she crushed everything in her way. It was inevitable that her view of social intercourse as an adversarial occupation in which she intended, and fully expected, to be the victor would bring into her into direct conflict with the glamorous young Frenchman who, like her, was self-possessed to the point of impudence.

It was to be a story that d'Orsay would tell for the amusement of others in later years. Long after both parties had died the story was retold with glee.

I have heard the Count tell, how, when he was in England for the first time (very young, very handsome, and not abashed), he was placed at some dinner-party next the late Lady Holland. That singular woman, who adroitly succeeded in ruling and retaining a distinguished circle, longer than either fascination or tyranny might singly have accomplished, chanced that day to be in one of her imperious humours. She dropped her napkin; the Count picked it up gallantly; then her fan, then her fork, then her spoon, then her glass; and as often her neighbour stooped and restored the lost article. At last however, the patience of the youth gave way, and on dropping her napkin again, he turned and called one of the footmen behind him. 'Put my couvert on the floor,' said he. 'I will finish my dinner there; it will be so much more convenient to my Lady Holland.'[12]

Such a remark incurred the displeasure of the queen of Holland Park, and her subsequent behaviour and letters demonstrate that she never forgave the slight. But d'Orsay's impudence was greeted differently a few miles to the east at 10 St James's Square, the fabulously appointed and richly decorated London house of the spendthrift Earl of Blessington.

CHAPTER FOUR

The 'Divine Bit of Blue'

ST JAMES'S SQUARE WAS A LONG WAY FROM TIPPERARY, WHERE on 1 September 1789 Margaret Power, later Countess of Blessington, was born. The third child of five, the eldest of whom died in infancy, she was physically frail, withdrawn and soulful, and her early years were far from cheerful. Thanks to a neighbour who took pity on the girl and taught her to read, young Margaret's literacy provided some internal refuge from the drunken, irresponsible and erratic behaviour of her father, a provincial dandy, snob, debauchee and opportunist social climber called Edmond Power.

'Mr Power was a fair, though not perhaps a very favourable specimen of the Irish country gentleman of some sixty years ago,' wrote an observer in 1855,

> fond of dogs, horses, wine and revelry, and very improvident and inattentive to all affairs of business. He was a fine-looking man, of an imposing appearance, shewy, and of an aristocratic air, very demonstrative of frills and ruffles, much given to white

48

cravats, and the wearing of leather breeches and top boots. He was known to the Tipperary bloods as 'a Buck,' as 'Shiver the Frills,' 'Beau Power,' and other appellations complimentary to his sporting character, rolicking disposition, and very remarkable costume.[1]

The woman who had been sufficiently impressed by this sporting character, with his 'rolicking disposition', imposing appearance and aristocratic air, to marry him was Ellen Sheehy. She was an ineffectual and slightly ridiculous figure who placed considerable importance in an ancestry that she could trace back to a twelfth-century Irish hero called Fitzgerald, who according to legend conquered Ireland with 140 men. Thus Margaret's upbringing alternated between the dressy, drunken activities of her father and the pious invocation of an illustrious lineage by her mother.

It was however not the twelfth-century heroics of her distant ancestor but the more recent conquest of Ireland by the English, culminating in the Battle of the Boyne in 1690, which had a direct impact on the childhood of young Margaret. A century later, at the time of her birth, discontent still simmered and latent Irish nationalism resurfaced at the time of the French Revolution. In 1796 France attempted an invasion of Ireland with a force of fifteen thousand men, forty-five ships and the Irish revolutionary leader Wolf Tone. The attempt was thwarted by delays and bad weather, but it increased tension in Ireland.

By 1797 Power had uprooted his family from the rural surroundings of Knockbritt and relocated to the relatively prosperous town of Clonmel. Hitherto Beau Power had been known as a Catholic and was even tacitly sympathetic to nationalistic aspirations. A Clonmel alderman, who had been a schoolfellow of one of Lady Blessington's brothers, recalls the arrival of the Powers in Clonmel thus:

When Mr. Power came to Clonmel, he was about thirty years of age; he was a good-looking man, of gentlemanly appearance and manners. He was then married. His first wife was a Miss Sheehy, of a highly respectable family. He engaged in the business of a corn-merchant and butter buyer. Subsequently he became proprietor of the Clonmel Gazette, or Munster Mercury. The editor of it was the well-known Bernard Wright. The politics of the paper were liberal – Catholic politics – Power was then a Catholic, though not a very strict or observant one.[2]

Catholic though he may have been, he was also a socially ambitious spendthrift. In a country given over to brawls and brigandry, populated by an illiterate and drunken peasantry, the elite was composed of absentee aristocrat landlords who owned vast tracts of Ireland, over which they exercised quasi-feudal power. Social advancement was to be found only by toadying to the English rulers. The resurgence of Irish nationalism, coinciding with the inevitable British paranoia resulting from the attempted French invasion of Ireland, gave Power the opportunity he sought to ingratiate himself. At the time measures against suspected nationalists or French sympathisers were severe: possession of so much as a letter written in French could lead to a severe flogging.

During these uncertain times, Power came to the notice of the local viceregal representative Lord Donoughmore, who made him a magistrate. Sensing social preferment, perhaps a pension, maybe even a baronetcy – how well he would have liked the sound of Sir Edmond Power Bart – Power took to his new role with alacrity. He renounced his faith, embraced Protestantism and set about hunting rebels as if they were vermin. Soon his duty on behalf of the English became an obsession and a pleasure, acquiring 'in a short time the character of a terrorist, in the district that was the sphere of his magisterial duties. The hunting of suspected rebels, of persons thought to be disloyal in the late rebellion, even so long as four and five years after its complete suppression became a favourite pursuit of Mr Power.'[3] As well as installing him as his local enforcer, it was Lord Donoughmore who helped set Power up as proprietor of the *Clonmel Mercury*; and during this time Power's house became a favourite meeting place of soldiers garrisoned at Clonmel.

However, the energy he invested in his work on behalf of Lord Donoughmore meant that his business suffered, and in an effort to revive his fortunes he entered into partnership with Messrs Hunt and O'Brien of Waterford and embarked on an ambitious programme of store and warehouse construction. Yet ironically his involvement with Donoughmore and the viceregal regime in Ireland would destroy his business prospects. The newspaper foundered when it was prosecuted for a libel. Power's warehouses were burned down, apparently out of revenge by people he had oppressed, and his partners terminated their involvement with him. After these acts of arson, Power's demeanour worsened and he began to brutalise his wife. 'His violence', recalled Lady Blessington in later years, 'which had formerly been of a political kind only, now became a sort of constitutional irascibility, his temper more and more irritable, his habits irregular and disorderly, he became a terror to his wife and children. He treated his wife with brutality.'[4]

It would have been therefore with some surprise that he learned that his daughter Margaret, although only fourteen years old and in his eyes a mere schoolgirl, had attracted the attention of two captains of the 47th Foot Regiment, recently stationed at Clonmel. Captains Murray and Farmer both paid their compliments. While flattered by the attention of Murray, she found the approaches of Maurice St Leger Farmer disconcerting. She was therefore distressed when her father announced that she would not be returning to school but marrying Farmer instead.

She protested in vain. It seems that Farmer had made pecuniary proposals that were to Power's advantage, and on 7 March 1804 the couple married. She soon came to experience Farmer's violence at first hand. It is with almost clinical detachment that her friend and biographer Madden notes, 'Captain Farmer was subject to fits of ungovernable passion at times so violent as to endanger the safety of himself and those around him; and at all times there was about him a certain wildness and abruptness of speech and gesture, which left the impression on her mind that he was insane.' She lived with Farmer for about three months, during which time he struck her repeatedly and locked her up whenever he left the house.

When he was ordered to join his regiment, then at the Curragh of Kildare, she, refusing to go with him, returned to her father's house. A few days after rejoining his regiment Farmer, in the midst of a quarrel and doubtless in the grip of one of his mad rages, drew his sword on his colonel. Shortly afterwards he was persuaded to sell his commission and go to India in the service of the East India Company. His wife declined to accompany him. Her treatment in the bosom of her family was not a great deal better than that which she had experienced in her marital home. Power resented what he perceived as the mess that his daughter had made of a marriage which would have been advantageous to him. Moreover, he feared that her failed marriage would blight the matrimonial prospects of his other daughters.

Margaret's return to her father's house in the summer of 1804 would, however, have coincided with the arrival in the area of the Tyrone militia, the lieutenant colonel of which was the extravagant Viscount Mountjoy, later Earl of Blessington. Mountjoy would have encountered Margaret Farmer at her father's house, where life was made so unpleasant for her that she spent part of the time elsewhere in Ireland. She is variously reported at Tullow in County Waterford and Cahir in Tipperary. Nevertheless she was back at her father's house three years later, and it would have been at around this time that she met Captain Jenkins of the 11th Dragoons. Suave, easy-going and rumoured to expect a considerable inheritance, he would have been exactly the sort of suitor that Power sought for his daughter Ellen.

But it was Margaret who caught his eye. Even prior to her marriage to Farmer, there was gossip about 'her alleged love of ballroom distinction, and intimacy with persons remarkable for gaiety and pleasure'.[5] It is therefore safe to assume that while she may have been cowed by the experience of a short brutal marriage and an unsettled family life, there was an engaging vivacity about her. Besides, by 1807 her beauty, for which she would later become famous, had matured somewhat from that of the pretty schoolgirl who had caught Farmer's eye.

Late in the afternoon or early in the evening of 21 April 1807, Edmond Power and his yeomanry were out on one of their rebel hunts when they encountered a young man carrying a pitchfork. Spotting the notorious Edmond Power mounted on horseback, at the head of his murderous band of thugs, the young man fled. Power then drew a handgun and shot him. Bleeding heavily, the young man was bound, then tied to a servant mounted on a horse and taken to Power's house. Here, even by the brutal standards of the time, the sight of the young man made an impression on the teenaged Margaret that would remain with her all her life. Later, as Marguerite, Countess of Blessington, she would recall the man, 'pale and ghastly, his head sunk on his breast, his strength apparently exhausted, his clothes steeped with blood'.[6]

The man died the following morning and his body, according to grisly custom, was hung outside the court house, where it was seen by his mother, a widowed peasant woman, who subsequently tried to commit suicide by slitting her throat. Such was the notoriety of this killing that even in this lawless corner of the country there was an inquest and, although he was acquitted, Power was removed from the magistracy. His decline was complete, but failure had been impending for a few years.

In the aftermath of the shooting by Power of the peasant, Jenkins persuaded Margaret to escape under his protection and the couple moved to Dublin and then to his estate in Hampshire. Accounts vary of her time here. It is rumoured that wild orgies took place where Margaret, who had metamorphosed into a stunning-looking young woman, would dance naked on the dining table for the amusement of the male guests. Certainly such behaviour would not have been out of character with the description given in the letters of Lady Bulwer Lytton. She thought Lady Blessington 'was one of the blackest hearted women I ever heard of'.[7] When it came to besmirching Lady Blessington's reputation, Lady Bulwer Lytton went at it with alacrity; 'every one knows', she wrote in a letter of February 1855, 'when her first Cavaliero, Captain Jenkins, voudrais s'en defaire, actually put her up to auction, *en costume de Paradis* (!!), on the public mess table, and after this creditable fashion she ran the gauntlet of the whole regiment'.[8]

A staunch defender of Lady Blessington's reputation, her biographer Michael Sadleir, provides an alternative view, contending that the unpleasant sexual experiences she had undergone with her husband 'had permanently diverted her sexual impulses into another channel'. Sadleir chooses not to dwell on what this other channel might have been, but feels 'it may be assumed that the physical element in their prolonged cohabitation was neither important nor long-lived'.[9] Instead Sadleir has the deracinated Irish beauty sitting demurely in Hampshire, nourishing her mind with the contents of Jenkins's library.

Whatever the truth, her retirement in Hampshire acted as a catalyst for the young woman. Whether or not she was Jenkins's sex toy, her reputation would be compromised as that of a kept woman. Yet at the same time she was to emerge as a remarkably well read and conversationally adept woman, who would captivate some of the leading intellectuals of the early nineteenth century with her wit and beauty. She would be seen as the sexy bluestocking or, as one visitor to her house was to dub her, that 'divine bit of blue'.[10]

*C*HAPTER FIVE

Her Comical Earl

AT THE AGE OF SEVENTEEN CHARLES JOHN GARDINER, VISCOUNT Mountjoy, found himself at the head of a family with a reputation as a pillar of the Anglo-Irish Ascendancy and owner of a vast estate with numerous tenants. He was an extremely rich young man; during the early years of the nineteenth century his income was in the region of £30,000 a year,[1] about £1,350,000 in today's terms. He overspent wildly and yet was an indulgent landlord, never harassing his tenants even when he himself was in need of funds. By the early 1850s the Mountjoy Estate would end up in the encumbered estates court, a financial farrago. But for decades the income from his estate and money raised on it would enable Viscount Mountjoy, later Earl of Blessington, to treat life as one long shopping spree, buying friends, lovers, houses, carriages, boats and young men.

The fortune that Lord Blessington was to enjoy had been founded by his great-grandfather, Luke Gardiner, who may have died fashionably in Bath in 1753, an MP and Privy Councillor, but whose early life had apparently been spent in the service of the White family at Leixlip Castle. He was succeeded in his estates by his son Charles, whose eldest son Luke rapidly established himself as a staunch and energetic supporter of the Anglo-Irish Establishment. Privy Councillor and colonel in the Dublin Militia, such was Luke Gardiner's standing that in 1789 the Mountjoy title, which had belonged to his grandmother's family and had been extinct since the death of her uncle in Bordeaux at the turn of the seventeenth and eighteenth centuries, was revived and bestowed upon him in the form of a barony – raised to a viscountcy in 1795. By this time his second son, the future Earl of Blessington, was entering his teens. From Eton he went to Christ Church, Oxford.

During the eighteenth century the Gardiners had been a typical Irish family on the make, an example of what toadying to Ireland's English rulers could bring. It was doubtless such a blueprint that the hapless 'Shiver the Frills' Power had hoped to follow; the difference was that by the 1790s the Gardiners had arrived.

The Mountjoy Arms was the name of the coaching inn on Main Street, Newtownstewart in County Tyrone, in what is now Northern Ireland. Baron, later Viscount, Mountjoy set about making his estate a model of agricultural enlightenment and clearly intended the eponymous Mountjoy Forest to be another monument to his family. Described as 'the most extensive and cultivated forest in Ireland',[2] with a circumference of between seven and eight miles, this was the subject of an ambitious reforestation plan; the years between 1790 and 1802 saw the plantation of 200,000 trees.

As well as his estate Mountjoy was proud of his son; as his first boy had died in infancy and as his other six children would be girls, there was a tendency to spoil and indulge the young Charles John.

His father's great fondness for him had contributed in some manner to the taste he had acquired in very early life for gorgeous ornaments, gaudy dresses, theatrical costumes and

military uniforms. At the period of the volunteering movement in Ireland, about 1788 or 1789, when the boy was not
above six or seven years of age, his father had him equipped in
a complete suit of volunteer uniform, and presented him thus
to a great concourse of people with a diminutive sword in the
poor child's hand, on the occasion of a grand review at
Newtownstewart, at the head of the corps that was commanded by his Lordship.[3]

But Mountjoy did not have long to dote on his son, his forest, his
estate or his new title. A mere three years after his elevation to viscount, he was dead: killed by several musket balls and numerous
pike wounds, at the evocatively named Three Bullet Gate in the
Battle of New Ross, ambushed by rebels while commanding his
regiment.

It was doubtless because of his family's reputation rather than
because of any intrinsic personal ability that the orphaned Lord
Blessington was sent to London as a representative Irish peer. In
1809 he made his House of Lords debut speaking in favour of a
motion for a vote of thanks to Lord Wellington, later duke and
victor of Waterloo, for the victory at Talavera in the Peninsular
campaign.

His speech was neither controversial nor especially scintillating.
'No general was better skilled in war, none more enlightened than
Lord Viscount Wellington,' he declared. 'The choice of a position at
Talavera reflected lustre on his talents; the victory was as brilliant
and as glorious as any on record. It was entitled to the unanimous
approbation of their lordships, and the eternal gratitude of Spain and
this country.'[4]

As Madden notes laconically, 'His Lordship seldom attended his
Parliamentary duties, and very seldom spoke.'[5] This cannot be said to
have been a loss to parliamentary oratory, but it is to his credit and

demonstrative of his good nature that he is recorded as having been opposed to George IV's vindictive charges against his queen, the excitable Caroline.

It was instead as a jewelled-up man of fashion that he wished to establish himself, hanging out at such louche establishments as Watier's, the glamorous but short-lived dining and gambling club founded by the Prince of Wales's chef Jean Baptiste Watier. 'No brighter youth danced in satin breeches and velvet coat at Almacks; none gayer gave delicious suppers in the lamp-lit bowers of Vauxhall Gardens.'[6]

In later years Byron would recall with some fondness a camp yet amiable figure, 'in all the glory of gems and snuff boxes, and uniforms and theatricals, sitting to Strolling, the painter, to be depicted as one of the heroes of Agincourt'.[7] Perhaps this militaristic pose recalled the antics of the six-year-old child at the head of the Tyrone militia. The infant militiaman had matured into a good-looking young aristocrat; his portrait by Holmes shows a dashing, if slightly vacant-looking, young man with an aquiline nose, sensitive features and wavy hair striking a Byronic pose – a deliberately unbuttoned tunic visible underneath a fur-collared coat. He adored dressing up. When not posing as a warrior of Agincourt he found time to sit for a portrait showing him as Achilles, dragging the body of Hector behind his chariot.

As well as embellishing himself he set about remodelling and extending the family seat. In 1807, in line with the interests he had developed at Eton, at Oxford and in London, he built an impressive kitchen, wine cellars and a large, extravagantly decorated theatre. And, having built his theatre, he established in his late twenties and early thirties a three- or four-week season of theatricals at Mountjoy, during which time professional actors and actresses would come from Dublin and London to perform. For about a month each year Mountjoy would take on the air of an early-nineteenth-century Irish Glyndebourne, with the upper echelons of

Irish Society descending on the house to enjoy the young lord's lavish hospitality. Even thirty years after Lord Blessington's last visit to his estate, when he, his wife and d'Orsay were all dead, tenants living in hovels on the Mountjoy Forest Estate would recall with awe 'the wonderful doings' of Blessington. Even though they could not remember exactly what parts he played in his private theatre, his costumes were recalled: 'the dresses he wore were very grand and fine'.[8]

At about the time he set up his theatre and established his theatricals as a fixture on the Irish social calendar he became involved with the woman who would become his first wife. Major Browne, one of his fellow officers, was ordered abroad and left his attractive wife in Viscount Mountjoy's care. The two promptly began an affair. Years passed, Browne was presumed dead and his wife's affair with the young spendthrift viscount settled into an open domesticity. She bore two illegitimate children whom he was happy to acknowledge as his: Charles John Gardiner was born in 1810, followed a year later by Emily Rosalie. Their parents then decided to regularise their arrangement and had just got married when Major Browne returned. Mountjoy dealt with the problem in a way that would become characteristic – he bought the man off. A definite figure is never stated but 'four or five figures'[9] is mentioned. The sum of around ten thousand pounds, worth in the region of four or five hundred thousand pounds today, is probably about right.

Shortly afterwards Major Browne died. Mountjoy married his widow and they had two further, legitimate children, Harriet Anne Gardiner born in 1812 and a year later an heir, Luke Wellington Gardiner. However, the following year, while on a tour of France, his wife died. Mountjoy proved himself as theatrical and lavish in grief as he was in amateur dramatics and wife-buying. The funeral was 'the talk of three European capitals'.[10]

Lord Mountjoy's grief at the loss of his lady was manifested in a funeral pageant of extraordinary magnificence, on the occasion of the removal of her remains to England, and from thence to Ireland. One of the principal rooms in his Lordship's Dublin residence, in Henrietta Street, was fitted up for the mournful occasion at an enormous cost. The body placed in a coffin, sumptuously decorated, had been conveyed to Dublin by a London undertaker of eminence in the performance of state funerals, attended by six professional female mourners, suitably attired in mourning garments, and was laid out in a spacious room hung with black cloth, on an elevated catafalque covered with a velvet pall of the finest texture, embroidered in gold and silver, which had been purchased in France for the occasion, and had recently been used at a public funeral in Paris of great pomp and splendour, that of Marshal Duroc. A large number of wax tapers were ranged round the catafalque, and the six professional female mutes, during the time the body lay in state, remained in attendance in the chamber in becoming attitudes, admirably regulated; while the London undertaker, attired in deep mourning, went through the dismal formality of conducting the friends of Lord Blessington who presented themselves to the place where the body was laid out, and as each person walked round the catafalque, and then retired, this official, having performed the lugubrious duties of master of the funeral solemnities, in a low tone, expressed a hope that the arrangements were to the satisfaction of the visitor.[11]

At a cost of three to four thousand pounds, such arrangements should have been at the very least satisfactory. In fact they were rather more than satisfactory; one of Blessington's more worldly and social friends, 'well acquainted with such pageants', considered 'the magnificence of it was greater than that of any similar *performance* of private obsequies he ever saw'.[12]

His wife interred in a suitably lavish fashion, the easily bored Blessington took a holiday. He went to England and spent a few weeks in Hampshire with his old friend Captain Jenkins. Here he met Margaret Farmer, perhaps remembering time spent at her father's house. At any rate intimacy between the free-spending young aristocrat and the Jenkins ménage grew. Jenkins is listed among guests at a dinner given by Blessington at the latter's house on Henrietta Street in Dublin towards the end of 1815.[13] And both Jenkins and Mrs Farmer appear again at a house party at Blessington's Mountjoy Forest Estate in September 1816.[14]

Although nominally still married to the unstable and increasingly dissolute Maurice St Leger Farmer, it would appear that, while perhaps not accepted into the most morally demanding of circles, Margaret was welcomed by such broadminded hosts as Lord Blessington as the mistress of Captain Jenkins. Besides it was not long before Blessington began to take an interest in Mrs Farmer on her own account.

At this time, in her later twenties, Margaret Farmer was a bewitchingly beautiful woman, who had used her time as a semi-recluse in the Jenkins house to improve her education. Blessington, whose prodigality was matched by a magpie-like acquisitiveness that extended from snuff boxes through paintings and houses to people, was clearly taken with her. He had recently lost one attractive wife and was in need of another. When he wanted something he would bend his entire will to its possession: his life was to be littered with projects. If he can be described as having had strength of character it was in this direction; he would allow himself to become totally consumed by an enterprise. Easily susceptible to the charms of a new object or person, once seduced he was determined in its acquisition until he had either succeeded in his desired end or become distracted by something more exciting. For him acquisition was an addiction. His soul was restless, he needed to fill his life with diversions and he did so regardless of cost. This was, after all, a man who had built a theatre in a distant region of a lawless and uncouth province of early-nineteenth-century Britain, itself no crucible of culture. What Blessington wanted, he tended to get; if there was a problem he threw money at it. Having met and been taken with the desirable Mrs Farmer, it was therefore inevitable that he would offer the easy-going Jenkins ten thousand pounds for her. Jenkins accepted.

Having bought her, Blessington then set about wooing her. According to some idiosyncratic sense of propriety he seems to have wanted to do the 'right thing'. There was perhaps a need to be thought well of by all parties. Having recompensed Jenkins, he set up Mrs Farmer in Manchester Square in London and paid court to her in the most respectful manner. Although a frequent visitor to the house in which he had established her, he was, according to those who saw him there, 'never unaccompanied by some mutual friend or acquaintance'.[15] There is something touching in Blessington's propriety, especially as Mrs Farmer can hardly be considered to have had a reputation to protect. She was still married to a madman whom she had deserted and she had spent the last few years living openly in the house of another man. Although Blessington could have done what he liked with Mrs Farmer, he appears to have been intent on possessing her in a way that was entirely proper. Pretty, intelligent and alluring, she was his dream wife. Divorce proceedings were initiated against Farmer, who had recently returned from a lengthy sojourn in the East Indies.

Rather obligingly Farmer died, falling from a window after a long bibulous evening with some friends at the King's Bench Prison. This was not as odd as it may sound. Discipline at this debtors' prison was so relaxed that by 1828 it was described as 'the most desirable place of incarceration in London'.[16] Those who could afford it purchased 'freedom of the Rules', which enabled them to roam the taverns in three square miles around the prison. Those who could not buy access to the surrounding area had to make do with the resources within the prison's high walls: in the courtyard hatters, tailors, barbers, oyster salesmen, even piano makers plied their trade, and there was no shortage of drink. The King's Bench was awash with alcohol: thirty gin shops operated there selling 120 gallons of Mother's Ruin a week, and richer prisoners entertained guests to dinner prepared by a chef. Farmer's defenestration in October 1817 was just another accident. Perhaps the most unusual aspect of the affair was that 'the party had drunk four quarts of rum'[17] rather than the locally available gin. Farmer's death allowed Blessington to marry his widow.

On 16 February 1818, Margaret Farmer entered the church in Bryanston Square the widow of a captain on half-pay and left it Marguerite, Countess of Blessington. The couple honeymooned in Ireland, where Blessington gave a reception for his wife at his house in Dublin and then descended on his Mountjoy Forest Estate, where tenants and servants greeted the couple rapturously. Ireland held unhappy memories for the new Countess of Blessington, however. This was to be the first and last time she visited her husband's estates as châtellaine.

It was instead in the heart of fashionable London, at 10 St James's Square, a house bought and sumptuously redecorated by Blessington in early 1820, that she was to reinvent herself. By the spring of that year she was already giving dinners and collecting social scalps. 'Miladi', wrote barrister, wit and politician Joseph Jekyll, 'keeps an album and desires all her literary friends to write in it to perpetuate their autographs.'[18] Over the ensuing three years, she was to emerge as the most lavish, intelligent and captivating London hostess of her generation.

Her portrait by Lawrence shows a fresh-faced woman who

looks barely out of her teens, instead of the twenty-eight-year-old who married Blessington. Her flawless white breasts descend into the deep décolletage of a diaphanous gown, where they are parted by a suggestively located corsage. Her hands perhaps appear a little plump. The only clue to her age is the knowing hint of a smile that appears to tug at the right-hand corner of her mouth, the effect of which only heightens her mysterious sex appeal. As well as being the most fashionable painter of his day – his portraits commanded a price of seven hundred guineas and there was a waiting list – he 'specialised in flattering "improvements" to those of his subjects who were past their prime or possessed of unfortunate features'.[19] It would appear that his portrait of the new Countess of Blessington, however, did not and indeed could not improve on nature.

Lady Blessington's portrait by Lawrence was the most talked-about painting in the Royal Academy Exhibition of 1821. Present on the opening day of this exhibition, P. G. Patmore (author, journalist, editor and father of the celebrated Victorian poet Coventry Patmore) described the work as 'Lawrence's celebrated portrait of Lady Blessington – one of the finest he ever painted'. He was also able to examine the subject at close quarters. 'She was leaning on the arm of her husband, Lord Blessington,' and while the free-spending earl was 'gazing in admiration on the portrait', Patmore 'saw how impossible it is for an artist to "flatter" a really beautiful woman'. So excited was he by the sight of this woman that he said, 'I have seen no other so striking instance of the inferiority of art to nature . . . as in this celebrated portrait of Lady Blessington. As the original stood before it . . . she fairly "killed" the copy, and this no less in the individual details than in the general effect.' He added, 'I have never since beheld so pure and perfect a vision of female loveliness, in what I conceive to be its most perfect phase, that, namely, in which intellect does not predominate over form, feature, complexion, and the other physical attributes of female beauty, but only serves to heighten, purify and irradiate them; and it is this class of beauty which cannot be equalled on canvas.' He pronounced her 'a star to kneel before and worship'.[20]

Even compensating for Patmore's hyperbolic gallantry, it is safe to assume that Lady Blessington was a bewitchingly beautiful woman, whose attractiveness resided in a complex cocktail of pulchritude, notoriety, vivacity and intelligence. She was without doubt one of the beauties of the age. By the time the dashing Count d'Orsay strolled into her drawing room one evening in the autumn of 1821, she was the most discussed woman of her day. This meeting between two of the most stylish and controversial figures of London then must have been an intriguing spectacle. Each would have formulated notions about the other. Perhaps d'Orsay expected a younger, prettier version of Lady Holland, a woman whose social and cultural pretensions he would prick with his insolence. Perhaps Lady Blessington felt that it was her duty as a fashionable hostess to inspect this extraordinary young Frenchman whose looks and behaviour were making him the talk of London. Lord Blessington would of course have been perfectly happy to gratify his wife's whim.

However, it seems that the meeting took a radically different turn, affecting the three people in a way that they could never have imagined. 'The young Count made a most favourable impression wherever he appeared; but nowhere did it pierce so deep or so lasting as in the heart of his charming hostess of the magnificent *conversaziones, soirées,* dinners, balls, breakfasts and suppers, that followed each other in rapid succession in that brilliant mansion in St James' Square.'[21]

There amid the burnished splendour of the London mansion that Lord Blessington had created as a springboard for his wife's entry into high Society, all three protagonists saw each other at his or her best. In later years Lady Blessington would stage-manage her appearance in a drawing room, arranging herself carefully in a chair in an aspect calculated to arouse a favourable response. It was an art of which she had doubtless made herself mistress by her early thirties. Having posed long enough for Sir Thomas Lawrence to create his portrait she would have fine-tuned that look of kittenish playfulness: a suggestion of a smile on those rosebud lips, her limpid grey-green eyes looking up through her eyelashes, her delicate hands fidgeting with the latest novel or volume of verse and so allowing the candlelight or perhaps the rays of the setting sun to catch the fire in the stones of her rings.

D'Orsay, meanwhile, at the start of his adult life must have been a wonderful sight: self-assured yet still in possession of the boyish charm that had caught Vigny's attention at the Pension Hix. Although already a rising social star, he had yet to acquire the worldliness of age or to affect the ennui of the man of fashion. Speaking in heavily accented French, he must have evinced a slight hint of vulnerability beneath his precocity that would have spoken to the vulnerability that despite her glittering carapace was at the core of Lady Blessington's personality. Perhaps also a sense of physical attraction was kindled within Lady Blessington by d'Orsay, and this was a sensation that, as a childless woman of thirty-two with her life apparently sorted out, would have come as a surprise. She might reasonably have thought that such sexual feelings had been extinguished by the actions of her first husband and that she had just put that part of her life to one side, devoting herself to the social and cultural conquest of London, with the Earl of Blessington as her consort. Maybe looking at this young man she experienced sexual desire and felt it better to direct these risky emotions in a maternal direction.

The two people appear to have experienced an instant attraction for each other, and Lord Blessington, who seems to have stopped at nothing in the quest for his wife's comfort and happiness, would have been glad of it. Kindness seems to have been one of Blessington's most prominent characteristics and if, as it seems, his wife's attraction to d'Orsay was immediate he would have seen the difference it made to her mood and encouraged it. Moreover his own sense of the theatrical would have warmed to the young, beautiful, epicene Frenchman. The chemistry of human attraction would have an extremely complex effect on these three people. 'I believe, and I like to think, that had Count d'Orsay fallen into good hands, he might have been a great many things that he was not,' noted Gronow, adding ominously, 'Unfortunate circumstances, which entangled him as with a fatal web from his early youth, dragged him downwards and led him step by step to his ruin.'[22]

But this is a view that ascribes an almost childlike pliability to d'Orsay's nature, which is at odds with the spirited and hot-blooded character who made such an impact on people as diverse as the Duke of Wellington and Lady Holland. It raises the intriguing notion that d'Orsay was rendered pliable by his love for either Lady Blessington or her husband – possibly both – or alternatively that he was an amoral and opportunistic adventurer who knew a good thing when he saw it. Perhaps sensing the potential for powerful attraction and the intricate emotional dynamics of the situation, he made himself especially agreeable that evening in St James's Square, praising Lady Blessington not just for her looks, which she must have known were stunning, but for her intellect, for which she seemed to want to nurture an even higher opinion. D'Orsay might also have taken care to make Lord Blessington think well of him, perhaps complimenting him on the decoration of the house or his dress.

At this point it is perhaps instructive to view d'Orsay's behaviour against the background of his upbringing. Two things stand out about the environment in which he was raised: its splendour and its instability. He had been petted and spoiled as a child prodigy. Character traits that might have been rounded and smoothed by more practical parenting were instead accentuated and made much of by a household dominated by women; the result was a complex and probably quite sensitive character whose external manifestations were eccentricities of dress and toilet, and an exaggerated self-possession. Once he had stepped over the threshold of the Blessington house in St James's Square he would have felt at home in a splendidly decorated milieu whose governing spirit was the enigmatic and strong-willed Lady Blessington.

Moreover, he cannot have failed to learn of Lord Blessington's remarkable riches, doubtless inflated by popular gossip. While d'Orsay had developed a talent for spending money with grace and imagination, his position was anything but secure. His parents had never had money, but rather corrosively they had grown up with a sense that, had history treated their family circumstances differently, had Anne Franchi been the wife of the king rather than his mistress, had somehow the fabled wealth of their tax-farming forebears survived the French Revolution, they would not have been cheated of the rank and riches that they felt were theirs. Such feelings would have been passed on to young Alfred.

D'Orsay was mixing with the fast set of his day, but this could not continue indefinitely. As regards a career he had no particular desire to take the one open to him and enter the peacetime army of a defeated superpower and spend the coming years as an officer in the army of a monarch he instinctively loathed. It is impossible to tell exactly how much d'Orsay's warmth of manner that evening was assisted by the knowledge, however subconscious, that the wonderful Blessingtons might take his life in an entirely different direction to the one in which it seemed it must inevitably lead. There is little reason to suppose that on their first meeting he saw them as surrogate parents. At most perhaps he envisaged a harmless flirtation with Lady Blessington, or maybe he saw Lord Blessington as man under whose patronage his leaning towards the arts might flourish.

However, he certainly came away that evening pleased with the two fascinating people he had met and feeling a curious warmth towards them. After all, the powerful mixture of splendour, beauty, scandal and apparently limitless wealth must have made him feel at ease, reminding him a little of his childhood in Napoleon's Paris. And between the kindness of Lord Blessington and the beauty of his wife, what could there possibly be not to like?

CHAPTER SIX

Ménage à Trois

D'ORSAY STREAKED ACROSS THE FIRMAMENT OF FASHIONABLE London like some exotic comet. Then, like a comet, he disappeared. His English holiday was over; he had come as part of the official French delegation to assist at the coronation of George IV and had stayed on to conquer fashionable Society, outrage Lady Holland and dazzle the Blessingtons. But his military career required his presence in France.

After the defeat of Napoleon various members of the Bourbon family had been restored to a number of European thrones: France of course, also Naples and Spain. But civil war in Spain had forced the Spanish king Ferdinand VII to adopt a constitution that greatly reduced his power. In Louis XVIII's view this was hardly satisfactory; he saw it as a dangerous resurgence of republicanism. It was inevitable that the ageing French king would want to safeguard the monarchist principle and help a relative in trouble at the same time. However, given that Napoleon had fared so badly in Spain, never fully subjugating the country and in the end being driven out by Wellington, the omens for French military intervention in the affairs of Spain were not favourable. Nevertheless the prospect of an expedition across the Pyrenees to restore a Bourbon despot was the talk of French military circles in 1822. It would eventually take place in 1823 and prove to be a surprise success.

D'Orsay's father was by now a prominent general — in September 1815 after Napoleon's defeat at Waterloo, General d'Orsay had been made commander of the second brigade of the first division of the infantry of the Garde Royale to reward him for not siding with Napoleon, and by 1820 he was appointed commander of the order of the Légion d'Honneur.[1] Because of this, and because d'Orsay himself was a member of the Garde Royale, a commission obtained through the nepotism of his grandmother, it was expected that he would take part in the invasion. In the meantime he was posted to Valence in southern France, 'a town of considerable extent, but its streets are narrow, irregular, and dirty'.[2]

From being the precocious darling of fashionable London, mixing with statesmen, writers, artists and aristocrats, he was thrown on to the scant society of a garrison in provincial France with its seedy billets, uncouth colleagues and tedious military routine. The dandified twenty-two-year-old with his exaggerated manners and flamboyant accessories, such as a solid gold dressing case given to him by his doting grandmother, did not fit in. In later life he would recall the first few days of his career in the Garde Royale thus: 'I had only joined my regiment a few days, when an officer at the mess-table used disgusting and impious language in speaking of the Blessed Virgin. I called on him to desist; he repeated the foul language he had used; I threw a plate of spinach across the table in his face; a challenge ensued; we fought that evening on the rampart of the town.'[3]

Although religion does not seem to have played a particularly important role in d'Orsay's life, there is a swagger and a vastness of scale in fighting a duel over an oath that would have appealed to his flamboyant nature. Indeed d'Orsay's entire, albeit brief, military career seems to have been characterised by an exaggerated sense of chivalry. It seems that in army life, just as at the dining table of Lady Holland and in the salon of Lady Blessington, he delighted in striking a pose. His dandyism was finding another outlet: if forced into the inimical surroundings of a garrison in an out-of-the-way French town he would at least behave in an idealised manner. While he took issue with the strong language and irreligious imprecations of his fellow officers, 'he was greatly beloved by the men, whose comforts and interests he looked to with the utmost care'.[4] And their affection for him was matched 'only by the admiration excited by his feats of strength, and superiority over his comrades in all manly exercises'.[5]

It is also during his military career that some early evidence of the genuine benevolence of d'Orsay emerges. Among those who knew him later in his life, his great kindness and altruism were almost universally lauded. And Madden recalled a few early instances of d'Orsay's gallantry:

> Some of the traits of his garrison life, though trifling in themselves, are too characteristic to be left unnoticed. At the provincial balls, where his repute as a man of fashion, of family, and of various accomplishments had made itself known, and rendered him a leading object of attention; he used to be jeered by his brother officers, for his apparent predilection for persons not remarkable for their personal attractions, as he made it a practice to single out the plainest girls present to dance with, and to pay the greatest attention to those who seemed most neglected or unnoticed. There was no affectation of any kind about him; whatever he did that appeared considerate or amiable, was done simply from natural kindness of disposition.

On one occasion, living out of barracks, he lodged at the house of a widow, with a son and two daughters; the son, a young robust man of a violent temper, and of considerable bodily strength, was in the habit of treating his mother and sisters with brutality. Comte d'Orsay, one day, while in his room, hearing a loud noise and tumult in the apartments of his hostess and her daughters, on the ground floor, descended to ascertain the cause, and finding the young man offering acts of violence to his mother, fell upon him, and notwithstanding the powerful resistance of his formidable opponent, whose rage had been turned against him, inflicted such severe chastisement on him, that quarter was soon called for. The Count then, with his characteristic quietude of manner, in the midst of any excitement or turmoil, ended the scene, by assuring the subdued bully, that any repetition of his violence on his family, would meet with punishment far exceeding in severity that which he had the trouble of bestowing on that occasion.[6]

But d'Orsay was not long to endure the ignominy of domestic violence at his lodgings, brother officers who took the Virgin's name in vain and plain dancing partners. Nor would he have to face the danger or discomfort of invading Spain.

On 25 August 1822, the Earl and Countess of Blessington, accompanied by Mary Ann Power, Lady Blessington's youngest sister, left London for the continent. It had been mooted that Lady Blessington should accompany her husband on a tour of his Irish estates. However, three years of life as a fashionable hostess, being painted by Lawrence, fêted by the leading men of the day and gossiped about by their wives and mistresses, had hardened her antipathy towards Ireland into a rigid detestation of the place. As Marguerite, Countess of Blessington she had no wish to return to the country where she had been mere Sally Power – drunk's daughter, bolter and woman of dubious morality. Ireland was a place that held only bad memories for her. She was adamant on the subject; her eloquence and her passionate aversion to a visit to Mountjoy impressed those who saw her. Writing to her on 27 July 1822, the novelist, travelling companion of Byron and habitué of St James's Square John Galt was struck by the force of her feelings.

> My Dear Madam
>
> On Monday evening I was so distinctly impressed with the repugnance which your Ladyship feels at the idea of going to Ireland, that I entered entirely into your feelings; but upon reflection, I cannot recall all the reasonableness of the argument, a circumstance so unusual with respect to your Ladyship's reasons in general, that I am led to think some other cause at the moment must have tended to molest you, and to lend the energy of its effect to the expressions of your reluctance.[7]

Galt was writing from Liverpool, where he encountered 'scores and hundreds, and the thousands of the poor Irish in quest of employment'. Rather like asylum seekers in England in the early twenty-first century, these economic refugees were a social problem viewed with jealousy by the 'common people'. Much of the blame for the plight of the Irish and the potential friction with the common people of England was apportioned to absentee landlords such as Blessington, who, while admittedly one of the most enlightened and personally kind, was also a high-profile, high-spending, London-based socialite. The letter plainly urges Lady Blessington to change her mind, as so many factors 'combine to form such a strong case for my Lord's journey, that nothing but the apprehension of your Ladyship's indisposition can be filed against it'.

Certainly Galt seems to have been in no doubt about Lady Blessington's ability to manage her husband, as he confides that the

Irish 'journey, however, to be really useful, should be one of observation only, and I am sure you will easily persuade him to make it so'. Lady Blessington could indeed persuade her husband to do pretty much as she wanted, and to forestall a visit to Mountjoy 'the Countess pleaded ill-health'.[8] Blessington capitulated.

Barely a fortnight after his letter from Liverpool Galt wrote to Lady Blessington from Edinburgh. 'I need not say that, although I regret that the journey to Ireland is not to take place, I am much more concerned on account of the cause which has occasioned the change, than the loss of pleasure I should have had in visiting Mountjoy.'[9] The 'cause' might have been Lady Blessington's 'ill health'. It is likely that the prospect of finding herself faced with a visit to her unhappy Irish past was the stimulus that prompted her to look for alternative projects to dangle in front of her husband. If London could not produce sufficient diversions to prevent Lord Blessington fretting about the flood of Irish poor into Liverpool, then perhaps a protracted tour of Europe might absorb his attention more fully. And while they were touring the continent they could of course look up the dashing young count who had made such an impression the preceding autumn. Given Lady Blessington's romantic disposition, it is not difficult to see how she would choose when faced with the prospect of a damp miserable autumn in Ireland or following the sun and the dashing young count south. And given Lord Blessington's touching desire to make his wife happy, it seems to have been outside his power to deny her anything for long.

But, once she had nagged and cajoled her husband into postponing the Irish visit in favour of a trip to Europe, Lady Blessington experienced some uncertainty. 'Yet now, that the moment of departure is nearly arrived, I almost wish I was not going. Yes, the quitting home for an indefinite period, makes one thoughtful. What changes, what dangers may come before I sleep again beneath its roof!'[10] Although she did not know it, it would be eight years before she would see St James's Square again, and her life would have changed beyond recognition.

After a rough crossing of the Channel they made their way to Paris, which they reached on 31 August, in time for Lady Blessington to celebrate her thirty-third birthday the following day. This was Lady Blessington's third visit to Paris.[11] And by coincidence, during an earlier visit to the French capital in 1820, they had even examined the Hôtel Craufurd with a view to renting it[12] – though, to judge from what Lady Blessington wrote in her journal, this was a whimsical business, undertaken more for entertainment than with any serious intention of taking the house.

Lady Blessington's journal of her Parisian visit in the late summer of 1822 records the observations and actions of a typical wealthy English tourist. She noted the arrival of the autumn/winter fashions: 'the ladies have added to their summer costume, a warm shawl, thrown over the shoulders with a grace peculiar to Parisians'.[13] And with some satisfaction she was already able to think of herself as a seasoned gourmet: '*la cuisine française* has greatly degenerated even within my memory'.[14] Like so many British travellers after her, she complained about the use of garlic, which had apparently been recently introduced to Parisian cuisine by Spaniards. She went to the Tivoli and had a ride on La Montagne Russe: a roller-coaster in fake ice modelled on one in St Petersburg and erected in Paris after the arrival of the Allies in 1815. As she filled her journal with page after page of remarks about the contents of the Louvre, she was completing her reinvention from small-town Irish slattern to woman of quality. Typical is her appraisal of one master: 'The exuberant *embonpoint* of Rubens' women disgusts me; they appear designed to attract the admiration of graziers or butchers, only.'[15]

While the excursions, cultural visits and dinners went on, so, it seems, did some serious negotiations with the d'Orsay family. Lord Blessington was once more in the grip of an obsession. Doubtless encouraged by his wife, but also motivated by acute personal desire, he was on another shopping binge.

> It was the peculiarity of Lord Blessington to throw himself with complete *abandon* into any passion or pursuit that came in his way, and to spare no expense or sacrifice of any kind, to obtain, as soon as possible, the fullest enjoyment that could possibly be derived from it; and no sooner was the object so ardently desired accomplished, the expense encountered, and the sacrifice made for its attainment, than the zest for its delight was gone; other phantoms of pleasure were to be pursued, and no sooner grasped than to be relinquished for some newer objects of desire.[16]

Thus while Lady Blessington was at the Louvre offering her censorious opinions on Rubens, her husband was, quite probably, locked in negotiations with the d'Orsay family over the future of their son. As is the way with addicts, Blessington required ever greater highs and, having purchased his last two wives for ten thousand pounds apiece, it would not be unnatural, given his craving, that he should also wish to purchase the ultimate male companion.

Hitherto he had dealt with complaisant Englishmen, Browne and Jenkins, easy-going friends of his for whom ten thousand pounds represented ample compensation for the absence of a wife or mistress. But with the worldly d'Orsays Lord Blessington was attempting to punch above his weight. Ranged against him were Madame Craufurd, the accomplished international courtesan who in her day had broken hearts everywhere from the Court of Württemberg to the offices of the East India Company; her accomplished daughter by the King of Württemberg; and of course the wily negotiator General Count d'Orsay, who had spied for Austria, been one of Napoleon's favourite generals and then changed sides again to find himself now at the centre of Royalist Society through the judicious marriage of his daughter to the Duke de Guiche. General d'Orsay had lived on his wits and charm during three of the most turbulent decades Europe had ever witnessed: as a negotiator he would have been more than a match for the good-natured, flamboyant, extravagant, sexually confused, indecisive, phenomenally rich Irish peer.

The family must have seemed impressive to Blessington. Indeed the earl and the general were to become friends; in 1825 General Count d'Orsay accompanied Blessington on a visit to his Tyrone estates.[17] Doubtless the good looks of d'Orsay *père* did nothing to hinder Blessington's infatuation with the family and its glamorous son.

On his side General Count d'Orsay, his daughter advantageously married, needed to arrange a suitable settlement for his son. With the d'Orsay family wealth plundered during the Revolution and Madame Craufurd reduced to letting the Hôtel Craufurd to wealthy tourists, there were few prospects for his son. Isolated military excursions such as that into Spain aside, the army could not offer the scope for rapid promotion that it had when all of Europe was at war. In any case, being a shrewd man of the world, the general saw that his son's talents lay in leading fashion not armies and conquering drawing rooms not continents. Presumably too he was able to draw on his own experiences as a good-looking, fashionable man of expensive tastes and limited means. He wanted the best for his son and presumably thought Blessington was in a position to offer it.

D'Orsay was to be one of Blessington's most expensive purchases. No mere one-off ten-thousand-pound payment would suffice. It seems that General Count d'Orsay wanted to set his son up with an income for life and that during September 1822 in Paris an agreement was reached that suited all parties. Certainly by 23 March of the following year there was no secret about the ménage. 'D'Orsay is established with them,' recorded Henry Edward Fox, son of Lord and Lady Holland, on encountering the Blessingtons at dinner on the

Riviera, 'and, she says, is to marry Ld B.'s daughter, whom he has never seen and who is only 13. This, I suppose, is only a blind.'[18] Blind or not, it was plainly an arrangement that satisfied General Count d'Orsay, the Earl of Blessington, his countess and presumably Alfred d'Orsay. Business concluded, Lord Blessington rewarded himself with a little light shopping and engaged a cook, 'one of the most accomplished artistes'[19] who had worked for Napoleon.[20] Then on 10 September the Blessington circus lumbered off to the South of France. One French wag on catching sight of the caravanserai observed that, such was the paraphernalia, 'One would suppose, that instead of a single family, a regiment at least, were about to move.'[21] And at the head of this regiment was the thirty-three-year-old Countess of Blessington, wallowing in every luxury that imagination could conceive and money could buy in early-nineteenth-century France. Luxury had become a way of life. 'I could not cheerfully resign a *dormeuse à doubleressort*, with its library, soft cushions, and eiderdown pillows, its nécessaire à déjeuner et à dîner, safely stowed in a well, and its innumerable other little comforts, without a sigh of regret,'[22] she confided to her journal.

As their cortège rumbled south, Lady Blessington filled up her journal with accounts of a visit to Voltaire's house in Ferney, the unwelcome attentions of mosquitoes, the purchase of a charger called Mameluke from the Count d'Hautpoul and so on. Then on 15 November the chaste tone of her journal changes, and a heightened sensuality becomes evident. 'We begin already to be sensible of an increased mildness in the temperature as we advance,' she records.[23] They had arrived in Valence. Although no mention is made of d'Orsay by name in her published journals until after her husband's death — before that he is coyly and euphemistically referred to as 'a gentleman of our party' — his presence can be felt in numerous ways. For instance Count d'Orsay's hero Napoleon is invoked with growing frequency; the 'house, in an obscure street, was pointed out to us',

presumably by d'Orsay, 'in which Napoleon Bonaparte, when a lieutenant in the artillery, spent many months'.[24]

It is possible to imagine her dabbing decorously at her glowing
forehead and perspiration-glistened breasts as she sits on the soft
cushions of her carriage surrounded by her travelling library, writing
her journal. 'The aspect of the people of the south is very different
to that of those we have lately quitted. Here, dark sparkling eyes,
clear brown complexions, and an increased animation of manner,
characterize the inhabitants. The men are, for the most part, tall and
athletic; but the women are so peculiarly round-shouldered, and
stoop so much, as to look as if they were deformed.'[25] Of course few,
if any, were as tall and as athletic as Count d'Orsay, and Lady
Blessington was herself a most pleasing contrast to the round-
shouldered, stooping and deformed local women. Like many British
women after her, Lady Blessington had fallen victim to the charms of
southern Europe.

D'Orsay now made the decision to resign his commission, and
five days later the party moved on down the Rhône to Avignon, where
they would spend the winter, and where they would meet the Duke
and Duchess de Caderousse Grammont, who had a château near by at
which they gave 'frequent entertainments'.[26] It was during this winter
in Provence that the relationship between the Blessingtons and
d'Orsay deepened. The Caderousse Grammonts were relatives of
d'Orsay's by marriage as was Count Sebastiani, who was in command of a Corsican regiment in Avignon. Indeed, as Christmas
neared, d'Orsay seems to have introduced the Blessingtons to a circle
composed either of relatives by marriage of his sister or military per-
sonnel, presumably recommended by his father, or friends he had
made during his time as a soldier in the South. Among their acquaintances at this time were an ex-soldier said to be 110 years of age, the
commander of a military hospital, the hospital's inmates and sundry
officers. Although he may have been embarking on a new life under

the sponsorship of Lord Blessington, d'Orsay did not turn his back on his old life. It was as if he were weighing up the relative merits of a life in the army and life in the household of Lord Blessington.

For her part Lady Blessington seems to have revelled in the social life afforded by regiments in small-town France. Maybe it was, unconsciously, a chance to revisit her past as a child and young woman in Ireland as she wished it might have been, with the senior officers paying her the respect owing to the spouse of a visiting British peer accompanied by the son of a prominent, decorated general. Certainly d'Orsay's friendship afforded her insights into military life 'such as are rarely allowed to travellers',[27] and forming 'an acquaintance with the commanding officers of many of the regiments in garrison towns through which we have passed'[28] was the social staple of their lives during the winter of 1822–1823. Perhaps d'Orsay was giving the Blessingtons a chance to see him in his preferred habitat and presumably allowing them to judge him favourably. For instance, her opinions of the relationship between officers and men chime almost exactly with the accounts of d'Orsay's behaviour as an officer that we saw earlier: 'A good understanding, approaching to friendship, subsists between the officers and soldiers; and it is difficult, with our notions of the distance and hauteur which a strict attention to discipline requires, to believe that a perfect subordination can exist where so much good will is visible. Yet such is the case. A frank, manly confidence is evident in the manners of the soldier towards his officer; but this demeanour is however entirely free from a disrespectful familiarity.'

She might have been describing d'Orsay himself rather than the officer caste in general. Certainly d'Orsay would have been the lens through which she viewed provincial French life, which, while nothing like as grand as the circle she had been creating for herself in London, was pleasing, perhaps even refreshing in its unpretentiousness. (The extent of their social circle at this time, centring on soldiers and d'Orsay's sister's in-laws, gives a snapshot of what d'Orsay's life might have been had he not embarked on life with Lord Blessington's patronage: a peacetime version of his father's career.) Lady Blessington would appear to have been genuinely happy at this time, and although Provençal high Society was almost an oxymoron, the Blessingtons and d'Orsay entered into the social life that the area afforded with an unfeigned enthusiasm, with Lady Blessington enjoying herself so much that she occasionally 'played truant'[29] to her journal, seduced by the delicious informality, by the *douceur de vivre* and increasingly by her glamorous guide.

Lady Blessington too was faced with an alternative existence; for the first time in her life she seemed to get under the skin of a different way of life. Through d'Orsay she no longer saw France and the French as a tourist. Moreover she began to understand a subtly different role for women in society, as she writes in her journal on New Year's Eve 1822:

The French women are very pleasant companions; so easily amused, and so naturally disposed to be amusing. They have more animal spirits than the English; but it never degenerates into aught approaching boisterousness. But this extreme facility of pleasing and being pleased, argues a want of that sensibility which renders English women so captivating. A French woman seems born to amuse, and to be admired; an English woman to interest, and to be loved. A man must have a more than common share of vanity, who could imagine that a French woman, however she might profess to like him, would break her heart at his loss. She is too *spirituelle*, too vivacious, and too prone to be diverted, to indulge a settled melancholy; but an English woman, with her naturally soft and reflective character, her power of concentration, and the gentle pensiveness which is a characteristic of her countrywomen, conveys an impression that her happiness would be for ever destroyed by the loss of the object of her affection; and this impression has a powerful influence over him who loves her.[30]

As the new year wore on, there were few aspects of the French character that were not met with delight by Lady Blessington; from acting to dancing to relations with their domestic staff, all were seized upon with glee. With the benign affluence of Lord Blessington in the background and the dashing young d'Orsay acting as a tour guide, winter passed pleasantly.

With the arrival of spring it was time to move on to the coast. Italian influence sprawled along what is now the French Riviera. Upon her arrival in Cannes on 2 March 1823, Lady Blessington may have seen only some unwashed fisherwives knitting and a few piles of fruit, but she wrote 'of all that I have seen of France, this part of it is by far the most beautiful, and resembles the notion I have formed of Italy'.[31] The area around Cannes also held a special resonance for d'Orsay, as it was where Napoleon had landed on his doomed return from Elba in 1815.

And if Cannes was French but felt Italian, Nice, where the Blessington baggage train pitched up later that March at the height of the Mistral, was then known as Nizza and had not yet been ceded to the French by the Kingdom of Sardinia (which also ruled Turin until 1860). Italy in the years following the death of Napoleon was little more than a collection of Austrian puppet states. When the Blessingtons arrived in the early 1820s, the Risorgimento of 1871, independence and the emergence of the unified state of Italy were still half a century in the future. Count Camillo di Cavour, future Prime Minister of Sardinia and one of the chief architects of an independent Italy, was not yet a teenager. But the slow move to nationhood had begun, with violence. The Carbonari, the leading secret society and resistance movement, had already attempted uprisings in Naples and

Turin. But, for the moment, Italy remained fragmented. Power in the south resided in the hands of the recently restored Bourbon Kingdom of Naples and the Two Sicilies. Rome and the Papal States came under the rule of the Pope, while to the north there was a jumble of autonomous duchies, Austrian provinces and the Kingdom of Piedmont.

Today Italy is a carefully marketed land of extra-virgin olive oil, undulating cypress-dotted hills, frescos and espressos. At the beginning of the nineteenth century it was exotic and mysterious: a land of brigands, a place of strange and ancient buildings, redolent of a dangerous pre-Christian culture. Edward Gibbon had finished his epic history of the Roman Empire barely thirty years earlier. Pompeii had been discovered a mere forty or so years before that. The treasures of Florence, Rome and Naples had yet to be overrun by the Baedeker-reading bluestockings. It was still sufficiently exotic to be an adventure, but d'Orsay and the Blessingtons would be the last generation of travellers to experience it thus. The mid-1840s would see Dickens writing to Count d'Orsay to complain of Rome being overrun by 'hundreds of English people with hundreds of Murray's Guide Books'.[32]

Nice, at the time the Blessingtons visited it, was established as a winter resort for consumptives and had something of an expatriate British community. The Blessington–d'Orsay party amused itself much in the manner that affluent tourists today might: sightseeing, dinner-partying and yacht-hopping. At a dinner which seems to have taken place in Menton,[33] the charmingly dowdy resort town that finds itself on the border of modern-day Italy and France, the Blessingtons and d'Orsay encountered Henry Edward Fox. A fickle and precocious young man of d'Orsay's age, he had been sent abroad to avoid what his parents saw as unsuitable romantic liaisons. With a congenital hip deformity he may understandably have felt some animus towards the near perfectly formed Count d'Orsay, and his quick mind allowed him to express his opinions in a caustic fashion. It was at this dinner that he learned, apparently from Lady Blessington, about the proposed marriage of d'Orsay and Blessington's younger daughter. As we have seen, Fox rapidly came to the conclusion that this was a smokescreen behind which Lady Blessington, and perhaps even her husband, could hide their involvement with the young count.

If d'Orsay had made fun of Fox's mother Lady Holland by suggesting that he should eat his dinner off the floor so that he might better be able to retrieve her dropped cutlery, Fox returned the insult with interest in his diary description of Lady Blessington. 'She is not at all pleasant, very vulgar and very abusive; laughs at Lds Grey and Thanet, especially at the former, for making love to her, which she says would be ridiculous to any woman but to her it was *insolent*. She told him, 'Are you vain enough to suppose that if I was inclined to play the fool with anybody, you would be the person I should choose?'[34]

In return, Lady Blessington was less harsh in her judgement, describing him as 'lively, and *très spirituel, mais un peu espiègle*. He abounds in anecdotes; some a little malicious, but all amusing and well told.'[35] Lady Blessington's journal, later published as *The Idler in Italy*, does not record whether or not the distinguished statesman and future Whig Prime Minister Lord Grey made a pass at her. Instead she confines her disclosures to such domestic trifles as the absence of a teapot at their *auberge*, the Hôtel de Turin, and the macabre sight of local children playing with human skulls that had come from a local graveyard.

From Menton onwards the roads, built by Napoleon and known today as the Corniches, deteriorated and the rest of the journey had to be made by mule. It is entertaining to imagine the train of mules, most of the baggage having been sent ahead by sea, plodding along, carrying the demure Lady Blessington, her sister, the well-dressed

Count d'Orsay and that slightly absurd figure, the Earl of Blessington.

Uncomfortable though the transport may have been, it seems to have prompted Lady Blessington to greater heights of lyricism. She was overcome by the thyme-scented air and began pondering the tendency for eternity to be 'unchanging, enduring'. Entries in her journal are littered with chasms and grottoes, shadows and skulls, and to read of her journey along the Italian Riviera one would think she and her party were journeying through the wilder corners of Bram Stoker's imagination rather than the pleasant coastline that is today one of the world's most celebrated holiday destinations.

Conveniently a human skull appears under the feet of one of the mules and, unable to pass up the opportunity of a lengthy reverie on the transience of human life, Lady Blessington is off again with a Pavlovian passage about the most Romantic of subjects – death.

Lady Blessington's metaphysical musings were perhaps understandable. With every step of their mules, they were being brought nearer to Genoa and Lord Byron – the wild genius, the bad boy of Europe, the sell-out success of whose poems had been eclipsed only by the immorality of his behaviour, who seemed to drive women, and men, mad with desire. His epic affair with Lady Caroline Lamb, who had pursued him with a shameless ardour, was probably the most scandalous liaison of the Regency period. Byron's reputation and behaviour fascinated and then scandalised England, making it advisable for him to move to the less morally exacting and meteorologically warmer climate of Italy.

*C*HAPTER SEVEN

Byron and Genoa

'I HAVE SEEN LORD BYRON; AND AM DISAPPOINTED!' BEGAN THE entry in Lady Blessington's journal for 1 April 1823.[1] However, Byron had met the young Count d'Orsay and had been anything but disappointed. It was at Genoa that spring that the d'Orsay legend really began.

Depending on which of Byron's biographers one believes, by the time the Blessington–d'Orsay party arrived in Genoa, Lady Blessington 'was already interested in d'Orsay',[2] or the 'young French aristocrat was said to be Lord Blessington's lover, for whom his wife, rumoured to be uninterested in men sexually, served as a beard'.[3] However, there is no doubt about Byron's status: he was the most notorious man in Europe. In 1812, he had made a fiery, radical debut speech in the House of Lords and printed the first two cantos of *Childe Harold*, which was to be a publishing phenomenon. His celebrity spread rapidly beyond England across Europe. Largely uncritical fame was to last four years, years that included frenzied socialising, homosexual relationships and well-documented affairs with Lady Caroline Lamb, Lady Oxford and Lady Frances Wedderburn Webster, as well as an infamous affair with his half-sister Augusta Leigh, to whom some of his most moving verse was dedicated.

Ironically it was his attempt to slow down his fast image by marrying the respectable Anne-Isabella 'Annabella' Milbanke and the scandal surrounding the breakdown of this marriage, amid rumours of rape, incest and sodomy, which forced him into exile. He left Britain in 1816 and embraced various revolutionary causes across Europe. By the time the Blessington–d'Orsay party caught up with him he was living with an attractive Italian noblewoman, Countess Teresa Guiccioli, at the Casa Saluzzo – in the words of the spiteful Henry Fox, 'a very pretty villa at Albaro, a little out of the town'[4] that had been rented for him by Mrs Shelley.

At a distance of almost two centuries it is easy to say that Byron was an important figure, but it is almost impossible to comprehend his power over the imagination of the then civilised world. As a member of the House of Lords, he was a legislator of one of the most powerful nations on earth. As a poet, he was hugely successful and also profoundly influential and liberating. His reputation as a dangerous sex symbol was cemented by the circumstances in which he had left Britain. In addition his credentials as a revolutionary were impeccable: from about 1820, he had been involved with subversive activity in Italy and at around the time he met d'Orsay he was preparing to take part in the Greek Revolution. A rebel perpetually in search of a cause, he was to die young. When he met d'Orsay Byron was barely thirty-five. Just over a year later he would be dead.

As he and Byron had been young men about town together in the second decade of the nineteenth century, it was Lord Blessington who knocked on the door of Byron's house and it was he, together with Count d'Orsay, who was admitted to the poet's rented villa. It is the period of intimacy with Byron that is perhaps the best known of d'Orsay's life, not least through Lady Blessington, who drew heavily upon her time with the poet for both *Idler in Italy* and *A Journal of Conversations with Lord Byron*. In the latter published account of time spent with Byron at Genoa, she managed to stretch out an acquaintanceship of barely two months into a pair of plump volumes of reminiscence. It is possible that in referring to Casa Saluzzo as a 'pretty villa', Henry Fox was trying to be a little over-worldly. Lady Blessington describes it as 'a fine old palazzo, commanding an extensive view, and with spacious apartments, the front looking into a courtyard and the back into the garden'.[5]

By other accounts too, Byron's retreat seems to have been a delightful spot with 'a wide view over olive woods and vineyards that stretched to the bases of the purple Apennines'.[6] The grounds were not merely those of a rented villa, but 'a stately garden, with orange-trees and cedars, terraces and fountains',[7] while the 'smell of the narcissus which he [Byron] loved hung heavily in the air'.[8] The natural geography of the Ligurian Riviera is stunning and the setting could not therefore have been more arresting, right down to the exotically uniformed chasseur standing guard in the vestibule. The setting had all the elements of one of Byron's own poems. And yet if the visiting party had expected to find a Byronic hero closeted in this little palace, ravishing a virgin in the famous curtained and corniced bed surmounted by the motto 'Crede Biron', or casting brooding glances out to either the purple Apennines or the cerulean Mediterranean, they were to be disappointed.

Instead they found a lively, scrawny little man, whose baggy clothes hung from him like rags, a man dying to catch up on London gossip and at the same time complaining that English visitors to the area had turned him into a tourist attraction. No doubt polite exclamations over the view and Byron's greetings to his old carousing partner and to the exotic-looking d'Orsay took up some time, before Lord Blessington announced that Lady Blessington and her sister were waiting in the carriage outside. The superficial pretext for dropping in on Byron had been to escape spring showers; 'a rainy forenoon was selected for the drive to Byron's villa. That shelter was necessitated, and that necessity furnished a plea for a visit which would not have been without some awkwardness under other circumstances.'[9]

At once Byron hurried into the courtyard and moved as quickly towards the carriage as his lame foot allowed him. 'You must have thought me quite as ill bred and *sauvage* as fame reports', he said, handing the ladies down from the carriage, 'in having permitted your ladyship to remain a quarter of an hour at my gate: but my old friend Lord Blessington is to blame, for I only heard a minute ago that I was so highly honoured. I shall think you do not pardon this apparent rudeness, unless you enter my abode – which I entreat you will do.'[10] If anything Lady Blessington seems to have been disappointed at not being treated in a more dramatic and Byronic manner; 'were I to point out the prominent defect of Lord Byron, I should say it was flippancy, and a total want of that natural self-possession and dignity which ought to characterize a man of birth and education'.[11]

D'Orsay however was happy to take people as he found them. Rather than be disappointed that the man who wrote *Childe Harold* was not quite the detached and moody Adonis suggested by Richard Westall's portrait of 1813, he was able to take delight in the man's conversation about the likes of Tom Moore and Douglas Kinnaird. Byron's lover the Countess Guiccioli was later to recall that 'Byron from the first liked d'Orsay; he was clever, original, unpretending; he affected to be nothing that he was not.'[12]

Lady Blessington noted that 'His [Byron's] voice and accent are particularly clear and harmonious, but somewhat effeminate'.[13] Might some sublimated femininity within d'Orsay have made an impression upon Byron, who had a history of falling for gorgeous young men? And might not Byron's effeminacy have appealed, albeit again subliminally, to the young count? Lady Blessington reported that they stayed a long time. Moreover, when they suggested that they leave, 'he so warmly urged our stay' that even the servants wore expressions of surprise that 'evinced that they were not habituated to see their lord display so much cordiality to visitors'.[14] Yet for some reason Byron did not talk to d'Orsay. It is almost as if he were too self-conscious to do so, babbling on instead about his old haunts and mutual friends to Lord Blessington, beseeching his visitors to stay, even when he professed to decry sensation-seeking English visitors. It was of course probably true that d'Orsay was on his best behaviour, careful not to offend his patron's famous friend.

During the Blessington–d'Orsay visit, Henry Fox, their dinner guest at Menton, turned up and – in addition to penning his customary swipes at the Blessingtons – observed, 'D'Orsay was with them, and to my surprise I found that Ld Byron could not, or would not, talk French.' And yet, as soon as they were gone, Byron is supposed to have said that 'He was sorry not to converse with d'Orsay. Having lived so long out of the world it was rather an amusement to him to see what sort of an animal a dandy of the present day is.'[15] Given Fox's eagerness to denigrate d'Orsay and the Blessingtons, it is safe to assume that Byron saw more than a mere clothes-horse when he gazed upon the young count.

Indeed accounts of Byron at this time depict him as a man aged beyond his years, emotionally weary, disillusioned, inveighing against the cant and hypocrisy of life in London. His exaggerated sense of his own age was one of the first things to strike Lady Blessington about him. 'Though now but in his thirty-sixth year, Byron talks of himself as if he were at least fifty, nay, likes to be considered old.'[16] But then he had reason to feel weary. The year before he met d'Orsay had been a tumultuous one for him. In January he had broken with his publisher John Murray. In April his daughter Allegra had died in a convent. In July his friend Shelley, with whom he had been intending to launch a publication called *The Liberal*, had drowned. And in August, in a particularly macabre scene, he had watched as Shelley's partly decomposed corpse had been exhumed and cremated by the Cornish adventurer Edward John Trelawny on the beach at Livorno.

> The heat from the sun and fire was so intense that the atmosphere was tremulous and wavy. The corpse fell open and the heart was laid bare. The frontal bone of the skull, where it had been struck with the mattock, fell off; and, as the back of the head rested on the red-hot bottom bars of the furnace, the brains literally seethed, bubbled, and boiled as in a cauldron, for a very long time.[17]

Such a scene doubtless put Byron in touch with his own mortality in the most powerful and graphic way imaginable. In the end he could face looking at the remains of his friend no longer and 'withdrew to the beach and swam off to the Bolivar [his yacht]'.[18] But the memory was to remain with him, and he apparently believed that Shelley's ghost haunted northern Italy.

D'Orsay, young, talented, good-looking, beautifully dressed, physically all but flawless and very much alive, must have been a vivid contrast to the events of the preceding August on the beach at Livorno. He was the antidote to Byron's ennui. If intelligently superficial does not sound like too much of an oxymoron, it is probably a quality along these lines that appealed to Byron. He saw perhaps himself as he may have liked to have been in his youth. Byron was obsessed by youth, in particular by the evanescence of his own. His nature was a restless one of extremes: if he could no longer be young and enthusiastic, then he would be old and cynical. Anything as bourgeois and boring as middle age would simply not be countenanced.

In d'Orsay he saw a young man taking pleasure in clothes and gewgaws, plainly having the time of his life, travelling in the greatest

style with one of the biggest spenders of early-nineteenth-century
Europe. While frivolous, this show of high fashion certainly appealed
to Byron. He apparently said that at this stage of his life he had 'two
points of ambition – the one to be thought the greatest poet of his day,
and the other a nobleman and man of fashion, who could have arrived
at distinction without the aid of his poetical genius'.[19] He was also
doubtless touched by d'Orsay's peculiar charisma. It is clear that
Byron was fascinated by the man. The day after meeting him, he
wrote a letter to the poet Tom Moore (who was to be his first biographer) recounting his visit:

> Your other allies, whom I have found very agreeable personages,
> are Milor Blessington and *épouse*, travelling with a very hand-
> some companion, in the shape of a 'French count' (to use
> Farquhar's phrase in the *Beaux Stratagem*,) who has all the air of
> a *Cupidon déchaîné*, and is one of the few specimens I have ever
> seen of our ideal of a Frenchman *before* the Revolution – an old
> friend with a new face, upon whose like I never thought that we
> should look again.[20]

The same day Byron also wrote to Lord Blessington, ostensibly to
convey news about the war in Spain, in which d'Orsay was to have
taken part, and after a couple of lines his thoughts turn to the
Frenchman. 'I shall be very glad to see your friend's journal. He
seems to have all the qualities requisite to have figured in his brother-
in-law's ancestor's Memoirs. I did *not* think him old enough to have
served in Spain, and must have expressed myself badly. On the contrary, he has all the air of a *Cupidon déchaîné*, and promises to have it
for some time to come.'[21] Again he uses that curious term 'Cupidon
déchaîné', Cupid on the loose, with its suggestions of sexual playfulness. Presumably Byron had made a comment about the current
French involvement in Spain and had given the impression that he

thought d'Orsay had fought with the French against Wellington in the Iberian campaign of 1807–1814. This note was probably intended as an oblique apology to d'Orsay, or Blessington, whose vanity might have been wounded at the assumption that his young protégé/lover was actually a middle-aged war veteran rather than a choice, epicene youth. It is also interesting to note that d'Orsay is still defined in part by his sister's marriage, the journal offered to Byron is compared to that of a Grammont, and yet there is the sense of an idea or image of d'Orsay emerging, an image that he would grow into as time passed.

As well as writing this letter Byron went into Genoa and presented himself at the Albergo della Villa, the hotel at which d'Orsay and the Blessingtons were staying. The party had just finished what Lady Blessington, not a woman ever to eschew a fashionable linguistic borrowing, calls their 'déjeuné à la fourchette', when Byron sent up two printed cards, which he followed in person. He seems to have been on fine form, especially for a man who only the day before had been complaining of becoming a tourist attraction. He spent over two hours laughing and gossiping.

He eventually 'took his leave, laughingly apologizing for the length of his visit, adding that he was such a recluse, and had lived so long out of the world, that he had quite forgotten the usages of it'.[22] He also took Count d'Orsay's journal. Within three days he had read it and on 5 April he returned it to Blessington with an extremely kind letter:

> I return the Count d'Orsay's Journal, which is a very extraordinary production, and of a most melancholy truth in all that regards high life in England. I know, or knew personally, most of the personages and societies which he describes; and after reading his remarks, have the sensation fresh upon me as if I had seen them yesterday. I would, however, plead in behalf of some few exceptions, which I will mention by and by. The most singular

thing is, *how* he should have penetrated not the fact, but the *mystery* of the English *ennui* at two-and-twenty. I was about the same age when I made the same discovery, in almost precisely the same circles, – (for there is scarcely a person mentioned whom I did not see nightly or daily, and was acquainted more or less intimately with most of them,) – but I never could have described it so well. *Il faut être Français,* to effect this.

Byron goes on to say that d'Orsay's journal:

is a very formidable production. Alas! our dearly-beloved countrymen have only discovered that they are tired, and not that they are tiresome; and I suspect that the communication of the latter unpleasant verity will not be better received than truths usually are. I have read the whole with great attention and instruction. I am too good a patriot to say *pleasure* – at least I won't say so, whatever I may think. I showed it (I hope no breach of confidence) to a young Italian lady of rank, *très instruite* also; and who passes, or passed, for being one of the three most celebrated belles in the district of Italy, where her family and connections resided in less troublesome times as to politics, (which is not Genoa, by the way,) and she was delighted with it and says that she has derived a better notion of English society from it, than from all Madame de Stael's metaphysical disputations on the same subject, in her work on the Revolution. I beg that you will thank the young philosopher, and make my compliments to Lady B. and her sister.[23]

He followed this endorsement with a postscript giving d'Orsay information about clubs of which he had been a member: Watier's ('the Dandy Club') and the Alfred, 'the most *recherché* and most tiresome of any'.

On 22 April Byron wrote to d'Orsay himself:

My dear Count d'Orsay (if you will permit me to address you familiarly), – You should be content with writing in your own language, like Grammont, and succeeding in London as nobody has succeeded since the days of Charles the Second and the records of Antonio Hamilton, without deviating into our barbarous language, – which you understand and write, however, much better than it deserves.

My 'approbation', as you are pleased to term it, was very sincere, but perhaps not very impartial; for, though I love my country, I do not love my countrymen – at least, such as they now are. And, besides the seduction of talent and wit in your work, I fear that to me there was the attraction of vengeance. I have *seen* and *felt* much of what you have described so well. I have known the persons, and the re-unions so described, – (many of them, that is to say,) and the portraits are so like that I cannot but admire the painter no less than his performance.

But I am sorry for you; for if you are so well acquainted with life at your age, what will become of you when the illusion is still more dissipated? But never mind – *en avant!* – live while you can; and that you may have the full enjoyment of the many advantages of youth, talent, and figure, which you possess, is the wish of an – Englishman, – I suppose, but it is no treason; for my mother was Scotch, and my name and my family are both Norman; and as for myself, I am of no country. As for my 'Works', which you are pleased to mention, let them go to the Devil, from whence (if you believe many persons) they came.

I have the honour to be your obliged, etc., etc.[24]

In just over three weeks d'Orsay, in part through his journal, had won the respect, admiration and friendship of the greatest living

English poet and perhaps the most inspirational thinker of his time. The journal is believed to have been destroyed by its author, as many of those described therein later became his intimates. It is fascinating, if futile, to speculate how the friendship between d'Orsay and Byron might have grown had the latter survived the illness that arose out of his doomed mission to Greece. However, at the time of reading Count d'Orsay's journal, Byron's Greek adventure was still in the future. He had only recently become interested in the cause of Greek revolution and, although he had been elected a member of the London Greek Committee in March 1823, he did not learn of his election until 23 May.[25]

During April and most of May 1823, Byron's letters to Blessington constantly refer to '*your* Alfred', 'the illustrious Chevalier Count D'Orsay' and so on.[26] He even goes as far as saying that there are some 'strange coincidences between a part of his remarks, and a certain work of mine now in MS. in England'.[27] Here Byron is probably referring to *Don Juan*, cantos VI–XIV of which appeared during the latter half of 1823. In the middle of May he writes to his cousin Lady Hardy in Florence, describing d'Orsay as 'very young and a beauty, of which last advantage he is fully aware, but he is not at all disagreeable and I should suspect that the women find him more formidable than dreadful'.[28] The vanity to which Byron alludes was doubtless fuelled by Byron's kindness to the young man, while the impression of extreme youth heightened by beauty was perhaps demonstrated by flashes of d'Orsay's characteristically spirited behaviour, which a less charitable observer might have thought spoilt and petulant.

During the spring of 1823 Byron and the Blessington–d'Orsay party saw a great deal of each other. There were dinners together, including one at which Byron, shrugging off concerns about his weight (according to Lady Blessington, 'Nothing gratifies him so much as being told that he grows thin . . . and he frequently asks

"Don't you think I am getting thinner?" or, "Did you ever see any one so thin as I am, who was not ill?"")[29], greedily enjoyed a second helping of 'plum pudding *à l'Anglaise*'.[30] They sat together on the flower-filled balcony of the hotel and watched the sunset. Byron attempted to buy Lady Blessington's horse. Lord Blessington bought Byron's yacht the *Bolivar*, fitted out with luxurious marble baths, soft couches and guns, which the poet attempted to remove before Blessington could take possession of it.[31] D'Orsay made two drawings of Byron, one of which would later form the frontispiece of Lady Blessington's journal *Conversations with Lord Byron*. They rode out together on sightseeing expeditions, where they frequently encountered 'persons, almost all of them English, who evidently had taken that route purposely to see Lord Byron'.[32]

The sight that greeted these early-nineteenth-century celebrity-spotters must indeed have been a strange one. Byron, at best a mediocre horseman, made up for his lack of finesse in the saddle by a fantastically gaudy appearance, as Lady Blessington noted:

> His horse was literally covered with various trappings, in the way of cavesons, martingales, and Heaven knows how many other (to me) unknown inventions. The saddle was *à la hussarde* with holsters, in which he always carried pistols. His dress consisted of a nankeen jacket and trousers, which appeared to have shrunk from washing; the jacket embroidered in the same color, and with three rows of buttons; the waist very short, the back very narrow, and the sleeves set in as they used to be ten or fifteen years before; a black stock, very narrow; a dark-blue velvet cap with a shade, and a very rich gold band and large gold tassel at the crown; nankeen gaiters, and a pair of blue spectacles, completed his costume, which was any thing but becoming. This was his general dress of a morning for riding, but I have seen it changed for a green tartan plaid jacket.[33]

Perhaps this was the very same green tartan jacket in which Byron was depicted in a head-and-shoulders study by d'Orsay completed in May 1823.

In contrast to Byron's ill-conceived equestrian attire, pictures of d'Orsay on horseback show a virile young man, exquisitely dressed in clothes that hug each contour of his magnificent body. With the increasingly corpulent, flamboyant Earl of Blessington puffing along and Lady Blessington atop her 'very highly-dressed' horse Mameluke, which Byron attempted to buy, they must have made an eyecatching group.

Then, on the evening of 1 June, they all gathered for the last time to say farewell. The Blessington–d'Orsay ménage was moving on the following day. According to his biographer Moore, the bidding of adieus was an emotionally charged affair for Byron, the poet resting his head on the arm of a sofa and bursting into tears. Indeed Moore makes much of the sense of refreshment that friendship with the Blessingtons and d'Orsay had brought about. Lady Blessington too recalled 'tears that flowed plentifully down his cheeks', adding that 'his voice was inarticulate, and his lip quivered' when he tried to make light of his emotion.[34] However, this emotional response is balanced by his friend John Cam Hobhouse's protestation that such behaviour on Byron's part was 'very unlike him'.[35] They exchanged gifts and finally Byron rode away.

It seems that Byron spent at least some of that night thinking about d'Orsay. Shortly before the Blessingtons and the count left Genoa, a letter arrived from Byron addressed to Lady Blessington ostensibly requesting the return of a cameo of Napoleon and urging her to accept a small chain instead. Then, affecting an afterthought, he added, 'I also enclose a ring, which I would wish *Alfred* to keep; it is too large to *wear*; but it is formed of *lava*, and so far adapted to the fire of his years and character.'[36]

Life on the Ligurian Riviera had not consisted only of unalloyed enjoyment, the renewing of old friendships, the forging of new ones, gift-giving, yacht-buying, light-hearted outings, jolly dinners and sightseeing trips. Nor was the leave-taking of Lord Byron the only shadow cast on the Blessington–d'Orsay party's stay in Genoa.

On 6 April, news reached Lord Blessington of the demise of his one legitimate son, little Lord Mountjoy, who had died on 23 March. For five days Blessington gave himself entirely over to his grief and then made a pact to talk about it no more.

Indeed while he remained in Genoa and busied himself with his usual pastimes of sightseeing, eating, shopping and spending time with d'Orsay, Blessington seemed to be able to keep at bay the grief and the fears that his son's death awoke in him. However, the party's impending departure from Genoa evidently made him nervous and on the eve of their resuming their travels, he penned the following codicil to his will:

> Having had the misfortune to lose my beloved son, Luke Wellington, and having entered into engagements with Alfred, Comte d'Orsay, that an alliance should take place between him and my daughter, which engagement has been sanctioned by Albert, Comte d'Orsay, general, &c. in the service of France, this is to declare and publish my desire to leave to the said Alfred d'Orsay my estates in the city and county of Dublin, (subject, however, to the annuity of three thousand per annum, which sum is to include the settlement of one thousand per annum to my wife, Margaret, Countess of Blesinton, subject also to that portion of debt, whether by annuity or mortgage, to which my executor and trustee, Luke Norman, shall consider them to be subjected), for his and her use, whether it be Mary (baptized Emily), Rosalie Hamilton, or Harriet Ann Jane Frances, and to their heirs, male, the said Alfred and said Mary, or Harriet, for ever in default of issue, male, to follow the provisions of the will and testament.

I make also the said Alfred d'Orsay sole guardian of my son Charles John, and my sister, Harriet Gardiner, guardian of my daughters, until they, the daughters, arrive at the age of sixteen, at which age I consider that they will be marriageable.

I also bequeath to Luke Norman my estates in the county of Tyrone, &c., in trust for my son, Charles John, who I desire to take the name of Stewart Gardiner, until he shall arrive at the age of twenty-five, allowing for his education such sums as Alfred d'Orsay may think necessary, and one thousand per annum from twenty-one to twenty-five.

Done at Genoa, life being uncertain, at eight o'clock, on the morning of Monday, June the second, one thousand eight hundred and twenty-three.

Blesinton[37]

'Life being uncertain' – poor Lord Blessington. All the shopping opportunities and delicious young Frenchmen to keep him company could not blot out the uncertainties of life. He had probably been up all night worrying about the future and decided to exorcise his fears by writing this codicil.

At first sight, it seems a remarkable document: his wife, his children, his family estates are apparently placed at d'Orsay's disposal. And if the codicil seems unusual, then the will that he signed later that summer when visiting England was even more favourable to d'Orsay. The codicil seems to have been something of a 'quick fix', a rough sketch of his intentions put down in a hurry under the pressure of his son's death and Blessington's unusually heightened awareness of his own mortality. The will that was drawn up later that summer, on 31 August, is a more formal and elaborate expression of Blessington's fears and wishes.

EXTRACTED FROM THE REGISTRY OF HIS
MAJESTY'S COURT OF PREROGATIVE,
IN IRELAND.

This is the last will and testament of me, Charles John, Earl of Blessington, of that part of the united kingdom called Ireland. I give Luke Norman, Esquire, for and during the time he shall continue agent of my estates, in the county and city of Dublin, and in the county of Tyrone, twelve hundred pounds per annum, in lieu of receivers' fees. I appoint Alfred D'Orsay, Count of [   ], in France, Luke Norman, Esquire, and Alexander Worthington, Esquire, my executors; and I give unto each of them one thousand pounds. I give to Isabella Birnly, Michael Mc Donough and John Bullock, one hundred pounds each. I give and devise my real and personal estate to said Alfred D'Orsay, Luke Norman, and Alexander Worthington, for the following purposes. First, for the payment of two thousand pounds, British, per annum, (inclusive of one thousand pounds settled on her at the time of my marriage,) to my wife, Margarette, or Margaret, Countess of Blessington; and I give to her all her own jewels, requesting that she may divide my late wife's jewels between my two daughters at the time of her decease. I give to Robert Power and Mary Anne Power one thousand pounds each. I give to my daughter, Harriet Anne Jane Frances, commonly called Lady Harriet, born at my house at Seymour Place, London, on or about the 3d day of August, 1812, all my estates in the county and city of Dublin, subject to the following charge. Provided she intermarry with my friend, and intended son-in-law, Alfred D'Orsay, I bequeath her the sum of ten thousand pounds only. I give to my daughter, Emily Rosalie Hamilton, generally called Lady Mary Gardiner, born in Manchester Square, on the 24th June, 1811, whom I now acknowledge and adopt as my daughter, the sum of twenty thousand pounds.

In case the said Alfred D' Orsay intermarries with the said
Emily, otherwise Mary Gardiner, I bequeath to her my estates in
the county and city of Dublin. The annuity of two thousand
pounds per annum, British, to be paid to my beloved wife out of
the said estates. I give to my son, Charles John, who I desire may
take the name of Stuart Gardiner, born in Portman Square on
the 3d day of February, 1810, all my estates in the county of
Tyrone, subject to the following charges; also the reversion of
my Dublin estates in case of male issue of said daughters. In case
of male issue, lawfully begotten, I leave these estates to the
second son of Alfred D'Orsay and my daughter; or if only one
son, to him, in case of failure to male issue, to go to the male issue
of my other daughter. My estates are to be subject in the first
instance to the payment of my debts. I give to my wife the lease
of my house in London, at the expiration of which the furniture,
books, &c. &c., are to be removed to the intended residence at
Mountjoy Forest; and I direct that the said house be built according to the plan now laid down, and do empower my said
executors to borrow money for the said purpose. I give to my
wife all my carriages, paraphernalia, and plate. I give to my son,
Charles John, my plate, wardrobe, swords, &c., &c., &c. I
appoint Alfred D'Orsay guardian of my son, Charles John, until
he arrives at the age of twenty-five years, the settlement of
twelve thousand pounds to be null and void on his obtaining
the Tyrone estates. I appoint my beloved wife guardian of my
daughter, Harriet Anne; and I appoint my sister Harriet guardian
of my daughter, commonly called Lady Mary. I give to Isabella
Mc Dougal, of Perth, one hundred pounds per annum for her
life, it being bequeathed her by my first wife, Mary Campbell,
Viscountess Mountjoy. I give to the National Gallery, intended
to be formed in London, under royal protection, my picture of
the 'Three Graces,' by Sir Joshua Reynolds, with a desire that

'the gift of Charles John, Earl of Blessington,' may be affixed to the said picture, as an encouragement to others to contribute to the said collection. I give to my sister, Harriet Gardiner, five hundred pounds per annum for her natural life. I revoke all other wills, by me made, and declare this to be my last will and testament; In witness whereof, I have to this my last will, contained in five sheets of paper, set to the first four my hand, and to this, the fifth and last, my hand and seal, this 31st day of August, 1823.

This document, fascinating in its own right, shows just how complex, not to mention expensive, Blessington's life had become. It demonstrates his affectionate and generous nature and it is rather touching to note that as well as providing for the future of his family, he also wishes to see his mania for architecture and decoration survive him, with direction for the building and furnishing of a new house, along with the poignant lines empowering the executors to borrow money for the purpose – although of course further debt was the last thing his estate would require.

The codicil and ensuing will would seem to indicate that Blessington was head over heels in love with d'Orsay and would do all in his power to keep him. But viewed in the perspective of Blessington's warm and benign nature, it takes on a different tone. The death of his heir would have naturally focused his mind on the future of his family. Perhaps Byron's closeness to and high opinion of d'Orsay helped cement Blessington's view that in the count he had a catch he could not possibly let get away.

By today's moral standards the idea of locking one or other of his two young daughters into a prearranged marriage with a man neither had met, who was probably his lover and who many thought was also their stepmother's lover, seems unpalatable. However by early-nineteenth-century standards this union could have been construed as merely careful planning on the part of a benevolent father. After all, if in Blessington's eyes d'Orsay was the finest man on earth, either one of his daughters should have been pleased to be given the opportunity to delight their father by marrying his dearest friend. Moreover there is the strong sense that in some muddled way, now that his only legitimate heir had died, he wanted d'Orsay as his son and heir. He sensed, not incorrectly, that beneath the younger man's veneer of vanity lay a substantial, well-intentioned character. After all, he had had several months to form a judgement of d'Orsay's character, and he must have noticed the lightening of his wife's spirits since the count had joined their party.

Having decided to involve d'Orsay so closely in plans for her family and fortune after her death, it is entirely in character that Blessington would want to complete formalities as rapidly as possible. Another spur to the speedy completion of his plans was his obsessive concern about his health. He complained vociferously to Byron about his gout. Later in his party's travels down through Italy, it was most likely Lord Blessington's fear of oppressive heat and the risk of contracting malaria that caused them to leave Rome in a great hurry. Lady Blessington almost says as much in her diary entry for 14 July: 'Left Rome yesterday, driven from it by the oppressive heat, and the evil prophecies dinned into my ears of the malaria. I have no fears of the effect of either for myself, but I dare not risk them for others.'[38]

Nor was it just gout, malaria and excessive heat that worried Blessington, who 'was very susceptible of cold, and had a horror of a "thorough draught"'.[39] D'Orsay said that Blessington was able to detect the change in the air caused by a key left crossways in a lock, and although this may have been one of the count's jokes it illustrates the obsessive nature of Blessington's worries about his wellbeing. On one occasion he was concerned lest a friend fall into the sea, and when he was assured that the man could swim, he answered

'Yes, yes, that's all very well, but I shall catch my death driving home in the carriage with him.'[40]

It is difficult to enter the mind of anyone, let alone that of an excitable, generous, impulsive, eccentric, bisexual, hypochondriac, early-nineteenth-century Irish peer shortly after the death of his heir. However, it is probable that these and other concerns were racing through his mind as the sun rose on the morning of 2 June. And having put his fears down on paper in this form, he probably felt a little better and was thus enabled to put mortality from his mind and throw himself into the business of travelling.

Given his generous nature he intended only good to come of his last wishes. Instead, he laid the foundations for d'Orsay's ruin, his wife's disgrace and his daughter's lasting unhappiness. Seldom has so much domestic destruction been accomplished before eight in the morning.

CHAPTER EIGHT

Dolce Far Niente

LUCCA, FLORENCE, SIENA, RADICOFANI, ROME, TERRACINA . . .
during the early summer of 1823 the Blessington caravan meandered
through Italy. Their passage down the Italian peninsula was rapid, but
they took in the sights. They stopped to handle gems crafted by
Cellini and visit the studio of Bartolini — both doubtless formative and
instructive experiences for d'Orsay, who would later deck himself
with jewels and turn his elegant hands to sculpture. Rome was almost
deserted for fear of malaria, yet they spent just over a week there
and, given their hectic schedule, sightseeing became a round-the-
clock business: the Colosseum by moonlight, the Vatican by
torchlight, a brief encounter with the Pope and so on.

During their time in Rome, they visited the Rome residence of
Napoleon's sister Pauline.

> Went over the Villa of the Princess Pauline Borghese, who is at
> present absent from Rome. The temple is worthy of the goddess:
> it is an exquisite specimen of French taste, and all its decorations

announce it the residence of a Parisian *petite-maitresse*. Though in very delicate health, and no longer in her *premiere jeunesse,* Pauline is said still to retain much of that beauty and symmetry which rendered her such an object of universal attraction at the court of Napoleon. The portraits of her are very lovely, yet I am told they scarcely render her justice. One of the apartments of her villa (that, I believe, appropriated for taking *café*) *is* fitted up in the Egyptian style, and in it, on a slab of marble, stands an urn, with a suitable inscription, containing the heart of General Le Clerc, the first husband of the Princess, who died in Egypt.

A chapel or an Oratory would be a more fitting place for this melancholy *memento mori*; but the Princess Pauline thinks differently, and likes to contemplate it while sipping her *café*.[1]

A year earlier Count d'Orsay had been facing, at best, a life of provincial obscurity in the military service of a monarch towards whom he felt personal antipathy; at worst he might have been disfigured, maimed or killed as part of the French force invading Spain. Now here he was trailing through Italy in the greatest imaginable luxury, his future secured by the will of his doting older patron.

Spoiled by a devoted grandmother during his childhood, admired by his peers and lusted after by his elders for his physical attributes, it would have taken an iron will to resist being seduced by the glowing opinion of him formed by others. And why should he not have a high opinion of himself? When he looked at his ring of lava, he thought of Byron. He had just traipsed around the palace of the notorious Pauline Borghese, sister of his hero Napoleon. At Carrara he had seen the busts of the Duke of Wellington, who had singled out the young d'Orsay in pre-Waterloo Paris, and he had admired other 'modern works' including 'Canova's colossal statue of Napoleon'.[2] Wandering through the ruins of Napoleon's European dream meeting and charming the greatest men of the day, d'Orsay already felt himself to be on the fringes of celebrity and no doubt imagined a great future for himself. His fortune seemed secured through an alliance with one of Lord Blessington's daughters. Flattered and admired, readily seduced by comforts and growing every day into an ever more confident and glamorous young man, it was inevitable that he would become dazzled by and then complacent about his new way of life, which was about to take another luxurious turn.

On 17 July, 'Naples burst upon us from the steep hill above the Campo Santo, and never did aught so bright and dazzling meet my gaze,' wrote Lady Blessington.[3] A vista of palaces and towers and domes sprawled before them. To their left lay 'a chain of mountains, with Vesuvius, sending up its blue incense to the cloudless sky'. As a backdrop lay the island of Capri, 'a vast and brilliant gem', sparkling in the azure waters of the Mediterranean. To the right lay the Baia peninsula, beyond it the isle of Ischia. So struck were the travellers with the perfect, balanced beauty of the panoramic scene spread out in front of them that they ordered their postilions to halt a while on the brow of the hill, so they could better drink in the beauty of the view. 'The scene', recalled Lady Blessington, 'was like one created by the hand of enchantment.'[4]

It was an apt simile as there was to be no place where d'Orsay's life would take on a more enchanted, carefree and Arcadian tint than in Naples, which would be his home for the next two and a half years. When Napoleon ran Europe, Naples had been ruled by his brother Joseph. And after he had been sent off to occupy the newly acquired Spanish throne, Napoleon's brother-in-law, the dashing, brave, scheming, treacherous and stupid Marshal Murat, ruled in Joseph's place – though before long, using Naples as his power base, he turned against the emperor. Later Murat was defeated by the Austrians, against whom he had tried to rally Italy under pretext of national unity. He was finally executed by firing squad after a characteristically flamboyant attempt to retake his former kingdom with a force of 250 and seven feluccas, little more than oversized rowing boats.

The man from whom he had tried and failed to wrest the city of Naples was Ferdinand III of Sicily, IV of Naples, a scion of the Bourbon dynasty, who in the summer of 1815 had been returned by the British navy to the throne of Naples. He had first sat on this throne in 1759 as a child king aged only eight. On his return Ferdinand declared himself king of the Two Sicilies: in thus uniting Naples and Sicily, he became, as well as Ferdinand IV and III, Ferdinand I of the new kingdom.

His restoration in the summer of 1815 was not a pompous state occasion, but an emotional family reunion. The king, a 'dignified eighteenth-century figure', could never, according to Harold Acton,

> play an Olympian role. He was as emotional as these kindly people who idolized him, and as free from affectation. His genuine simplicity stirred their warm hearts; Murat's flamboyance had merely appealed to their eyes. They never dreamt of judging him according to his prowess: they saw him as a genial old paterfamilias whose all-too-human weaknesses were comprehensible and endearing; they accepted him as their true King by divine right. And they were comforted by the survival of a cherished institution.[5]

Public demonstrations of affection for the returning monarch reached their climax on 19 June, when Ferdinand appeared at the San Carlo Theatre. Such was the tumult that the king broke down in tears and, when his bust was brought on to the stage, the audience clapped and cheered for thirty minutes.

However happy Ferdinand's subjects were to see him return, his was a kingdom struggling with an acute identity crisis. Now an old man, and forced to compromise, the king 'could not help disliking the survival of so many Napoleonic institutions'.[6] Nevertheless, the Code Napoléon had become the legislative foundation of his domain and it was clear that various Napoleonic institutions would have to stay, if only for the smooth running of the country. It was, as Acton says, 'decided to leave things as much as possible as they had been under Murat without saying so'.[7]

But it was not all bad news for Ferdinand; at least Murat and his wife Caroline, Napoleon's sister, had, very considerately, decided to subject all his royal palaces to a programme of restoration, renovation and redecoration. 'The present sovereign and his family are said to have been hardly able to recognise their ancient abodes, when they returned from Sicily; and expressed no little satisfaction at the improvements that had taken place. Ferdinand is reported to have said that Murat was an excellent upholsterer, and had furnished his palaces perfectly to his taste,' recorded Lady Blessington on a visit to the Palazzo Portici on 31 July 1823.[8]

When d'Orsay and the Blessingtons arrived that summer, Naples's Napoleonic past was very recent history. Like much of the rest of Europe it may have been returned to Bourbon rule, but it was still a city bearing the imprint of the years of Napoleonic influence. Moreover, it was a pleasure-loving city to which a certain type of Englishman flocked after the Napoleonic Wars. As well as classical scholars, those who fled scandal in England gravitated to the relaxed Mediterranean metropolis, described by Stendhal in 1817 as 'the only capital in Italy'.[9]

The omnipresent image of a smoking Vesuvius, the quick-changing succession of rulers (Joseph, Murat, Ferdinand) and a host of occupying forces (sometimes French, sometimes Austrian, with a strong British naval presence hovering just beyond the bay) were potent incentives to live life for the moment. Naples, with its crooning *lazzaroni*, or vagabonds, its earringed manservants, its exotic ice-cream-guzzling nobility, its elderly monarch who, though well into his seventies, when not out hunting was still capable of flirting with visiting *danseuses* and opera divas, its eccentric expatriate community, its many Roman remains, antiquities and archaeological ruins, was the sun-drenched, lotus-eating, *carpe diem* capital of Europe.

'Who that has seen Naples can wonder that her children are idle, and luxuriously disposed?' wrote Lady Blessington. 'To gaze on the cloudless sky and blue Mediterranean, in an atmosphere so pure and balmy, is enough to make the veriest plodder who ever courted Plutus abandon his toil and enjoy the delicious *dolc'e far' niente* of the Neapolitans.'[10] If the Neapolitan atmosphere could have such an effect on the 'veriest plodder', what on earth would it do to the young Count d'Orsay?

D'Orsay and the Blessingtons checked into the Hotel Gran Bretagna, on the fashionable Strada de Chiaja, on the evening of 17 July. The chic location had one considerable drawback: the noise of the evening promenade. Lady Blessington had soon seen and heard her fill of the nocturnal pageant of rumbling carriages, thronged ice-cream shops, noisy watermelon pedlars, portable macaroni ovens illuminated by paper lanterns, and gaudily decorated mobile *sorbetto* and lemonade vendors. 'The noise of the Strada de Chiaja of an evening is so overpowering that a longer *séjour* in this hotel is not desirable,' she recorded tersely two days after her arrival.[11]

Lord Blessington was a master at dealing with such irritants. His response was, as usual, splendidly out of proportion to the problem. He, his wife and their protégé, the delightful d'Orsay, went house-hunting. Within two days they had looked at half the palaces in Naples and its immediate environs. One in particular stood out.

The Palazzo Belvedere was a proper palace. An imposing house, perched high on the hill of Vomero and reached through exotic pleasure grounds expensively stocked with rare plants and trees, it belonged to the Prince Belvedere. The prince had been a cardinal, but when he inherited the title and the considerable fortune that accompanied it, the pope gave him dispensation from his vows to marry and start a family.

Intended as a summer residence, the Palazzo was a splendid overblown wedding cake of a building. Lady Blessington described it as forming:

> three sides of a square; the fourth being an arcade, that connects one portion of the building with the other. There is a court-yard, and fountain in the centre. A colonnade extends from each side of the front of the palace, supporting a terrace covered with flowers. The windows of the principal salons open on a garden, formed on an elevated terrace, surrounded on three sides by a marble balustrade, and inclosed on the fourth by a long gallery, filled with pictures, statues, and alti, and bassi-rilievi. On the top of this gallery, which is of considerable length, is a terrace, at the extreme end of which is a pavilion with open arcades, and paved with marble. This pavilion commands a most enchanting prospect of the bay, with the coast of Sorrento on the left; Capri in the centre, with Nisida, Procida, Ischia, and the promontory of Misenum to the right; the fore-ground filled up by gardens and vineyards. The odours of the flowers in the grounds around this pavilion, and the Spanish jasmine and tuberoses that cover the walls, render it one of the most delicious retreats in the world.[12]

Internally the palace's five salons, billiard room, chapel, sacristy and numerous bedroom suites offered an abundance of decoration: Oriental alabaster architraves, marble tables crowded with vases and ornaments of agate, rock crystal and malachite, and walls crammed with paintings. Its theatricality appealed to Lord Blessington, an appeal doubtless heightened by the exquisite pleasure of seeing the clean-limbed, muscular d'Orsay strutting around the *piano nobile* of this imposing building, the heels of his highly polished boots clicking against the cool marble floors.

And for d'Orsay it must have been the culmination of his dreams, dreams that he had probably never even really allowed to form in his mind. Here was a house more magnificent than the Hôtel Craufurd, a residence that even equalled the fabulousness of the Hôtel d'Orsay, which he knew of only through stories from his father. In later life repossession of or compensation for the *objets* and artworks seized from his family house would become an obsession, but for the moment d'Orsay allowed himself to revel in his new surroundings.

They were all delighted with the place, and as usual whatever Lady Blessington and d'Orsay wanted, Lord Blessington and his banker, in Naples 'a most gentlemanly and obliging' Mr Price, would supply.[13] However, it was judged that a few home comforts were required. A French upholsterer was engaged, almost a dozen cleaners were set to work scrubbing the walls and floors, a small army of earringed Neapolitan servants, dressed to look like London footmen, was engaged and a contract was entered into with a cook. Presumably the torrent of English wealth released by the gentlemanly and obliging Mr Price was sufficient to extinguish the natural '*dolce far niente* of the Neapolitans'. Within two days of their first visit, the Palazzo Belvedere began to wear what Lady Blessington called 'a more habitable aspect' and 'now that curtains, carpets, and other adjuncts to comfort are beginning to be placed, the palazzo is assuming an aspect of English elegance joined to Italian grandeur, that renders it a delightful residence'.[14]

And on 25 July, almost a year after they had left St James's Square, the Blessingtons, and d'Orsay were able to take up residence in their Neapolitan fantasy palace. Their first visitors were the Prince and Princess of Belvedere, who came to offer their new tenants use of the family box at the Opera, a useful venue for socialising, seeing and being seen, and left perfectly astonished at the elaborate and costly changes that the eccentric Earl of Blessington had wrought on their house.

The presence of d'Orsay and the Blessingtons in the Palazzo Belvedere was a source of considerable interest to Neapolitan Society, and not merely because of the extravagant expenditure or the intriguing nature of the ménage. Their neighbour at the adjoining Villa Floridiana, the widowed Princess Partanna, was a figure of considerable importance. Otherwise known as the Duchess of Floridia, she had been King Ferdinand's mistress and, after the death of his wife Queen Caroline, had become his secret wife. Queen Caroline had died in September 1814 and the morganatic marriage of Ferdinand to the widowed princess took place on 27 November of the same year. He was sixty-three. She was forty-four. He had given the villa to the duchess, leaving the deeds under her plate at breakfast on his birthday.

By the time d'Orsay and the Blessingtons became her neighbours in 1823, the middle-aged duchess shared more than the king's bed. She exercised considerable control over the ageing monarch, and a sufficiently wily courtier could influence the outcome of Council meetings through judicious flattery of the royal consort. She came to perform a key role in the government of the kingdom, and the Villa Floridiana was where she held a court of her own during the spring and summer.

Seldom can politics have been conducted in such exotic surroundings. D'Orsay and the Blessingtons would often stroll in the gardens of the Floridiana. 'We have free ingress to the beautiful gardens of the Floridiano [*sic*],' wrote Lady Blessington,

> which join ours, and in which the trees, plants, and flowers of every country are skilfully raised. Grottos, of considerable extent, are perforated in the huge rocks that intersect the grounds; a bridge, of fine proportion and of cut stone, is thrown across a vast chasm to unite them. Terraces of marble well executed, representing fauns, satyrs, and nymphs, with vases, and groups of sculpture, ornament the gardens. A menagerie is, in my opinion, the only drawback to this charming place, as the

roaring of lions, and screams of the other wild beasts, are little
in harmony with so Arcadian a spot. Never were wild beasts
more carefully attended, or more neatly kept. Their cages are
made to resemble natural caverns, and are cut, in fact, in rocks;
and the keepers remove every unsightly object, and preserve
the dens as free from impurity, as are most children's nurseries in
England.[15]

She made no mention of the eighteen kangaroos that were a
noteworthy component of the duchess's private zoo. Nevertheless
the presence of a well-kept menagerie next door must have added
to the sense of unreality that characterised the living conditions of
the Blessington–d'Orsay ménage à trois.

Wittingly or otherwise, they had also made themselves a component of southern Italy's human zoo. Theirs was the sort of 'act'
entirely calculated to captivate the social circus. Within a couple of
days of their arrival in Naples they had broadcast their presence with
an explosion of English cash and French savoir-faire. Eschewing the
relative anonymity of an hotel, they had toured the grand houses of
the area that were available for rent, and had chosen one of the most
splendid available, locating themselves at the centre of the scheming
cauldron of Neapolitan politics.

Either they had no idea of the stir their arrival had caused, or
they did not really care. Perhaps Blessington's considerable wealth
insulated them from gossip. However, the arrival of this intriguing
trio in this southern European city was an event. Blessington's generosity and extravagance, d'Orsay's precocity and charisma, Lady
Blessington's fondness for the Mediterranean way of life and her own
increasing confidence in herself as a person, not just as the female
adjunct of her husband, combined fatally to create an impression of
high-profile sybaritic abandon that would titillate and entertain
locally, but when viewed from England – relayed by members of the

expatriate community and the dozens of Englishmen passing through on the Grand Tour – would outrage and scandalise.

However, the ripples spreading outwards from the splash of their arrival in Naples would take time to reach London. In the meantime, d'Orsay's Neapolitan years were the crucible in which many of his extravagant tastes were formed. Subsequent interests of his such as the aviary that became such a talking point among the smart set of 1830s London – with the speaking crow that was taught to say '"Up, Boys, and at 'em": a phrase which, with its head on one side, it would deliver with a comic gravity that made the Duke of Wellington roar with laughter',[16] and the 'very pigeons' that according to Bulwer Lytton had 'trousers down to their claws and have the habit of looking over their left shoulder'[17] – can be traced to his lengthy sojourn in Naples. His flair for decoration too was nurtured during this time. As well as strolling amid caged beasts, he was poking around royal palaces and even looked around the king's wife's bathroom – more of a white marble swimming pool with white marble ottomans, marble flower stands and gilt metal fixtures – which furnished him with ideas for future schemes.

The sense that Naples acted as a finishing school for the striking young man is borne home by the elaborate entertaining and complicated gastronomic arrangements the party enjoyed. At one of the more memorable dinners over which d'Orsay presided, the French cook at the Palazzo Belvedere 'encaged a poor goldfinch in a temple of spun sugar, as an ornament for the centre of the table, for the third course; and the poor bird, while the *convives* were doing honour to the *entremets*, and *sucreries*, fluttered through the temple and beat his wings against its sugary pillars, till they were encrusted with its clammy substance'.[18]

There is a considerable case for calling life at the Palazzo Belvedere a fairytale existence. It was the very definition of *douceur de vivre*, sipping iced tea in the 'delicious pavilion, at the end of the terrace',[19] or dining in the cabin of Byron's yacht the *Bolivar*, bought by Blessington, in which the poet had written much of *Don Juan*. Days were also leavened with learning; the abundance of classical sites in the neighbourhood made for a fascinating variety of excursions. As one visitor to the Palazzo Belvedere recalled, such trips were the subject of considerable studious preparation. 'The day before their execution every authority, ancient and modern, that could throw a light upon the subject, was consulted, and notes collected to illustrate the object of inquiry.'[20]

Often d'Orsay's mind and body found themselves being nourished simultaneously. Take a visit to Pompeii in August 1823, described by Lady Blessington:

> The Forum Vinalia was the spot fixed on for our halting-place; and, on arriving there, we found a *recherché* collation spread on the tables, shaded by weeping willows, the bright foliage of which formed an agreeable protection against the scorching rays of the sun. The table covered with snowy napkins, and piled with every dainty of the united *cuisine à-l'anglaise, française, and* Neapolitan; from the simple cold roasted meats and poultry, to the delicate *aspics, mayonnaises, Galantine de volaille, pains de lièvre aux pistaches, pâtés de Pithiviers, salades d'homard et d'anchois*, and *la Poutarga*, down to all the tempting *friandises à-la-napolitaine*, formed as picturesque an object to the sight, as a tempting one to the palate. Sir William Gell was eloquent in his praises of our superiority over the ancients in the noble science of gastronomy; asserted that Pompeii never before saw so delicious a *déjeuner à-la-fourchette*, and only wished that a *triclinium* was added to the luxuries, that he might recline while indulging in them: a position, however, which I should think far from agreeable when eating.[21]

The bon vivant Sir William Gell who called for the triclinium was probably the leading classical scholar of his generation. A former chamberlain to the late Queen Caroline, Gell had made extensive visits to classical sites in Turkey and Greece. Before moving to Naples in 1820, he had lived in a house built amid the ruins of Domitian's Palace in Rome. Nevertheless he wore his unparalleled scholarship lightly and, as well as classical lore, he was interested in noticeable clothes, probably influencing d'Orsay's taste in apparel. Always good humoured, in spite of the gout, which dictated that he be carried around in a chair or propel himself at speed in a wheelchair along the marble floors of the palaces to which he was welcomed, he was a most engaging antiquary and a unique tour guide for grand English visitors to Naples, including the novelist Sir Walter Scott.

But Gell was just one member of a social circle, the diameter of which was impressive. From the Archbishop of Taranto to the impeccably mannered astronomer Giuseppe Piazzi, who discovered the first minor planet and named it Ceres; from the poet Casimir de la Vigne to the sculptor Sir Richard Westmacott, matters spiritual and scientific, literary and artistic, were all covered. And all the time the curious came to meet d'Orsay, his high-spending patron and the charming countess: a torrent of princes, dukes, earls, viscounts, counts, young men on the Grand Tour and serving military officers poured through the alabaster doorjambs of the Palazzo Belvedere.

In November 1823, the Palazzo acquired an additional resident – a young architect called Charles James Mathews. The son of an actor who was an old friend of Lord Blessington, Mathews had just completed four years studying under Augustus Charles Pugin, father of the celebrated Gothic architect Augustus Welby Pugin, who designed the Houses of Parliament. Having settled d'Orsay in the Palazzo Belvedere Lord Blessington had left his wife in the company of his young friend and travelled back to London to vote in favour of Catholic emancipation. While in London he looked up his old friend

Mathews senior and conceived a liking for the drawings and the person of Mathews junior. He declared that Mathews junior should travel immediately to Ireland to make his debut as an architect by building a new house at Mountjoy. Dozens of plans were drawn up, altered and discarded. As Mathews recalled later, 'I was shrewd enough to discover very soon that my chief charm lay in my acquiescence with his whims, and patience with his vacillations.'[22] The house never got built, but Mathews proved himself to be sufficiently acquiescent to be invited to accompany Lord Blessington to Naples.

Charles Mathews was good company. Whether he became Blessington's lover is debatable. He certainly cheered the mercurial earl's spirits as they journeyed southwards and the couple became intimate, with Mathews providing an endearing description of the comical earl in bed wrapped in a shawl, wearing a large flannel nightcap surrounded by his books and his ludicrously expensive accessories. During their journey they encountered Lady Blessington's sister, Mrs Purves, who was travelling the continent with her lover Charles Manners Sutton, Speaker of the House of Commons, who later became her husband and was elevated to the peerage with the title of Lord Canterbury.

On Mathews's arrival in Naples in the autumn of 1823 he described Count d'Orsay as 'then a youth of nineteen'[23] when, depending on the year of d'Orsay's birth, he was either twenty-two or twenty-three years old. Perhaps the architect was confusing d'Orsay's age with his own: Mathews was born in 1803. There is however no mistaking his admiration for d'Orsay, which is excessive in the homoerotic hyperbole it piles on the glamorous Frenchman.

I have no hesitation in asserting [that he] was the beau ideal of manly dignity and grace. He had not yet assumed the marked peculiarities of dress and deportment which the sophistications of London life subsequently developed. He was the model of all

that could be conceived of noble demeanour and youthful can-
dour; handsome beyond all question; accomplished to the last
degree; highly educated, and of great literary acquirements;
with a gaiety of heart and cheerfulness of mind that spread happiness on all around him. His conversation was brilliant and
engaging, as well as clever and instructive. He was, moreover,
the best fencer, dancer, swimmer, runner, dresser; the best shot,
the best horseman, the best draughtsman of his age. Possessed of
every attribute that could render his society desirable, I am sure
I do not go too far in pronouncing him the perfection of a youthful nobleman.[24]

The two young men became inseparable or, as Mathews put it, 'I
may say without exaggeration, bosom friends.'[25] Presumably much to
the delight of Lord Blessington, this pair of young men shared the
manly, physical pursuits of 'fencing, pistol-shooting, swimming,
riding',[26] as well as more sedentary occupations such as reading and
drawing. 'It is true that in everything I felt myself more like his pupil
than his equal,' recalled Mathews; 'but this modesty on my side never
for a moment drew from him the slightest manifestation of the superiority he could not but be aware that he possessed.'[27]

However, it would not be long before Mathews's unequivocal
admiration of the young count would give way to rivalry and
animosity.

CHAPTER NINE

A Duel Narrowly Averted

AT FIRST MATHEWS SLOTTED INTO THE AGREEABLE ROUTINE OF life at the Palazzo Belvedere with the ease of the missing piece of a jigsaw puzzle. As Lord Blessington's latest young amusing male toy, a pet architect, he was given a desk in the large room in which the house's occupants 'worked' at their quasi-intellectual tasks. 'In one corner of the large salon stood Lady Blessington's table, laden with books and writings; Count d'Orsay's in another, equally adorned with literary and artistic litter.' As well as concentrating on making the cut of his trousers the talk of Neapolitan high society, d'Orsay also developed his talent as an artist sketching some of the visitors to the Palazzo. 'Miss Power's and mine completed the arrangement, while Lord Blessington strolled and chatted from one to the other, and then dived into his own sanctum, where he divided his time between fresh architectural schemes for his castle in the air, and the novel of "De Vavasour," on which he was busily engaged.'[1]

De Vavasour, an historical novel, did eventually struggle into print a couple of years later. It is often said that everyone has at least one book inside them; in Lord Blessington's case it seems as if it would have been better for the book-buying public if *De Vavasour* had stayed there. 'Don't read Lord Blessington's Reginald de Vavasour . . . duller than death,' was the verdict of one critic.[2] However, for all its faults, *De Vavasour* did actually come to fruition, which Blessington's grandiose architectural schemes, upon which Mathews worked, did not. Frustrated, Mathews found different ways to entertain himself and the other inhabitants of the Palazzo Belvedere. A clue to the direction that Mathews's diversions would take is contained in Lady Blessington's description of a certain feature of the Palazzo.

Along with shopping and the company of attractive, amusing young men, the stage was of course one of Lord Blessington's chief preoccupations, and as well as the chapel, the billiard room and the old masters the palace also had an open-air theatre. 'Among the various *agrémens* of the pleasure-grounds of the Palazzo Belvedere is a theatre, formed of trees and plants, the proscenium elevated, and of verdant turf, and the seats of marble; the different rows divided by cut box and ilex, which grow so luxuriously, as to screen the passages of which they form the separation.'[3]

Lord Blessington would have compared his own theatre on his estates in Ireland with the magical setting of the theatre at the Palazzo Belvedere, and Mathews, knowing of his patron's fondness for the performing arts, realised that he must sing for his supper somehow or other. If his architectural drawings were to remain forever two-dimensional, he would find another way of demonstrating his versatility as a house guest and continue to endear himself to Lord Blessington. The son of an actor, Mathews was a talented mimic. He would later become a celebrated thespian and much loved figure of the Victorian stage. His memoirs and reminiscences were judged to be of such importance that they were edited posthumously by Dickens.

In the 1820s, Mathews's renown on the London stage was still in the distant future but it was in the lotus-eating atmosphere of the

Palazzo Belvedere that the first inklings of his later fame became apparent. 'In the cool of the evenings we all repaired to a charming loggia overlooking the bay,' he wrote,

> and here a succession of amusements, springing out of the fun and fancy of the moment, passed away the moonlight hours. Visitors poured in in endless variety, and the charms of music and playful wit were brought into action.
>
> I had soon picked up many imitations of Neapolitan manners and peculiarities and gave frequent dressed representations of the characters I had collected, while not a week passed but I had added one or two Neapolitan songs, which given in the grotesque dialect of the peasantry, and with guitar accompaniment, were always welcome contributions.[4]

Young Mathews was having a ball: singing songs, performing little sketches, admiring the dancing of the tarantella, dressing up, never quiet for a moment, dashing about and generally acting as court jester. His letters home to his mother are filled with enthusiastic accounts of the party in costume for a fancy-dress dinner, trips into the country, his increasing command of Italian, and the grand folk he was meeting. He even writes home that 'there is great talk of going into Egypt, as Lady B. has a very great desire to see the Pyramids. She wishes to know what would be your opinion about my going too. I tell her I am sure that wherever I go with *her* you will be perfectly satisfied. Have I not said right?'[5]

With Mathews working his way ever deeper into his host's and hostess's affections, d'Orsay felt he was becoming sidelined. Blessington was of course easily distracted and given his tendency, once having achieved his aim, of moving on to the next bauble, the count was concerned that his place in Blessington's pantheon might be supplanted by Mathews. But there was nothing calculated to offend d'Orsay in Blessington's interest in the architect. If anything Blessington was probably unaware of the intensity of his favour and the concomitant distress of its withdrawal. In any case, d'Orsay might have begun to take the Blessingtons for granted. Nevertheless, for someone who had basked in the earl's sunny disposition for many months, d'Orsay found it difficult to share his favour with another. Moreover, Mathews knew just how to flatter Lady Blessington, and anyone who pleased Lady Blessington pleased her husband too. Of his hostess in fancy dress, Mathews wrote to his mother, 'I never in my life saw anything so perfectly beautiful. I would have given a hundred pounds for you to have seen her. You never saw such a darling as she was altogether.'[6] There is also a poignancy about an aside in Mathews's letter to his mother about the Egyptian trip:

> They all desire their kindest love to you and my father to whom, of course, my best love. Count d'Orsay is rather piqued at your saying nothing about him in your last letters and desires me to send his love. I tell him that if you were to hear him speak English – which he does in the prettiest manner – that you could not refrain from kissing him. I hope you are enjoying yourselves at this season, as we are here, with all sorts of fun.[7]

It is unclear whether Mathews meant this mention of d'Orsay to his mother to be anything more than playful. Probably not. Neverthless there was enough here to wound d'Orsay's sense of pride. After all, he was capable of being goaded into histrionic over-reaction, as his behaviour at Lady Holland's dinner table and in the regimental mess had demonstrated. Perhaps, as he got to know the Frenchman, Mathews felt emboldened to make gentle fun of his exaggerated courtesy, and, given his effective mimicry and his capacity to amuse, perhaps he raised a smile from Lord and Lady Blessington at d'Orsay's expense.

Perhaps Blessington had artlessly attempted to find d'Orsay a friend of his own age. Perhaps by introducing another young man into the domestic ménage, he had hoped to dispel potential grounds for gossip. D'Orsay, however, saw things differently: his ego and his confidence growing, he might have ruminated that, as someone who had been hunting with Wellington and become Byron's friend, to be outdone by a young architect, little more than a mere tradesman, was an insult. Mathews's popularity must have brought the essentially precarious nature of his apparently gilded existence into sharp focus. Charming, handsome, well dressed, witty and charismatic as he was, d'Orsay's continued existence as a member of the early-nineteenth-century jet-set depended entirely on the whims of Lord and Lady Blessington. Perhaps at night he would fret that, as easily as he had been written into Lord Blessington's will, he might be written out, or that Mathews might somehow marry Blessington's other daughter.

Come the summer of 1824 d'Orsay's simmering temper and discontent were brought to the boil in the emotional pressure cooker that was the Palazzo Belvedere. Events took a dramatic turn at the end of July.

There are two versions of the genesis of these events. One, as recalled by Mathews in his memoirs, sets the scene on the morning of 31 July 1824. After breakfast, Lord Blessington suggested a cruise on the *Bolivar*, over to Castellamare. The yacht was one of Blessington's favourite toys. To the perpetual irritation of his household he was constantly proposing little sailing trips that frequently resulted in the party being becalmed for several hours, bored by the company of the over-enthusiastic skipper Captain Smith and roasted by the fierce Mediterranean sun.

The notion of a cruise that morning was not greeted with enthusiasm. The ladies declined, pleading fear of the heat. D'Orsay, perhaps revealing his childish ego and wanting to get his own back at

Blessington for favouring Mathews, flatly refused to indulge his patron without even bothering to veil his distaste with an excuse. Not to be put off, Blessington mentioned the idea to Mathews. But the architect was no keener, offering the excuse that he had a pressing sketch to make. 'As you please,' said Lord Blessington. 'I only hope you will really carry out your intention; for even your friend Count d'Orsay says that you carry your sketch-book with you everywhere, but that you never bring back anything in it.'[8] Stung by the normally good-natured earl's catty remark, Mathews turned on his heel, and poor Lord Blessington was left to go sailing with only the overly hearty old sea-dog Captain Smith for company.

After his departure the atmosphere at the Palazzo Belvedere could have been pierced by one of the épées with which Mathews and d'Orsay used to fence in friendlier days. Lady Blessington, probably feeling guilty about having turned down her husband's offer of a day's sailing, seems to have lectured d'Orsay on his discourtesy to Lord Blessington. Mathews meanwhile smarted from his employer's rebuke.

The other story, recounted by Lady Blessington's biographer Madden, takes place before an evening carriage ride. In Madden's version of events, a mildly drunk Lord Blessington, ribbing Mathews with the words 'So Mr. Charles, I understand that there are sad complaints against you on the score of idleness; Count d'Orsay tells me that you always take your sketch-book with you, but not always to make sketches.'[9] They then get into the carriage, where 'galled with the piquant manner in which Lord B. had mentioned it', Mathews 'in a half-laughing way' raised the subject with d'Orsay.[10]

Thereafter the two accounts are roughly convergent in recollection of the exchange in the carriage which became rather heated. As Mathews recalled, he himself snapped, '"I have to thank you, Count d'Orsay, for the high character you have given me to Lord

Blessington, with regard to my diligence." "Comment?" said the Count.'[11] Mathews immediately began to wish that he had not mentioned the subject; following his lecture by Lady Blessington, d'Orsay was in a foul temper. 'I saw the fire flashing in his eyes,' wrote Mathews,

> and changed my tone: 'I should have been more gratified had you mentioned to me, instead of to his lordship, anything you might have—'
>
> 'Vous êtes un MAUVAIS BLAGUEUR, par Dieu, la plus GRANDE BÊTE, et BLAGUEUR que j'ai jamais rencontré, et la première fois que vous me parlez comme ça, je vous CASSERAI LA TÊTE et je vous JETTERAI PAR LA FENÊTRE.'
>
> Such words as these, before two ladies and the servants, I did not conceive were answerable, and remained silent. Lady Blessington, in order to end the affair, said: 'Count d'Orsay, I beg you to remember I am present, and that such language is not exactly what I should have expected before me.'
>
> 'Pardieu,' said the Count, and, I regret to say, proceeded to lengths in reply to her ladyship passing all I had believed possible.[12]

The scene is tinged with farcical unreality – two sulking boys slinging insults at each other while Lady Blessington, who must have heard far coarser modes of expression at her father's house in Ireland, appeals to Count d'Orsay to spare her delicate feminine sensibilities. But things got worse.

The party returned to the Palazzo and took a stroll in the garden, before each retired to his or her room. D'Orsay immediately scribbled a hot-tempered note, which was delivered to Mathews.

If you had had any knowledge of the world, you would have understood that it is indispensable to know one's place in it – that is a matter which, above all things, you ought to learn. You would avoid by so doing the trouble of being taught that the friendship which people have for you is no excuse for your taking a tone which it is necessary to lower, especially when you address a person who does not forget who he is. If you had taken a proper tone, you would have learnt that in conversation with milady before milord, we took occasion to remark that you had let slip the opportunity of making sketches at Capri, and further, that it was a pity you did not devote more time to drawing. If you find anything offensive in these words, I am at a loss as to their meaning, and as they were only uttered in conversation by milady to me, I was far from thinking they could annoy you. Further, and on another point, you have no right to assume an arrogant air and an unbecoming manner in reproaching me with what I said. You have placed me under the cruel necessity of putting you in your proper place, but you might have avoided it all if you had remembered to whom you were speaking.[13]

As a masterpiece of pompous, self-justifying *folie de grandeur*, d'Orsay's note is pretty near faultless. Its arrogance is breathtaking. It has to be admitted that in the early nineteenth century social divisions were considerably more marked than today. However, the Blessington–d'Orsay *ménage* can hardly be said to have been a conventional one, and certainly it was not one that would have withstood rigorous social scrutiny. Indeed d'Orsay might have done well to heed his parting advice that Mathews ought to have 'remembered to whom he was speaking': he was himself a penniless young spendthrift, who had effectively been sold by his parents to the Blessingtons; the bearer of a French title admittedly, but one purchased relatively recently by a socially ambitious, *arriviste* ancestor. Perhaps subconscious

recognition of his own inadequacies had prompted him to this stinging and snobbish attack on his former friend.

The dawn of Sunday, 1 August did not bring with it a restoration
of cordial relations between the inmates of the Palazzo Belvedere.
Mathews awoke and sent the following note to d'Orsay:

> I have slept and thought over your letter and the words with
> which you honoured me yesterday, and as it seems to me that
> neither nobility nor superior strength give you any right to insult
> me so grossly before ladies, and especially before servants, I
> hope you will not refuse me that satisfaction which I feel con-
> strained to demand of you.[14]

The letter ended, 'Monsieur le Comte, j'ai l'honneur d'être, Votre
serviteur, C.J.M.'[15] The irony was not lost on d'Orsay.

The servants at the Palazzo were kept busy that morning, because
shortly afterwards Mathews had his note returned to him with these
icy paragraphs from d'Orsay:

> Your letter goes further to prove how little knowledge you have
> of the world. You should know that a letter ought not to be so
> flippantly ended, and as I hope that some good may come out of
> all this quarrel, profit by this piece of advice.
>
> As to the satisfaction you desire, I will give you as much as
> you please. Name the place and the weapons; in fact everything
> you think most fitting for your personal satisfaction. I return
> your letter, as its tone does not incline me to preserve it.[16]

It would seem that the swords and pistols with which the two young
men had played but a few months earlier were to be put to graver use.

As soon as he had read d'Orsay's letter, Mathews went into
Naples to the house of Richard Madden, a young medical student

who had befriended the Blessingtons. Madden would later become a pioneer of homeopathy and, as we have already seen, write a rambling three-volume life of Lady Blessington. He agreed to act as Mathews's second and advised the architect to return to the Palazzo Belvedere, so as not to arouse the suspicions of the household. As it was, Mathews need not have worried about his covert behaviour. On his return to the Palazzo he found that d'Orsay had already asked Lord Blessington to act as his second. By now in a terrible state, Blessington said that he would have nothing to do with the duel and that he was upset that such a state of affairs should have come about.

Mathews, 'thinking it not quite agreeable to sit at table with the Count',[17] cleared off into Naples, intending to stay away from the Palazzo Belvedere until the matter had been settled. There he received a hurriedly penned letter from Lord Blessington:

My Dear Mathews,

I considered it proper to state to Count d'Orsay, that I could not take any part in the very disagreeable affair that has taken place, except that of a mediator. I assured Count d'Orsay that you had no intention of speaking to him in an improper tone, or questioning him in an impetuous or disrespectful manner. The Count had imagined the contrary, and meant to express that if you did not change your tone towards him, that he would have recourse to violence; for the use of any words beyond the expression of such intentions he says as follows: 'Si j'ai employé plus de, paroles qu'il étoit suffisant pour lui exprimer mes intentions j'en suis fâché.' The Count says also: 'Je n'ai pas eu l'idée de le rebaisser dans ses propres yeux.' The Count acknowledges to me his regret for the quarrel and the violence of his temper. That violence has not yet sufficiently subsided to make him perceive fully to what improper lengths his violence has carried him; but as you declared to me that you had no intention of speaking improperly, and the Count declares he spoke from misconception, and is sorry for language used in anger, and without intention of lowering you in your personal esteem, I should wish you to speak further on the subject to your friend before you take any steps which must make the breach wider. Having consulted Mr Madden, I am sure he will give you the best advice, and you can this evening let me know his sentiments.

I cannot conclude without repeating that you were highly to blame in speaking on the subject at all, however I deeply regret the consequences that have arisen from your ill-timed and injudicious appeal.

I wish I had sufficient influence over the Count to persuade him to say everything consoling to you, but his having denied the intention of wounding your feelings must be so far satisfactory, and 'evil words hurt only the speaker.'

Believe me yours very sincerely,

BLESSINGTON.

Excuse the haste of this scrawl; you may guess why I hasten it.[18]

There is something unseemly about poor Lord Blessington having to grovel to both his boyfriends, but the kindly older man was doubtless distraught about the tensions between his two young friends. Even if it had cost what little dignity he possessed, he felt he had found a suitable way for the young men to extricate themselves from the situation. He was wrong.

Mathews looked over the letter and handed it to Madden, who read it closely and considered that it did not meet the required criteria for calling off the duel. Only a suitably worded letter from d'Orsay would suffice, and Madden wrote to tell him so.

Monsieur Le Comte

On a subject of importance, I can hardly trust to my bad French; I therefore have recourse to the only language I can distinctly make myself understood in.

If I felt less embarrassed in addressing you on the subject of a late unhappy misunderstanding between you and Mr. Mathews, I should hope to be able to convince you that the character of an officious man cannot be more disagreeable in your eyes than it is in mine, and that I have undertaken the office of mediator on the present occasion (though not without reluctance) not less from my friendship for Mr. M. than from my high respect for you. I should have done so indeed, even had I not stood committed to Mr. M. by promise, before I was acquainted with the name of his antagonist, when I considered that the exposé to a stranger of this misunderstanding might be prevented by the interference of a mutual acquaintance.

Pardon me, Monsieur le Comte, if I presume to offer a few words in the way of counsel and observation. I have too high an opinion of your understanding to fear you will be offended by receiving them when honestly given, even from an humbler individual than myself.

I can very well conceive some momentary annoyance (the cause of which might not be apparent to Mr M.) extorting from you those expressions, which no gentleman should hear in the presence of a lady, although, in a cooler moment, in all probability, by you forgotten or regretted. I can very well understand, in your observation about Mr. M's neglect with respect to drawing, &c., the friendliness of your intentions, but permit me to add, if what followed had been suppressed, the feelings of Mr. M. had been spared a severe trial.

Depend upon it, Monsieur le Comte, that persons of inferior rank are ever tremblingly alive even to an imaginary slight or insult from a superior; and when you reflect that the epithets that stand for limits of separation between *noble* and *plebeian* are but arbitrary distinctions between man and man you will best consult the nobility of your nature by practising the honourable condescension of a brave man by making a trifling atonement for a hasty injury.

It is with a full knowledge of your manly spirit that I demand an acknowledgment, on the part of Mr. M., of your having been betrayed by anger into those hasty expressions, which only those who do not know you could think of attributing to intentional incivility.

I have the honour to be Monsieur le Comte, with the highest respect,

Your obedient, humble Servant

R. R. MADDEN[19]

This skilfully worded, subtly flattering document, appealing to d'Orsay's nobility of spirit as well as to his sense of lineage, seemed to be the emollient that the situation required. In the evening this reply was sent:

My dear Mr Madden

I am very far from being sorry that Mr. Mathews has chosen you for his second, my only fear having been that he might choose somebody else. I am also far from being offended at any of your remarks. When I esteem anyone, his opinion is always welcome.

In principle the matter is, as you know, very simple. I was asked if Mathews had drawn anything at Capri. I replied no, but that he always carried his chalks and sketch-book to do nothing with, and that, with his great abilities, it was a pity it should be so. Lord Blessington had not sufficient courage to speak to him on the subject, without bringing in my name, and Mathews took the matter up with me in so lofty a tone, that I was obliged to bring him to reason, after explaining to him that my remarks had only been prompted by my interest in him. He continued in the same manner, and I then told him that the first time he took the same tone with me, I would throw him out of the carriage and break his head. I give you the quarrel word for word. The only difference I made between him and anyone else, was that I only said to him what I would actually have done to any other person who had treated me in the same manner. If I accompanied my threat with offensive and unbecoming language, I am sorry, for his sake as well as for my own; for I should be wanting in self-respect if I used unduly violent language.

As to your remark about the difference of rank, it is useless, for I never attach importance to rank which is so often compromised by so many fools. I judge people for what they are, without enquiring who their ancestors may have been and if my superior had adopted the same tone of reproach as Mathews did, I would assuredly have done to him what I only said to Mathews, whom I love too much to degrade in his own eyes. I feel it would be ridiculous not to admit that I was wrong in using unnecessarily hard words, but at the same time I do not wish to deny them – such for instance as my proposal to throw him out of the carriage. If Mathews wishes satisfaction, I will give him as much as he likes, acknowledging at the same time the goodwill he has shown in choosing you for his second. This affair is as disagreeable for you as it is for all of us, but at least it will not alter the friendship of your devoted

Comte d'Orsay[20]

Mathews returned to the Palazzo the next morning and shook hands with d'Orsay, who was about to embark on a long-winded explanation-cum-apology, only for Mathews to cut him short with the words, 'My dear Count, I beg you, let's speak no more about it, I have completely forgotten about it.'[21] And so the business was happily resolved – almost.

A day or two later Mathews entered the drawing room to find Lady Blessington lying ill on a sofa. With her were Miss Power and d'Orsay, the latter in tears. On seeing Mathews, the count, in a state of heightened emotion, once more asked for Mathews's forgiveness, in front of Lady Blessington, and implored him to put the whole matter from his mind, asking him to promise that the incident would be completely forgotten. Mathews, himself now quite affected and not a little embarrassed, assured the count 'over and over again, that it had long been banished from my thoughts'.[22]

It seemed that Mathews had emerged from the affair with greater credit, or perhaps more accurately less shame, than d'Orsay. However, if Mathews triumphed in this non-duel, it was d'Orsay who would eventually get what he wanted.

By the end of the year Mathews had left Naples and was sufficiently far away from the Blessington–d'Orsay ménage for d'Orsay to write to him affectionately in December 1824. He opened his letter thus: 'It is useless for me to repeat how much we have regretted your absence, you can have no doubt of that. Let it be enough for you to know that there is a great void in your place which no one can fill.'[23] A void d'Orsay would make sure that no one, expect perhaps himself, would attempt to fill.

Apart from throwing the complex emotional tensions at the Palazzo Belvedere into sharp relief, this incident is also illuminating about d'Orsay's character. The hotheaded gallantry, exaggeratedly chivalric behaviour and easily bruised honour are firmly established traits. It seems that he was actually rather fond of flying into an histrionic rage over something petty. In reading his letters, it is clear that there is a malicious joy in the exquisite snub and the killing put-down – 'I return your letter, as its tone does not incline me to preserve it.'

But d'Orsay's swagger masked considerable insecurity. The extent of his self-doubt, or rather his acute sensitivity to the opinions of others – in spite of the exaggerated dandiacal indifference he affected – is made clear in an undated letter probably written in the 1830s, to his friend Dr Quin. Written at midnight, it concerned a meeting Quin had had with an anonymous peer with whom d'Orsay had clearly fallen out. D'Orsay said that he felt he had been spending his life outside Quin's door; he explained that he had presented himself early in the day in the hope of waylaying him and speaking with him about this meeting. D'Orsay's letter reveals that, although Quin and he had obviously talked about this character at considerable length, d'Orsay wanted to go over the subject again.

He complained that the peer in question had transferred his affections to d'Orsay's own parents, with whom the man had become friendly on a recent visit to France. Then he proceeded to recount several instances in almost obsessive detail when he considered that the peer had snubbed him: once outside Quin's house, 'He greeted me with such a cold manner that several days later the Easterly thermal still hasn't warmed me up.'[24] D'Orsay added that he had seen the man at the Opera and that he had not deigned to turn his head to look in his direction. He was also upset that he had been greeted strangely by him at the house of a well-known painter. Similarly at the house of a duke (perhaps Beaufort), he had been greeted with a handshake that was far from warm – 'He gave me a handshake like a wet fish.'[25]

So powerfully affected was he by the man's froideur that he said he could hardly believe it was the same man with whom he and Quin had spent such enjoyable evenings and had such 'witty conversations. You say it's my fault that we're no longer friends, and you scold me for my "thin skin".'[26] The letter reads almost like that of a wounded lover, and perhaps there had indeed been some attachment to the anonymous peer, whom d'Orsay suspected of abandoning him because he believed himself to be an 'homme d'état' and was always surrounded by a crowd of courtiers who flattered his 'amour propre' and impeded him from using his common sense.

What this letter demonstrates quite clearly is that d'Orsay's carapace of accomplishments was just that. His letter of the 1830s sheds light on the motivations of the actions of the younger man. Beneath his glittering and haughty exterior, he was easily hurt. Any slight, however trivial, or even imagined, would be carefully noted and pondered upon by the hypersensitive count. It would fester in his mind. If this personality trait was still in evidence in London a decade later, a time when d'Orsay's image was a much more highly crafted creation and when his standing as a man of fashion was almost unassailable, it is fair to assume that d'Orsay as a young man was even more emotionally sensitive and touchy.

Moreover, it exposes one aspect of the dynamic of the relationship between d'Orsay and Lady Blessington. Much as it would have appealed to this former Irish nobody to play the grand lady and stage a convenient attack of the vapours, or whatever it was that early-nineteenth-century ladies of quality succumbed to when faced with strong language, a bad atmosphere and the prospect of a duel, there is also the sense that she realised just how much she cared for d'Orsay, almost as a son for whom she had incestuous feelings, rather than as a lover.

Her admonition to d'Orsay and the tear-soaked drawing-room scene smack strongly of parental disappointment, tinged with relief at a disaster only narrowly averted. Much as a parent might scold a child who has caused a domestic accident but avoided serious injury, so Lady Blessington was ticking off Count d'Orsay who, essentially an affectionate man, was upset and ashamed to have caused her so much obvious grief.

D'Orsay was an artistic and sensitive person who was coming to maturity. In his efforts as a dandy, artist and sculptor he had yet to make his mark. But at the time of his sojourn in Naples he was beginning to establish a style of dress and behaviour that would remain with him for the rest of his life. It is ironic that he would eventually make more use of his sketchbook than Mathews. From his early sketches of Byron in 1823 until Lady Blessington's death the output of drawings, and later of portraits and sculptures, tended to increase with each year. It is also significant that d'Orsay's mother saw Lady Blessington as acting *in loco parentis*. Shortly before her death, the Countess d'Orsay spoke with 'great earnestness of her apprehensions for her son, on account of his tendency to extravagance, and of her desire that Lady Blessington would advise and counsel him, and do her utmost to counteract those propensities which had already been attended with embarrassments, and had occasioned her great fears for his welfare'.[27]

And very late in his life when, a pale wreck of his former self, he was facing death, he admitted to Madden, his face streaming with tears, in a state reminiscent of that summer morning in 1824, 'In losing her I lost every thing in this world – she was to me a mother! a dear, dear mother! a true loving mother to me!'[28] The emotional geometry at the Palazzo Belvedere was nothing if not complex.

CHAPTER TEN

A Change of Scene

BOREDOM, DRAUGHTS, DOUBTLESS LORD BLESSINGTON'S obsessive concern with his health and perhaps even the lingering memory of the duel that almost was, militated against another winter in the Palazzo Belvedere. By the autumn of 1824, d'Orsay and the Blessingtons had moved to the Villa Gallo at Capo di Monte. The Neapolitan royal family, doubtless impressed by the quality of improvements made by Lord Blessington, immediately rented the Belvedere themselves.

Described by Lady Blessington as 'less fine, but infinitely more comfortable' than the Palazzo Belvedere,[1] the Villa Gallo was still an opulent house with fine pleasure grounds, abounding in grottoes, rustic bridges, limpid streams and exotic vegetation. Here life continued much as it had before Mathews had arrived at the Belvedere: sights were seen and visitors welcomed, among them Henry Edward Fox, who had first spent time with the Blessington–d'Orsay party in Menton.

Byron dead, his mistress Teresa Guiccioli was now conducting an affair with the sharp-tongued Fox. The sexual side of their relation-ship had commenced on 8 August. Of their first night together Fox wrote that she 'received me as those females receive one, who makes such occupations not their pleasure but their trade'.[2] As ever Fox was blunt in his appraisal of his new lover. 'She has a pretty voice, pretty eyes, white skin, and strong, not to say turbulent, passions. She has no other attraction.'[3] He nevertheless added that he spent every night in August with his lover and it seems to have been an interesting, if less than restful relationship. 'With T. G. I had various quarrels and hys-terics: she is jealous and exigeante and troublesome. Poor Ld Byron! I do not wonder at his going to Greece.'[4]

After numerous quarrels and reconciliations Teresa left Naples on 15 October and Fox was to have followed had he not fallen from his horse the following day, while on his way to the Villa Gallo, and seri-ously hurt his ankle. 'You will be astonished at reading the date of this letter both as to time & place – *Villa Gallo on the last day of October*!!! When you have I conclude long ago settled that I ought to be at Paris,'* wrote Fox to a friend on 31 October, 'I was riding up here on my old gray pony – the beast tumbled down & came with his whole weight upon my ankle – my good luck & nothing else that I can guess prevented the fracture of my leg but I received a horrid bruise & though it is now nearly 18 days since it happened I am only beginning to walk.'[5]

But if his correspondent was surprised that Fox was still in Naples, it was nothing compared to Fox's surprise that, forced to convalesce at Villa Gallo, he found himself actually liking his hosts, in particular d'Orsay. 'I have been taken the greatest care of by this family – indeed I never can feel sufficiently grateful for all the kindness I have met with,' continues his letter of 31 October, 'd'Orsay I am extremely

---

* Fox's parents had decided to spend the winter in Paris, and he had already sent his servant ahead to meet them.

fond of – he has great frankness openness & warmth of character – quite unlike the race of die away effeminate selfish dandies whom he only resembles in being recherché in his toilette – He has a 1000 real good qualities & many talents – in fact I am glad to have had an opportunity of improving an acquaintance into a friendship & nothing but my accident would ever have made me know him or think of him as I do.'[6]

A month after his accident, Fox still lingered at Villa Gallo. 'Here I still am – I *could* go – I *can* walk but I wait on,' he writes in a letter of 15 November, 'partly because I am so well nursed, partly because I am so well attended by a surgeon here in whom *strange to say* I have confidence, and *partly* though I do not like to own such a reason just out of curiosity to wait till I hear what my family think & how they take my accident.' As well as curiosity about the reaction of his parents, he had become increasingly close to d'Orsay:

He has great meatiness of character & is when well known a very agreeable member of society – It is a very bad thing for any one to live as he does in such a narrow circle completely – it forms prejudices and ends by making one narrow minded – haughty & weighing every trifle in the actions of others beyond their real value – living up here as I do I see little of Naples or its inhabitants it seems to me as if I was in a [*sic*] English country house suddenly placed by . . . [an] Aladdin genie within gun shot of Naples —The habits – hours – conversations [are] such as one would find in some Hall or Priory or Abbey in a distant province of Albions isle.[7]

During the four weeks since he sustained his injury Fox seems to have radically altered in character. The sniping tone of his earlier journal entries has vanished, he no longer seems to be the querulous individual addicted to socialising. 'Society is necessary for me,' he once confided to his journal,[8] and yet weeks afer a relatively minor injury he shows no sign of wanting to hurry back into the social maelstrom. Instead he seems a far happier, calmer and more contented man, clutching at excuses for staying on at the Villa Gallo, where the good-natured d'Orsay would read aloud to him in the evening.[9] Fox's volte-face is typical of many who spent a protracted period in d'Orsay's company. It is almost as if the force of the Frenchman's character and charisma worked as a spell. From Fox's account of his stay, d'Orsay is not just a good-looking, well-dressed, cultured, amusing and interesting specimen; he emerges as, to use an undervalued adjective, a nice man. 'Towards d'Orsay', wrote Fox from the Villa Gallo on 22 November, 'I entertain warmer feelings & fully return the affection he professes & which therefore I feel confident he feels for me – he is sincerity & frankness itself.'[10]

And through the deepening and mutual affection that he feels for d'Orsay he is inclined to become tolerant of Lady Blessington:

The kindness of my hostess towards me and the extreme partiality she either feels or professes for me prevent my saying anything in disparagement of the beauty, talents and good qualities which far better judges than I am see and admire in her. Though perhaps I am either blind or stubborn, I cannot be ungrateful or ever forget her hospitality and attentions to me . . . It rather hurt me, as I felt myself acting with duplicity (although I never made any sort of professions), but it hurt me not to be able to like Ly Blessington as I should wish to like her; but she has exactly the defects that suit least with my character and that cross all my prejudices and wound all my little peculiarities of opinion and disposition. I have already given my opinion of her and d'Orsay, and have sometimes thought that I ought to correct it in consequence of the subsequent kindness I have met with; but I have determined not. It is a lesson not to judge too hastily or too severely. First impressions are sometimes wrong, and as it is my art always to see the worst first, I should have very often to cancel. The ridicules and defects I there point out struck me at the time. I saw but them, and did not wait to discover that under Alfred's dandy exterior there beat a warm and generous heart; or could I foresee that I ever should have occasion to feel so much gratitude towards Ly B. as I at present do.[11]

Fox's accounts of his soujourn with d'Orsay provide a fascinating glimpse of life inside the ménage. Whereas the cheerful and active young Mathews was a threat to d'Orsay's position in the household, Fox, crippled at birth and recovering from a riding accident, was not. So, unthreatened, d'Orsay felt that he was able to turn the full force of his charm and personality on to Fox. And, basking in the sun and warmth of d'Orsay's charm, goodwill and kindness, Fox found himself liking the man he had hitherto written off as a feckless dandy. But, dazzled though he was, he was not blinded by d'Orsay. He liked the man in spite of the dandiacal pose rather than because of it. The 'marked peculiarities of dress and deportment' to which Mathews alluded and which would account for d'Orsay's later celebrity and glamour had begun to develop. These were affectations that Fox disliked, but he was able to see beyond them and glimpse the caring, kind and congenial man that was as much, if not more, the real d'Orsay than the outrageous fop.

Fox stayed until 4 December, then moved to the Gran Bretagna, the hotel in which the Blessingtons and d'Orsay had commenced their stay in Naples, and prepared to leave, journeying first to Rome and eventually joining his family in Paris, in March of the following year. Before he left, he made a summing up of his stay in Naples: 'the summer I have passed here has been the happiest I ever have or most likely ever shall pass'.[12] The final paragraph of his Neapolitan diary is devoted to d'Orsay and offers a shrewd and perceptive character sketch of the Frenchman who was now in his mid-twenties.

My friendship with Alfred is a warm one, but quite different from any I feel or ever have felt for anybody else. I admire some of his qualities and talents, and think he is by nature goodhearted and full of many estimable feelings and impulses; but vanity, vanity with a good deal of false exaggerated pride, have so disfigured his character that they have turned his merits almost into defects. Besides, the fatal liaison with such a woman as Ly Blessington is calculated to do him a terrible deal of harm, living as he does the solitary life of an idol incensed by flattery all day long.[13]

It is an acute appraisal of what two and half years in sybaritic Naples had done to d'Orsay, and possibly even he and Lady Blessington realised that to stay longer would not be healthy. By February 1825 d'Orsay and the Blessingtons were on the move again, via Rome, to Tuscany where the household would divide its time between Florence and Pisa.

Life broadly followed the same sort of pattern that it had in Naples. For almost eighteen months the programme was one of dinners and entertainments. Blessington was in good spirits: the delicious dandy, fashionable novelist and rising diplomat young Lord Normanby, attached to the British legation, was as fond of the stage as the eccentric earl and had a private theatre constructed at his villa, which became one of the centres of expatriate activity in Florence in the 1820s. Towards the end of the decade the cast list read like a roll call of fashionable and aristocratic London Society: as well as Lord and Lady Normanby, the players included 'Sir Hedworth and Lady Williamson, Lord Fitzharris, Lord Albert Conyngham, Messrs. Craven, Nightingale, Dundas, Aubry, Phipps, Bligh, Antrobus, Thelluson, Sitwell, St. John [and] E. Villiers'.[14] The enigmatic Russian plutocrat Prince Demidoff also had his own company of actors and used to throw lavish theatrical evenings at his palace, the malachite furniture of which made a great impression on Lady Blessington and doubtless on d'Orsay.

Once again d'Orsay was wheeled out as the 'idol' of both Lord and Lady Blessington, and there is the entertaining conceit of the Frenchman growing daily into his role as an outrageous dandy, in a bizarre society where the overt thespianism of the rival acting troupes and of the stage-obsessed trio of Blessington, Normanby and Demidoff spilt over into the strange and no less theatrical goldfish-bowl existence of these gilded expatriates wafting about Europe. The reports that filtered back to London must have made for fascinating and titillating gossip, evoking a world of decadent abandon.

There were characters so exotic that they needed no specially constructed theatre or attendant troupe of actors to enhance their appeal. For instance, the immensely fat Prince Borghese, the erstwhile husband of Napoleon's sister Pauline, lived much of the time in Florence. Such was his obesity 'that he dare not indulge in repose in a horizontal position; and sleeps either in his carriage, in which he drives about during the greater part of the night, or in a large chair, constructed for the purpose'.[15] Meanwhile in Pisa, at Byron's old address the Palazzo Lanfranchi, there were the Prince and Princess Carragia. The princess, an elderly woman in Oriental garb, compensated for her fading years with some of the biggest and best jewels in Europe. On a visit in April 1827, Lady Blessington rhapsodised over one particular necklace, 'a single row of pear shaped diamonds',[16] while the men puffed on pipes with amber mouthpieces and handles encrusted with rubies, sapphires, emeralds and diamonds.

These were also times of gastronomic experimentation. Typical of the increasingly colourful life that d'Orsay led at this time, smoking gem-set pipes and meeting preposterously corpulent royalty, was a spring dinner in Pisa, 'at the Archbishop of Mitylene's', at which the count 'partook of a repast in which many Turkish and Greek dishes were introduced'. Among them was 'a pillaw, the rice served with which was so admirably dressed that, white as snow, and very hot, each grain might be separated from its neighbour without being crushed: yet it was perfectly boiled. A kid, roasted whole and stuffed with pistachio nuts, was delicious. The dinner was sumptuous, consisting of three courses, *à-la-française*, besides *hors-d'oeuvres*; among which were caviare and various other Russian delicacies.' Then followed a succession of 'sweet things composed of flowers, and not only tasting, but impregnated with the odour of them. One cake of rose leaves was a *chef-d'oeuvre*; and another of orange flowers, was pronounced worthy of being served with nectar.'[17] After dinner there was Turkish coffee and rosewater-filled pipes for the gentlemen.

Among the guests at this dinner was d'Orsay's sister, who had arrived in Pisa with her husband the Duke de Guiche. The two households spent time together and Lord Blessington must have looked with an almost paternal pride on d'Orsay and his sister. He was fixated with the idea of the d'Orsay family as a whole: a gifted and glamorous dynasty of which young Alfred was the brightest ornament. That summer of 1825, the restless earl had disappeared for a visit to his estates in Ireland and, although the idea had not appealed to his wife or to d'Orsay, he had managed to persuade d'Orsay's father to accompany him. Now in Pisa Blessington cannot have been immune to the attraction of d'Orsay's sister, 'one of the most lovely and fascinating women of her day',[18] and her dashing husband, the Duke de Guiche, who 'looks like *the beau idéal* we form to ourselves, of Le Chevalier Bayard, "*sans peur et sans reproche*"'.[19]

As well as seeing his family while in Pisa, d'Orsay made a couple of friendships that would stay with him for a long time. There was Walter Savage Landor, the bluff poet, author, and unconventional radical who would prove to be a loyal friend to Lady Blessington in future crises. Another friendship dating from his time in Tuscany was with Alphonse de Lamartine, the nearly man of French politics in the late 1840s whose bust d'Orsay would sculpt over twenty years later. In the mid-1820s he was just another young poet, introduced to d'Orsay by the Marquis de la Maison-Fort, French minister to the Florentine court.

Lamartine was an interesting specimen, and Lady Blessington provides an intriguing portrait of a man who seemed not to be able to decide between public life and the arts. He was, rare among poets of the day, neatly turned out, well mannered and not at all Byronic in his pose:

> I have seen M. de Lamartine, and greatly like him. He is very good-looking and distinguished in his appearance, and dresses so perfectly like a gentleman, that one never would suspect him to be a poet. No shirt collars turned over, an apology for a cravat, no long curls falling on the collar of the coat; no assumption of any foppishness of any kind; but just the sort of man that, seen in any society, would be pronounced *bien comme il faut*. His features are handsome, and his countenance is peculiarly intelligent and intellectual; his manners are polished, and his conversation is brilliant and interesting. He has a *presence d'esprit* not often to be met with in the generality of poets; and a perfect freedom from any of the affectations of manner attributed to that *genus irritabile*. The truth is, that though gifted with a very glowing imagination, and a deeply reflecting mind, Mons. de Lamartine has been called on to act a prominent part in the scenes of actual life, which has compelled him to exercise his reasoning faculties as much, as his genius has led to the exertion of his imaginative ones: hence he presents the not common union, of a clever man of business, a well-bred man of society, and a poet; and appears to advantage in all three *rôles*.[20]*

* It is intriguing to note by contrast the acerbic Henry Fox's opinion of Lamartine: 'a poet, a dandy, and a diplomat, in about the third or fourth classes of each department'.

If Lady Blessington's description seems familiar, perhaps it is because she is, in a curious way, venting her feelings for the multi-talented d'Orsay. It may also be possible to see a hint of imaginative longing in her observation that Lamartine is, like d'Orsay, 'very well disposed towards the English; and no wonder, for he is the husband of an English lady'. Moreover, like Lamartine, d'Orsay was about to become the husband of an English, or at least Irish, lady. Four years had passed since the summer of 1823, when Blessington had written the codicil to his will at Genoa; now the arranged marriage between one of his daughters, it didn't really matter which, and d'Orsay was at last to take place.

CHAPTER ELEVEN

Marriage à la Mode d'Orsay

IN SPITE OF THE VARIOUS INTERESTING ACQUAINTANCES STRUCK up, the first seven or eight months of 1827 seem to have been largely bathetic for d'Orsay and the Blessingtons. Nothing, it seems, could match the *douceur de vivre* or indeed the weather of Naples. A letter written by Count d'Orsay from Pisa on 24 January that year is full of complaints.[1] He whinges about the weather, about plans for a winter journey that had been adandoned, about the fact that his sister would have returned to Paris had it not been for the advice of French doctors and about the poor quality of Pisan houses compared to those in Paris, although he grudgingly admits that the change of scene has done his sister good. 'We are living on the Lung Arno – our house is adequate yet miserable –' he writes; 'it is difficult to be able to content oneself with it when one has lived in such Italian houses as the Belvedere et the Villa Gallo, of which we have in truth some very pleasant memories, that at least is a consolation.'[2]

But if d'Orsay had hoped for a swift return to Naples he was to be disappointed. The summer saw him in Tuscany and likely to remain there for some time, for on 7 August Lady Blessington wrote to Charles James Mathews from Florence of 'a change having taken place in our plans, which ensures our being here for another month or two . . . Our winter quarters are not yet decided on, & we hesitate between Rome & Genoa as we are pledged to go where the Duchesse de Guiche does.' She added that, ever restless, 'Lord B—embarks this day at Leghorn for Naples* but will be back by the 1st of September my Birthday.'[3]

But soon the listlessness of their existence would be galvanised by the impending marriage of d'Orsay to one or other of Blessington's daughters, who were living with Blessington's sister in Dublin. This union would assume the proportions of an international diplomatic incident. As he knew neither of them, it mattered little which of the daughters d'Orsay chose. In the end he selected the younger, legitimate one. Her name was Harriet. A girl barely fifteen years old, she was taken from school without any knowledge of the world, acquaintance with Society, or its usages and forms and summoned to Italy for the count to marry. Having returned from his cruise Blessington set about arranging the ceremony.

'That the Blessingtons should seriously have intended to celebrate this indefensible marriage under official auspices in Florence, showed a misapprehension of the atmosphere of the English community which, on the part of the Countess at any rate, is very unexpected.'[4] Although a trifle sententious, Michael Sadleir's appraisal of the situation seems fair.

However, when viewed from their perspective, the attitude of

---

* Members of Landor's family had fallen ill during the summer and, according to Michael Sadleir, 'When the sick children were at last out of danger, their father was near collapse with anxiety and sleeplessness. Blessington therefore persuaded him to sail to Naples and back in the *Bolivar*' (Sadleir, p. 113). It is presumably to this trip that Lady Blessington alludes.

d'Orsay and the Blessingtons is anything but unexpected. Count d'Orsay and the Blessingtons inhabited a fantasy world, insulated from reality by their own high opinion of each other and of course by Lord Blessington's wealth. Even Fox, who once again turns up and dines with the Blessingtons in Florence on 25 October, had experienced the almost narcotic power of life within d'Orsay's charmed circle. But by that autumn he had shaken off the intoxication of convalescence and returned to his caustic form: 'The dinner was dull. The hostess, d'Orsay, and even that besotted idiot Ld B., recounted as usual the universal flattery and admiration with which they were hourly dosed, and scrupled not to assure us how well they deserved what they did receive and more to boot.'[5] D'Orsay had come to believe his own mythology.

The members of the ménage felt that they were living outside or above the normal strictures of London Society: Lord Blessington busily chasing amusement and beginning various projects from writing fiction to remodelling his Irish seat; Lady Blessington reinventing herself as a *femme sérieuse* and hostess on the European model; and d'Orsay perfecting his dandiacal pose, all the time feeding off the attention and the praise of others. But just because they did not want to follow the mores of English Society does not mean that they escaped being judged according to them, not least by those of its members who had been hostile to Lady Blessington and her attempt to establish herself as a London hostess.

Though they might have thought that physical distance rendered them all but invisible to London eyes, the opposite was true. Much as the cult of Byron had been fuelled by exaggerated rumours about his conduct and his way of life in Italy, to the extent that Lady Blessington had professed herself disappointed by his actual appearance, so the life that d'Orsay was leading with the Blessingtons became a subject of conjecture and gossip around London. After all, the Blessingtons had been absent from London for years. What was it that kept them away?

Was their way of life so dissipated and immoral that it could be countenanced only in the part of the world that had sheltered Lord Byron when he had been forced to leave Britain in disgrace?

The French minister through whom d'Orsay had met Lamartine was a friend, and complaisant enough when it came to the subject of d'Orsay's marriage to one of Blessington's daughters. Lord Burghersh, the English minister in Florence, was a different matter. He had just returned from a period of leave and presumably his opinions were those prevailing in fashionable circles in Britain. He was scandalised at the behaviour of the d'Orsay–Blessington party. When Lady Blessington and Harriet met with Lord Burghersh to discuss plans for the marriage, they discovered that he was against it. As an added insult to the French minister in Florence he suggested that, even if the union were to take place, the English ceremony would have precedence over the French one. A throwaway remark in a letter written by Lady Holland in August 1831 raises the possibility that Lord Burghersh was only acting out of compassion for the teenage Lady Harriet. 'Ly J[ersey] says Ld Burghursh [*sic*] refused to allow the marriage they celebrated in his house in Florence, in consequence of a private message from Lady Harriet declaring her reluctance to the union.' Lady Holland had the good sense to add, 'All this may or may not be true.'[6]

But much as Lord Burghersh may have represented Establishment outrage at the proposed marriage, not all opinion ran against it. Having enjoyed the friendship of the party and just returned from a most refreshing cruise aboard the *Bolivar*, Walter Savage Landor fired off the following letter of sympathetic outrage.

DEAR LADY BLESSINGTON: – If I could hear of any wrong or any rudeness offered to you, without at least as much resentment as you yourself would feel upon it, I should be unworthy, not only of the friendship with which you honour me, but of one moment's thought or notice. Lord B. told me what had occurred yesterday. I believe I may have said, on other occasions, that nothing could surprise me, of folly or indecorum, in Lord Burghersh. I must retract my words, – the only ones he will ever make me retract. That a man educated among the sons of gentlemen could be guilty of such incivility to two ladies, to say nothing of condition, nothing of person, nothing of acquaintance and past courtesies, is inconceivable, even to the most observant of his behaviour, throughout the whole period of his public life. From what I have heard and known during a residence of six years at Florence, I am convinced that all the ministers of all the other courts in Europe (I may throw in those of Asia and Africa) have never been guilty of so many unbecoming and disgraceful actions as this man. The only person for whom he ever interested himself was a Count Aceto, the most notorious gambler and profligate, who had been expelled from the Tuscan and the Lucca States. And now his conscience will not permit him to sanction a father's disposal of his daughter in marriage with almost the only man who deserves her, and certainly the very man who deserves her most.

I said little in reply to Lord B., only to praise his coolness and forbearance. Nothing can be wiser than the resolution to consider in the light of diplomacy what has happened, or more necessary than to represent it, in all its circumstances, to the administration at home, without which it cannot fail to be misinterpreted here, whatever care and anxiety the friends of your family may display, in setting right the erroneous and malicious. I hope Count d'Orsay sees the affair in the same point of view as I do, and will allow his resentment to lose itself among feelings more congenial to him. Lord B., I do assure your ladyship, has quite recovered his composure; I hope that you have, too – otherwise, the first smile on seeing him at Rome will not sufficiently reward him for his firmness and his judgment.

> With every good wish in all its intensity to the happy couple,
> and with one good wish of much the same nature to Miss
> Power, – I remain your ladyship's very devoted servant.[7]

Thus convinced once more of their own rectitude, and comfortable in
the warm glow of righteous indignation, the party moved from
Florence to Naples, stopping at Rome en route.

On 16 November, just before leaving Rome for Naples, d'Orsay
had tried to convince Henry Fox to act as a witness at the marriage
ceremony. To Fox's credit the request caused him considerable unease,
his former warm feelings for d'Orsay conflicting with the distaste he
felt obliged to demonstrate.

> After dinner I went to the Blessingtons, who are now established
> at the Palazzo Negroni, where I found a whist-party. D'Orsay
> took me aside to ask me to be a witness to his marriage, which is
> to be hurried up immediately. I was much distressed and could
> not refuse, much as I lament and disapprove of the proceeding,
> which seems to me one of the most disgraceful and unfeeling
> things ever committed. I own I always hoped that something
> would occur to prevent it. I made an evasive answer to d'Orsay's
> request, determined either openly to refuse or quietly to avoid
> compliance.

> Nov 17
> In the morning I was annoyed with Alfred's request, and at last
> I thought the most manly and proper manner was frankly to
> speak the truth, and to tell him I considered his marriage as ill-
> calculated to advance his happiness or his credit, and that I
> begged to decline being present. I put it entirely upon my regard
> for him, as I did not choose to say the real truth or how abom-
> inably I thought he was sacrificing the happiness of a poor child

to his own convenience, or rather to the indulgence of his passion for Ly B.[8]

Fox's position is an odd one. Much as he professes distaste for the eccentric domestic arrangements of d'Orsay and the Blessingtons, he seems to be one of their more frequent visitors. Two days later, on 19 November, he is round for dinner again, where he comments censoriously on the corruption of Count d'Orsay's fiancée: 'I am sorry to see that they have made poor Lady Harriet (who was before well educated) listen with childish pleasure to the heartless doctrines and selfish ribaldry of her worthless mother-in-law.'[9]* Quite what claims Harriet had to being well educated is unclear. Besides, if as had happened to d'Orsay himself, and as would be entirely normal, the count and the Blessingtons had made her feel that she was a part of a rather special and wonderful family, why should she not respond with 'childish pleasure'? In the end, after the party had reached Naples, neither Harriet's former education nor widespread censure was sufficient to avert the marriage. On 1 December 1827, aged fifteen years and four months,[10] Lady Harriet Frances Gardiner became Countess d'Orsay.

Within a few days the young couple returned to Rome, to begin their married life under the same roof as Lord and Lady Blessington. On 8 December, d'Orsay wrote a triumphant letter to Landor saying that the marriage had eventually been completed and that the British minister in Florence had been guilty of ignorant stubbornness in his handling of the matter. As belligerent as ever when faced with an affront to his dignity, the Frenchman said that he had just written to inform him that he was completely ignorant of his duties. 'I hope he took my letter badly,' wrote d'Orsay to Landor, 'as I would have great pleasure in cutting off the tip of his nose.'[11]

---

* That is, stepmother (Harriet's mother by law since marriage to her father).

The day after the count had written this letter to Landor the exultant mood still prevailed at the Blessingtons' Rome headquarters. The omnipresent Fox was round at the Palazzo Negroni to heap opprobrium on the happy couple:

> From Lady Compton's I went to the Blessingtons. They are just returned from Naples, where they have triumphantly effected the nefarious marriage of poor Lady H. Gardiner. They are proud of what they have done and expected me to congratulate and approve. I behaved as civilly as I could, feeling as I do the strongest detestation and contempt for Lady B., and great sorrow at d'Orsay's weakness and folly in being humbugged and blinded by the machinations of that b . . . I like him notwithstanding all his ridicules, and I must ever lament his infatuation for her having made him guilty of one of the most disgraceful and odious proceedings I ever heard of.[12]

The marriage completed, the teenage Countess d'Orsay seems to have slipped into the background. By March of the following year, 1828, a visitor to the Palazzo Negroni had this to say about the young countess.

> Lady Harriet was exceedingly girlish-looking, pale and rather inanimate in expression, silent and reserved; there was no appearance of familiarity with any one around her; no air or look of womanhood, no semblance of satisfaction in her new position were to be observed in her demeanour or deportment. She seldom or ever spoke, she was little noticed, she was looked on as a mere school-girl; I think her feelings were crushed, repressed, and her emotions driven inwards, by the sense of slight and indifference, and by the strangeness and coldness of, everything around her; and she became indifferent, and strange

and cold, and apparently devoid of all vivacity and interest in society, or in the company of any person in it.[13]

The picture is of a frigid, joyless, clinically depressed young woman – hardly the perfect partner for the fun-loving young count. Certainly the gossip circulating among the Anglophone expatriate community in Rome in the spring of 1828 was that the Count and Countess d'Orsay did not have a sex life. Indeed all heterosexual activity at the Palazzo Negroni had ground to a standstill. According to Fox, Lord Blessington had confided to Lady Elinor Butler that his was the most chaste of all houses in Rome. 'Lord Blessington describes to her the extreme chastity of each member of his family. Ly B. has a spine complaint, which prevents him from exercising his matrimonial duties. D'Orsay has not and will not consummate his marriage, and he himself does not think it's worth the trouble to make any search among dirty Italian women.'[14]

This tantalising image of a sexually frustrated household is conveyed by Fox without any of his customary gloss, gloating or vitriolic asides about Lady Blessington. A number of constructions can be placed on these apparently sexless marriages. The first is that Lord Blessington and Count d'Orsay were continuing a homosexual love affair. The second is that Lady Blessington and d'Orsay were continuing an affair: that she was lying to her husband about back pain and that d'Orsay had no interest in sex with a pale, cowering child. The third is the intriguing possibility that Lady Blessington had simply decreed that sex was out of bounds. By the early 1830s it was an accepted tenet of Society gossip 'that Lady Blessington had made it a sine qua non that Ct. d'Orsay was not to consummate his nuptials for four years'.[15]

Lady Blessington's biographer of 1933, Michael Sadleir, presents her as a selfless protector of poor Harriet's virginity. According to Sadleir Lady Blessington accepted the marriage only on condition that d'Orsay refrain from sex with his wife for the first four years of their marriage. Sadleir has no difficulty in seeing it as the perfectly natural action of a concerned woman:

> Unfortunately she made one inevitable though, as matters turned out, disastrous calculation. She failed to foresee that scandal would so irrevocably link her name with d'Orsay's that when, in a few years' time, he actually became the husband of Lord Blessington's daughter, the world would assume them guilty of a stratagem of a peculiarly ugly kind. Even her plea that the girl enjoy four years of immunity from sex experience was turned to her discredit, and humane consideration taken by gossip for jealousy.[16]

Sadleir realises that Lady Blessington's actions are, even on the most charitable interpretation, decidedly odd, and goes to considerable lengths to vindicate her:

> It was of course generally assumed in society that Lady Blessington was d'Orsay's mistress, and that in view of her general record she could on no occasion be given credit for any motive save the most selfish and contemptible. It follows, therefore, that her rumoured insistence on the non-consummation for four years of the d'Orsay marriage must be attributed either to jealousy or self-interest, no more respectable impulse being within the bounds of possibility. But unfortunately neither jealousy nor self-interest makes sense. If she were jealous, why limit her demand to four years? Was she likely to be less jealous in 1832 than in 1828? As for self-interest, what possible *material* advantage could she derive from having secured to d'Orsay's wife four years of virginity? Her interest was all the other way. She and d'Orsay were as familiar with the terms of Lord

Blessington's will as any of their enemies, and would realise that the birth of a son to Harriet was the only certain guarantee that her property would remain perpetually under joint Blessington–d'Orsay control. Is it not obvious that the Lady Blessington of current gossip (a being without scruples, a mere piratical adventuress) would have welcomed the consummation of d'Orsay's marriage as a necessary overture to the so desirable pregnancy?

However, he does concede that 'It is very likely that she did in fact insist that Harriet be left alone until, at nineteen, she could more clearly understand what marriage meant.' He proposes this rationale: 'When one recalls Lady Blessington's own first sexual experience, and that she was virtually the age of Lady Harriet when handed over to Farmer, it seems not only natural but almost inevitable that she would have determined to save her step-daughter from the shock of even a modified version of her own suffering.'[17]

Whatever the sexual dynamic among the residents of the Palazzo Negroni, any interest that d'Orsay may have had in his young wife was about to be overtaken by a new passion that would remain with him until he died.

Rome in the late 1820s was a smallish city, with around two hundred thousand inhabitants. It was a curious conurbation, peppered with farm animals, smallholdings and vineyards that contrasted with the pomp, ceremony and intrigue of the Vatican, all set against a backdrop of crumbling ruins that made the place look like one large Piranesi engraving. By the end of the decade it was becoming clear that Pope Pius VIII was dying, and the political temperature rose as plotters and secret police followed each other around the streets. Occasionally the situation boiled over into minor skirmishes, gun battles, arrests and deportations.

With the exception of the former King Joseph (first of Naples, then of Spain), who had fled to America with most of his wealth intact, every surviving sibling of Napoleon, as well as the formidable Madame Mère, the Bonaparte materfamilias, owned or rented a palazzo in Rome. The importance that the former emperor had attributed to the Eternal City was indicated by the title he had bestowed on his son: the King of Rome. By the time d'Orsay, his young wife and his parents-in-law were established at the Palazzo Negroni, the Bonaparte family more or less ran Rome's winter social season. As Lady Blessington wrote approvingly, 'The Bonaparte family are greatly esteemed and respected at Rome; where they expend much money, not only in a liberal hospitality, but in extensive charities.'[18] If you were rich enough, which the d'Orsays and Blessingtons certainly were, Rome was an entertaining city in which to spend the winter, with a surfeit of balls and dinners. In this highly social atmosphere d'Orsay was emerging as the town's style leader. For instance a fashionable French artist, Cottenet, is noted as adopting a mode of dress described as 'a studious imitation of d'Orsay in his square-cut coat and his shirt sleeves doubled back over the coat half-way towards the elbow'.[19]

It was inevitable that in the course of such frenetic socialising during the first four months of 1828 a high-profile new arrival like d'Orsay would come into contact with members of the Bonaparte clan. In fact, as a man of fashion one could barely venture out of one's palazzo in the Rome of the late 1820s without bumping into a Bonaparte or tripping over some former Napoleonic monarch. Lady Blessington's journal of the time is littered with encounters of this kind. For instance, 'Walking in the gardens of the Vigna Palatina yesterday, with our amiable friend the owner, Mr. C. Mills, we were surprised by the arrival of the Prince and Princesse de Montfort,* and their children, with Madame Letitia Bonaparte, or *Madame Mère*,

---

* The prince was Jérôme Bonaparte, ex-King of Westphalia, and Napoleon's youngest brother.

as she is generally called, attended by her chaplain, *dame de compagnie*, and others of their joint suite.'[20] Or 'Spent two hours yesterday with the ex-King and Queen of Westphalia, at present known as the *Prince* and *Princesse* de Montfort. Jerome Bonaparte is sensible, well-informed, and well-bred, with a good natured kindness of manner, that detracts not from the dignity acquired by having possessed sovereign power.'[21]

In addition to the excitement of mixing with Bonapartes, the friendship between d'Orsay and Jérôme Bonaparte had particular resonance for the count. Jérôme had married a daughter of the House of Württemberg, of which d'Orsay himself, through the activities of his grandmother, the sexually energetic Madame Craufurd, was a member, albeit an illegitimate one. He was Jérôme's wife's second cousin; this was doubtless a link that reinforced the friendship of the two men.

Even though they no longer 'possessed sovereign power', these scions of the Bonaparte dynasty milked their former status for all its worth. There is an almost Ruritanian preposterousness about the way Jérôme ran his household. 'An etiquette, bordering on that of royalty, is kept up in his palace. Visitors are conducted by a Chamberlain, to the presence of the ex-King and Queen, who give them an audience in the *grand salon de reception*, attended by *une dame d'honneur, et un gentilhomme de chambre*.'[22]

However ridiculous the regal rigmarole of the deposed, discredited, nepotistic puppet monarchs that Napoleon had installed on the thrones of Europe might seem in the perspective of history, at the time it must have been impressive. D'Orsay was moving in the company of those who had known the great Napoleon, not merely as a political figure, or as the distant ruler of a vast European empire, but as a sibling or son. He was undoubtedly bewitched by the sense of grandeur that came with the Bonapartes, who, though shorn of their power, still carried with them many of the souvenirs and trappings of the time when Europe was a family business divided up between the Bonaparte brothers. Coming from an obscure Corsican background, Napoleon compensated for a less than affluent childhood by plundering Europe for art treasures; he treated conquered countries as little more than cash machines and art galleries from which he took whatever appealed to him.

The late emperor's acquisitiveness and magpie taste for splendour seems to have been a family trait. Lady Blessington's eye for detail provides an intriguing snapshot of the lifestyle of the deposed Napoleonic despot of the day:

> The palace in which the Prince and Princess de Montfort reside is a very large one, containing a fine suite of apartments, richly and tastefully furnished. Two rooms are appropriated to memorials of the Emperor Napoleon; one is hung with engravings of all his battles, in which he of course is the conspicuous object; and the other contains prints from all the portraits painted of him, from his first step on the ladder of glory to the pinnacle: underneath which are a second series of prints from pictures painted since his reverses, concluding with one representing the last scene of the drama of his eventful life, his death-bed, and tomb at St. Helena. Three of the hats worn in battle, and sundry pairs of gloves used on the same occasions, are placed in glass cases beneath the engravings of the actions where they were worn. Here, surrounded by all the memorials of his greatness, closed by that of his humble tomb in exile, there was ample food for reflection; and no more striking example of the instability of human grandeur, and the nothingness of ambition, could be given. The next room contained a series of portraits in oil, by the best French artists, of the Emperor Napoleon in his imperial and military costume; and the resemblance between him and the Prince de Montfort, struck me as being very remarkable. There

was a warm sentiment of fraternal affection in thus dedicating these apartments to the memory of the Emperor, that showed how fondly his memory is cherished, and kept apart from the every day business of life by his family; and in viewing these memorials of him, strong evidences of the feeling were visible in his brother. A large gallery was filled with full length portraits of the Prince and Princess de Montfort, painted when they sat on the throne of Westphalia, with various other pictures, representing them at different periods of their regal career, surrounded by portraits of all the individuals of the imperial family.[23]

Among the members of the Bonaparte dynasty that d'Orsay would have met in the spring of 1828 was Hortense Bonaparte, then styled the Duchess de Saint-Leu. Former Queen of Holland, née de Beauharnais, daughter of Empress Josephine, stepdaughter of Napoleon, even rumoured at one time to have been his lover, Hortense had effectively functioned as the First Lady of France during Napoleon's Hundred Days and had offered him refuge at Malmaison after his defeat at Waterloo. She had been married to Napoleon's younger brother Louis, who was rumoured to have been homosexual. Their marriage was not a happy one. In August 1808 he had written to her, 'My only consolation is to live away from you, to have nothing to do with you and nothing to expect of you. Adieu, Madame.'[24]

Louis and Hortense did however have two sons who survived into adulthood. The elder, Prince Napoleon, lived with his father. Prince Louis, the younger, born in April 1808, lived with his mother, spending summers in Switzerland and winters in Rome. By the time d'Orsay would have met him twenty years later, Prince Louis had become 'a fine, high-spirited youth, admiraby well educated, and highly accomplished, uniting to the gallant bearing of a soldier all the politeness of a *preux chevalier*'.[25] Another opinion of the young prince was given by Lord Fitzharris, later the third Earl of Malmesbury, who met the young prince the following year and described him as 'a wild, harum-scarum youth riding at full gallop down the streets to the peril of the public, fencing and pistol-shooting, and apparently without serious thoughts of any kind, although even then he was possessed with the conviction that he would some day rule over France'.[26] Whether this trigger-happy youngster was at that time genuinely thinking of ruling France can be questioned, but another twenty years thence, on 10 December 1848, he would be elected president of France and would later seize power and become known as Napoleon III. During the two turbulent decades which would see him mature from just another wild young European hotblood into a major world leader of the second half of the nineteenth century, one of his most staunch, loyal and vocal supporters would be Count d'Orsay.

As the nephew of Napoleon I, he was as yet unable to present himself as the great Bonaparte's heir and successor. The King of Rome, Napoleon's son by his second wife Marie Louise, daughter of Emperor Francis I of Austria, was still alive, albeit resident in Austria where he was known as the Duke of Reichstadt, a frail young man, effectively a prisoner in the court of his maternal grandfather. Technically he could be known as Napoleon II, as his father had abdicated in his favour after Waterloo, although as a four-year-old living in Vienna at the time his practical experience as Emperor of the French was limited. Nevertheless it was to this sickly Austrian youth that Bonapartists looked as the pretender to the imperial throne of France. Besides, even if the Duke of Reichstadt were to die, Prince Louis' elder brother Prince Napoleon would assume the mantle of imperial pretender.

As well as sketching, dressing and getting to know the Bonapartes, another d'Orsay pastime in Rome was his fondness for issuing challenges to duel. Upon a slight, whether actual or imagined, he could usually be counted on to overreact splendidly and such slights were not infrequent. However much d'Orsay and the Blessingtons were accepted at the houses of the Bonapartes, there were still members of expatriate British Society who were outraged at what they perceived to be the scandalous nature of the ménage, and their indignation had been stoked by the marriage of Alfred d'Orsay to the fifteen-year-old Harriet.

The vendetta against d'Orsay and the Blessingtons started by the British minister at Florence Lord Burghersh was continued in Rome by his stepmother the Countess of Westmorland. Lady Westmorland was a key figure in the Rome of the time. An autocratic hostess, she would often sleep all day and then remain awake all night, expecting her friends and guests to do the same. She was fond of dressing up, cut a striking figure, was educated and well connected and could be a generous patroness. In 1821, her attention had been caught by the artist Joseph Severn, who had travelled to Rome with Keats. 'Her ladyship is a most superior woman,' wrote Severn in a letter to his sister, 'having all the really English nobility in her and much learning – she is about thirty-eight and is a very noble looking lady – the charm in her manner from the many accomplishments blended down in this lady of fashion is very astonishing. She is a beautiful musician and a poetess and seems to be quite acquainted with all the great persons of the time.'[27]

She was also a meddling virago and, towards the end of the 1820s, she was decidedly middle aged. Severn now described her to his father as 'a most queenly person' who had become even more imperious and eccentric with age.[28] She cannot have reacted well to the news that the glamorous Countess of Blessington was in town, and by early February 1828 she was plotting against her. Her pretext for instigating a campaign against d'Orsay and the Blessingtons was that they had been received socially by the French ambassador, the Prince de Laval-Montmorency, when in her view they should have been ignored. 'I then drove and walked with Lady Westmorland in the Villa Borghese,' recorded Fox in his journal for 4 February. 'She is in a great state of indignation at Laval's receiving Lady Blessington. Her language on the subject is more vehement than proper, and Laval is the object of her actual contempt.'[29] Indeed over the ensuing weeks the French ambassador would be bombarded with letters from her on the subject. Three days later she was still 'very busy in making war upon Laval for receiving Ly Blessington. She wants the English ladies to refuse going to his house in a body.'[30]

Lady Westmorland had found an ally in young Henry Fox, who, having run into Lady Blessington at a ball on 16 February, showed that he had fully recovered from the kindness she and d'Orsay had shown him:

> I hate harshness to a woman for such venial misdemeanours, but if ever there was an occasion to be harsh, it is upon a woman of Ly Blessington's trade, who, having persuaded a drivelling drunkard to marry her, dishonours him and makes the future misery of his young daughter by sacrificing her at 15 years old to a worthless adventurer, whom, as the husband of this poor child, she may contrive to keep in the house on the score of relationship. It is one of the basest and most barbarous transactions I ever knew.[31]

The feud simmered on for a month before d'Orsay waded in with a characteristically excoriating letter to Lady Westmorland on 18 March, raking up her less-than-spotless past and suggesting that he would expose her for the mad, meddling harpy she was. If his past epistles threatening to carve up Lord Burghersh's face or putting Mathews in his social place are any indicators of his style, d'Orsay's bile-steeped pen was at least as mighty as his sword. That he unleashed his considerable epistolary powers on a woman demonstrated that he was not overly restrained by any chivalric sensibilities.

The effect was devastating. Three days after the letter, Fox called on Lady Westmorland and found her in a terrible state:

> She was in her dressing-gown, her hair about her neck, and sadly harassed and broken. Three days ago she received a most horrible, libellous letter from d'Orsay, threatening if not to murder, to insult and outrage her, and alluding to all the disgusting, malicious reports calumny has, at various times, propagated about her. Much as she deserves some punishment for her interference in everybody's business, I cannot but feel most deeply her being exposed to a similar insult from such a beast as d'Orsay. The letter, of which she did not shew me the copy she has preserved, but out of which she repeated some sentences, is the most infamous ever penned. She gave it last night to Laval, and said, 'Celà appartient, Monsieur, à la France et pas à moi.' He is weak and bad, nor will he insist, as he should do, upon d'Orsay being trundled out of the Papal States.

'I want her to apply directly to the Pope,' writes Fox, who describes her as 'broken and oppressed by this infamous outrage. I cannot bear to see her so. Nervous and irritable as she is, a blow of this sort may drive her mad or even kill her.'[32]

News of the scandal was soon all over Rome, with d'Orsay rumoured to be showing copies of his letter quite freely about town. For her part Lady Westmorland seemed to be descending rapidly into a form of nervous breakdown, paranoiacally imagining that she was being 'spied upon by emissaries from Casa Blessington'.[33] She constructed a lengthy letter to the French ambassador to answer d'Orsay's allegations, though in the view of one who read it it was rather 'too full of God and the Devil'[34] to be entirely effective.

Fox attempted to whip up support for Lady Westmorland, but it seems that d'Orsay's behaviour and the conduct of the Blessington family was considered preferable by Rome's expatriate community to Lady Westmorland's malicious meddling. Fox's success in marshalling support for her was limited. Lord Arundel, he noted, one of the few prominent Englishmen in Rome to side with Lady Westmorland, 'feels as few among the English here, I am sorry to say, *do* feel, but as all ought, and is very desirous something should be done to protect Ly W. from the insults of a ruffian'.[35] But on the whole most people were just as 'desirous' to avoid being drawn into conversation on the subject and, as Fox remarked, 'were anxious not to express opinions of which they have, I suppose, enough feeling left to know they should be ashamed'.[36]

Unsuccessful though Fox's attempts to poison public feeling against d'Orsay may have been, news of his campaign soon reached the count, and matters reached a head on Sunday 6 April, a searingly hot day, when most of fashionable Rome had gathered in St Peter's Square to see the Benediction. The Blessington carriage stopped near the obelisk to watch the Pope bless the crowd, as did Fox's. 'The family tried to catch my eye and bow,' recalled Fox, 'but I carefully avoided their recognition.'

D'Orsay must have been upset by the slight, and the sensitive and thoughtful side to his nature cannot have failed to ponder it. The following morning he returned to Fox a snuff box that Fox had given him. With it was a typically terse note: 'Je vous renvoye votre souvenir, car je ne veux rien garder qui puisse pour un instant me rappeler votre ingrate et fausse personne. ALFRED D'ORSAY'.[37]

From the count's point of view it is easy to see why he should consider Fox false and ungrateful. After all, d'Orsay and the Blessingtons had nursed him when he was injured and had extended their hospitality to him on numerous occasions. Fox had repaid past kindness with a public slight. Now d'Orsay intended to provoke Fox into challenging him to a duel.

Fox was rattled. 'It took me some time to decide what I should answer, anxious as I am to avoid a duel both for my own sake and for Lady Westmorland's — a duel being the only thing to restore d'Orsay's character to the level of a gentleman, and being, I have no doubt, his object in writing to me.'[38] After a while, Fox wrote the Frenchman a mealy-mouthed note. In it he said that he was glad that d'Orsay had returned the gift because it would doubtless have been painful for him to hang on to it and look at it. Fox went on to suggest that the sight of the snuff box would have been a constant reproach because Fox was neither ungrateful nor false, and that Fox's fond memories of d'Orsay's goodness merely made him all the more upset at his current conduct. There was no hint of a challenge to a duel.

That evening he went to see Lady Westmorland, who was attempting unsuccessfully to get the Hanoverian minister involved in the affair.

I told Ly W. of d'Orsay's note to me. There is scarcely any other woman on earth to whom such a secret could be confided with safety. She, however, acted, as I was sure she would, with courage and sense. She felt that till the paper putting him below the level of a gentleman, in consequence of his letter to her, was signed by all the most distinguished people here, my refusing to fight him would be impossible. That even if it were signed, I should not be justified in so doing, and that the only way to prevent d'Orsay recovering his character by a duel is to keep out of town, where he may find occasion to provoke me to the necessity of challenging him. She was pleased at my confidence in her, and not sorry at the prospect of *une affaire d'honneur*, though chagrined and distressed at d'Orsay, whom she justly thinks below the par of a gentleman, being likely to retrieve his character.[39]

It was a win–win situation for d'Orsay. Either he would engage Fox in a duel, which the disabled Fox would in all likelihood lose, or his intended combatant would be forced into the ignominious action of fleeing town: an action that, despite Fox's gloss on the semantics of whether d'Orsay was strictly speaking below the level of a gentleman, would be widely construed as craven. Fox fled.

On 10 April Lady Westmorland wrote to Fox to say,

> The night before last at half past ten the Governor of Rome waited upon the French Ambassador, and informed His Excellency that it was the wish of His Holiness that Count d'Orsay should quit Rome. The Ambassador declined conveying the information, as not having authority as Ambassador or influence as an individual. The Governor added that the correspondence was in his possession, and that the opinion of His Holiness and himself was to be seen by the promptitude of their measures. This scene took place in public. I understand the Governor is a very energetic and determined man, and I suppose there is no doubt, therefore, that the measure will be executed immediately.[40]

As it turned out, Lady Westmorland's belief that d'Orsay would be drummed out of the Papal States was premature and misplaced. A couple of days later d'Orsay was still about town and, by the 15th, word was that Laval had seen the Pope himself and had d'Orsay's expulsion reversed.

This endorsement of d'Orsay's actions against her enraged Lady Westmorland further. She began to nurse ever more spectacular paranoid fantasies, including one that d'Orsay was in some way in league with the secretaries of the French Embassy. Even Fox, who returned to Rome after a week, grew tired of her. The prospect of a duel between him and d'Orsay was tacitly dropped.

When he and d'Orsay bumped into each other a week after the reversal of the expulsion order, they diplomatically avoided each other's gaze, although d'Orsay was noted by an observer of the scene to have 'looked extremely distressed and pale' at meeting his former friend.[41] The idea of d'Orsay being visibly upset by the encounter is rather touching. It speaks of his sensitivity, and of the store he put by Fox's friendship and his upset at what he would have seen as Fox's betrayal.

In the end it was Lady Westmorland who left, for Florence. She still wrote frequently of her persecution, but at least one recipient of these letters 'noticed that she had transferred many of her former champions into the ranks of the agents of darkness'.[42] She did not return to Rome until the middle of June,[43] by which time d'Orsay, his wife and his parents-in-law were long gone.

The whole affair was entirely ridiculous, but if nothing else it underlines the festering ill-will that was felt in certain quarters towards d'Orsay. A powerful and significant section of English Society seemed keen to destroy him. Strangely enough given d'Orsay's impudent behaviour towards her and the gossip that reached her about d'Orsay — 'People are full of of stories about Ly Blessington, Ly M. Ross*, d'Orsay, & sad trashy squabbles, quite contemptible'[44] — Fox's mother Lady Holland was remarkably level headed about Lady Westmorland. In a letter of 9 May to her son she poses the quite reasonable question, 'But why will Lady W. in a foreign country be the *Custodian* of the morals of the town?' Moreover, displaying a mother's gratitude, she is well disposed towards Lady Blessington and d'Orsay: 'I have had a good will to Lady Blessington ever since she lodged, tended and nursed you so kindly when you had your fall; & you then, I thought, praised her & d'Orsay for qualities beyond their deserts.' But she added ominously that d'Orsay was 'not esteemed in this country at all'.[45]

* Lady Mary Ross, daughter of Robert, second duke of Leinster.

On the day that Lady Holland wrote to her son, the Count and Countess d'Orsay and the Earl and Countess of Blessington left Rome. They would spend the summer travelling north through Italy and into France. The lack of esteem in which they were held in fashionable London Society did not seem to bother them greatly.

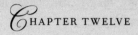

CHAPTER TWELVE

Paris Fashion

BY JUNE 1828 COUNT D'ORSAY, HIS WIFE AND THE BLESSINGTONS had reached Paris, putting up at the Hôtel de Terrasse on the Rue de Rivoli. Before they had finished dinner on the evening of their arrival, they were joined by d'Orsay's sister and brother-in-law the Duke and Duchess de Guiche, both no doubt eager to look over their brother's new wife. Amid happy greetings, the reunited family adjourned to the salon and chatted late into the night, the air fragrant with the scent of orange trees wafting in from the Tuileries, over which the hotel looked. Rather less agreeably the hotel was also filled with the 'loud reverberation of the pavement, as the various vehicles roll rapidly over it'.[1]

As in Naples a noisy street would be the cue for the Earl of Blessington to look for a new house. The ensuing days were pleasurably passed in a mixture of house-hunting, socialising, shopping, a visit to the venerable octogenarian Madame Craufurd, a dinner at the Duchess de Guiche's, a night at the Opera to see 'the *début* of the new *danseuse* Taglioni'[2] and a military review at the Champ de Mars. On this occasion they were able to get their first sight of France's king, the reactionary, strongly religious Charles X, who had succeeded his brother Louis XVIII in 1824. The king 'looked well', noted Lady Blessington approvingly, 'his grey hair and tall thin figure giving him a very venerable aspect'.[3]

By now Charles X was well into his seventies, having been sixty-seven when he ascended to the throne. His presence as ruler of France, three and a half decades after his brother had been guillotined in the Place de la Revolution, was as much of a spur for those who opposed the regime as it was a comfort for those émigrés who supported him and had benefited from a law passed in 1825 compensating them for lands siezed during the Revolution. The sense of a return to the status quo ante was fuelled by the overtly *ancien régime* tone of his lavish coronation ceremony in Rheims Cathedral and the religious revival over which he presided. The Church was perceived as supportive of the monarchy. The 'tone of society at Paris' was accordingly characterised by a 'ceremoniousness of manner, reminding one of *La Vieille Cour*, and probably rendered *à la mode* by the restoration of the Bourbons'.[4]

Families of courtiers such as that of d'Orsay's brother-in-law the Duke de Guiche, whose elderly father the Duke de Grammont had been faithful to his sovereign during adversity, were typical beneficiaries of Charles X's reign. Through his family connections Count d'Orsay found himself once more at the centre of political and social activity. Quarters to reflect this eminence were required and duly located. 'At length, we have found a house to suit us,' wrote Lady Blessington, 'and a delightful one it is; once the property of the Maréchal Ney, but now belonging to the Marquis de Lillers. It is situated in the Rue de Bourbon, but the windows of the principal apartments look on the Seine, and command a delightful view of the Thuillerie [*sic*] Gardens. It is approached by an avenue bounded by fine trees, and is enclosed on the Rue de Bourbon side by high walls, a large *porte cochere,* and a porter's lodge; which give it all the quiet and security of a country house.'[5]

The Hôtel Ney was perhaps the most desirable house to come on to the market in Paris during 1828. Exquisitely appointed, the decoration of the exterior walls alone had cost a million francs.[6] It had been on offer for only three days before Lord Blessington snapped up the house, unfurnished, for what even Lady Blessington admitted was a high rent. As we have seen, Ney was the most glamorous and valiant of Napoleon's marshals, created Prince de la Moskowa and dubbed the 'bravest of the brave' by Napoleon after his dashing exploits on the retreat from Moscow.[7] It was with Ney and Wellington that d'Orsay had gone hunting as a boy. And after the defeat of Napoleon at Waterloo it was at the Hôtel Ney that the Princess de la Moskowa was told of her husband's imminent execution for having sided with Napoleon during the ultimately abortive putsch of the Hundred Days.

These resonances would certainly not have been lost on d'Orsay as he strode into the splendid residence, his new home in Paris, a paradigm of the splendour enjoyed by the Napoleonic elite. Entering the house through a conservatory, visitors were assailed by every decorative device from the innovative use of plate glass to the invocation of classicism in pilasters topped with Corinthian capitals; gilding, stucco and *trompe l'oeil* abounded, fireplaces were magnificent; and military trophies mingled with decorative art created by the leading painters of the day.

The mood of rooms ranged from the sad irony of the colonnaded Salle de Victoire with its figures of Victory proffering laurels to the innovative elegance of an octagonal dressing room panelled with mirrors. While some rooms sound as though they bordered on the kitsch, such as:

> a *salle de bain* of an elliptical form; the bath, of white marble, is
> sunk in the pavement, which is tessellated. From the ceiling

immediately over the bath hangs an alabaster lamp, held by the beak of a dove; the rest of the ceiling being painted with Cupids throwing flowers. The room is panelled with alternate mirrors and groups of allegorical subjects finely executed; and is lighted by one window, composed of a single plate of glass opening into a little spot of garden secluded from the rest.[8]

The house was offered unfurnished. But what for others might have been an inconvenience was for d'Orsay and the Blessingtons a welcome opportunity to shop for fine furniture. To her 'surprise and pleasure' Lady Blessington found that any quantity of excellent furniture could be rented 'by the quarter, half, or whole year'. Within forty-eight hours even a sprawling house like the Hôtel Ney could be filled with the costliest, gaudiest furniture known to man. It was, she noted approvingly, 'a usage that merits being adopted in all capitals'.[9] Moreover, if they liked they could buy the furniture at the end of the term, deducting rental already paid – it seems to have been an early form of hire purchase. Within a short while the Hôtel Ney was stuffed with sofas, bergères, fauteuils, consoles, clocks, tables, chiffoniers. D'Orsay's and Blessington's delight at decorating this splendid house was infectious. 'We feel like children with a new plaything,' wrote Lady Blessington.[10]

Typical of Lord Blessington's sweetness towards his wife were the special plans he had for her bedroom, which he kept secret from her as a surprise. It was one of his finest creations to date. It bore all his usual hallmarks of lavish expense, but, even by his standards, his wife's Parisian bedroom went well over the top.

The bed, which is silvered, instead of gilt, rests on the backs of two large silver swans, so exquisitely sculptured that every feather is in alto-relievo, and looks nearly as fleecy as those of the living bird. The recess in which it is placed is lined with white fluted silk, bordered with blue embossed lace; and from the columns that support the frieze of the recess, pale blue silk curtains, lined with white, are hung, which, when drawn, conceal the recess altogether.

The window curtain is of pale blue silk, with embroidered muslin curtains, trimmed with lace inside them, and have borders of blue and white lace to match those of the recess.

A silvered sofa has been made to fit the side of the room opposite the fire-place, near to which stands a most inviting *bergère*. An *écritoire* occupies one panel, a book-stand the other, and a rich coffer for jewels, forms a pendant to a similar one for lace, or India shawls.

A carpet of uncut pile, of a pale blue, a silver lamp, and a Psyche glass, the ornaments silvered to correspond with the decorations of the chamber, complete the furniture. The hangings of the dressing-room are of blue silk, covered with lace, and trimmed with rich frills of the same material, as are also the dressing stools and *chaise longue*, and the carpet and lamp are similar to those of the bed room.

A toilette table stands before the window, and small *jardinières* are placed in front of each panel of looking-glass, but so low as not to impede a full view of the person dressing in this beautiful little sanctuary.

The *salle de bain* is draped with white muslin trimmed with lace, and the sofa and *bergère* are covered with the same. The bath is of white marble, inserted in the floor, with which its surface is level. On the ceiling over it, is a painting of Flora scattering flowers with one hand, while from the other is suspended an alabaster lamp, in the form of a lotos.

A more tasteful or elegant suite of apartments cannot be imagined.[11] Lady Blessington added without a shred of irony, 'The effect of the whole suite is chastely beautiful.'[12] Her 'chastely beautiful' retreat took a mere three days to create.

The scale and style of d'Orsay's return to Paris, the city he had left as a penniless soldier six years earlier, was a great source of satisfaction to the young count. He was living at the best house Lord Blessington's money could afford, he dined with dukes, marquises and counts. His family was intimately connected with the ruling house (his Napoleonic enthusiasm was not such that it stopped him enjoying life in the Paris of Charles X). He stormed the world of Paris fashion.

D'Orsay was emulated in Paris by a number of influential young men of the day, including one of particular resonance – Count Walewski, illegitimate son of Napoleon by the Countess Walewska, conceived during the summer of 1809. Although only a teenager, the young Walewski was judged by one visitor to Paris at the time to be 'very like' his father.[13] It must therefore have been a considerable thrill and a source of great pride for d'Orsay that young Walewski, a mini-Napoleon in looks, emulated his style. He copied d'Orsay right down to such details as having six changes of gloves to see him through a day and having a child groom, or 'tiger', bouncing up and down on the back of his carriage.[14]

Walewski was also one of the founder members of the Cercle de l'Union, a club established on the English model by de Guiche and d'Orsay in 1828. According to Charles Yriarte, a chronicler of the emerging Paris club scene of the mid-nineteenth century, de Guiche and d'Orsay were 'the first to introduce anglomania into France'.[15] The Cercle de l'Union was also a meeting place for the diplomatic corps from the British Embassy: many British ambassadors from Lord Stuart de Rothesay, an intimate of d'Orsay's clique, onwards were regulars at the Cercle de l'Union.

Moreover, its significance as a meeting place for d'Orsay and his smart friends notwithstanding, the foundation of the Cercle de l'Union was to prove highly influential in a wider context. It was a catalyst that prompted a shift of the social power base away from the female-dominated salons that had moulded society in France since the late eighteenth century to an all-male environment where men of similar interests and social background would socialise. In 1828 the Cercle de l'Union was an interesting novelty; by 1843 there were an estimated 1928 *cercles* in France, with a total membership of 121,858.[16]

Even more overtly Anglophile was the New English Club on Rue de Mont Blanc that is mentioned in the scurrilous London newspaper the *Age*. This establishment was a place where politics and pleasure, notably gambling, collided. 'The *Ecarte* firm, or bank, is composed of Mr. Henry Baring, American Church, and a *retainer* of the Duke of Wellington's, who forwards *private despatches* to Downing-street,' noted the *Age*, adding that d'Orsay's friend Count Walewski lost heavily there during the winter of 1828–1829. As well as acting as a listening station for Wellington's administration, the New English Club seems to have played a significant part in shaping French policy and government: 'here, it is said by the Parisians, was first started the idea of forming the present French Ministry, a report that is entitled to some credit, when it is known that the Duke de Grammont, the Duke de Mouchey, Duke de Polignac (brother of the Minister), Duke de Choisseul and the Duke de Dino, with Monsieur Talleyrand, a brother of the celebrated statesman, are all of them leading members'.[17] These same names appeared regularly on the guest list at dinners given or attended by Count d'Orsay and it is difficult to imagine that d'Orsay was not a member of the New English Club.

As a further part of his Anglomania, d'Orsay was instrumental in establishing racing as an acceptable pastime for the Parisian beau monde. In a report of the last day of the official Paris Races, 11 October 1829, at which 'His Majesty and the Royal Family appeared highly delighted with the sport',[18] d'Orsay is mentioned frequently as a better, and 'The Count d'Orsay was, on the whole, the principal winner.'[19] His jockeys wore green colours and triumphed at the Bois de Boulogne. There were times when he was not content just to participate as an owner but appeared as a jockey too; for instance, on 4 March 1830 he took part in a steeplechase.[20] His success in nascent French racing circles was crowned on 5 September of the same year, when he received the sum of six thousand francs as the Prix Royal won by his horse Malsina.[21]

D'Orsay may have been an Anglomaniac, but the feeling was not entirely reciprocated. 'The Blessington family do not succeed well at Paris. D'Orsay is censored for his treatment of his poor wife, & laughed at for his dress, which is composed of sky blue pantaloons of silk & other strange mixtures.' So wrote Lady Holland sniffily to her son in January 1829. 'He wears his shirt, without a neckcloth, fastened with diamonds & coloured stones – in short a costume that men disapprove as effeminate and nondescript.'[22]

Such voices as Lady Holland's were however in the minority at the beginning of 1829. It must have seemed to d'Orsay that life stretched ahead of him as one long glittering social event, punctuated by sporadic bursts of decorating.

'Lord B— set out for London to-day, to vote on the Catholic question, which is to come on immediately. His going at this moment, when he is far from well, is no little sacrifice of personal comfort; but never did he consider self when a duty was to be performed.'[23] The Catholic question, to which Lady Blessington refers in this entry in her journal, was that of Catholic Emancipation, perhaps the single most contentious issue in British politics in the late 1820s. It was the cause of a notorious duel between Lord Winchelsea and the Duke of Wellington at Battersea.

In the summer of 1828, the Catholic Irish activist Daniel O'Connell was elected to represent County Clare in Parliament, but as a Roman Catholic was unable to take his seat. However, as a barometer of the strength and temperature of public opinion in Ireland, O'Connell's landslide victory was taken very seriously by the Prime

Minister, the Duke of Wellington. 'Throughout the late summer and autumn of 1828,' writes the duke's biographer Christopher Hibbert, 'Wellington, who had gradually come round to the belief that, with civil war threatening in Ireland, something must be done for the Catholics, persisted in his efforts to bring the King round to less intransigent views about them.'[24] Ultra-conservative factions of the British Protestant elite aside, Wellington's biggest problem was the king. George IV, his bigotry stoked by his mischievous brother the Duke of Cumberland, clung to his virulently anti-Catholic views. Eventually, despite threats of abdication by the king and at least one attempt to change the government, Wellington gained the king's consent to the proposed measure.

Blessington may have been an absentee landlord *par excellence*, but he was a kindly one. To be able to do real and lasting good appealed to him. Moreover, to feel himself to be a part of the legislative process, instrumental in bringing off this historic measure, would doubtless have bolstered his self-esteem. He was a fool, but a sensitive and caring one. There must have been times looking around the sumptuously decorated Hôtel Ney, his countess scribbling her saccharine journal, Count d'Orsay gadding about town returning to change his gloves and clothes, and his daughter the Countess d'Orsay behaving, in the words of one observer, like a Cinderella,[25] that he longed to achieve something of substance. The Catholic Relief Bill was to be that something.

Lady Blessington urged him not to go to London but merely to send his proxy. For once Blessington was not to be swayed by his wife. Perhaps she did not protest enough, preferring instead to spend her time shopping, gossiping, driving and partying in Paris with Count d'Orsay. Or perhaps he felt it was time to rekindle the extinct embers of his lacklustre political career. Besides, the Duke of Wellington himself was taking a personal interest in the business.

Blessington left Paris, and it is reassuring to know that his trip was not all hard work – while in London he found time to tear himself away from his political activities to attend a theatrical dinner. In due course, the bill was passed with a majority of just over a hundred. The effect on Lord Blessington of having participated so decisively in the future of his country and having set the British on the path to religious tolerance was beneficial. He returned, bearing gifts of course (he obviously managed to make it out to the shops while in London), to be garlanded by the laurels of his wife's praise:

> Lord B— arrived yesterday, and, Heaven be thanked! is in better health. He says the spring is three weeks more advanced at Paris than in London. He is delighted at the Catholic Question having been carried; and trusts, as I do, that Ireland will derive the greatest benefit from the measure. How few, with estates in a province where so strong a prejudice is entertained against Roman Catholics as exists in the north of Ireland, would have voted as Lord B— has done; but, like his father, Lord B— never allows personal interest to interfere in the discharge of a duty! If there were many such landlords in Ireland, prejudices, the bane of that country, would soon subside.[26]

The Catholics emancipated, Lord Blessington turned his mind to the more serious business of putting a roof over the heads of his family. While he had been away the household had amused itself in the usual fashion: Lady Blessington shopping and reading the fashionable novels of Hugo and d'Orsay's school chum Vigny; Count d'Orsay with his horses, clothes and young male friends; and Countess d'Orsay perfecting her manner of wounded neglect. The one inconvenience had been the offer made by a duke to rent the Hôtel Ney for either fourteen or twenty-one years. As the d'Orsays and Blessingtons '[did] not intend to remain more than two or three years more in Paris',[27] it was decided that they would leave the house when the year for which they had rented it expired.

Eventually they found a house 'newly built and freshly and beautifully decorated'[28] on the Rue Matignon, near the Champs-Elysées and the Rue Saint-Honoré. Lord Blessington of course called for lavish alterations to be made with all speed, regardless of cost. 'It will be beautiful when completed,' wrote Lady Blessington, 'but nevertheless not to be compared to the Hôtel Ney.'[29] It was to be a comfortable, albeit comparatively modest, family home once an additional room had been constructed, a grove of orange trees planted, a fountain installed, one large aviary built, one smaller heated aviary added for good measure, a fresco depicting their beloved Italian countryside painted, and numerous trailing plants included for decorative effect.

However, Lord Blessington would not live to walk among his orange trees, feed the birds or enjoy the calming effect of a gently tinkling fountain.

His Lordship had returned from London only a few days, when one forenoon, feeling himself slightly indisposed, he took some spoonfuls of eau de Melisse in water, and rode out, accompanied by his servant, in the heat of the day, along the Champs Elysées.

He had not proceeded far, when he was suddenly attacked by apoplexy, and was carried home in a state of insensibility, where all means were resorted to in vain, for his relief.

On the 23rd of May, 1829, thus suddenly died Charles James Gardiner.[30]

The last entry in Lady Blessington's journal prior to her husband's death was unintentionally prophetic. On the subject of the impending move she wrote that they would gladly 'remain where we are, for we prefer this hôtel to any other at Paris; but the days we have to sojourn in it are numbered'.[31] Lord Blessington's were numbered less generously than most and it would be 'a chasm of many months',[32] not until September in fact, before Lady Blessington would write again in her journal, by which time other, more malicious pens would have been busy.

CHAPTER THIRTEEN

Blackmail and Revolution

THE COUNT D'ORSAY, WHO A SHORT TIME SINCE MARRIED a daughter of the late Lord Blessington, continues to reside with his wife and noble mother-in-law, but from some reason or other their *only* visitant of rank is the Duchesse de Guiche – more it were not polite of us to tell. (The *Age*, 23 August 1829)[1]

Alfred d'Orsay, with his pretty pink and white face, drives about *à la* Petersham, with a cocked-up hat, and a long-tailed cream coloured horse. He says he will have seventeen thousand a-year to spend, others say seventeen hundred: he and my Lady go on as usual. The Duchesse de Guiche visits there in solitary womanhood; indeed, she says it is a great bore, and she can stand it no longer. (The *Age*, 27 September 1829)[2]

What a *menage* is that of Lady Blessington! It would create strange sensations were it not for one fair flower that still blooms under the shade of the Upas. Can it be conceived in England,

Mr. AGE, that Mr. Alfred d'Orsay has publicly detailed to what degree he has carried his apathy for his pretty interesting wife, and has boasted of his continence? This young gentleman, Lady Blessington, and the virgin-wife of sweet 16, all live together. You surely must remember a lady, who, some fifteen years ago, was acting wife to Captain J., of some dragoon regiment. As he had nothing but his spurs and his whiskers, Mrs J. used to levy taxes, on her friends, according to the system here called *les contributions indirectes*. Petersham introduced her to a Lord who, like a fool, married her. (The *Age*, 11 October, 1829)[3]

The Count makes the most loving of *beaux fils* to his *belle mere* (*à la mode de Bretagne*.) They are scarcely ever asunder. Lady Blessington is really a charming woman. (The *Age*, 7 March 1830)[4]

During the late 1820s and early 1830s the *Age*, founded in 1825, was the scourge of those in public life. It specialised in witty, scurrilous gossip, muckraking, innuendo and outright abuse, seasoned with a bit of lightweight news reporting. Very quickly after it was founded the *Age* and its reporters seemed to be everywhere that mattered: at the races, in the clubs, in boxes at the Opera, in the chop houses, in boudoirs, in taverns, with sportsmen and rakes, with those in public life and with their mistresses. As one of its own editorials put it, 'The *Age* is everywhere, and everywhere there is something to be picked up either for the information or amusement of our readers.'[5]

However, readers were not the *Age*'s only source of income. The newspaper 'flourished on a wholesale system of blackmailing', and its attacks on private life 'led Chief-Justice Denman to remark that everyone within range of [its] influence was living under the greatest of tyrannies ever known'.[6] The system worked simply enough. Proof copies of articles were forwarded to their subjects, or word was got to them that private papers had been purchased by the *Age* for publication, with the suggestion that on payment of an appropriate sum the matter would be dropped. At times the sums involved were significant. The editor of the *Age* was once accused of, and did not deny, 'extorting £5000 [nearly a quarter of a million pounds in today's values] to suppress the particulars of some long since forgotten intrigue in which certain members of the Court and a general officer were said to have been mixed up'.[7]

The warped genius, founder and editor of the *Age* was Charles Molloy Westmacott. He is spoken of variously as the son of 'Susannah Malloy [*sic*], landlady of the King's Arms Tavern in Kensington';[8] 'the son of a sweep named Molloy, living in some street off the Strand';[9] and even the son of the sculptor Westmacott.[10] However, as the last suggestion for his paternity was put about by Charles Molloy Westmacott himself and denied by the sculptor's family,[11] it can be discounted with reasonable safety.

The emergence of a scandal-hungry press coincides with d'Orsay's burgeoning fame. The first such newspaper was *John Bull*, which was launched in 1820 to support the Tory party and the king in his campaign against his estranged queen, Caroline. It attacked anyone who sided with the queen, finding their weakest spot and preying upon it mercilessly, plainly eschewing delicacy and not even bothering to hide behind innuendo: raking up affairs, illegitimate children and so on. 'There is the most infamous newspaper just set up that was ever seen in the world – by name John Bull. Its personal scurrility exceeds by miles anything ever written before',[12] wrote one outraged reader, who nonetheless had familiarised himself with the paper and the scandals it delineated.

John Bull put Society in uproar, but it was also irresistible. As one aristocratic woman and patroness of Almack's put it, 'I am told it is clever but very abusive.'[13] Those who were lampooned in it tried to use their influence to exclude from Society those who took the paper.

Then came libel actions, which secured the newspaper's success. Soon *John Bull* was selling ten thousand copies a week, and the scandals and inner secrets of the aristocracy were no longer items of tittle-tattle to be discreetly whispered at dinners, suppers and balls, but the property of anyone sufficiently literate to read a newspaper.

After the arrival of *John Bull* came the *Age*, again a notionally Tory paper, and a Whig weekly called the *Satirist*, but in both cases political principle was secondary in importance to private peccadillo. Neither paper was respectable. 'Macaulay once stigmatised a particularly disgraceful proposal as being too bad even for the editor of the *Satirist* to have made to the editor of the *Age*.'[14] Even so, both papers were widely read.

The editor of the *Age* was apparently horsewhipped on more than twenty occasions. Charles Kemble, playwright and friend of Count d'Orsay, had once felled him with a stick in public in the Covent Garden Theatre for having insulted his daughter Fanny in print. Likewise another man who came to be a friend of d'Orsay's in later life, the radical MP Thomas Slingsby Duncombe, 'soundly castigated him'.[15] It was doubtless to guard against further sound castigation that the *Age*'s office acquired 'a stalwart Irishman, armed with a stout shillelagh, whose duty it was to receive irascible visitors, who demanded to see the editor'.[16]

It is slightly curious that for once, given his love of issuing challenges to anyone who gave offence, real or imaginary, d'Orsay did not cross the Channel, fight his way past the shillelagh-wielding Irishman and challenge or horsewhip the offending editor. Perhaps it was that Charles Molloy Westmacott was rather too common for d'Orsay to want to dignify his insult with a challenge to a duel. After all if Charles James Mathews had been a borderline case, then to fight Molloy would have been *infra dig.* in the extreme. Then again the count might have realised that to storm into the offices of the *Age* would have been as counterproductive as it was ridiculous.

The symbiosis is obvious. The *Age* needed characters such as d'Orsay, and d'Orsay's vanity would have been fuelled by exposure in the emerging press. Although it would be going too far to say that he deliberately courted the attention of the nascent popular newspapers, at least while he was living in Paris in the late 1820s, the intrusion of the *Age* into his increasingly public 'private' life is important, in that it marks the transition from being mentioned in private letters and journals to a more public fame. He became public property.

In many ways d'Orsay was an early media celebrity and as time went on his relationship with the press became increasingly ambivalent. In London he would socialise with journalists and popular novelists. In certain instances he doubtless connived in placing stories and items calculated to help him in some of the desperate attempts to make money that would characterise his later life. And he would become increasingly happy to play up to the image of himself as a dazzling dandy and brilliant leader of fashion with limitless financial resources. The problem was that, when he wanted to escape from the colourful, but one-dimensional, caricature that had been created with his tacit consent by popular opinion and the popular press, he would find it very difficult.

It would of course also have been true that to respond to Westmacott's demands in d'Orsay's customary hot-headed manner would have been to provoke an even bigger scandal. Perhaps, now with Lord Blessington dead and himself the master, as he saw it, of a large fortune, he felt he had no need to be worried by press reports across the Channel in London. D'Orsay had a remarkable ability to appear unaffected by various crises. Perhaps Lady Blessington persuaded him not to travel to London to challenge, pay off or thrash the man. After all, it was about the last thing that she needed when widowed, in a foreign town and running an impressive household on what were increasingly unsure finances.

She may perhaps have been beginning to awake from the perpetual dream that had been marriage to Blessington. His death hit her very hard and, although it could not have been described as a passionate relationship, a deep and genuine affection had united Lady Blessington and her late husband. After his death she did not write in her diary for months and, when she did, her entry for the entire month of September 1829 amounts to a few mournful lines describing her grief. October begins in a similar vein. 'Ill, and confined to my chamber for several days. My physician prescribes society to relieve low spirits; but in the present state of mine, the remedy seems worse than the disease.'[17] Entries continue to be patchy. 'Some months have elapsed since I noted down a line in this book,' she wrote in May of the following year. 'When once Death has invaded our hearths and torn from us some dear object on whose existence our happiness depended, we lose all the confidence previously fondly and foolishly experienced in the stability of the blessings we enjoy, and not only deeply mourn those lost, but tremble for those yet spared to us.'[18]

As it was, the fourth mention of d'Orsay and Lady Blessington in the *Age* has the air of bringing the business to an unsatisfactory close for both sides: a sort of draw, in which Westmacott was neither paid off nor chased through the courts. This must have been a relief to Lady Blessington, since she was in no state at all to countenance a protracted campaign against the editor of the *Age*. She was simply too depressed.

And of course, there was a kernel of truth to the *Age*'s innuendo. It is interesting to note that, after the death of Lord Blessington, d'Orsay began to be mentioned by name in Lady Blessington's diary. Hitherto, as we have seen, he had lurked under such vague allusive descriptions as 'a gentleman of our party'. But gradually, as Lady Blessington eases herself back into Society, and her journal fills out with accounts of visits, walks and dinners, giving the impression of a far busier social life than hinted at by the *Age*, d'Orsay emerges from the shadows of the journal. This suggests some subliminal guilt on Lady Blessington's part. Perhaps the shock of her husband's death prompted a degree of greater honesty in her diary writing. Or perhaps she was just acknowledging d'Orsay's increasing importance as the significant male figure in her life: whether as lover, social passport or emotional support.

Another reason for d'Orsay's apparent lack of reaction to Westmacott's sniping was that he was having too good a time in Paris. For instance, heavy snowfall during the winter of 1828–1829 had rendered the Parisian streets 'not only nearly impassable for pedestrians but exceedingly disagreeable to those who have carriages'.[19] However, what was nearly impassable for common folk and exceedingly disagreeable even for those who had carriages was, for d'Orsay and his circle, an excuse to go for a sleigh ride through the streets:

The sledge of the Duc de Guiche, in which reclined the Duchesse, the Duc seated behind her and holding, at each side of her, the reins of the horse, presented the form of a swan, the feathers beautifully sculptured. The back of this colossal swan being hollowed out, admitted a seat, which, with the whole of the interior, was covered with fine fur. The harness and trappings of the superb horse that drew it were richly decorated, and innumerable silver bells were attached to it, the sound of which was pleasant to the ear.

The Duchesse, wrapped in a pelisse of the finest Russian sable, never looked handsomer than in her sledge, her fair cheeks tinged with a bright pink by the cold air, and her luxuriant silken curls falling on the dark fur that encircled her throat.

Count A. d'Orsay's sledge presented the form of a dragon, and the accoutrements and horse were beautiful; the harness was of red morocco, embroidered with gold. The Prince Poniatowski and Comte Valeski [*sic*] followed in sledges of the ordinary Russian shape, and the whole cavalcade had a most picturesque effect. The Parisians appeared to be highly delighted with the sight, and, above all, with the beautiful Duchesse borne along through the snow in her swan.[20]

And if the calvacade of sleighs was eye-catching by day, its appearance after dark was even more striking:

The swan of the Duchesse de Guiche had bright lamps in its eyes, which sent forth a clear light that was reflected in prismatic colours on the drifted snow, and ice-gemmed branches of the trees, as we drove through the Bois de Boulogne. Grooms, bearing lighted torches, preceded each sledge; and the sound of the bells in the Bois, silent and deserted at that hour, made one fancy one's self transported to some far northern region.

The dragon of Comte A. d'Orsay looked strangely fantastic at night. In the mouth, as well as the eyes, was a brilliant red light; and to a tiger-skin covering, that nearly concealed the cream-coloured horse, revealing only the white mane and tail, was attached a double line of silver gilt bells, the jingle of which was very musical and cheerful.[21]

The predatory overtones of d'Orsay's sled with its dragon design and tigerskin covering attracted much attention, and Lady Blessington recorded that the sight of these young aristocrats careering through the streets and parks of Paris in their opulent sleighs 'has greatly pleased the Parisian world, and crowds flock to see them as they pass along'.[22] Once again there is the sense that d'Orsay had become some sort of fashion-led celebrity, bringing out the crowds to marvel at his lavish conveyance. But Lady Blessington pointed out, 'in former days sledges were considered as indispensable in the winter *remise* of a grand seigneur in France as cabriolets or britchkas are in the summer'.[23] If anything, this overtly old-fashioned behaviour, evoking shades of the *ancien régime*, must have inflamed feelings of discontent among opponents of Charles X.

Through his sister's marriage to the Duke de Guiche, d'Orsay found himself at the heart of legitimist society in Paris. The Prince de Polignac, the king's favourite, was an intimate of d'Orsay's, but rather more interestingly d'Orsay was also openly friendly with those who were implacably opposed to the Bourbon regime.

In late 1829, two rather unlikely guests attended a dinner party at d'Orsay's and Lady Blessington's house on the Rue de Matignon. Thiers and Mignet were liberal historians. Thiers was a revolutionary firebrand, tirelessly energetic; Mignet a thinker and theorist. According to Lady Blessington, Mignet looked like Byron. Thiers was a 'modern Prometheus'[24] fizzing with energy and reforming zeal. 'The countenance of Monsieur Thiers is remarkable. The eyes, even through his spectacles, flash with intelligence, and the expression of his face varies with every sentiment he utters. Thiers is a man to effect a revolution, and Mignet would be the historian to narrate it.'[25]

In what she wrote Lady Blessington was either closer to the truth than she realised, or she was extremely well informed. At about the same time as they were enjoying dinner in the lavish surroundings of the house Lord Blessington had remodelled, Mignet and Thiers were engaged in setting up and editing the *National*. This was a new newspaper, the inspiration for which had come from Talleyrand and the backing from an Orleanist banker called Lafitte. Thus, while his brother-in-law was advising the king, d'Orsay was consorting with those who wished to dethrone him and install the Duke d'Orléans, a cousin of Charles X and the next in line to the French throne after Charles' family. D'Orsay's political position is encapsulated in two words used by Lady Blessington to describe his behaviour in a non-political situation, when she talks of his 'frank naïveté'.[26]

D'Orsay was drawn to the romanticism of the Napoleonic cause. But, as an essentially fair-minded person, had he given the issue much thought, he would probably have favoured a liberal government. Besides, as a contrapuntal stance it would have seemed fashionable, daring and controversial to espouse liberal views, much as it had been chic to appear at the royal stag hunt as a precocious youth on an English horse with a plain saddle, when all others had heavy riding gear. Yet there is no doubt that he relished the power, cachet and convenience of being, through his sister's marriage, part of a family that was so plugged in to a current of power.

He liked to have the best of all possible political worlds. Rather charmingly he saw no reason why he should not enjoy the choicest elements of the political buffet on offer in Paris at the time. With his considerable charisma and physical charm he could carry off a life in which he mixed with revolutionaries and Royalists. Even so, while he doubtless had some influence and might have begun to think of himself as something of a political fixer, a delusion that was to become stronger in later years, it is unlikely that he was ever taken seriously by any political heavyweights. D'Orsay's readiness to enjoy the pastimes and privileges of the Bourbon elite while flirting with opposition elements and at the same time fostering romantic nostalgia for a Bonapartist Europe might have made perfect sense to him, but marked him out as a shiftless dilettante to those who took their politics more seriously. If not a champagne socialist, d'Orsay can probably be described as a Bollinger Bonapartist.

In the summer of 1830 elections were held for the Chamber of Deputies, and the Polignac ministry, a central plank of Charles X's rule since the previous year, was defeated. Bearing in mind that this was a time when universal male suffrage, let alone allowing women to vote, was still a radical pipe-dream and that the electorate in France at that time was under less than a hundred thousand (largely comprising the landed elite and higher echelons of the urban bourgeoisie), this was a serious blow to the king. If the upper portion of society was against him, what did the unenfranchised masses think?

Charles X was in no mood to find out what his subjects wanted, let alone acquiesce to them. He set out to reverse the defeat and at the end of July issued the 'Four Ordinances': dissolving the newly elected Chamber of Deputies, banning the publication of any pamphlet or newspaper unless authorised by his government, reducing the electorate by 75 per cent (restricting the vote to the wealthiest members of society, those more likely to support him) and calling a new election. It was in effect a *coup d'état*: disbanding government, imposing blanket censorship and rigging the election.

'I remember Count d'Orsay telling me that on the day previous to the appearance of the celebrated ordonnances,' wrote Captain Gronow in later years,

> his sister the Duchesse de G—, niece by marriage to Prince Polignac, and a violent Royalist, was seated at the piano, playing and singing with triumphant vigour, '*La victoire est à nous,*' when suddenly the music-stool gave way, and the beautiful duchess lay sprawling on the floor. D'Orsay, who was a Liberal, assured her, laughingly, that this fall in the midst of her Legitimist song was *de très mauvais augure*, and a bad prognostic for the success of the party to which she belonged. He did not at the time believe his own prophecy, so firmly did the Bourbons appear to be established.[27]

Charles X, the titular head of the Bourbon family, did not share Gronow's optimistic appraisal of his family's fortunes. He clearly felt threatened and wanted to turn back the political clock. His thinking was, not unreasonably, influenced by what had happened to his family. He saw tumbrils and guillotines lurking behind every hostile newspaper article and every piece of public abuse. He said as much to his ministers.

The revolutionary spirit survives in its entirety among the men of the Left. In attacking the ministry it is really royalty that they resent, it is the monarchical system that they want to reverse. Unfortunately, Gentlemen, I have more experience on this point than you, who were not old enough to have seen the Revolution. I remember what happened then: the first retreat that my hapless brother made led to his downfall . . . They pretend that they are only angry at you, they say to me: 'Dismiss your ministers and we will come to an understanding.' . . . I will not dismiss you; first of all, Gentlemen, because I have an affection for you all and because I give you my full confidence, but also because, if I gave in to their demands this time, they would eventually treat us like they treated my brother . . .[28]

Had Charles X actually backed up his paranoia and his ordinances with a show of military force, the occupation of newspaper offices, the arrest of known opponents and a period of martial law on the streets of Paris, he might have succeeded. However, the majority of his crack troops were still in Algiers, where the French had achieved a victory that marked the beginning of a French colonial presence in North Africa that would last until the latter half of the twentieth century. Perhaps he hoped that military success abroad might help his domestic reputation. But, if anything, Charles X seemed in thrall to his own notion of divine right; he appeared to believe that the fact that he said something made it so. It seems that, if he thought about it at all, he banked on support based on a mixture of political apathy and underlying public loyalty. Unfortunately for France's last legitimate king, neither existed.

It was d'Orsay's dinner guest Thiers, and his colleagues on the *National* who made the first move of public opposition to the king's decrees, with a manifesto urging resistance. 'Shops and workshops in Paris were closed on 26 July: the King, as though to model himself on

Louis XVI, spent the day hunting.'[29]* Not all Charles X's courtiers shared his spectacular complacency. D'Orsay's brother-in-law the Duke de Guiche had dashed off to the royal château Saint Cloud 'the moment he had read the ordonnances'.[30] According to Lady Blessington, had de Guiche's advice been followed, the ordinances would not have been issued. But events were already taking their course. Coming back from a late drive on 26 July Lady Blessington noticed a crowd of youths outside the hotel of the minister of finance, shouting 'Vive la charte!' and 'A bas les ministres!' 'A patrol passed close to these persons, but made no attempt to disperse them, which I think was rather unwise, for, encouraged by this impunity, their numbers, I am told, increased rapidly.'[31] The days known as 'Les Trois Glorieuses', when the citizens of France would once again rise up and dispose of another hated king, had begun.

Revolution was becoming something of a habit in France. Rather like drink, the French had got a taste for violent political upheaval and were in danger of becoming addicted to the stuff. It was Voltaire who put it succinctly when he made the observation, 'Les Français goutent de la liberté comme des liqueurs fortes avec lesquelles ils s'envirent.'[32] This particular exercise in public uprising during the summer of 1830 was to be recorded and romanticised in Delacroix's impressive canvas *Liberty Leading the People*, a painting that would later find its way on to the nation's banknotes.

At the time it must have seemed anything but romantic. Paris echoed to the sound of firearms being discharged, gunsmiths were looted, street lanterns smashed, cobbled streets torn up, barricades

---

* The closure of shops and workshops does not seem to have reached the status of a paralysing general strike. As Lady Blessington wrote in her journal on 27 July: 'Yesterday the business of life flowed on in its usual current. The bees and drones of this vast hive were buzzing about, and the butterflies of fashion were expanding their gay wings in the sunshine' (*Idler in France*, vol. II, p. 150).

erected, houses shuttered, dead bodies paraded through the city. The mob clashed with troops loyal to the Crown under the command of the Duke de Raguse (the former Napoleonic marshal Marmont), his orders relayed from the king by d'Orsay's brother-in-law de Guiche who, in plain clothes, made the perilous journey to loyalist forces two or three times a day.

It must have seemed like a ghastly replay of the events of 1789. The descent of the country into another blood-bathed orgy of slaughter seemed a real and frightening possibility, especially to those like d'Orsay's grandmother Madame Craufurd, who locked herself into her house and fearfully bewailed her misfortune at having to endure a second French Revolution. To have lived through one revolution was unfortunate but to have to endure two must have been torture. 'For myself,' said the once formidable Madame Craufurd to Lady Blessington, 'I have little fear' – though her blanched cheek and trembling hand told another story –

> but for those dearer to me than life, what have I not to dread? You who know the chivalrous sentiments of the Duc de Guiche, and the attachment entertained by him and my granddaughter for the royal family, will understand how much I have to dread for them from the vengeance which their devotion to their sovereign may draw on their heads. *They* are not, as you are aware, timeservers, like so many others, who will desert their king in his hour of need. No; they will brave death, I am assured, rather than forsake in adversity those whose prosperity they shared.[33]

Had she known about it, she would have been even more disturbed by the behaviour of her grandson. D'Orsay seems to have treated the events of 'Les Trois Glorieuses' as a gripping adventure. As a high-profile member of a prominent Royalist family, he might have been wise to keep his head down. But d'Orsay was a liberal too and, besides, the whole thing was terribly exciting, with plenty of scope for heroic swashbuckling. While other aristocrats cowered in their *hôtels particuliers*, sheltering behind shuttered windows, the *portes cochères* guarded by burly Swiss servants, d'Orsay simply could not resist getting out and about as Paris erupted.

'Comtes d'Orsay and Valeski [*sic*] have just returned,' wrote Lady Blessington late in the evening of 27 July,

and state that they have been as far as the Place de la Bourse, where they saw a scene of the utmost confusion. The populace had assembled there in great force, armed with every kind of weapon they could obtain, their arms bared up to the shoulders, and the whole of them presenting the most wild and motley appearance imaginable. They had set fire to the Corps de Garde, the flames of which spread a light around as bright as day. Strange to say, the populace evinced a perfect good-humour, and more resembled a mob met to celebrate a saturnalia than to subvert a monarchy.

Comtes d'O— and V— were recognised by some of the people, who seemed pleased at seeing them. On returning, they passed through the Rue de Richelieu, which they found in total darkness, all the lanterns having been broken. Comte d'O— luckily found his cabriolet in the Rue de Menars, where he had left it, not being able to take it farther, owing to a portion of the pavement being broken up, and had only time to reach the club-house in the Rue de Gramont, in the court of which he placed his cab, before the populace rushed by, destroying every thing they met, among which was the carriage of the Prince Tufiakin. A considerable number of the members of the club were assembled, a few of whom witnessed, from the balcony on the Boulevard, the burning of the chairs placed there, the breaking of the lamps and other depredations.[34]

On the morning of 28 July the tricolour was flying from the towers of Notre Dame, while what Lady Blessington described as 'the white flag of the luckless Bourbons, as often stained by the faithlessness of its followers, as by the blood of its foes',[35] was still fluttering from the column in the Place Vendôme. D'Orsay's house on the Rue Matignon was suddenly on the front line. Breakfast was interrupted by the arrival of two doctors seeking refuge from the battle that raged on the Champs-Elysées and the Rue Saint-Honoré. Five minutes later the party moved from the breakfast table to the drawing room to watch a gun battle take place on the street. 'We have now entrenched ourselves in the front drawing-rooms,' wrote Lady Blessington that morning, 'with the external shutters, which are stuffed to exclude noise, closed, but which we open occasionally, in order to see what is going on. Sitting in darkness, with the sound of firing, and the shouts of the people, continually in our ears, I can hardly bring myself to think that all that is now passing is not a dream.'[36]

As the day drew on, the temperature rose and Paris boiled with rumours: several regiments had gone over to the liberals; the royal family had fled to Belgium; the city was about to be torched. Paris descended into anarchy.

Periodically d'Orsay would venture out or send his servants to gather information. One of his stable lads, when defending the count's stables on the Rue Verte, 'evinced a courage and enthusiasm that remind one of all we read of the old Imperial Guard',[37] and turned up outside the house on the Rue Matignon covered in blood and gore. Brandishing a huge sword he pounded on the gate and shouted up, 'order the gate to be opened, that I may lay at the feet of my generous master the trophies I have won with this trusty sword'.[38] His trophies amounted to a pair of silver-mounted pistols and a sabre, but they prompted d'Orsay to think of the art treasures in the royal collection, now exposed to looters and vandals. Lady Blessington reported:

Comte A. d'O— sent two of his servants (Brement, formerly drill-serjeant in the Guards, and now his porter, and Charles who was an hussar, and a brave soldier) to the Tuilleries to endeavour to save the portrait of the Dauphin by Sir Thomas Lawrence – an admirable picture. His instructions as to its emplacement were so correct, that the servants found it instantly, but torn in pieces, and the fragments strewed on the floor.

These men report that even in this feat a strange mixture of the terrible and the comic was exhibited, for *while* a dead body was placed on the throne of Charles the Tenth, some men appeared in the windows of the palace attired in the gold and silver tissue dresses of the Duchesse de Berri [the king's widowed daughter-in-law], with feathers and flowers in their heads, and fans in their hands, which they waved to the multitude beneath, with all the coquettish airs and graces of *would-be-fine* ladies.

The busts of Charles the Tenth were broken and trampled upon; the wardrobes of the royal family were scattered, torn, and thrown among the people, who seemed to regard them only as trophies of the victory they had achieved, and not for their intrinsic value.[39]

Every building that symbolised the Bourbon regime was attacked with ferocity and sacked, and those objects too big to loot were destroyed. D'Orsay's nephews had to be evacuated and his sister's house was besieged by the mob, who positioned two pieces of artillery in front of its gates. 'I hardly knew whether to be thankful or sorry that her brother Count Alfred d'Orsay was not at home when this news reached us,' wrote Lady Blessington, 'for he would certainly have proceeded to her house, and would probably have, by his presence and interference, rendered her danger still greater.'[40]

And yet, in the midst of this devastation, d'Orsay and indeed his

sister behaved with remarkable sang-froid that bordered on reckless-
ness. Ida de Guiche rebuked a tradesman for removing a royal warrant
from the outside of his shop, telling him that having sought the right
to display the royal arms he ought to have the bravery to defend
them. D'Orsay went to considerable pains to arrange the funeral of
the son of a family friend who had received the patronage of the
Duke de Guiche, had been enrolled as royal page only a week or two
earlier and had been shot dead at the Hôtel des Pages.

This young page was just one of an estimated two thousand
people who had died in Paris by 29 July, with 90 per cent of the casu-
alties occurring among the rioters.[41] But for d'Orsay this death was
more than a mere statistic. Hearing that the child had no relatives in
Paris at that time, the count took it upon himself to make elaborate
arrangements for the young boy's funeral. This action was undertaken completely without ulterior motive and is entirely in keeping
with d'Orsay's almost perverse kindness – the attitude that led him to
partner the plainest women at those rural dances of his youth. There
is also a dandiacal quality to this gesture, that of ensuring proprieties
and social rituals are observed even at a time when the fabric of society was being ripped to shreds. D'Orsay pursued a cultivation of
temperament as well as dress, and the events of 'Les Trois Glorieuses'
gave him the backdrop against which to set these traits and foibles.

If one accepts that as a dandy d'Orsay saw himself as an artist,
with himself as both medium and finished work, then the stimulus of
the upheaval around him would have been exhilarating – a chance to
set his exquisite persona against the backdrop of the barbarity of civil
war. To some eyes his behaviour might have seemed trivial and slight,
but, as he saw it, he was above mere politics and represented a dignity
and refinement that transcended the events of the day: there was of
course a romanticism about his *grandes gestes* – whether attempting to
rescue works of art or to conduct a proper burial – that allowed him
to feel infused with a nobility of spirit. Moreover, the death of Lord

Blessington had of course changed the dynamics of the household. D'Orsay was now the dominant male presence and it was a role he relished. Given the self-referential nature of the count's domestic life and the power of the spell that he wove, Fox's account of an enchanted convalescence in Naples testifies eloquently to the subtle force of his personality. Those near to him would have been caught up in his image of himself and would then have fuelled it further with their own quasi-worship of him.

On 30 July d'Orsay 'returned from seeing the last sad duties paid to the remains of the poor young page. He brings the intelligence that the royal family left St Cloud last night,' recorded Lady Blessington, 'and are now at Versailles. This step proves that they consider their case hopeless.'[42] The king tried to offer a compromise but events had overtaken him, and his situation was indeed without hope. Considering himself under threat at Versailles he moved to Rambouillet. Here he abdicated in favour of his grandson, naming the Duke d'Orléans as lieutenant general.

Once again it was too little, too late. A municipal council formed mostly of deputies had, by 30 July, elevated itself to the position of provisional government. And a document drawn up by Mignet and Thiers had been posted on the city walls calling for the Duke d'Orléans to be placed on the throne by the populace, which he was, without any reference to a role for Charles X's grandson. Thus the legitimate line of succession was broken. The deposed monarch headed into exile in Britain and the Duke d'Orléans became King Louis-Philippe, a distant member of the Bourbon family, but more significantly a popularly appointed monarch: the people's king in every respect.

The first few days of August were filled with rumours that Charles X had changed his mind and decided to retake the throne with a strong military force that had gathered around him at Rambouillet and even that Napoleon's son would be called upon to rule France. However, on 4 August Charles X and his party had 'taken the route to Cherbourg',[43] and thence into exile. Of his former courtiers few chose to accompany the deposed monarch to the coast. Among those who demonstrated a vestigial loyalty was d'Orsay's brother-in-law the Duke de Guiche, who would see the old king safely out of France before returning to Paris to dispose of the dauphin's property, with the intention of then following the king into exile at Holyrood.

By the evening of 6 August sufficient calm had returned to the streets of Paris for d'Orsay to suggest an evening stroll with Lady Blessington in the Champs-Elysées. The scene of furious fighting, this thoroughfare resembled a battlefield. The ground had been churned up, the trees damaged and destroyed: an air of eerie desolation hung over the famous boulevard. As they walked they saw a crowd gathered around a man who was reading aloud from a proclamation nailed to one of the few trees that remained standing. Mildly curious, d'Orsay and Lady Blessington went towards them.

'We paused for a moment to hear it,' recorded Lady Blessington,

when some of the persons recognising my companion, shouted aloud, '*Vive le Comte d'Orsay! Vive le Comte d'Orsay!*' and the cry being taken up by the mass, the reader was deserted, the fickle multitude directing all their attention and enthusiasm to the new comer. We had some difficulty in escaping from these troublesome and unexpected demonstrations of good will; and, while hurrying from the scene of this impromptu ovation to the unsought popularity of my companion, I made him smile by hinting at the danger in which he stood of being raised to the vacant throne by those who seem not to know or care who is to fill it.

Comte d'O— was as much puzzled as I was how to account for this burst of enthusiasm, for, taking no part in politics, and all his family being attached to the legitimate cause, this demonstration of regard appears more inexplicable. It seems, however, to establish one fact, and that is, that though the monarch has fallen into disrepute with the people, the aristocracy have not, and this alone proves how totally different are the feelings of those who have effected the present revolution with those of the persons who were engaged in the former one, a difference, perhaps, not more to be attributed to the change produced in the people by the extension of education, than in the *noblesse* by the same cause, aided by the habits and feelings it engenders.[44]

How like Lady Blessington to seek to extrapolate a wider judgement on the educative state of the French nation from one spontaneous act of enthusiasm from a crowd drunk on the revolutionary spirit of the occasion. It is unlikely that the crowd encountered by d'Orsay and Lady Blessington that evening, who were probably of limited literacy if they needed to have a proclamation read to them, evinced much in the way of intellectual distinction between a degenerate monarch and a member of the aristocracy.

It is more likely that they recognised, in d'Orsay, a popular man about town and perceived in him a 'star quality'. Indeed at over six feet in height, seeming taller in his top hat, and impeccable in his perfect clothes, he must have been a figure in stark contrast to the devastation around him. Maybe d'Orsay was puzzled by his rapturous reception, but this bemusement might have been a trifle disingenuous. Perhaps instead it was the thoroughness of his success that surprised him: his fame travelled well beyond the salons of the *vieux hôtels*; there was a quality about him that made his appeal unusually broad. D'Orsay was becoming the people's dandy, a consummate showman who enjoyed a symbiotic relationship with his 'fans', feeding off their adulation and in turn radiating a charisma that stoked their mania for him.

Over the coming decade d'Orsay's star quality was to reach its zenith. Back in London crowds would turn out to watch him drive in the Park 'in faultless white kid gloves, with his shirt-wristbands turned back over his coat-cuffs'.[45] Awestruck provincials would line the route of his carriage as he took country rides just to gawp at the spectacle he presented. 'A striking figure he was in his blue coat with gilt buttons, thrown well back to show the wide expanse of snowy shirt-front and buff waistcoat; his tight leathers and polished boots; his well-curled whiskers and handsome countenance; a wide brimmed glossy hat, spotless white gloves. He was the very beau-ideal of a leader of fashion,' is how Lord Lamington remembered d'Orsay on a ride to Richmond. 'I was greatly interested in noting the admiration with which he was regarded,' he said, adding that the people of the suburbs gazed at d'Orsay 'as at a superior being'.[46]

Lady Blessington's joke that he might be raised to the throne of France was echoed by the 'sporting folk' in Britain, who came to refer to Count d'Orsay as 'King of the French'.[47] He was to be 'seen in all places where fine fellows do congregate as the observed of all observers'.[48] A mere four years after this encounter with an enthusiastic crowd of fans on the Champs-Elysées, his fame would be seen as an established fact of life in Europe in the second quarter of the nineteenth century. He was to become so famous that *Fraser's Magazine* would pronounce that his story 'has been written by so many illustrious authors, especially of the hebdomadal press, that we willingly excuse ourselves from entering upon it here'.[49]

D'Orsay was perhaps the first modern media celebrity: his every move chronicled, examined and exaggerated by the nascent tabloid press of the day. Where Brummell had been a dandy who had achieved fame through an old-fashioned route, becoming a favourite at court, d'Orsay's dandified antics had caught the imagination of a broader public. His was a time when aristocrats were the leaders of fashion, yet also a time when democracy was making itself felt, albeit within the framework of a constitutional monarchy. He perfectly embodied the spirit of the age. Posh yet populist, just as Louis-Philippe was the people's king, so d'Orsay was the people's dandy.

Before long Paris life for d'Orsay settled back into the comfortable routine of dinner parties, with such architects of 'Les Trois Glorieuses' as Thiers and Mignet featuring prominently as guests. However, even d'Orsay began to realise that to stay in Paris would be impractical: there was Lord Blessington's estate to sort out. Besides there was also another, altogether more pressing reason for d'Orsay to leave Paris. He became convinced that his wife Harriet was having an affair. His marriage can most charitably be described as a curious arrangement. One suspicious aspect of the familial dynamic had been exposed in the *Age* and he had no desire for further scandal.

There were rumours linking Harriet and the dashing Lord Castlereagh, who like many English people of quality passing through Paris had been to dinner with d'Orsay. But the more embarrassing liaison being gossiped about was between Harriet and the Duke de Chartres. Described as an 'exceedingly handsome young man'[50] with an interest in the arts, the Duke was the eldest of five sons, all of whom were good-looking and accomplished. But he was no ordinary man about town. His father was the Duke d'Orléans, who by August 1830 had been elevated to the throne of France as King Louis-Philippe. Thus by the late summer of 1830 Harriet d'Orsay's name was no longer linked with the son of a distant member of the ruling family, but rather with the heir to the throne of France. Furthermore the next in line had something of a reputation as a ladies' man and, though 'very handsome and amiable', was 'accused of flirting instead of occupying himself with politics'.[51] Harriet denied that there was any substance in the rumour. Nevertheless, in the years following her marriage she had grown from being the pale adolescent wafting around in the background of whatever grand palace her father had rented, into an alluring and beautiful woman,* who would a few years later catch the attention of the Turkish ambassador to Paris.[52]

At around the same time she certainly made a lasting impression on the journalist George Augustus Sala, who was at school in Paris in the 1830s. 'I remember her as a charming lady, with lustrous eyes,' he wrote in his memoirs at the end of the nineteenth century,

> who dressed her hair in what I have always held to be the most bewitching fashion – a bunch of ringlets on each side of the head, such as you see in the portraits of Henrietta Maria, and in those of some of the beauties of the Court of Charles II. Lady Harriet d'Orsay was really the heroine of a story which has been told in at least twenty forms of twenty different ladies of fashion. She was presiding at a stall at a *vente de charité*, or bazaar, held in aid of the funds of some asylum or another, when there came up the young Duke of Orleans, son and heir of King Louis Philippe. The Duke, after some polite small talk, began to extol the beauty of her hair; and, indeed, her Henrietta Maria *coiffure* had never looked glossier and softer than it did this day. 'Oh!' said His Royal Highness, 'if I could only possess one of those enchanting ringlets!' 'How much would Monsieur give for one?' asked Lady Harriet, gravely, 'Five thousand francs?' 'Five thousand francs!' repeated the Duke; 'a mere *bagatelle*!' 'Six thousand francs?' 'Anything so charming a lady chose to ask.' 'I will not be extortionate,' pursued Lady Harriet; 'We will say five thousand.' And then she very composedly produced a

---

* On 1 January 1838, Harriet Countess Granville wrote to Lady Carlisle that 'Mrs White, Lady Harriet d'Orsay's sister, has been to a soirée, and is coming to the ball – nice-looking, like her sister, without the beauty.' To the Duke of Devonshire on 18 November of the same year she included Harriet in a list of 'Our Beauties'. (Gower, The Hon. F. Leveson (ed.). *Letters of Harriet Countess Granville*, London: Longmans & co., 1894 pp. 254–5 and p. 274.)

dainty little pair of scissors; snipped off the adorable Henrietta
Maria ringlet; wrapped it in silver paper, and handed it, with a
smile and a curtsey full of graceful dignity, to the Duke. His
Royal Highness looked very straight down his nose; and returning Lady Harriet's salute, stalked somewhat gloomily, away. But
his Privy Purse duly forwarded the money the next day.[53]

It would appear that with the change in the Countess d'Orsay
had come an awakening of her sexual appetite. Certainly there was no
shortage of men passing through the house to pay her compliments
and flirt with her. To be smitten by d'Orsay you either had to bask in
the uninterrupted sun of his personality, which of course was at his
discretion, or to accept him *in toto*: his charm, vanity, kindness, touch-
iness, generosity, insecurity – everything. It seemed that d'Orsay
never really expended enough time trying to charm his wife and,
unhappily for domestic harmony, the older she got, the less enthralled
she became with her husband, particularly as the bond between him
and her stepmother was as close as, if not closer than, it had been
during her father's lifetime.

And then there was the sex. In spite of the compact made to preserve her virginity for the early years of her marriage, it is unlikely
that d'Orsay put any great store by the prospect of a full and energetic
sex life with his wife when the time arrived. There is perhaps something of Captain Jesse's verdict on Brummell, namely that he 'had too
much self-love ever to be really in love', and for a man of d'Orsay's
vanity, sex involved too many other people to be entirely satisfying for
long.

By November 1830 Count d'Orsay, his wife and his stepmother-
in-law, the widowed Countess of Blessington, were on their way back
to London. It was not a return that Lady Blessington was anticipating
with any pleasure. 'I ought to feel pleased at leaving Paris, where the
heaviest trial of my life has occurred, but *here* I have now learned to

get inured to the privation of his society, while in England I shall have again to acquire the hard lesson of resignation.'[54]

She was returning to London an older woman, with a truculent, frustrated and unhappily married stepdaughter of increasing sexual allure, and a stepson-in-law who was fast achieving international celebrity and notoriety on a scale not seen since Byron. Moreover, without Lord Blessington to protect her, she realised that polite Society back in England was waiting to pounce at the first sign of social failure or moral irregularity. It is not without reason that she wrote, 'the present is cheerless and the future clouded'.

Chapter Fourteen

Return to London

I WENT YESTERDAY TO WINDSOR TO THE FUNERAL OF the late King. I went in the morning with Lady Georgiana Fane to Sir Andrew Barnard's room in the Castle. He and Lord Fife went with us to see the Lying in State. It was in one of the old State Rooms in the Castle. The coffin was very fine and a most enormous size. They were very near having a frightful accident for, when the body was in the leaden coffin, the lead was observed to have bulged very considerably & in fact was in great danger of bursting. They were obliged to puncture the lead to let out the air & then to fresh cover it with lead. Rather an *unpleasant operation*, I should think, but the embalming must have been very ill done.[1]

So wrote the diarist Mrs Arbuthnot on 16 July 1830. It was thus in a puff of foul-smelling gas that George IV left this England and this life, taking with him the Georgian Age that had begun in 1714, when his great-grandfather found himself George I of England. With one king dying in London, and revolution and the dethronement of another monarch in Paris, it must have seemed that a new world order was being installed.

William IV took the throne in England, but at times it appeared that there was barely any rule at all. In the month that d'Orsay returned to London it seemed to some that London would go the way of Paris. There were rumours that 9 November, Lord Mayor's Day, was to be marked by widespread civil disobedience that bordered on revolution. It was feared that bombs would be planted in factories, members of the government would be murdered, the City would go up in flames and the king would be the subject of an audacious kidnap attempt when he arrived at the Guildhall. The event was postponed for a few days and, as it happened, disruption was minimal. But riots continued up and down the country during the early 1830s, with factories and the country estates of the aristocracy and gentry being a focus for violence, reflecting rural discontent and concerns about the pace of industrialisation; while in London reactionaries, not least the Duke of Wellington, received death threats. During this time Apsley House, the duke's London residence, was often under siege from the mob.

It is probably to William IV's credit that his rule was not marked by more serious flare-ups. Formerly the Duke of Clarence, brother of the late king and a career sailor, William was an eccentric with decidedly populist tendencies. One story has him walking down St James's arm in arm with an old shipmate roaring with laughter; another tells of a prostitute who rushed up to him and embraced him, shouting 'God Bless You, Billy, My King!'[2] Gronow noted one incident when the king was 'going down to prorogue Parliament' and, the state carriage not being ready in time, 'swore he would order a hackney-coach and go to the House in that humble vehicle'.[3] Given recent events in Paris, the change of king from a bloated, vain, gluttonous recluse to a down-to-earth old sea-dog probably came at the right time to defuse a similar upheaval in London. Moreover William emerged as a surprisingly able statesman and, although he is remembered chiefly, if at all today, as the monarch who preceded Victoria on the British throne, it was during his rule that the Reform Bill was piloted through Parliament, ushering in sufficient electoral change to avert revolution. As the *Dictionary of National Biography* puts it, William IV 'displayed the instincts of a statesman; refused to swamp the majority in the House of Lords which (1832) rejected the Reform Bill (originally brought in in 1831) by creating new peers, but owing to a circular letter sent by him to the Tory peers, a hundred of them absented themselves from the division and the bill became law' on 7 June 1832.[4]

It was in the middle of this excitement that d'Orsay, his wife and his stepmother-in-law arrived. They settled into the old house in St James's Square, but soon it was decided that they would move: 10 St James's Square was expensive to maintain, and the house held too many associations with the late Earl of Blessington for any of them to be happy in it. It would not have been comfortable for Lady Blessington to be reminded daily of her late husband, d'Orsay would have wanted a place on which he could set his stamp and perhaps they even thought that a different address might have done some good for d'Orsay's wife.

Much as Lady Blessington had been happy to enjoy her late husband's largesse, she was prudent where he had been prodigal. For a while she sub-let the vast house, fully furnished, to the Windham Club, for £1350 per annum[5] (over sixty thousand pounds today). However, with an annual head rent of £840,[6] she was left with barely £510 a year, which, while a reasonably useful sum, was further eroded by repairs that needed to be made to the house.

As almost every other aspect of society was changing in the England of the time, d'Orsay and Lady Blessington took the decision to launch a new style of salon for London's social, artistic, literary and political elite. They chose to locate it in fashionable Mayfair, in a house in Seamore Place. Lady Blessington recommenced her career as a London hostess in the midst of the London palaces of the country's richest aristocrats.

As a salon queen Lady Blessington had two or possibly three principal rivals. The tyrannical Lady Holland still ruled over her austere salon at Holland House, much as she had nine years before when, seated next to d'Orsay at dinner, she had repeatedly dropped her cutlery. Almost as intimidating was Lady Charleville, with her formal manners, deep voice and habit of addressing everyone as 'Sir' or 'Ma'am'. A woman of Irish extraction who had lost the use of her legs while still a young woman,[7] she only ever appeared seated, which according to one contemporary, gave her 'the appearance of a queen upon her throne'.[8] However, it was by her friendship with the Dowager Lady Mountjoy, Lord Blessington's stepmother, and in her role as the mother of Lord Tullamore that Lady Charleville was to impact upon Lady Blessington.

And then there was old 'Corky', or the Countess of Cork and Orrery as she was more properly known: a celebrated London hostess for at least half a century, she had been a friend of Dr Johnson and had remained a dedicated if theatrical socialite subject to mild bouts of kleptomania. By the time Count d'Orsay and Lady Blessington returned to London, she was well into her eighties. In Disraeli's novel of 1837, *Henrietta Temple*, she is the thinly disguised model for the Viscountess Dowager Bellair, 'the last remaining link between the two centuries'.[9] Disraeli provides an evocative description of the portly, gaudily clad little woman who 'had witnessed revolutions in every country in the world' and who was able to remember 'Brighton a fishing-town, and Manchester a village'.[10]

Almost as much of a cherished institution as Corky was her macaw, the subject of a book called *Memoirs of a Macaw of a Lady of Quality*. This bird had nibbled at George IV's stocking and bitten a chunk out of Lady Darlington's leg. Its reputation reached its zenith on 'the great evening when the conservatory was fitted up to look like a Brazilian forest, with tin palm trees, a stuffed alligator and an artificial upas-tree, on which the macaw was solemnly enthroned to display his master-trick of drawing out, clipping and smoking a cigar'.[11]

With the autocrat, the invalid and the crank ranged against her, Lady Blessington deployed her formidable armoury. She had a bulging address book of salon habitués from her days in St James's Square, as well as extensive contacts throughout Europe. Then there was her talent for extravagant entertaining, honed to perfection during almost a decade of continental high living. Having spent a number of years away from England she was also politically neutral (a valuable commodity at a time when Society was divided by the question of Reform). And while she was no longer in the first bloom of youth, there was still a powerful attraction about her. In the right setting with low lighting, dressed 'in a richly coloured gown of velvet or satin, cut very low so that her superb shoulders and arms shone with a sort of dazzling warmth in the candle-light',[12] she seemed little altered from the celebrated portrait by Lawrence that had been the talk of the Royal Academy Summer Exhibition a decade earlier. Indeed one visitor to Seamore Place in January 1832 said of her, 'Miladi has doffed her widow's weeds, and was almost in pristine beauty.'[13]

Her most potent weapon, however, was the tall, elegant, exotic, charismatic and celebrated Count d'Orsay. The house they chose on Seamore Place was rented for five years from Lord Mountford. D'Orsay then set about recreating a Mayfair version of the splendour they had surounded themselves with in the Palazzo Belvedere in Naples and the Hôtel Ney in Paris. Decorated from designs by d'Orsay[14] and furnished with the fruits of almost a decade of continual shopping in the major cities of Italy and France, the creation was remarkable.

D'Orsay's plans for Seamore Place were an exercise in set design as much as domestic decoration. The house's status as a home for d'Orsay, his wife and Lady Blessington was secondary to its use as a space for lavish and virtually constant entertaining. Lady Blessington received visitors between eight p.m. and midnight every night.[15] After dinner a second wave of guests would arrive to join in the repartee before dispersing to their clubs for more late-night conversation or gambling. Occasionally she took a break from this punishing party-giving schedule to attend the Opera or theatre.

To succeed as a hostess, she needed a suitable launchpad for her social ambition. D'Orsay duly delivered a suite of rooms, which even the late Lord Blessington would have been proud to have created. The principal stages were an octagonal dining room with mirrored walls 'reflecting every motion',[16] clearly inspired by an almost identical room at the Hôtel Ney; and a long library, the walls of which were decorated with gold, mirrors and beautifully bound books that guided the visitor's eye to an impressive window running the width of the room overlooking Hyde Park.

The Park itself had altered considerably since d'Orsay had first seen it as a teenager. The vast 20-foot-high bronze of a naked Achilles made from cannon captured by Wellington and erected by the 'women of England' to honour 'Arthur Duke of Wellington and his brave companions in arms' in 1822 was still a talking point. This bronze Achilles features prominently in many engravings of the time; apart from being a very large piece of public art, it was the first nude statue to go on general view in England. In addition to this astonishing sight, the fashionable architect Decimus Burton had been busy during the 1820s designing smart new lodges for Hyde Park Corner, Grosvenor Gate, Stanhope Gate, and Cumberland Gate, as well as the screen at Hyde Park Corner and the imposing Constitution Arch, which today finds itself marooned within several lanes of fast-moving traffic. And in 1826 a bridge had been put across the Serpentine, altering the Park for ever.

From being a piece of countryside next to Mayfair that in the previous century had been a venue for duels and a hunting ground for highwaymen, Hyde Park was rapidly being transformed into a polite urban amenity where the rich could flaunt their latest horses, carriages and women. Much as Brummell had stood in the window of White's a generation before, so d'Orsay would while away the odd half-hour gazing out at the Park from the window of the library at Seamore Place.

To compete with such an engrossing view, the interior would have to provide a rich seam of conversational possibilities and it is to such an end that the knick-knacks gathered over the years in Europe were displayed. At dinner Lady Blessington often chose to occupy a chair ordered by George IV for a meeting with Louis XVIII. The contents of Seamore Place amounted to a small museum of mementoes of the famous: a clock that had belonged to Marie Antoinette, a fender with eagles that had been owned by the Empress Josephine, snuff boxes given as gifts by Louis XIV, as well as numerous pretty little *objets* that had once been the property of such celebrated figures as Ninon de Lenclos and Madame de Pompadour. That Lady Blessington saw herself as the inheritor of the wit, grace, style and sexual attractiveness of these *femmes fatales* was made abundantly clear through the careful location of the famous Lawrence portrait. It was hung with strategic precision, opposite where new visitors to Seamore Place and those bearing letters of introduction would sit during their first interview with Lady Blessington herself.

To *objets* of intrinsic beauty to which the patina of previous ownership brought the lustre of history, d'Orsay added such striking novelties as decorating the dinner table with fruit and flowers displayed in Sèvres porcelain rather than with the ancestral plate that most hosts chose for garnishing their dining rooms. Disraeli called it 'the most charming of modern houses'.[17] According to Joseph Jekyll, 'it was a house of bijoux'.[18] However, it is an American journalist,

Nathaniel Parker Willis, who leaves the most vivid description of the salon in Seamore Place.

A friend in Italy had kindly given me a letter to Lady Blessington; and with a strong curiosity to see this celebrated authoress, I called on the second day after my arrival in London. It was 'deep i' the afternoon,' but I had not yet learned the full meaning of town hours.* 'Her Ladyship had not come down to breakfast.' I gave the letter and my address to the powdered footman, and had scarce reached home, when a note arrived, inviting me to call the same evening at ten.

In a long library lined alternately with splendidly-bound books and mirrors, and with a deep window of the breadth of the room, opening upon Hyde Park, I found Lady Blessington alone. The picture to my eye as the door opened, was a very lovely one – a woman of remarkable beauty half buried in a *fauteuil* of yellow satin, reading by a magnificent lamp suspended from the centre of the arched ceiling; sofas, couches, ottomans, and busts arranged in rather a crowded sumptuousness through the room; enamel tables, covered with expensive and elegant trifles in every corner; and a delicate white hand relieved on the back of a book, to which the eye was attracted by the blaze of its diamond rings. As the servant mentioned my name, she rose and gave me her hand very cordially; and a gentleman entering immediately after, she presented me to Count d'Orsay, the well-known Pelham of London, and certainly the

* A novel of the early 1840s gives the following explanation of the hours kept by the fashionable elite of London of the day. 'The time was morning; that is, although the sun had been dipping a full hour from his altitude, it was still, in the world of fashion, the beginning of the day, and the beginning of the day is generally understood to come under the denomination of that division of the hours' flight.'

most splendid specimen of a man and a well-dressed one, that I had ever seen. Tea was, brought in immediately, and conversation went swimmingly on.[19]

The scene was one of unalloyed opulence: the carefully stage-managed presentation of the spotlit Lady Blessington, engulfed in an overstuffed yellow satin armchair, her pale hand weighed down with diamonds. And d'Orsay entering on cue, speaking English with 'a very slight accent'[20] that doubtless added to the attraction of this handsome man whose carefully tailored clothes emphasised the toned curves of a physique in its prime.

The whole effect teetered on the brink of camp. It must have seemed to the visiting American journalist that he had stumbled into a living representation of one of the 'Silver Fork' novels of Society life that were in vogue at the time. In Seamore Place's sumptuous soap opera Lady Blessington played a sultry, seductive role. Willis was bewitched. Here was a rich seam of sensational copy for his readers, while, for d'Orsay and Lady Blessington, Willis was a conduit for spreading their celebrity across the Atlantic and into the status-hungry New World. It seems to have worked, in that in 1846 d'Orsay's name would be appended as author to an American book entitled *Etiquette; or A Guide to The Usages of Society with a Glance at Bad Habits*, priced at 25 cents and written by someone else entirely.

Willis resumed his account:

In the evening I kept my appointment with Lady Blessington. She had deserted her exquisite library for the drawing-room, and sat, in fuller dress, with six or seven gentlemen about her. I was presented immediately to all; and when the conversation was resumed, I took the opportunity to remark the distinguished coterie with which she was surrounded.

Nearest me sat Smith, the author of 'Rejected Addresses' –

a hale, handsome man, apparently fifty, with white hair, and a very nobly-formed head and physiognomy. His eye alone — small, and with lids contracted into an habitual look of drollery, betrayed the bent of his genius. He held a cripple's crutch in his hand, and, though otherwise rather particularly well-dressed, wore a pair of large India-rubber shoes — the penalty he was paying, doubtless, for the many good dinners he had eaten. He played rather an *aside* in the conversation, whipping in with a quiz or witticism whenever he could get an opportunity, but more a listener than a talker.

On the opposite side of Lady Blessington, stood Henry Bulwer, the brother of the novelist, very earnestly engaged in a discussion of some speech of O'Connell's. He is said by many to be as talented as his brother, and has lately published a book on the present state of France. He is a small man; very slight and gentleman-like; a little pitted with the smallpox, and of very winning and persuasive manners. I liked him at the first glance.

A German prince, with a star on his breast, trying with all his might — but, from his embarrassed look, quite unsuccess-fully — to comprehend the drift of the argument; the Duke de Richelieu; a famous traveller just returned from Constantinople; and the splendid person of Count d'Orsay, in a careless attitude on the ottoman, completed the *cordon*.[21]

A revered man of letters, a prominent diplomat and Member of Parliament, a token couple of young European aristocrats and of course the magnificent Count d'Orsay — it was just another evening at Seamore Place. Willis is plainly in awe of 'the distinguished coterie', and after dinner the coterie became even more distinguished:

Toward twelve o'clock, Mr. Lytton Bulwer was announced, and
enter the author of 'Pelham.' I had made up my mind how he
should look, and, between prints and descriptions, – thought I
could scarcely be mistaken in my idea of his person. No two
things could be more unlike, however, than the ideal of Mr.
Bulwer in my mind and the real Mr. Bulwer who followed the
announcement. I liked his manners extremely. He ran up to Lady
Blessington with the joyous heartiness of a boy let out of school;
and the 'how d'ye, Bulwer?' went round, as he shook hands
with every body, in the style of welcome usually given to 'the
best fellow in the world.'[22]

Edward George Earle Lytton Bulwer, later Edward George Earle
Lytton Bulwer-Lytton, Lord Lytton, stalwart pillar of the Victorian
Establishment, was *the* popular novelist of the late 1820s and 1830s.
With the publication of his novel *Pelham or The Adventures of a
Gentleman* in 1828, the same year that he celebrated his twenty-fifth
birthday, Bulwer had caused a sensation. In its way the book altered
people's lives, encapsulating the spirit of the new urban dandy. And in
detailing the way of life and preoccupations of this exotic creature,
Pelham was a lifestyle primer for aspiring dandies, teaching them how
to dress and behave. Sterner moralists found it seditious and dangerous, and later in his life Bulwer would feel the need to bowdlerise
this, the seminal dandy novel, in order for it to meet the more exacting moral standards of Victorian England.

But on the occasion of his midnight arrival at Seamore Place to
receive the plaudits of this fashionable salon, he was a young, flashily
dressed, successful novelist, revelling in his fame. It was natural that
he would fall into d'Orsay's orbit. And his unhappy marriage to the
clever, pretty, extravagant, outspoken and hot-tempered Rosina meant
that he was out of the house until all hours. According to Willis's
account, this jolly soirée at Seamore Place did not begin to break up

until 3 a.m. when the gouty Smith staggered to his india rubber-clad feet and hobbled off on his crutches.

Soon Willis was back for another evening, which this time finished with a sing-song around the piano. Indeed it is in his recollection of this dinner party in the summer of 1834 that he makes a telling observation: 'after Lady Blessington retired from the table', he writes, 'everybody else seemed to feel that light had gone out of the room'.[23] It was of course customary for women to leave the dinner table for coffee, allowing the men to talk among themselves. However, it was only Lady Blessington who left the dinner table at Seamore Place, because she was the only woman at the table. No woman who valued her reputation could risk going to dinner at Seamore Place – especially after the scandalous events of 1831.

*C*HAPTER FIFTEEN

Break-up of a Marriage

ON 18 JULY 1831 JOSEPH JEKYLL WROTE ABOUT A LITTLE DINNER that Lady Blessington gave at Seamore Place. The guest list was select: Lord Wilton, General Phipps, Jekyll and of course Count d'Orsay. The evening was a success: '*Cuisine de Paris exquise*', enthused Jekyll.[1] The only slight disappointment was d'Orsay's wife, Harriet, who appeared to be unwell. 'The pretty melancholy Comtesse glided in for a few minutes, and then left us to nurse her influenza.'[2]

Influenza was not the only thing that Harriet was nursing. Her listless distaste for life with her husband and her stepmother was hardening into an active antipathy, and there were those in London who were only too keen to exacerbate her dissatisfaction. In the early part of 1831, Lord Blessington's elder sister arrived in London with her niece Emily, Harriet's sister. Countess d'Orsay got into the habit of slipping out of Seamore Place early in the day, 'every day to her aunt, in her aunt's carriage'.[3]

Life in Seamore Place had settled into the quasi-nocturnal routine that Willis described. Like Brummell before him, it would seem that d'Orsay liked the day to be well aired before he got out of bed and launched himself into it. After dinner would come the post-prandial chatter and drinking, followed by a late-night prowl of the clubs. He would not get to bed much before three or four o'clock in the morning. It would have been easy for his wife to slip away from dinner, pleading some illness or other, and withdraw to her room early in the evening, getting up fresh and early, picking her way quietly through the servants, opening the shutters and tidying the debris of the previous evening – or perhaps even the servants would still be in bed – to find her aunt's carriage waiting for her outside Seamore Place. Given that Lady Blessington would not be out of bed for several hours yet and d'Orsay had probably only got to sleep a couple of hours earlier, it would have been easy for Harriet to spend the morning with her aunt and be back under the marital roof before anyone could notice that she was missing.

Moreover, d'Orsay was increasingly absorbed in the role he was creating for himself as London's leading man of fashion, and so involved was he in the excitement of assuming Lord Blessington's role as spendthrift-in-chief and experimenting with bold new fashions in interior design that he had no time to worry about his wife. There was nothing calculated in his neglect: if nothing else his loyalty to the memory of Lord Blessington would have militated against outright cruelty to her. However, if she wanted to mope about the house feeling sorry for herself, then d'Orsay was too busy to stop her. In truth, she was not content to waft about the theatrically adorned rooms of Seamore Place watching her stepmother and her husband develop their bizarre quasi-Oedipal relationship, especially when her early-morning coach rides enabled her to have conversations with her aunt that filled her mind with anti-d'Orsay propaganda – soon she began to see her husband as the means by which her family had been robbed of Lord Blessington's fortune. It was perhaps typical of d'Orsay's self-absorption that he failed to see what was going on under his own roof and that, from being an easily guided girl, his wife was becoming a strong-minded young woman who was being turned against him. Although kind and generous, there was also an arrogance of the spoilt child about d'Orsay that blinded him to many things.

Countess d'Orsay's life was not without its moments of consolation. It was rumoured that she was conducting an affair with Lord Tullamore, the son of Lady Blessington's salon rival, Lady Charleville. Tullamore was a friend of d'Orsay and a member of the fast set that included the hardened gambler Lord Sefton. Lady Charleville did not wish to believe that her married son was having an affair with Countess d'Orsay. As she wrote in a letter dated 4 August:

> I do not believe one word of poor Countess d'Orsay living with Ly Blessn. Suspicion may fall on her; but the fact seems to me that Ct d'Orsay is extremely clever & agreeable exactly in his way, with abundance of demi connaissances, & the presumption of being the Arbiter Elegantiarum of Dandyism . . . & so, precisely to the taste of my poor conceited dear Child, who has goût enough to find his other companions very dull! His career and his wife's must be one of luxury and vanities, and if he had more to support it I dare swear he wd be less foolish than one half of those he associates with![4]

It is possible to detect in Lady Charleville's letter some sort of respect for d'Orsay as the most interesting and intellectually active of Tullamore's circle, as well as the fear that it is d'Orsay and not his wife who will corrupt her son. Indeed it would seem that at the time there was a school of thought (although how well attended that school was is unknown) that d'Orsay was actively attempting to involve his wife in an affair with Tullamore. This would provide him with the grounds to divorce her, leaving him free to to enjoy the money, which came to him via the marriage, with Lady Blessington.

Sadleir, Lady Blessington's biographer of 1933, who is always keen to present d'Orsay in an unfavourable light, describes him as 'utterly non-moral' when 'money and his own material interest were involved'.[5] He may have been vain, and this period of his life, with his burgeoning fame, seems to have marked the beginning of increasing self-delusion about his abilities and his expectations, but he was not a devious man. Sadleir's is an unduly harsh assessment, probably born out of a desire to rehabilitate Lady Blessington's reputation, which entered history very stained and spotted. However, Lady Blessington was not a weak-willed woman at the mercy of what Sadleir would have posterity see as a feckless exquisite. She had dragged herself out of the mire of a provincial Irish background, extricated herself from one potentially lethal marriage of her father's design, embarked on an altogether more agreeable one and reinvented herself as one of the most celebrated hostesses of her day. Instead she and d'Orsay's reputations were crafted by public opinion, itself manipulated by private individuals who for their own reasons, pecuniary or social, motivated by fear or jealousy, had taken against Count d'Orsay and Lady Blessington.

A more even-handed examination of d'Orsay's character would take into account the quality Lady Blessington identified as 'frank naïveté'. D'Orsay is unlikely to have spent much time scheming about how to embroil Tullamore and his wife in an extramarital affair. His self-regard and his exaggerated sense of honour would have militated against such an unchivalrous and underhand ploy. As regards the money, it is safe to say that he had little financial sense; he evinced a blithely optimistic attitude to life and finance that makes Mr Micawber seem a model of pessimistic pecuniary pragmatism. This, coupled with his congenital extravagance, was to contribute to his ruin.

Others were happy to pick over the future of the Blessington bequest, however, and as the summer wore on Harriet d'Orsay's

AUTHOR OF "A JOURNAL."

Published by James Fraser, 215 Regent Street, London.

Count d'Orsay by Daniel Maclise, 1834

Lady Blessington by Sir Thomas Lawrence, 1822

Lord Blessington, as drawn by
his son-in-law d'Orsay, 1828

Count d'Orsay by Sir George Hayter, 1839

An engraving of Gore House (1830) from *Old and New London*

Lady Blessington's salon at Gore House. *In foreground, from left*: William Thackeray, Hon. Mrs Norton, Rev. Dr Lardner, Edward Bulwer Lytton, Count d'Orsay, Benjamin Disraeli, Lady Blessington, Daniel Maclise, Lord John Russell and Charles Dickens

Salone Grande at the Villa Belvedere, Naples

Seamore Place

George Byron by d'Orsay, 1823

The Duke of Wellington
by d'Orsay, 1845

Beny Disraeli.

Captain Gronow

Clockwise from left:
Benjamin Disraeli (1837),
Captain Gronow (undated) and
Edward Bulwer Lytton (1845),
all drawn by d'Orsay

Crockford's casino and 'Club House' on St James Stree[t,] engraved by William Tombleson from a drawing b[y] Thomas Shepherd, 18[2]

William Crockford
by 'R.S.'

A gaming table
at Crockford's,
engraved by Greco,
from Gronow's
Reminiscences, 1843.
Count d'Orsay
is pictured 'calling
a main'

*The Last Grand
Steeple Chase*, at the
Hippodrome
racecourse,
Kensington.
Engraved by Charles
Hunter after a
painting by
Henry Alken Jnr

Advertisements for d'Orsay perfume

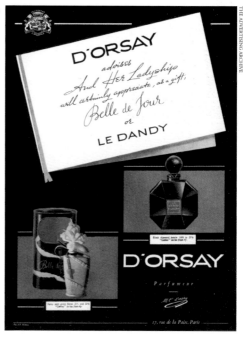

The Chambourcy house of the de Grammont family as it is today

Road signs in Chambourcy – the legacy of d'Orsay's and Lady Blessington's time there

Count d'Orsay's tomb in the town, also occupied by the remains of
Lady Blessington. He was interred there in August 1852

matutinal rides in her aunt's coach had the effect that this relative desired – one morning she left Seamore Place and did not return.

By the middle of August it was relatively common knowledge that Harriet d'Orsay had left her husband and gone into hiding. On the 16th Lady Holland wrote her son a chatty letter concerning politics in Ireland, the state of Europe, and rural unrest. In the midst of these concerns she mentioned that 'Lady Jersey had heard that Ly Harriet d'Orsay had quitted her worthless companion & joined her aunt, the wife of an Irish Bishop. I wish she may be able to annul her imperfect marriage & recover the enjoyment of her own property.'[6] It seems that amid the political and social upheaval the break-up of d'Orsay's marriage was being seen as social light relief, with which Society might divert itself from the tales of burning ricks in the country or the machinations of the Reform Bill.

On the day that Lady Holland was sitting in Holland House scribbling her letter of current affairs and gossip to her son, Lady Charleville was also writing a letter about her son and his entanglement with the d'Orsay household. 'Tullamore, it is but too true, never was out of the house; and affiche'd, by going on the Dicky with the party to races parties, park etc etc, his association with them. Whether the Ct. wished to get him to gamble or had the views imputed to him by everybody, I cannot be as convinced as others are. The poor young creature', she wrote of Harriet, 'was considered a wanton by those who cd. not believe in the impressions of early education, and who saw her with Lady Blessington.' However, 'the young victim no sooner was aware of the dangerous situation she was in, than she withdrew herself from Ly Blessington's House and is now under the protection of her family; but *where* is a conceal'd thing not to be trusted to paper.' For the first time she conceded that Harriet might be involved with Tullamore. 'If she loves Tullamore I do pity her from my heart: but at 19 she will soon get the better of a weakness too natural under such circumstances.'[7]

In a letter of 20 August to her daughter, Lady Charleville described a dinner at Greenwich at which both Tullamore and his wife seemed out of sorts, she retiring to lie down, 'over eated I fancy',[8] while Tullamore was 'clearly out of spirits – he told me that he had been *cupped* the night before'.[9] Lady Charleville took an indulgent view of her son's hangover, hoping that drink would alleviate his sufferings from 'agitation of mind, late sittings in the house and hot weather combined'.[10]

She then proceeded to discuss intimate details of d'Orsay's sex life, and the promise that he had allegedly made to Lady Blessington not to consummate his marriage for four years:

> This promise unluckily he kept for three years only – this last yr. he lived with his innocent poor wife which enraged the Lady and led to the last schemes now frustrated. Had it not been, Lady Harriet might have got back her fortune – as it is, she is to try only for an amicable separation, not a divorce, and to get half her income: poor little soul, she was a victim and an innocent one – think what a match for poor Tullamore £8000 pa [£360,000 in today's values] if he had been content to wait a little.[11]

There is a breathtaking callousness about Lady Charleville's calculation, all the more disturbing for its juxtaposition with an almost suffocating maternal indulgence that she herself described as the 'twaddle of an old woman'. Her son, however, seems to have behaved with rather less self-interest and rather more dignity than his mother would have credited him with. It would appear that Tullamore was keen to end speculation about his relationship with Harriet d'Orsay and had sought out Lady Mountjoy. On 23 August Lady Charleville wrote that Tullamore was 'truly happy that Lady MtJoy testified her approbation of his conduct, and really she desir'd I might tell him that she shd. always love him for his proper advice to Ly Harriet'.[12] In the same letter Lady Charleville does her best to depict Seamore Place as little better than a violent brothel, with 'a female cook who is lying in & has no husband', while the 'Count's violence was extreme he called her [Harriet] twenty *Catins* [prostitutes] and Lord Tullamore was the mark, because it is evident that she preferred him to Ld Forester and the rest of the pack'.[13]

Evidently life at Seamore Place was no bower of bliss, and one possible complexion to put on the events is that d'Orsay, notoriously prickly when his honour and amour propre were involved, was concerned that his wife was spreading her favours around a bit too freely for his liking – the role of cuckold is hardly compatible with that of fashion leader. Perhaps it was this state of affairs that had prompted him to have sex with his wife and break the covenant that he had made with Lady Blessington. Maybe he felt that if she was looking for sex, it was better that she found it at home.

The rumours that surrounded her in Paris had, to read between the lines of Lady Charleville's correspondence, followed her to London, where some considered her a wanton and where she had been clearly flirting with Tullamore, Forester and 'the rest of the pack'. Whether this flirtation actually amounted to anything other than the mild diversion of a young woman trapped in an unhappy marriage is not clear, but it would seem that Tullamore had taken pity on the young woman, whereupon she had coquettishly manipulated him, playing up her situation and suggesting to him that he perform the role of selfless knight to her damsel in distress. There seems to have been sufficient sense of chivalry in Tullamore for him to prove receptive to the notion, and if he himself was unhappy in his own marriage, the chance of dalliance with an attractive young woman would have been most welcome. As the following letter written by Harriet to Tullamore would seem to indicate, he had at the very least been a shoulder to cry on.

Dear Lord Tullamore

Our interview was so short on Satd. previous to my leaving town that I had not time to express my feelings as strongly as I should have wished on the subject of Cte d'Orsay's communications to you – At first I felt rather annoyed at your repeating them to me though I now believe that a friendly feeling for both parties induced you to do so – I cannot however in common justice to myself rest under such accusations – I wish to speak if possible calmly & dispassionately upon the subject & more in justification of myself than in accusation of others – Cte d'Orsay is perfectly aware that during our residence in Paris *had* I *even had every inclination* to act as he assumes me to have done I could not have put it into practice – All the persons who were in the habit of coming to the House must be aware that I was never alone with any of them except perhaps the one or two minutes that Lady B used to be sometimes putting on her bonnet – he knows that not a creature could come in or go out of the house without the knowledge of his [illegible] who was completely in his confidence & heeded his authority – & that I never had the power even had I the inclination of seeing anyone alone – this I can bring many to prove – likewise the same thing in S_ Place – As to what he says of Charles de Mornay there is something perfectly absurd in the idea of a professed Libertine being driven out of the house by the advances of a person of 16 – besides he visited constantly up to the day of his leaving Paris –

What is remarkable about this lengthy letter is its defensive tone. After the most perfunctory of preambles, she launches into detailed refutations of various accusations. Either she was so obsessed with their lack of justification and her own innocence that she could not wait to unburden herself. Or these stories were by now so well known

around Society that there was simply no point in her dressing up a
letter with polite 'small talk'. There is also some ambiguity to be
detected in this letter's tone; the desperation of a young woman of
character trapped in an invidious domestic situation mingles with
over-zealous protestations of innocence that might be over-
compensating for a guilty conscience. She continues:

> As to Mr Cradock I never was alone with him – the circum-
> stance he alludes to was utterly different to what he represents it
> as he knows perfectly well – I put all propriety out of the ques-
> tion – could there exist such madness as to allow of such a
> circumstance taking place in the presence of two people Miss
> Powers and young Ornano being in the room & the folding
> doors open between the drawing rooms – persons coming in
> and out every moment – As to Cte Waleski he never even was an
> admirer of mine – he was a great deal in the house but Cte
> d'O____y knows perfectly well that it was not for *me* – we never
> interchanged but common civilities except on one occasion in
> which he confided to me several things that had been repeated to
> him by Lady B_ about me. No! had he told me this I should
> d[amn] all & more than all that I have borne but *he* knows he
> never did – never could have done so – No – he must feel if he
> has *one* feeling left – that I have not deserved my fate at his
> hands – he did not love me – I did not please him that could not
> be helped – but *he* knows that when that ill fated marriage took
> place – I was young – (a child) – I was innocent – my heart was
> good and after that I was willing to obey him – & bore from him
> language & conduct that no one else would have endured that I
> have borne it unanswering (he will say that was fear) but also
> uncomplaining – for I hid my wrongs from my family & it was
> my constant aim and endeavor to put Him & Her in the best light
> to them – And what has been my return – As to Her I will not

trust myself to speak of her to you – suffice it to say that though she certainly showed me a fair face and repeatedly told me I was her only comfort etc etc she was at that very time injuring me in *every possible way* – I believe from what various people have told me & from what she wrote to me herself after I left them that she accuses me of *Ingratitude*!!!] – C'est un peut fort – I never before heard that it was necessary to be grateful for having been deceived betrayed insulted and reviled! – As to his conduct let him remember his letter to my Aunt – where he dares to insult the memory of my dead Mother – how will that [illegible] for him – I could fill volumes on this wretched subject but I do not wish to weary you any further indeed I have too long trespassed upon your patience – I have only one request to make of you which is that you show this to Count d'Orsay this I know you will not wish to do – but I insist upon it as an act of common justice – God who knoweth all things can judge between us as of course what Man who had every desire that his Wife should behave herself well would place her under the protection of a Person like Ly B_ set *her* up as an example for her to follow & respect her in such a manner as to induce every person coming to the House to pay her attentions that it would be impossible with prudence to receive – I might dwell long on this subject mais à quoi bon – the thing is as clear as day light – & even you must see it – it appears that He makes out that he told me before hand what I was to expect – I deny it *altogether*. I do not pretend to say he was in love with me or wished to appear so – *that* I acquit him of – but I would ask him whether he ever informed me that he was the Lover of my father's Wife whether he ever told me that it was his intention to blight every prospect & make my life a burden to me covering my name with insult & dishonor from what I have stated you may imagine how far the statements you hear are to be credited – I believe you

mentioned [abbreviation of title] Charles I shall merely say on
that head that I can prove that I ever was alone with him for *one
second* & that as soon as we heard from a friend of ours that his
attentions excited observation we instantly left Naples – I do
not wonder at anything they may choose to say of course it is
their part to make me appear in as bad a light as possible – but I
maintain & every right minded person will be of the same opinion that supposing *all* they said was perfectly true it does not in
the least alter the case as respects them – it does not extenuate his
conduct in the least – quite the contrary – it makes it worse.

The body of Harriet's letter makes her aim clear: by asking that it
is shown to d'Orsay she is effectively stating that this is an open letter,
her version of events and an account of her feelings. With her emphasis on naming witnesses to her behaviour and the invocation of such
quasi-legal terminology as 'act of common justice', 'God who
knoweth all things can judge between us', 'I deny it altogether', 'that
I acquit him of' and 'I can prove that', she is in effect giving a formal
statement, not to any legal power but to that rather more demanding
and exacting body, Society. If fashionable London was convening a
kangaroo court to judge the morality of life in Seamore Place, she was
pleading innocent to all charges that might be brought against her
and presenting society with a melodramatic scenario, in which she
was casting herself as a young, wounded, innocent terrorised by a
wicked husband who was the lover of her evil, duplicitous stepmother.
She finishes:

Those who will also ere long know much hitherto only suspected will also judge which has been the injured party –
whether I succeed or whether I do not it will be some consolation
that my story hitherto kept in the back ground will be brought to
light with *all the force of truth* nothing vague or contradictory or

unsubstantiated – Up to this time they have had considerably the advantage they had lived in the world (which I have not) & been very unsparing of their histories – now it will be my turn – & vague reports and fake accusations will not serve & whatever may be the result I do not imagine they will gain any additional credit by it – but now I must conclude hoping you will excuse my writing so long a letter on this painful topic & believe me

Always yr sincere friend

Harriette

Oct 13th

It is no use them thinking now to frighten me there was a time when the fear of exposing my father's name to obloquy & bringing my secret affairs before the curious eyes of a scandal loving Public may have intimidated me – but that day is gone by – I am now driven to desperation and prepared to face the worst.[14]

This hitherto unpublished letter shines further light into the murky sex lives of the d'Orsays and Blessingtons. Almost from the very date of their marriage there seem to have been worries about Harriet's fidelity. She does protest rather a great deal, perhaps too much, of her innocence of affairs. However, the image of a strumpet is at odds with the picture of the listless, sickly woman given by visitors to the various houses d'Orsay occupied. This letter also portrays d'Orsay as at some times indifferent to her and at others obsessively jealous to the point of accusing her of lusting after almost every man who crossed the threshold. Such obsessive behaviour is quite typical of d'Orsay – turning over in his mind a glance or a smile that his wife had bestowed upon a male visitor to their house and thus enlarging it until it became a sexual relationship.

For her part Harriet is quite happy to confirm unequivocally that d'Orsay was her stepmother's lover: such an accusation coming from someone who had lived under the same roof for four years has more weight than idle speculation and gossip from those outside.

From what she mentions of d'Orsay's communications with Tullamore, the latter is cast in a favourable light as being something of a mediator and even marriage counsellor. Indeed later correspondence shows that he remained on cordial terms with both parties and did his best to bring about as equitable a settlement to the tawdry business as he could. For example, d'Orsay wrote to him in October 1834:

Mon Cher Tullamore

Before leaving for Newmarket, I must thank you for the efforts you are making to smooth over the arrangements between Harriet and myself. The fact is that it's very hard to work out and I don't think that we'll be able to do so, since each party has such differing views. So it is with all the difficulty in the world that I've decided that only my lawyer should be in touch with the opposition, following the bad judgement they showed with their suggestions in Ireland: – For a long time I've been resolved (against the counsel of my advisors) that Lady Harriet should benefit from half of the proceeds of the properties in Ireland. To some, this has been viewed as an act of generosity, to me it seems merely one of fairness – whichever way, you can see that Lady Harriet's financial state would have been very different had she not married me, since she would have found herself with her 10,000 pounds paid to her, at least this way I have the consolation of feeling I'm helping her – She is embarrassed by this, and I would have felt the same way if I had not found friends who were very happy to assist me – l would be delighted if it were possible to come to an arrangement that allows Lady Harriet her freedom, and it now remains to be seen whether this can be carried out in a way that will not offend either party's honour. It is for this reason that Mr Powell must meet with Mr Harrison.

As far as the trial goes, threats and all that business make me laugh, I find myself defiant in the face of such things – I have more material goods than I alone know what to do with, and this should make them think again about their plans, so I'll let you decide whether I am a man who is easily intimidated. Although I confess I'd be angry to have nothing by which to remember what I owe Blessington – Many times I've tried to open channels of communication, but I keep fearing that people will think I am being pushy, yet you can see that by having an impartial inter-mediary many matters are pending. At the moment, if I follow the advice I'm getting, I'd have to reject any forms of commu-nication, apart from those we dared start in Ireland. You have to give me credit for wanting things to be fair, and since it's more than likely that they will become public after the turns events have taken, I'd be much happier if people could see this had been my intention from the outset. Lady Harriet has suffered, for she has a family who have access to many good counsels and yet they've been unable to find even one to help her now – that seems to me the main point – Anyway, enough of this, I'm leav-ing for J.h. tomorrow morning. On my return I shall see whether Powell has decided to meet with the collection of advi-sors and lawyers that Lady Harriet believes she needs to score points over those whom they're discussing.

I remain your devoted

Votre très devoué

d'Orsay[15]

As time advanced, d'Orsay's money worries would become more pressing. He wrote the following letter to Lord Charleville in June 1838:

Mon cher Charleville

[This is Lord Tullamore – he has inherited his father's title]

You wrote to me a few days ago to say that Lady Harriet 'had determined to abide by her agreement'. It appears she's mocking you because now, after all the papers have been signed and sealed, Mr Manning has just suggested that Mr Powell should make a change to the deed. I cannot consent to this and even if I were happy to, such a move is outside my powers. Delaying the conclusion of formalities, as she is demanding, is preventing me from lending her money, so she's losing out, as are her brother and others. It makes no difference to me, my affairs are in order and I've been told that the papers have been signed in front of reliable witnesses and are impossible to annul, even with all the dishonesty one might be tempted to bring into play. So my counsels don't see the point of me asking you to communicate to Lady Harriet that it is improper to go back on matters that are signed and sealed; to make objections that will delay the collection of 200,000 £S.

Be advised that it's not a sinecure that you've accepted by acting so obligingly as a trusted friend and trustee. This whole business must disgust you,

Votre très devoué
Alfred d'Orsay[16]

The marriage that the late Lord Blessington had intended to be his legacy descended into nothing more than a tawdry squabble for money.

After the breakdown of her marriage Harriet wound up in Paris, where she would sparkle at dinners and, during the late 1830s, live openly as the mistress of the Duke d'Orléans, about whom the story of the ringlet is told. After his death in a carriage accident she enjoyed the protection of numerous other aristocrats, until d'Orsay's death, when she returned to England, married and lived quietly near Sandringham. She reworked her life in print with contributions to *Ainsworth's Magazine* and a novel published in French in 1851, which appeared in England under the title *Clouded Happiness*. It was a camp, lurid, titillating Gothic romp relying heavily on melodrama, preposterous coincidence and, as first novels often do, a considerable amount of the author's own experience. Its milieu is raffish high Society seasoned with the odd brigand, its locations the capitals of Europe with particular reference to Naples. The male protagonist is called d'Arville, and it is interesting to note Harriet's prefatory remarks about him.

> In the character of Fernand d'Arville I have endeavoured to pourtray [*sic*] the restless sentimentality of the young men of the day, ardently seeking the delights of heedless pleasure, and leaving true happiness behind them; capricious and ungrateful, crouching beneath the temporary passion that consumes them, and imperiously domineering over that they have inspired; alternately ruthless tyrants and most abject slaves, open to the inculpation of innumerable faults, and yet without any sympathy for suffering, leniency to errors or compassion for remorse.[17]

If, as seems likely, d'Arville is a fictional reworking of d'Orsay, then twenty years after the events of the summer and early autumn of 1831, Harriet did not remember him with anything other than undiluted enmity. About halfway through *Clouded Happiness*, she pens a poignant paragraph: 'Life is but a chain of mingled grief and suffering, of which every individual holds a link; and that being undoubtedly the case, is it not our bounden, our sacred duty to entertain sentiments of forgiveness of offence, and eschew the delusive pleasures [of] revenge?'[18] Sadly Harriet d'Orsay never seemed able to entertain those elusive 'sentiments of forgiveness'. Others, however, found it easier to forgive. On 16 September, Lady Charleville wrote a long letter to her daughter in which she writes, 'Yesterday Ct d'Orsay sent me the portrait of Massaniello original by Salvator Rosa, which the princes of Belvedere at Naples have possessed since 1647 . . . & was part of Murat's pillage – I am to keep it a week.'[19] As well as being socially cognisant Lady Charleville was an art snob, and d'Orsay knew how to deal with snobs. It would seem that his charm and the loan of a rare early work by a fashionable seventeenth-century master were sufficient to erase from Lady Charleville's mind the calumnies with which her letters had been filled only weeks before.

CHAPTER SIXTEEN

The Glass of Fashion

SEPARATED FROM HIS WIFE, IT WOULD HAVE BEEN DIFFICULT FOR d'Orsay to remain under the same roof as his quondam stepmother-in-law without attracting outright social condemnation. Moreover, if, as Lady Charleville's assertion would suggest, Lady Blessington was upset by his sexual relationship with Harriet, the atmosphere would have been tense, especially as Harriet's sudden departure had placed Seamore Place under Society's magnifying glass. However irregular the relationship, and by this time there are reasonable grounds to suppose that d'Orsay had been the sexual partner of Lord Blessington, his wife and his daughter, certain conventions had to be observed. For all their originality and the undoubted strength of feeling between them, Count d'Orsay and Lady Blessington sought the approval of Society, while at the same time wanting to conquer it, she as its premier hostess, he as its chief dandy. Despite their marked eccentricity and the fact that they functioned at the limits of acceptable behaviour, they were still governed by the proprieties of the day – to conquer Society they had to remain in it. And so d'Orsay moved out of Seamore Place and round the corner to 22 Curzon Street.

In 1844, a novel was published which caused a scandal. Called *D'Horsay; or the Follies of the Day*, its author an anonymous 'man of fashion' was actually John Mills, a popular author and sporting novelist, compared to Surtees. It was less a novel and more a loosely connected series of louche scenes featuring thinly disguised portraits of leading characters of the day, involved in all manner of legally and morally suspect activities. It was suppressed shortly after publication and was regarded as unfit to reprint until more than half a century later, when those depicted between its covers were safely dead.

It is the sort of book it would have been very difficult to publish any later in Victoria's reign as its tone is, even now, mildly shocking – it accuses leading public figures of the day of group sex, the sharing of mistresses and the evasion of creditors, with only the flimsy figleaf of transparently obvious aliases. D'Horsay is of course d'Orsay, the Earl of Chesterlane is the Earl of Chesterfield, Lord Bitchfield is Lord Lichfield, the Marquis of Hereford is the Marquis of Hertford. Others do not even merit aliases and are just insulted. 'That swarthy, circumcised driver of the cabriolet' is the anti-Semitically loaded description of the future Prime Minister and royal favourite Benjamin Disraeli.

The book begins with a description of d'Horsay's house:

In the vicinity of Curzon Street, Mayfair, there was, and, for aught we know to the contrary, there may be, a house of strange and peculiar architecture. Its construction was such as to give an appearance of ample room, whereas, in truth, it was the veriest nut-shell of a place that can well be conceived. The wide door, which opened only in the middle, formed quite two-thirds of the front, and yet, to the casual observer, it would seem the portal of a mansion of imposing aspect. Never was there such a deceptive house! How it contrived to hug its neighbours so closely, and blend them, as it were, with its own bricks and mortar, is a mystery which we confess ourselves inadequate to solve. Sufficient to say, that if a house obtaining a character under false pretences is an indictable offence, this, of all others, should be selected for exemplary and condign punishment. The interior, too, had a correponding [*sic*] effect; for although elegant and refined taste was displayed in all its garniture and profusion of luxurious trifles, yet the same crafty attempt to appear above its size was palpable everywhere. Large mirrors, multiplying their reflected surfaces, and some cunningly devised to be approached by marble steps, gave an expansive semblance to the rooms, and all in all, 'to seem what it was not,' was declared in every brick, nook, and corner of this false and subtle edifice.[1]

Putting aside the authorial device of using the deceptive architecture of the house to indicate a similar trait in its occupant, the general description of the place has a ring of authenticity: the use of mirrors to create an illusion of space is very d'Orsay, as is the 'profusion of luxurious trifles'. Moreover, the portrayal of the house as little more than a pied-à-terre for d'Orsay sounds right, as he still spent much of his time at Seamore Place, acting as Lady Blessington's master of ceremonies.

It was at this juncture that d'Orsay's fame exploded. While Lady Blessington emerged from the scandal of Harriet's departure bruised, d'Orsay seems to have shrugged off any suggestion of impropriety and immersed himself fully in the social life of the city. Within a short time of his return to London, he appears to have reasserted the hold he had enjoyed over fashion in the London of the early 1820s, except that now as a man in his early thirties he exercised his influence with considerably more skill and panache. While d'Orsay's marital difficulties made Lady Blessington a pariah, they merely added to his exotic appeal.

'Although, of course, the aristocratic and rigidly virtuous British Matrons would have nothing to do with Lady Blessington, as usual, by that curious and very English convention, the lady's *chevalier* was a welcome guest everywhere and sought after by the most exclusive hostesses,'[2] is the analysis of the situation shortly after the break-up of d'Orsay's marriage given in an early-twentieth-century biography of William Harrison Ainsworth.

D'Orsay was a man in demand. 'We had a very brilliant reunion at Bulwers last night. Among the notables were Lords Strangford and Mulgrave, with the latter of whom I had a great deal of conversation, Count d'Orsay, the famous Parisian dandy,' wrote a breathless young novelist to his sister in March 1832.[3] The young novelist was Benjamin Disraeli, who five years before, while in his early twenties, had published the successful dandy novel *Vivian Grey*, albeit anonymously.

Disraeli was a man on the make, hoping to achieve social, literary and political success. The importance of d'Orsay's friendship to the younger ambitious man was considerable, as his obvious pride in the association reveals. 'D'Orsay attacked me yesterday in Bond St. attired with a splendor I cannot describe, so dishevelled were his curls, so brilliant his bijouteries and the shifting tints of his party-colored costume. He knows who I am,' he wrote, almost exultantly, in another letter a few days later.[4]

Far from being cast out, d'Orsay was sought out by fashionable Society. In fact there is an argument to be made that for a fast set of rich, or would-be rich, young men d'Orsay *was* fashionable Society. Certainly he was one of fashion's leaders. In *D'Horsay; or the Follies of the Day*, the eponymous protagonist's fashion credentials are clearly enumerated:

> The Marquis D'Horsay was, indeed, 'the glass of fashion, and the mould of form.' From the colour and tie of the kerchief which adorned his neck, to the spurs ornamenting the heels of

his patent boots, he was the original for countless copyists, particularly and collectively. Even the brow which the ducal coronet occasionally pressed, was proud to wear the hat imitated from the model, which every aspiring Tittlebat Titmouse of the age strove to copy in his gossamer. The hue and cut of his many faultless coats, the turn of his closely fitting inexpressibles [trousers], the shade of his gloves, the knot of his scarf, were studied by the motley multitude with greater interest and avidity than objects more profitable and worthy of their regard, perchance, could possibly hope to obtain. Nor did the beard that flourished luxuriantly upon the delicate and nicely-chiselled features of the Marquis, escape the universal imitation. Those who could not cultivate their scanty crops into the desirable arrangement, had recourse to art and stratagem to supply the natural deficiency. Atkinson and Rowland revelled in the attempts. From the extreme east to the far west ends of London, lights and shadows of the Marquis were plentiful as daisies in merry May. Wristbands, both false and real, were turned over cuffs of every dye and texture, and, in short, from the most essential article of the modish lion's dress to the most trifling, not an item was left confined to its pristine state of originality. And this general monomania was not restricted only to 'the fashion which adorned his person.' The style of his equipage, the richly ornamented harness, the dainty stepping of his cavalier horse, the very boots of the tiger-cub in attendance in the rear, were all objects of envy and close imitation. Many a hired nag has had reason to sorrow for the high-stepping example.[5]

A contemporary poem described d'Orsay thus:

> Patting the crest of his well-managed steed,
> Proud of his action, d'Orsay vaunts the breed;

A coat of chocolate, a vest of snow;
Well brush'd his whiskers, as his boots below;
A short-napp'd beaver, prodigal in brim,
With trousers tighten'd to a well-turn'd limb;
O'er play, o'er dress, extends his wide domain,
And Crockford trembles when he calls a main.[6]

The 1830s and early 1840s were d'Orsay's era. For a period of some fifteen or twenty years he effectively ruled male fashion, with his influence extending into areas as diverse as equestrianism, domestic décor, entertaining and even pets. It is almost impossible at such a distance to analyse and deconstruct d'Orsay's celebrity; it was just what d'Orsay did best. He was the ultimate dandy, a more interesting and complex character than Brummell. His stance on matters of dress was diametrically opposed to that of his dandy predecessor: Brummell favoured an elaborate simplicity that elevated the plain country costume of the day to that of the uniform of gentlemen. As his friend and biographer Captain Jesse put it:

His chief aim was to avoid anything marked; one of his aphorisms being that the severest mortification that a gentleman could incur was to attract observation in the street by his outward appearance. He exercised the most correct taste in the selection of each article of apparel, of a form and colour harmonious with all the rest, for the purpose of producing a perfect, elegant general effect.

Restraint was paramount: 'There was, in fact, nothing extreme about Brummell's personal appearance but his extreme cleanliness and neatness, and whatever time and attention he devoted to his dress the result was perfection; no perfumes, he used to say, but very fine linen, plenty of it, and country washing.'[7]

By contrast d'Orsay opted for sensory overload. Whereas Brummell affected to enjoy a stylish anonymity of dress, the count liked to dazzle passers-by with a polychromatic display; whereas Brummell would show but two links of his watch chain, d'Orsay would have at least a couple of chains looped across the front of his waistcoat; whereas Brummell's waistcoat was fastened with buttons of brass, d'Orsay favoured the glint of gold; and whereas Brummell eschewed perfume, d'Orsay was addicted to it, favouring 'gloves scented with eau de Cologne or eau de jasmin',[8] being 'in the habit of taking perfumed baths'[9] and using perfumed visiting cards supplied by Mitchell's, booksellers and stationers.

The world of fashion was as keen to follow d'Orsay into excesses of colour, texture and glitz as it had been eager to emulate Brummell's contrived simplicity of dress. By the mid-1830s fashionable London was doing its best to dress d'Orsay-style, and his appearance was 'servilely copied'.[10] The d'Orsay craze even reached the Houses of Parliament. In 1836, in one of Dickens's early parliamentary sketches Thomas Slingsby Duncombe, the well-connected radical MP and close friend of d'Orsay, is characterised as 'That smart-looking fellow in the black coat with velvet facings and cuffs, who wears his d'Orsay hat so rakishly'.[11]

One observer even claimed that 'he occasionally indulged in exaggerations which he must have very well known exceeded the limits of good taste: some said there was a spice of waggery in this proceeding, and that he enjoyed the fun of seeing how far he could exercise his influence. His fanciful waistcoats, rich in embroidery, soon became the *point de mire* of fashionable assemblies, and there was always a fierce contest among the young coxcombs of the day to be first to obtain a facsimile of the latest novelty the Count had brought out.'[12] At first this entertained d'Orsay immensely: he exerted power over others far richer and better born than he had been; numerous members of the aristocracy were his puppets. There was probably something of this spirit of marionettish mischief to be found in the story that he instructed the Earl of Chesterfield to dress just in blue, an instruction that Chesterfield was apparently only too happy to obey.

And of course when something special was required for an important party or costume ball, dozens of aristocrats and Society figures would seek out d'Orsay and canvass his opinion on what they should wear. It was with a curious mixture of weariness and pride that in May 1842 the count wrote to his friend Lord Lichfield, by then living in Naples, of the preparations for 'le Bal de la Reine' in May 1842, recounting the costumes to be worn by Chesterfield, Cardigan, Beaufort and others, adding that 'These men have taken me for their costumier, I've dressed about thirty of them.'[13] There is the sense here that having cast him as its costumier, fashionable society was not going to release him from that role – what had begun as fun and frivolity was eventually to become a prison. It was, however, a prison from which d'Orsay was never quite sure that he wanted to be released.

He was a centre of attention and, not content with his advice, some even wanted the clothes off his back. On one occasion Gronow, the diminutive dandy and diarist, dubbed Nogrow by d'Orsay, went so far as to ask him to give him a particularly splendid waistcoat. The exchange ran thus: '"Oh, my dear Count, you really must give me that waistcoat." "Wiz plésure, Nogrow," replied the Count, with a charming French bow and a courteous French smile; "but what shall you do wiz him? Ah! he shall make you one dressing-gown."'[14]

These colourful waistcoats were everywhere. 'I remember, with the vividness of only yesterday, a certain dinner party at 25 George Street, in the spring of 1835, "the season" when London is so gay and brilliant, after the dark English winter,' wrote one man of fashion, recalling, at the distance of almost half a century, a dinner party given by Lord Lyndhurst.

Among the guests on that occasion was the handsome and petted Count d'Orsay; somewhat late Disraeli appeared. His marked Jewish features, his coal-black hair, and especially one long, truant curl, which, with an expressive, impatient action he tossed back from his brow, impressed him sharply on my memory. At that time the waistcoat was the especial feature of a fine gentleman's attire. Disraeli exclaimed as he entered, 'What a beautiful pattern! Where did you find it my lord?' [The stuff was what we know under the general class of shawl pattern or Persian.] Upon this a general excitement prevailed, and all the guests simultaneously threw back their coats to allow a freer inspection of that portion of the dress beneath.[15]

It must have been a memorable, if cornea-searing, occasion. But with d'Orsay's talent for exuberant display came a hint of sexual ambivalence; Gronow was not alone in noting that 'he took as much care of his beauty as a woman might have done'.[16]

However d'Orsay saw his appearance as his passport to fame and a position in Society. The essential core of d'Orsay that had been revealed to those who had become intimate with him in his Italian days was increasingly obscured by 'marked peculiarities of dress and deportment'[17] which were the mannerisms and costume necessary for him to get into character and act out his role. His performances were rides in Hyde Park, drives to Richmond or out to Blackwall for a whitebait dinner, appearances at the ballet and the gaming tables. His nominal separation from Lady Blessington at Seamore Place enabled him to enlarge a sense of his own identity. He was no longer the exotic French hanger-on, but a star in his own right. A small holiday he took in Paris in the autumn of 1837 warranted column after column of humorous encomium in the weekly *Charivari*, reporting on such minutiae of his life as how he gave a guinea (around £50 today) to the boy who sold him the matches to light his cigar every day.* There was a remarkable appetite for d'Orsay stories, and in the flesh he was even more extraordiinary than represented in the press.

* Another version of the 'guinea for a light' story provides further illumination of d'Orsay's character and demonstrates an inherent kindness that lurked behind such apparent extravagance. According to an anecdote of the Countess de Bassanville, reported in Teignmouth Shore's biography of d'Orsay, the count stopped at an inn and was about to call for a light for his cigar, when a boy offered him the match with which he was about to light his own pipe.

> D'Orsay, who was struck by the boy's politeness and good looks, began to chat with him.
>
> 'From what country do you come?'
>
> 'From Wales, my lord.'
>
> 'And don't you mind leaving your mountains for the smoky streets of London?'
>
> 'I'd go back without minding at all,' answered the boy, 'but poor folk, can't do what they want, and God knows when I'll be going back to my old mother who's crying and waiting for me.'
>
> 'You're ambitious then?'
>
> 'I want to get bread. I'm young and strong, and work's better paid in London than at home. That's why I've come.'
>
> 'Well,' said d'Orsay, 'I'd like to help you make your fortune. Here's a guinea for your match. To-morrow, come to Hyde Park when the promenade is full; bring with you a box of matches, and when you see me with a lot of people round me, come up and offer me your ware.'
>
> Naturally enough the boy turned up at the right hour and the right place.
>
> 'Who'll buy my matches,' he called out.
>
> 'Ah, it is you,' said d'Orsay. 'Give me one quick to light my cigar.'
>
> Another guinea – and the Count said carelessly to those grouped around him –
>
> 'Just imagine, that I couldn't smoke a cigar which is not lit with one of this boy's matches – others seem to me horrible.'
>
> No sooner hinted than done; off went the matches and down came the guineas, and addresses even were given for delivery of a further supply. (Teignmouth Shore, pp. 121–2)

After such an endorsement the boy became the most sought after and presumably the richest match seller in town. A cynical eye might also note that d'Orsay was much taken by the youth's looks and manner and might suggest that more than a mere match was exchanged for the Count's guineas.

A full-dress entrance by d'Orsay was a jaw-dropping event, as Thomas Carlyle wrote to his brother a few weeks after the 'Phoebus Apollo of dandyism' had paid him a visit in the spring of 1839. D'Orsay, 'escorted by poor little Chorley [journalist on the *Athenaeum*], came whirling hither in a chariot that struck all Chelsea into mute amazement with splendour. Chorley's under-jaw went like the hopper or under-riddle of a pair of fanners, such was his terror on bringing such a splendour into actual contact with such grimness. Nevertheless, we did amazingly well the Count and I. He was a tall fellow of six foot three, built like a tower, with floods of dark auburn hair, with a beauty, with an adornment unsurpassable on this planet.'[18]

Once Carlyle's wife had recovered from the excitement of the 'prancing of steeds' and arrival of his carriage 'all resplendent with sky blue and silver, like a piece of the Coronation Procession', she wrote to her cousin with details of the count's dress: 'sky-blue satin cravat, yards of gold chain, white French gloves, light drab great-coat lined with velvet of the same colour, invisible inexpressibles, skin-coloured and fitting like a glove, etc., etc.'. She was struck by the contrast between the two men: 'Carlyle in his grey plaid suit and his tub chair, looking blankly at the Prince of Dandies; and the Prince of Dandies on an opposite chair, all resplendent as a diamond beetle, looking blandly at *him*'.[19]

It is almost as if, with his wardrobe and his paraphernalia, he was erecting a set of defences around himself through which few could pass to discover the essential man behind the finery. He had trained his temperament, but at the expense of the quality that had so impressed Byron in Genoa all those years earlier. Of course these were different times, a different town, and Byron and Carlyle were utterly different men. Yet each made a considerable contribution to shaping the ideals and sensibilities of their generations. And both men were curious about d'Orsay.

Carlyle was to become the Victorian essayist and thinker *par excellence*, and it was in 1833 that serialisation of his *Sartor Resartus* began. Ostensibly a book purporting to introduce readers to the work of an obscure German philosopher of clothing, it was in fact an exploration of a wide range of issues: Utilitarianism, religion, the need for heroes, the nobility of continence, the morality of work and so on. Although poorly received at first, it came to be seen as a defining work in British cultural history, which marked the end of Romanticism and ushered in the period that we know as Victorian. In 1855 George Eliot was able to write, 'there is hardly a superior or active mind of this generation that has not been modified by Carlyle's writings'.[20] Such was his eminence that, when he lay dying at his house on Cheyne Row in 1881, Queen Victoria had a watch placed on his house so that she might receive bulletins about the eminent man's health.

But although Carlyle and d'Orsay exchanged visits during the 1830s, there never existed between them the warmth that had flourished between the count and Byron. The most significant difference is that, by the time he met Carlyle, d'Orsay was on his way to becoming a specimen of a type, a casualty of his reputation: one wanted to see the spectacle rather than the man. The perspicacious youngster whose journal had so impressed Byron was disappearing behind the myth of the quintessential man about town and d'Orsay was at this time a willing participant in burying his other self – burning his journal and playing up to the image he had forged.

The reaction of the austere and cerebral Carlyles to the sensuous and decadent d'Orsay is interesting in that it is a highly articulate description of the impact that the Frenchman had on those who were not part of the aristocratic or self-consciously fashionable circles (at the time Chelsea was an unfashionable suburb and not the chic residential *quartier* it is today). As Carlyle noted, the immediate impression he made was with his imposing and dramatic appearance. To his impressive physique he added a new style of dressing that Mrs Carlyle so carefully records. This was a creation every bit as carefully prepared and meticulously worked as the cantos of Byron or the pages of Carlyle's *Sartor Resartus*.

Typically d'Orsay would wear a coat 'setting tight round the waist, and (that it may give a resemblance in the male form to that of the female) being very full in the skirts'.[21] The coat would be thrown back to such an extent that one of d'Orsay's imitators was described as giving the appearance of 'having lately been exposed to some strong gusts of wind in his front'.[22] The thrown-back coat would allow for ample display of perhaps a pair of waistcoats adorned by a chain or two and maybe a few seals dangling for effect. Gloves would be in the shade 'feuille morte' that he asked a banker in Frankfurt to source for him, or have a tint of primroses. The display would be finished off with a neckcloth that enveloped the chest and climbed to just below the chin. It was a killer look, to which at least three tailors are reported to have contributed.

In the preface to the 1902 edition of *D'Horsay; or The Follies of the Day*, d'Orsay's tailor is named as Cook. Henry Creed, at 33 Clifford Street, is mentioned elsewhere as having been another of his tailors. In 1961 Henry's grandson Charles Creed wrote that d'Orsay 'wore clothes splendidly, he knew everybody who was anybody, and whither he went the beau-monde followed', adding that 'They followed him to Henry Creed.'[23] According to Richard Walker, author of *The Savile Row Story: An Illustrated History*, d'Orsay's patronage was sufficient to assure Creed of 'fame and fortune for the family business'.[24]

A few doors along from Henry Creed, at 10 Clifford Street, was Herr Stultz. Stultz was a fashionable German military tailor who features in novels of the period including Thackeray's *Pendennis* and Bulwer's *Pelham*. According to one source,

> Herr Stultz made a wonderfully good thing of his French client's custom. All Fashion rushed to his show-rooms. Such was the

Count's *prestige*, that 'Tailor to M. le Comte d'Orsay' was a far more privileged title than 'Tailor to His Majesty.' It was said, moreover, that the client whose custom was so *prestigious* and so profitable, did not disdain to share its advantages. By a delicate arrangement, each time the integuments of this exquisite were sent home, he was to find a bank-note of a certain amount in one of the pockets – a little pocket-money, in fact. After a time, however, the tailor began to think he was paying too dear for his whistle, and that he might, perhaps, begin to relax in the liberality of his dividends; so he, one day, sent in a suit, *pur et simple*, with nothing but its own merits to recommend it. D'Orsay's surprise was extreme on discovering this departure from the established practice, on the regularity of which, moreover, he altogether relied; but he was equal to the occasion. Calling his valet, he told him to have Mr. Stultz's parcel returned to him for alteration, with a message to the effect that 'he had forgotten to line the pockets.'[25]

D'Orsay's taste in clothes was not restricted to garments of the greatest expense and most refined quality. There was a contrapuntal and daring quality about some of his clothing choices that set him apart from the mere follower of fashion, even rather expert ones like Bulwer or Disraeli. It was this inventive irreverence towards fashion that always kept him ahead of his imitators. Among the sartorial innovations with which he is credited is the paletot.

The paletot was a significant feature of nineteenth-century male dress in that it provided an alternative to fitted garments. In reality it was nothing more glamorous than a loose-fitting coat worn by mariners: a sort of early-nineteenth-century duffel coat or donkey jacket. Its impact on the polite dress of the day is described by Farid Chenoune in his *History of Men's Fashion*:

Around 1835 there emerged a fashion that provoked wariness among tailors – the overcoat. Its primary feature was that it did not hug the waist. Rather, it took up where the cloak had left off, since there were no horizontal seams anywhere, nor any pleats under the arms. The overcoat was neither frock coat nor tunic, and a simple overcoat in coarse broadcloth or ratiné fell straight like a sack. Double-breasted, back-vented, firmly buttoned and endowed with large pockets, it had nearly all the features of the sailor's coat that, according to legend, the Comte d'Orsay borrowed one rainy day.[26]

According to another source the legend surrounding the 'invention' of the paletot begins with d'Orsay being caught by a sudden downpour while out riding and finding that his groom had forgotten to bring a suitable outergarment.

D'Orsay was equal to this as to most occasions. He spied a sailor who wore a long, heavy waistcoat which kept him snug.

'Hullo, friend,' called out d'Orsay, pulling up, 'would you like to go into that inn and drink to my health until the rain's over?'

The sailor was naturally enough somewhat surprised, and asked d'Orsay why he was chaffing him.

'I'm not,' said d'Orsay, dismounting and going into the inn, followed by the sailor, 'but I want your vest, sell it me.'

He took out and offered the poor devil ten guineas, assuring him at the same time that he 'could buy another after the rain was over.'

D'Orsay put on the vest over his coat, buttoned it from top to bottom, remounted and rode on to town.

The rain passed over, the sun came out again, and as it was the proper hour to show himself in Hyde Park, d'Orsay showed himself.

'How original! How charming! How delicious!' cried the elegant dandies, astonished by d'Orsay's new garment, 'only a d'Orsay could have thought of such a creation!'

The next day dandies similarly enveloped were 'the thing,' and thus the paletot was invented.[27]

CHAPTER SEVENTEEN

Man about Town and Country, Man of Letters

D'ORSAY'S INFLUENCE EXTENDED WELL BEYOND THE TAILOR'S shop and the fashionable West End. Although his most visible talent was the creation of a wardrobe, his accomplishment and impact in other spheres were considerable. His reputation as a host and a gourmet was not confined to Lady Blessington's salon. He was friendly with the major chefs of the day, including Alexis Soyer of the Reform Club, to whom he wrote a charming note in a book of subscribers to one of Soyer's works.[1]

And when his friend Lord Chesterfield left his position as Master of the Royal Buckhounds, it was d'Orsay who organised a dinner for thirty friends at the Clarendon Hotel on Bond Street, which had acquired fame in the early years of the nineteenth century for its kitchen superintended by 'a French cook, Jacquiers, who contrived to amass a large sum of money in the service of Louis the Eighteenth in England and subsequently with Lord Darnley. This was the only public hotel where you could get a genuine French dinner, and for which you seldom paid less than three or four pounds'[2] (approximately

£150 in current values). D'Orsay's dinner for Chesterfield, at six guineas a head, cost around twice that. It was a prodigious blow-out of a dinner, in two phases:

Premier Service

Potages. – Printannier: à la reine: turtle

Poissons. – Turbot (lobster and Dutch sauces): saumon à la Tartare: rougets à la cardinal: fiture de morue: white bait.

Relevés. – Filet de boeuf à la Napolitaine: dindon à la chipolata: timbale de macaroni: haunch of venison.

Entrées. – Croquettes de volaille: petits pâtés aux huitres: cotelettes d'agneau: purée de champignons: côtelettes d'agneau aux pointes d'asperge: fricandeau de veau à l'oseille: ris de veau piqué aux tomates: côtelettes de pigeons à la Dusselle: chartreuse de légumes aux faisins: filets de cannetons à la Bigarrade: boudins à la Richelieu: sauté de volaille aux truffes: pâté de mouton monté.

Cote. – Boeuf roti: jambon: salade

Second Service

Rots. – Chapons, quails, turkey poults, green goose

Entremets. – Asperges: haricot à la Française: mayonnaise d'homard: gelée Macédoine: aspics d'oeufs de pluvier: Charlotte Russe: gelée Marasquin: crême marbre: corbeille de pâtisserie: vol-au-vent de rhubarb: tourte d'abricots: corbeille des meringues: dressed crab: salade au galatine. – Champignons aux fines herbes.

Relevés. – Soufflé à la vanille: Nesselrode pudding: Adelaide sandwiches: fondues. Pièces montées, &c &c.[3]

During the early 1830s he was also often to be found at Greenwich, eating whitebait. The seventeen-year-old Georgina Smythe, niece of Mrs Fitzherbert ('wife' of George IV before he married Princess Caroline), notes in her journal in August 1832 that one of her suitors, Lord Alfred Conyngham, 'was going to dine at Greenwich with d'Orsay',[4] and in July 1834 Disraeli too found himself invited out to 'a white bait dinner with d'Orsay and the dandies at Blackwall'.[5] Once again d'Orsay is adventurous rather than parochial. While remaining loyal to the cuisine of his native France – as the largely French menu, albeit with English additions, devised for Chesterfield shows – his enthusiasm for the small fried fish of the Thames indicates that he agreed with Eustache Ude, chef at his club Crockford's, who once said, 'I will venture to affirm that cookery in England, when well done, is superior to that of any country in the world.'[6] He would of course have been in a position to taste many of Ude's dishes, as he was an habitué of Crockford's and perhaps the most colourful gambler in town.

The 1830s was a time when gambling was reaching the proportions of a national mania. Since 1827 talk of modish architecture, new depths of dissipation and fresh heights of extravagance had been linked to 50–53 St James's Street. The site at the top of the street had been the subject of intense press speculation ever since four houses had been torn down to make way for a vast building designed by the fashionable architect Benjamin Wyatt. Until recently Wyatt had held the post of surveyor of Westminster Abbey and was responsible for numerous modish buildings, including Drury Lane Theatre, the Duke of York's Column and Londonderry House. The disruption of traffic to central London during the summer and autumn of 1827 caused by work at the top of St James's Street was further exacerbated when the Guard's Club, which adjoined the site, collapsed as a result of the construction work.

The project was the culmination of the dream of a former fishmonger, William Crockford. The building that was to bear his name was the grandest and most eye-catching project in St James's since White's had been given a new frontage by James Wyatt, father of Benjamin, in 1789. From 1828 until the mid-1840s William Crockford's eponymous club was the most talked-about gambling hell in the most talked-about street in the most talked-about city in the world. Behind its Wyatt-designed frontage, the aristocracy of England, and much of that of Europe, was systematically fleeced by the former fishmonger.

Shortly before he opened his eponymous club in 1827, the *Literary Chronicle and Weekly Review* estimated Crockford's personal worth at £300,000[7] (£13,500,000 in today's terms). He died in 1844 having amassed a fortune of £1,200,000, a sum that might have been greater had he not been given to rash speculation and unsuccessful business ventures towards the end of his life.

Born above a fishmonger's shop near Temple Bar in 1775, Crockford had started his career gambling in such taverns as the Tun on Jermyn Street and the Grapes on King Street. Although involved with betting on horses and at games of cards, it was with hazard, a forerunner of craps, that Crockford made his fortune and his name. Part of hazard's appeal lay in its simplicity. A player would simply bet other players that he would throw any one of five specified numbers (five, six, seven, eight and nine). The thrower's choice was known as a main. If he matched it, he took all the stake money. If he threw another number he neither won nor lost, but continued to throw until he repeated the number (known as chance) and won, or repeated his main and lost. Hazard was more than a mere gambling game; it was a mania – ruining its players financially and morally.

However, William Crockford prefigured the moral hypocrisy of the coming Victorian age. He suspended gaming on the stroke of midnight on Saturday – gambling on the Sabbath would have been anathema to him. And of course Crockford's was an all-male establishment. It was an epitome of the time, a physical symptom of the transition from the elegant savagery of the Regency to the bourgeois respectability of the Victorian era. It was rumoured that Crockford's fortune was founded on a hundred thousand pounds he had taken off an Old Etonian gambler 'Ball' Hughes and Lords Thanet and Granville during one night's session of hazard.[8] Hughes was later destined to become one of Crockford's 'deeper' players.

The genius of William Crockford was to take gambling out of private houses and back streets and turn it into a *grand luxe* pastime. Ostensibly he created a club where gentlemen of good standing in Society could gather and where gambling seemed offered as a mere afterthought. From the outset he intended his club to be exclusive. The entrance fee of thirty guineas (around fifteen hundred pounds today) was the highest in London. We can get an idea of contemporary expenditure from *A Practical Guide to the Peculiar Duties and Business of all Descriptions of Servants*, published in 1825, which informed its readers that a 'Widow or other unmarried Lady' with an annual income of only a hundred pounds 'may keep a Young Maid Servant at a low salary'. In other words Crockford was demanding, and receiving, a third of the sum of money on which a spinster could live genteelly, albeit modestly, for a year. Nor was mere money enough. The selection process of the committee was so rigorous that election to Crockford's was deemed more difficult, and therefore more sought after, than election to White's, Brooks's or Boodle's.[9] Crockford's was quickly dubbed the 'Ascot of Gambling'. Yet it was much more than a casino.

'No one can describe the splendour and excitement of the early days of Crockey,' wrote Gronow.

The members of the Club included all the celebrities of England, from the Duke of Wellington to the youngest Ensign of the Guards; and at the gay and festive board, which was constantly replenished from midnight to early dawn, the most brilliant sallies of wit, the most agreeable conversation, the most interesting anecdotes, interspersed with grave political discussions and acute logical reasoning on every conceivable subject, proceeded from the soldiers, scholars, statesmen, poets and men of pleasure, who, when the 'house was up' and balls and parties at an end, delighted to finish their evening with a little supper and a good deal of hazard at old Crockey's. The tone of the club was excellent. A most gentleman-like feeling prevailed, and none of the rudeness, familiarity, and ill-breeding which disgrace some of the minor clubs of the present day, would have been tolerated for a moment.[10]

The time to visit Crockford's was during the London Season, when Parliament was sitting and the nightly bank (the amount that Crockford put up and could in theory lose) was at a minimum of five thousand pounds. In fact the bank was routinely increased to twenty thousand pounds. The visitor would descend from his coach and mount the flight of shallow steps. Upon entering the club he would find himself in a hall illuminated by the very latest form of gas lighting, in itself a novelty. The proportions of this hall dwarfed those of many stately homes, with towering black scagliola columns enhanced with gilt capitals. To the left was the reading room, to the right the dining room.

Gaming and its select membership aside, the dining room was the chief attraction of the place. The chef was Eustache Ude, whose father had worked in Louis XVI's kitchen. Ude himself had worked for Madame Letitia Bonaparte and then come to England to cook for the Earl of Sefton, who paid him three hundred guineas a year. It was at Crockford's that Eustache Ude achieved his immense fame. Dinner at Crockford's was served from 4.30 p.m. until 6 p.m. And it was between these hours that it would be possible to taste Ude's famous dishes, for example the celebrated entrée of soft roes of mackerel baked in butter and served with a rich cream sauce that he had devised with the Earl of Sefton. And perhaps a dinner might be brought to a close with the famous pudding Boudin de cerises à la Bentinck, a dish of stoned cherries which Ude had created for the young Lord George Bentinck. At Crockford's, Ude was paid a starting salary of twelve hundred pounds a year, at the time a remarkable amount for a cook.

Progressing past the dining room to the foot of the grand staircase the visitor could gaze up to a ceiling of luminous panels of stained glass, from which was suspended a vast chandelier. The stairs led to the first-floor and what was dubbed the State Drawing Room. The effect of this suite of first-floor drawing rooms was overpowering. Panels painted in the style of Watteau alternated with mirrors that soared from the chair rail to the elaborate plasterwork of the cornice with its swirling acanthus leaves and classical Medusa-like medallions. Rich curtains framed sash windows that ran from floor to ceiling. Tables covered with blue and crimson velvet were scattered about the room. As the periodical *Bentley's Miscellany* recorded, 'Royalty can scarcely be conceived to vie with the style and consummate splendour of this magnificent chamber.' In a London that was full of bright shining edifices, including Nash's startling development at Regent's Park, which was completed in the year of Crockford's opening, the first-floor drawing room of 50 St James's was the nonpareil.

In all it was estimated that £94,000 was spent on decorating and furnishing Crockford's. Although the sum of £4,230,000 that this represents in today's terms is considerable, it is interesting to contrast it with the expense of constructing the Athenaeum, which opened in 1830: the building, designed by Decimus Burton, cost £35,000; a further £15,000 was spent on the club's interior decoration and the contents of the cellar.[11]

But the splendid public rooms, on which Crockford spent so freely, were little more than elaborate window dressing, partly intended to frame and partly to disguise activities on the floor above. The gaming room was located in comparatively modest surroundings on the second floor. The room itself was curiously intimate, in contrast to the rest of the club. It was almost as if the proprietor had instructed Wyatt to create a room in which gentlemen of fashion could relax, after behaving with decorum in the club's main rooms.

In the early decades of the nineteenth century it was customary to drink quantities of wines and spirits that would be unthinkable today. A couple of bottles of port were regarded as the minimum alcoholic refreshment a gentleman could expect to enjoy with his dinner. Dinner parties that began at six, seven or eight in the evening did not finish until one in the morning. 'There were then four and even five-bottle men,' recalled Gronow; 'and the only thing that saved them was drinking very slowly, and out of very small glasses.' Gronow went on to record with delighted awe that the 'late Lords Panmure, Dufferin, and Blayney, wonderful to relate, were six bottle men'.[12] Thus it was in a state of fairly advanced refreshment that many members headed for the gaming room. Given the quantities of fortified wine that had been taken it is hardly surprising that men like Lord Rivers lost £3400 at a game of whist merely because he forgot that the seven of hearts was still in. What is more, the same man was happy to lose £23,000 at a single sitting, which ran from midnight until 7 p.m. the following evening.[13]

The gaming room was pleasantly furnished and well lit. As the evening wore on it would become crowded with men, some hatted, some not, most of them dressed in blue coats, waistcoats and shirts with embroidered fronts and fancy studs. To ensure that the atmosphere retained its joviality, liveried footmen in breeches that buttoned at the knee circulated with trays of the 'very small glasses' that had been enjoyed earlier in the evening. At the centre of the room stood the large oval mahogany mass of the hazard table, covered in green cloth and marked with yellow lines demarcating the 'zones of speculation' and the odds between main and chance. Indentations in the middle at either side allowed croupiers and players calling main or chance to place themselves near the action. Hanging above the table was a large triple lamp, shaded to throw its soft light over the green baize, while at the same time protecting the players' eyes. The dice were of the finest ivory. Three new pairs were provided at the opening of play, at a cost of a guinea a pair. After an evening's gambling they were never used again. Various bowls, stacks of counters, dice cups and rakes completed the equipment.

Seated at a high chair in the corner of the room was Mr Page. Page supervised gaming, received players' losses, paid out their winnings and ensured that the pace of play never slackened. Walking around the room was Mr Gye, chief lieutenant of the proprietor. As Parliament and the social diversions of London wound down, the fashionable, the famous and the frivolous of the day poured in to Crockey's; and the room would fill with the hypnotic rattle of the dice and the cries of players calling for various numbers.

Crockford himself surveyed the scene quietly from a desk in another corner of the room. His appearance was in direct contrast to that of his customers. Even though he had already amassed a considerable fortune he had done little to improve his manner and bearing from that of a fishmonger. He was servile and cringing. His mode of speech was that of a hackney coachman. His cheeks were white and flabby. His mouth had been given an added ghoulish interest: it was filled with false teeth, or rather, following the dental practices of the time, healthy teeth pulled from corpses and set into his own jaw. The hands with which he issued his loans and accepted IOUs were pale, plump and so fleshy that his knuckles were completely obscured and described as 'soft as raw veal'. His dress was apparently 'common in the extreme', his only affectation being a vast white cambric cravat folded thickly around his neck in a parody of contemporary elegance.

While many parvenus sought to ape the manners of their social superiors, Crockford never attempted to 'better' himself – further evidence of his astute grasp of psychology. He played the role of humble servant, presenting himself as fawning and socially inept, merely an instrument of his masters' pleasure, supplying them with credit for their convenience, all the time creating an atmosphere where they were encouraged to gamble beyond their means. Outwardly at least, Crockford never appeared to be getting above himself.

Gronow recorded d'Orsay as being one of the high rollers at Crockford's, in that he played for the same 'enormous stakes' as Lords Lichfield and Chesterfield.[14] Indeed d'Orsay counted these and other heavy betters such as the Earl of Sefton as his friends, and his great popularity rested partly on his nonchalance as a gambler – what Gronow preferred to call 'the gentlemanly bearing and calm unmoved demeanour, under losses or gains, of all the men of that generation'.[15] But Gronow's account of the heyday of Crockford's, published between 1862 and 1866, had already had ample time to acquire a patina of nostalgia. D'Orsay's monthly income of one thousand pounds, substantial though it was, did not really equip him to gamble in such company. What is more, the character of imperturbable gambler was only one of the roles that he played. While others had fortunes to gamble, estates and houses to mortgage, d'Orsay did not. While others wagered thousands, the loss of a few hundred would be felt by d'Orsay. On one occasion his friend Disraeli, believing him to be cleaning up at Crockford's, approached him for a loan. The Frenchman's reply revealed how, with his finances as with much of his life, appearance was at odds with the reality of his situation. 'I swear before God', said d'Orsay, 'that I've not sixpence at my banker's now, having lost night before last, £325.'[16]

Nevertheless, at Crockford's appearance was all, and the sham glamour of this high summer of high stakes gaming was to last only until May 1844. On the 20th of that month a House of Commons Select Committee published a Report on Gaming that made numerous recommendations, which would curb gaming and indeed change it radically. It was also the month in which Crockford himself, the greatest casino operator England had ever seen, died. However, although Crockford's was the hottest address in town, there were numerous other operators who, having seen the success of Crockford, were keen to mimic him and for whom the patronage of a gambler such as d'Orsay would have been a coup – his tall figure at the hazard table was as much a part of the Crockford's experience as the chance to eat Ude's food. Indeed, one element of the d'Orsay legend concerns payments allegedly made to the court by various gambling hells to get him to keep his carriage outside the entrance.

Mills includes this part of the d'Orsay legend in *D'Horsay; or the Follies of the Day*. D'Horsay owes five thousand pounds to Bosky Tom, the proprietor of a fledgling gambling operation. He is unable to pay, and Bosky Tom puts a proposition to him:

'There's not such an advertisement,' continued Tom, regardlessly, 'for the tailor, hatter, coach-maker, horse-dealer, hosier, and bootmaker, in the world. I've often thought so, and often said so. Put all the papers together, morning and evening, and all the prospectuses, and all the placards on hoards, and all the walking sandwiches with boards before and behind, and all the perambulating wans, they'll never, I said to my partners, this very day, get such an advertisement as the Marquis *on wheels*.'

The Marquis was quite silent during this eulogistic notice of his value in the public gaze: but he looked as if it was anything than flattering unction to his vanity.

'Now, we're a young house,' continued Bosky Tom, 'and although doing a pretty stroke of business, still we should like to do more.'

'Very natural and praiseworthy,' said the Marquis.

'And you can assist us, Marquis, in carrying out the intentions.'

'Me!' exclaimed the Marquis, drawing himself upright in his chair and looking exceedingly astonished. 'No, no!' continued he, shaking his head as if a sudden unpleasant thought had entered there. 'I can never descend to occupation of a bonnet, however empty the exchequer and ghostly the chance of replenishing it.'

'Nor was I going to ask you,' replied Bosky Tom. 'All we want is for you to let your flashy cab stand for a couple of hours or so at the door, and for you to sit at the table and play as usual, with *our* money. There can be no objection to that, I suppose?'

'None in the smallest degree,' rejoined the Marquis, smiling a complete approval to the arrangement. 'The conception is in the mildest form disagreeable, if disagreeable at all, and that depends entirely upon the results of my nightly labours. Pray,' continued he, 'are my winnings to be carried to the old account or may I feel sufficient interest in the game to—?' and the Marquis slightly but significantly tapped that part of his trousers where a pocket might be supposed to be.

'Over a hundred,' replied Bosky Tom, 'and it must go to the

old score. Under that amount you may grab.'

'A liberal and, at the same time, judicious policy,' rejoined the Marquis. 'My cab and myself are at your service.'[17]

And what a cab it was. Hugh McCausland's 1948 book *The English Carriage* states that in 'the history of carriages the name of Count d'Orsay crops up frequently, more than one vehicle owing as much to his interest as a leader of fashion as to his coachmanship and an amateur knowledge of carriage design and structure that he added to his varied accomplishments, artistic, social and sporting'.[18] A man of fashion of the early nineteenth century would be known by his vehicles. In old age Gronow recalled that seeing d'Orsay 'driving in his tilbury some thirty years ago, I fancied that he looked like some gorgeous dragon-fly skimming through the air; and though all was dazzling and showy, yet there was a kind of harmony which precluded any idea or accusation of bad taste'.[19] The tilbury gig was a popular two-wheeled carriage built by the eponymous coach-builder. And as carriages at the top of the market were bespoke affairs, the scope for originality and personalisation was considerable.

One of the most fashionable types of carriage of the d'Orsay years was the curricle: the convertible sports coupé, so to speak, of carriages. A compact two-wheeler with a neat curvaceous body enhanced by large C-shaped 'cee' springs at the rear, folding leather hood, a dashboard raked forward over the backs of the horses, it accommodated two passengers comfortably with the option of seating for a groom between the springs at the rear. Unlike other carriages the horses were harnessed abreast with the curricle pole. 'Always provided that the horses were well matched in size and action, and that the balance of the vehicle was correctly adjusted with due allowance if a groom was carried, for his weight at the back, the result was a jaunty and extremely comfortable carriage with an easy, buoyant motion.'[20]

As well as the ride quality, it was the arrangement of the horses side by side and the difficulty and cost of acquiring a pair matched in size, power and appearance that accounted for the curricle's desirability. One rich eccentric got his vehicle up to look like something that Neptune might have driven, covered with shells and heraldic designs. As soon as he could afford it Dickens purchased a curricle. The Duke of Wellington had one in a violent shade of yellow with silver harness. D'Orsay's set were customers of the famed coach-builder Barker, from whom he ordered at least one curricle in 1836; and d'Orsay's name is still to be seen in the ledgers of Barker & Company held at the Science Museum.

It was with Barker that d'Orsay collaborated to create a one-horse version of the curricle. Called the cabriolet, a similar style of vehicle had been popular in France during the early years of the century. It was so swift that the horse's collar was frequently fitted with bells by drivers who liked to travel fast, to alert fellow road users to their presence. It was more manoeuvrable than other carriages and was distinguished by a tiny groom in livery called a 'tiger' who, clinging on to straps, stood on a small platform at the back. Among the refinements d'Orsay is said to have initiated was the practice of having the hood 'half-struck' or 'set back', which was deemed quite rakish and had the practical benefits of allowing unobstructed vision from the front, while oval windows set into the hood allowed the driver to look out to the side. It could be said that this was the vehicular equivalent of d'Orsay's penchant for wearing a coat open and thrust back to display fine waistcoats.

D'Orsay also gave his name to a style of dress coach. According to McCausland, 'one of the neatest introduced for less formal private use and with the appointments and accompaniments correspondingly modified, was the Chariot d'Orsay. The Count's excellent taste in such matters was here exemplified in a comparatively sombre chariot without unnecessary embellishments, with a simple box in place of the sumptuous hammer cloth, with unadorned panels and the accompaniments of plain harness and dark liveries.'[21] In deciding upon a deliberately plain look, d'Orsay was once more demonstrating his stylish contrapuntalism: as Marylian Watney's 1961 book *The Elegant Carriage* explains, 'Everything about the Dress Chariot was very ornate, being painted in the family's colours, with armorial bearings and crests on the panels, the latter being repeated on the harness and servants' livery buttons, and embroidered upon the hammer cloth.'[22]

The London d'Orsay of William IV's rule and the early years of the reign of Victoria essentially enjoyed the same pastimes as the young man who had won the admiration of Charles James Mathews. Indeed, the recollection of d'Orsay given by P.G. Patmore is uncannily reminiscent of young Mathews's awed account of the young Frenchman's abilities:

> Count d'Orsay was one of the very best riders in a country whose riders are admitted to be the best in the world; he was one of the keenest and most accomplished sportsmen in a nation whose sporting surpremacy is the only undisputed one they possess; he was the best judge of a horse among a people of horse-dealers and horse-jockeys; he was among the best cricketers in a country where all are cricketers, and where alone that noblest of games exists; he was the best swimmer, the best shot, the best swordsman, the best boxer, the best wrestler, the best tennis-player; and he was admitted to be the best judge and umpire in all these amusements.[23]

It is d'Orsay's status as one of the best cricketers in the England of the day that is perhaps most amusing. Nevertheless Patmore's account, albeit fulsome, of the count's status as a sporting star and arbiter as well as fashion leader in equestrian matters gives some idea of how eagerly each nugget of information about his stable and equipage was seized upon. 'It was a little fortune to his tiger to tell the would-be dandies dwelling north of Oxford-street where d'Orsay bought his last new cab-horse, or who built his tilbury or his coat,' and he was, said Patmore, the 'model by which all the male "nobility and gentry" of London horsed, equipaged, and attired themselves!'[24]

He was as keen on riding as he had been as a teenager when mounted for the Royal Stag Hunt in the Bois de Boulogne, and the minutest details of his equestrian style were studied, analysed and copied. 'As late as 1835', recorded one observer, 'it was the fashion for the swells or dandies of the period – Count d'Orsay, the Earl of Chesterfield, and their imitators – to tittup along the streets and in the Park with their toes just touching the stirrups, which hung three inches lower than in the hunting-field.'[25]

Appearing on horseback with d'Orsay in Hyde Park was a way of attracting the closest scrutiny. His notoriety coupled with his faultless turnout, which would have been examined with an almost forensic interest by the educated follower of fashion, made a ride through the Park with him a potentially nerve-wracking and unsettling experience, as Abraham Hayward wrote in a letter the day after a hack with d'Orsay in March 1838. 'I rode through the park yesterday with d'Orsay to the admiration of all beholders, for every eye is sure to be fixed upon him, and the whole world was out, so that I began to tremble for my character. But he is certainly one of the pleasantest fellows in town.'[26]

In fact throughout the 1830s d'Orsay was a fixture in Hyde Park. Whether the fashionable strip ran parallel to Park Lane or along the Park's northern perimeter, at least one feature was unchanging: d'Orsay's presence. For instance the diary of Georgina Smythe, who made her debut during the Season of 1832, has d'Orsay, who at this time was friendly with Count Tolstoy, a relative of the novelist and nephew of Princess Lieven with whom he was staying at the Russian

Embassy, cropping up with such frequency that his absence from the Park is an oddity that warrants comment.[27]

But if d'Orsay was absent from London it was because he was much in demand as a guest at country houses. It was as a member of a house-party at Lord Sefton's Stoke Farm in October 1834 that the politician Thomas Creevey wrote to his stepdaughter describing his fellow guest d'Orsay as 'the ultra-Dandy of Paris and London, and as ultra a villain as either city can produce'.[28] But it was not a reputation that stopped him receiving invitations to the country; in the raffish circles that he dominated, his complex domestic life only added to his attraction.

'My Dear Count,' begins a typical letter from his friend the painter Edwin Landseer,

> If you are the man I take you for you will immediately pack up your little all, and come to Redleap – his Lordship and Mr Dells both say they will be perfectly delighted if you can consent to this arrangement pray if possible come. You have no idea of the happiness we enjoy here – Charming garden beautiful pictures and very good shooting if you you [*sic*] can make good, only one day it would reward you and we might return – together – at all events write me a line – by return of post – you will sorely disappoint us all if you cannot leave home to join our party = If yr Lordship *could* travel by a coach there are lots going from C. X. every day – either to Hastings or Tunbridge Wells – they would put you down at Wats X. or Sevenoaks and I will send a Carriage to meet you if you will let me know at what hour you start.
>
> I write in extreme haste
> but am always most truly yrs
> Elandseer'[29]

One accomplishment that would have endeared him to his hosts was that d'Orsay was a good shot. In another letter Landseer wrote, 'I wish very much you would let me know what day or morning you could manage to go to Purdy's [*sic*]. I should like F Grant to see you shoot.'[30] James Purdey had the honour of supplying d'Orsay with a gun, an honour to which the count saw no reason to add the bonus of payment.[31] He did, however, put his Purdey to good use. In the letters and journals of the time, he is often mentioned as being off shooting with the likes of the politician and diarist Charles Greville, shooting at Bradenham as the guest of Disraeli[32] and staying more than once as the guest of Lord Carrington at Wycombe Abbey.[33]

He was also a resourceful and thoughtful guest, as this undated letter from a shooting party at Ranton Abbey in Staffordshire shows:

> My dear Doctor.
>
> Will you have the goodness to come at once at [*sic*] Lord Lichfield, by the next train which starts from Euston Square, at 6 oclock in the morning, and will bring you to Stafford, where a carriage will be in readiness to bring you here – Lord Lichfield has been shot in the Eye, through the upper Eye lid, and I think that the shot is lodged in the fleshy part near the nose, under the Eye lid. – We depend upon you to extract it, therefore dont loose [*sic*] a minute in coming.
>
> Believe me
> Yours most faithfully
> Cte d'Orsay[34]

It is possible to imagine d'Orsay taking command of the situation, calming everyone down and scribbling off a hurried note summoning a physician – in whom, he no doubt assured the injured Lord Lichfield, he had the utmost faith.

As noticeable in the hunting field as he was in Hyde Park or on the moors, he cut a prominent and imposing figure in Francis Grant's painting depicting a meet of the Royal Staghounds on Ascot Heath. Writing in the June 1838 number of the *New Sporting Magazine* about this picture, Nimrod described d'Orsay as appearing 'in all the glory of French-polish; satin neckcloth; the inside of his coat lined with kerseymere; leathers and boots to perfection'. He continued:

I never saw the Count d'Orsay in the field, but I have heard of his doings there, and especially on a horse called Shamrock, which he purchased at the stiff price of £400 from Mr Anderson. On him, I am told, he would ride a burst in right good form; and when missing, it was not to be attributed to want of pluck. In fact, he is said to have looked upon hunting – I speak now in the past tense, having reason to believe he has nearly given it up – chiefly as an arena on which adventures were to be sought, inasmuch as he would go out of his way to charge a large fence or a wide brook, after the manner of Don Quixote with the windmill, and not unfrequently meeting with a similarly disastrous fate.

Characteristic of the tact and generosity of the Count, I must be allowed to mention one circumstance. On the day of the great steeple chase in the Aylesbury country, a deer was to be turned out, but the number of horsemen present – about two thousand – was so great that the farmers demurred. As they were on their road home despairing of further sport, a liberal occupier of land rode up to Lord Errol, and said, if his lordship would order the deer to be sent to his house it should be turned out on his farm; and it was done accordingly. The next day the Count wrote to his wine merchant to send the said farmer four dozen of his best port wine, with his compliments.[35]

Typically d'Orsay sought to set himself apart from the rest: if he could not be the best huntsman in the field, he would demonstrate his difference by his heedless love of danger and by his generosity. But just because he wanted to distinguish himself did not mean he was chilly and aloof. He could be relied upon to join in any idiotic pastimes his host might decree reasonable to while away the days. Indeed while staying at Wycombe Abbey during December 1839 the weather was so bad that all thoughts of riding or shooting had to be abandoned. 'D'Orsay sent down a horse to Wycombe Abbey,' wrote Disraeli to his sister,

> but could not get out of the house the whole time he was there; even to pay you a visit which he greatly desired. It was so foggy that he was obliged to give it up. They had a roaring, robustious, romping party, of which he gave us very amusing details. Playing hide and seek, they got into the roof and Albert Conyngham fell thro' the ceiling of one of the rooms – an immense long leg dangling out. Carington came to look at it with his eye glass, but took it very good humouredly.[36]

Such was the breadth of d'Orsay's acquaintance that he was not just a guest at country houses where rakes got drunk, gambled, shot, hunted and fell through ceilings; he was also welcome in literary and political society.

William Harrison Ainsworth is typical of another sort of man with whom d'Orsay consorted. Born in 1805 in Manchester, the son of a solicitor, he studied law but married a publisher's daughter and embarked on a literary career. He worked as an editor and early in 1834 burst upon the London scene as the author of *Rockwood*, a popular version of the life of Dick Turpin. He was 'a handsome man, but it was very much of the barber's block type of beauty, with wavy scented hair, smiling lips, and pink and white complexion. As a young man he was gorgeous in the *outré* dress of the dandy of '36, and in common with those famous dandies d'Orsay, young Benjamin Disraeli, and Tom Duncombe, wore multitudinous waistcoats, over which dangled a long gold chain and numberless rings.'[37]

Yet, however dashing Ainsworth was, he was unable to compete with the cosmopolitan polish, urbanity and charisma of the older man. According to one observer Ainsworth had:

> a strongly developed and practical fancy for modelling his style after that of the elegant French Count. It is true he was a fine, well-proportioned fellow, and possessed chestnut curls on his head, and hair on his face in sufficient abundance to adorn it after a similar fashion, but it was a mistake all the same. He spared no pains and no expense to get himself taken for d'Orsay; in the Row, and passing rapidly on a mount of the same hue, he actually did contrive now and then to get a hesitating recognition from some of d'Orsay's slighter acquaintances; and when wearing evening dress he arrived, by careful study, at the exact angle at which his coat should be thrown open, to display a gorgeous waistcoat *en coeur*, with a snowy bediamonded shirt-front beneath it; but, somehow it wasn't at all the same thing, and only seemed to call attention to the vast difference between the two individuals who, nevertheless, had so much in common. It was simply, that grace, refinement, elegance, and *chic* were wanting in the imitation.[38]

D'Orsay subtly flattered men like Ainsworth by allowing them to treat him as an equal. It was the sort of friendship that was replicated with other younger literary men, who viewed d'Orsay in some way or another as a role model for their early lives: Disraeli, born in 1804; Thackeray, born in 1811; and Dickens, born in 1812. He revelled in their adoration and was evidently pleased to feature in their novels, barely disguised as a dashing figure under a variety of names; he even signed himself in one of his letters to Bulwer, 'Yours Glaucus, Mirabel, Crichton',[39] the names of characters based on him in various novels. The effect he had on these younger men was almost mesmeric. Carlyle, writing to his brother, described Dickens as 'dressed à la d'Orsay rather than well'.[40] But, in addition to imitating him in matters of dress, they turned to him in moments of crisis, looking to him as a man of the world. One notorious instance of the count being called upon as an arbiter in matters other than fashion occurred in May 1835.

On 2 May, the veteran Irish politician Daniel O'Connell made a spirited speech in Dublin branding Disraeli 'a blackguard', 'a ruffian', 'a liar both in actions and words' and for good measure 'a living lie'.[41] He then went on to make anti-Semitic remarks. O'Connell offered these insults after reading an account of a speech Disraeli had given at Taunton. The speech is disputed, but one report has Disraeli calling O'Connell, perhaps not inaccurately, 'an incendiary in politics'.[42] As O'Connell had once killed a man in a duel, he had vowed never to take part in one again. Instead he left it to his son, Morgan O'Connell MP, to defend his honour. Having just finished fighting a duel with Lord Avanley on behalf of his hot-tempered father, Morgan O'Connell must have been annoyed to find a note from Disraeli demanding that he resume his 'vicarious duties of yielding satisfaction' for the insults served up by his father.[43]

The following day Disraeli wrote to his sister in high spirits, emphasising the role d'Orsay had played in managing the affair. 'I went to d'Orsay immediately. He sent for Henry Baillie [later a Tory MP] for my second, as he thought a foreigner shd. not interfere in a political duel, but he took the management of everything. I never quitted his house until 10 o'ck when I dressed and went to the Opera. I believe an affair was never better managed. Everybody agrees that I have done it in first rate style, and nothing else is talked of.'[44] For

Disraeli the duel, and the way it was handled, would seem to have been as much a fashion statement and an opportunity for publicity as a potential fight to the death. He revels in the fashionable nature of it all and, as the postscript to his sister shows, he read his press avidly. 'Vicarious was a hit,' he scribbled exultantly '[no]body now uses any other word. All the paper[s] are *vicarious*.'[45]

Disraeli's father, however, was neither pleased about the duel, nor about the fact that d'Orsay was advising his son. But, in a letter written at the end of that week, Disraeli stoutly defends his friend: 'I do not know a more "experienced" or "better" head than d'Orsay's, or as good: all other men in worldly affairs are fools to him.'[46] As it was, the affair fizzled out a few days later with Disraeli being taken into custody by the police and bound over to keep the peace.

What is remarkable about d'Orsay's circle of acquaintance is its circumference. There were the senior political and artistic figures, relics of the days of Lord Blessington's sumptuous St James's Square establishment. There were the itinerant Eurotrash from his continental tour, for instance Teresa Guiccioli, mistress of Byron, then of Fox, who later became a friend of Lady Blessington's. There were dissolute aristocrats who gambled at Crockford's, and hunting and shooting friends including Lord Chesterfield, who at the end of 1834 was offered the Mastership of the King's Buck Hounds,[47] and Lord Sefton whose Stoke Farm near Slough was described as 'a beautiful *ferme ornée*'.[48] The young dandy novelists such as Bulwer, whose 1833 novel *Godolphin* was later dedicated to d'Orsay (the count described it as the 'best book of the genre that I have read'),[49] and Disraeli whose 1837 novel *Henrietta Temple* was likewise dedicated to d'Orsay and features a flattering portrait of him under the name Count Mirabel, obviously saw the tall, smart Frenchman as an ideal of male elegance and loyal friend. Then there were such demi-dandies as Ainsworth, a middle-class Mancunian who had propelled himself from the obscurity of the provinces to the centre of fashionable London. It was probably through Ainsworth that d'Orsay began his unlikely involvement with the Fraserians.

If one can speak meaningfully of anything like a 'counterculture' in 1830s London it was centred around *Fraser's Magazine*. For half a century *Fraser's* would dominate the world of magazines and periodicals. The Fraserians, as its contributors and associates became known, included some of the leading figures of Victorian cultural life. Edited initially by William Maginn, *Fraser's* was a reaction against the excesses, decadence and exclusive nature of Regency Society. Its tone was robust, earthy and proudly middle class, and its contributors were bound by a stout beer-drinking antipathy to the dandiacal preciousness of such writers as Bulwer, who was a frequent butt of the magazine's rumbustious criticism.

An 1834 drawing by the artist Daniel Maclise, whose images of literary figures of the day illustrated the magazine, shows the Fraserians gathered around a table for one of their editorial meetings-cum-drinking sessions. Though their individual features are faithfully reproduced, each man is identified by name. They are an impressive bunch, including Carlyle, Southey, Thackeray, Ainsworth, Coleridge and, on the far right, his well-oiled curls spilling over his coat collar, that 'ultra-dandy of Paris and London',[50] Count d'Orsay.

D'Orsay's presence in the midst of the Fraserians was odd, but it makes him more interesting. As the quintessential dandy, surely he was the standard bearer of a species whose extinction was the Fraserian goal. Moreover, d'Orsay's claims to literary importance were slender, resting upon little more than the elusive journal praised by Byron. Nevertheless, there he was; the Fraserian establishment obviously detected in d'Orsay characteristics other than the ability to wear clothes well. For all his elegant posing, he was a substantial character and in December 1834 he merited his own entry in the magazine's 'Gallery of Literary Characters', with an essay and an accompanying portrait by Maclise that d'Orsay felt made him look 'like a Drum Major'.[51]

But d'Orsay's presence amongst the Fraserians was not merely predicated on his charisma and capability for making himself liked. While the Fraserians might have been avowedly opposed to dandies in print, they quite liked them in person: ambivalent feelings are characteristic of an interstitial time, as when the established hierarchies and values of Regency England were giving way to a new and as yet not so clearly defined society. It also has to be said that part of d'Orsay's interest in the Fraserians resulted from Lady Blessington's own ambitions.

Though she was handicapped by all sorts of questions about her past and her morals, Lady Blessington's desire to succeed as a premier-league political and literary hostess had grown ever more intense. Following the success of her *Conversations with Lord Byron*, published in 1832, she was experiencing literary success on her own account and by the mid-1830s had acquired a reputation as a bankable novelist. 'She writes very poor novels,' was the opinion of the prickly Lady Holland, 'but obtains from them near £1000 pr am [per annum]. A name will sell any trash.'[52] A lively and intelligent woman, Lady Blessington was irked by the social straitjacket that she found herself wearing. But she made the most of her limited sphere of socialising: entertaining at home, being seen in the Park and appearing at the theatre and Opera. For the rest, d'Orsay had to be her eyes and ears, her proxy on the party circuit, reporting back to her on London's vibrant literary and social scene. When he reported being recognised in the street by d'Orsay, Disraeli wryly observed that he had 'I suppose been crammed by lady Blesinton'.[53]

From 1834, Lady Blessington began to edit *The Book of Beauty*. This was typical of a kind of publication known as annuals – saccharine collections of stories, verse and illustrations – that became fashionable at this time. Later she would become editor of another called *The Keepsake*. The friends that d'Orsay made out and about on the London scene were invited to dinner at Seamore Place and encouraged to contribute to *The Book of Beauty*. 'Dear Lady Blessington,' began a letter dated 31 May 1834 from Ainsworth.

> Rest assured that my best efforts shall be used to make my illustration of the engraving you have been good enough to send me worthy of the pages of *The Book of Beauty*. I like the subject, and will endeavour to do justice to it. The unknown dame has striking and beautiful features; rich in expression and charged with melancholy. Her dress, I conclude, is such as might belong to any lady of any modern European clime, so that I may lay the scene of my story where I please.[54]

'My dear Lady Blessington,' wrote Disraeli a little later that summer. 'I send you the tale, which I beg you to accept as a mark of my sincere regard; and to reject *without hesitation*, if, on perusal, you do not consider it suitable to your wishes. I shall be glad indeed if you consider it such, as it must always afford me lively satisfaction to be of service, however slight, to one whom I so much esteem.' He adds the postscript, 'I fear the MS. is not as fair as I cd. wish. My amanuensis is too busy to help me, and I broke down in the copying. Let me have a proof.'[55] Lady Blessington did consider the tale suitable and, after publication in November, Disraeli received 'a fine waistcoat' in payment.[56]

D'Orsay was effectively Lady Blessington's co-editor, schmoozing contributors and eliciting contributions with skill, grace and flattery, as this undated letter to Bulwer demonstrates:

> Lady Blessington dares not ask you for a few lines for her *Book of Beauty*. I have therefore come forward to beseech you to

search the wastepaper basket beneath your desk. You shall find there some fragments that would certainly be good enough to be the best in her book[57]

Your affectionate d'Orsay

A similar tone is evinced in the postscript to another letter to Bulwer. After writing a detailed account of Napoleon's tactics at Waterloo and the unreliability of his generals, he adds, 'Si Dimanche vous êtes par accident en Ville venez diner avec nous – Lady B. pense que son Book of Beautiy [*sic*] for next year will be damned if there is nothing by you, she is afraid of asking you knowing all your occupations if you have any old scraps in one of those drawers, will you give her one.'[58]

CHAPTER EIGHTEEN

Gore House

THE ELABORATELY CASUAL TONE OF D'ORSAY'S LETTERS
extracting contributions from his author friends belies Lady
Blessington's increasingly acute need to earn a living. The shock of
adjusting to life without Lord Blessington to underwrite her considerable expenses was beginning to make itself felt. The nature of her
existence was a neat definition of a vicious circle: she needed to maintain a splendid establishment to attract a glamorous intellectual circle
to contribute to her annual and furnish her with inspiration and support for her trashy novels to pay for the maintenance of the splendid
establishment . . .

To the scandal and legal complication of Harriet's departure from
Seamore Place, followed by d'Orsay's retirement round the corner to
Curzon Street, was added the distress of a burglary in the summer of
1833, when thieves broke in and stole 'plate and jewellery to the value
of about £1,000'.[1] Seamore Place did not hold happy associations for
Lady Blessington. She had taken the house at a time when she had
planned a full-dress assault on polite Society, but since polite Society

had not welcomed her to its heart, a house located so close to the centre of town was no longer necessary. Now in her mid-forties, she was inclining to matronliness rather than to the vivacity of her youth and, according to Sadleir, though 'she still visited the opera or the theatre, she did so with increasing reluctance; her famous green chariot – with its white wheels picked out in green and crimson, its driver and footman perched high above the normal level of their kind – was seen ever less frequently in Hyde Park; indeed the days multiplied when she never left the house at all'.[2]

Middle aged, beset by financial worries, fretting about the antics of her son–lover d'Orsay, working constantly, entertaining lavishly, yet shunned by soi-disant respectable society and putting on weight through infrequent exercise, Lady Blessington reinvented herself once again. In 1836 she abandoned any pretence at maintaining a social presence in fashionable central London and instead let that portion of Society over which she exercised influence come and visit her. She decided to move to the country, or at least to Kensington – which in the early nineteenth century was still semi-rural, with several acres remaining under cultivation by market gardeners until the 1850s – and negotiated a lease on Gore House. It was to be the location of her last and her most successful salon.

As well as a change of scene and style there might even have been some half-hearted motive of economy behind her relocation. Writing to Lord Durham about Lady Blessington's move Bulwer Lytton says that the house has cost her 'a thousand pounds in repairs, about another thousand in new furniture, entails two gardeners, two cows and another housemaid; but she declares with the gravest of all possible faces that she only does it for – economy!'[3] Perhaps she was hoping to economise on dairy bills with a couple of cows. But old habits did not die. As Madden notes, the 'new establishment was on a scale of magnificence exceeding even that of Seamore Place'.[4] Lady Blessington and d'Orsay were a fatal combination: the count's delusions and his obsessive maintenance of his persona were abetted and supported by a woman who was hopelessly in love with him.

Gore House was later demolished to make way for the Albert Hall. Constructed in the mid-eighteenth century for Robert Michell of Hatton Garden,[5] Gore House would now be considered a substantial residence. Originally a symmetrical Georgian mansion, with a grand balconied entrance flanked by two bays, which extended to the rear, the architectural harmony was destroyed by the addition of a later wing. A contemporary watercolour shows a three-storey house, with a further floor of what were presumably servants' quarters, illuminated by dormer windows, in the attic. It had a frontage of eight sash windows, overlooking the Park, but was protected from the road by a wall of about ten feet in height, a row of trees and two sets of heavy gates, each surmounted by a large lantern. Its chief attraction was the immense garden, three acres of which extended from the rear of the house towards the site now occupied by the Natural History and Science Museums of South Kensington.[6]

Among those who had lived in the house during the eighteenth century were Lord Drogheda and Admiral Lord Rodney. Its first famous nineteenth-century occupant was the anti-slavery campaigner William Wilberforce, who moved into Gore House in 1808, when it was in a state of some disrepair, and stayed there until 1821. 'We are just one mile from the turnpike gate at Hyde Park Corner,' he wrote contentedly of his house in around 1810, 'having about three acres of pleasure ground around my house, or rather behind it, and several old trees, walnut and mulberry, of thick foliage. I can sit and read under their shade, which I delight in doing, with as much admiration of the beauties of nature (remembering at the same time the words of my favourite poet: "Nature is but a name for an effect whose cause is God,") as if I were two hundred miles from the great city.'[7]

After 1821, when Wilberforce retired from the moderately rural Kensington to Morden, Surrey, 'two or three tenants of no particular importance'[8] occupied the house until Lady Blessington moved in fifteen years later. Wilberforce was the arch do-gooder, a paragon of political correctness, who entertained the great, the good and sundry leading evangelists; the sort of man who amused himself by strolling home 'from Hyde Park Corner, repeating the hundred and nineteenth Psalm in great comfort'.[9]* The contrasting character of the two well-known occupants of Gore House provided a talking point, not lost on the waggish author James Smith, who wrote the following verse:

> Mild Wilberforce, by all beloved,
> Once owned this hallowed spot,
> Whose zealous eloquence improved
> The fetter'd negro's lot;
> Yet here still slavery attacks
> When Blessington invites:
> The chains from which he freed the blacks,
> She rivets on the whites.[10]

D'Orsay moved to Gore House with her, albeit maintaining a pretence of propriety by ensconcing himself in what Bulwer called a 'cottage *orné*',[11] where he set about establishing his aviary. D'Orsay's cottage was actually part of a 'row of five houses called specifically Kensington Gore',[12] to the side of Gore House, which over the course of several years were modified by various occupants. They had, in the words of the journalist Leigh Hunt, 'an air of elegance, and even of distinction. They look as if they had been intended for the out-houses, or lodge, of some great mansion which was never built.'[13] Small but with a pleasant garden at the back and views over the Park at the

---

* This is the longest of the Psalms, extending to a hundred and seventy-six verses, full of pious self-congratulation, and of rebukes of its deriders' (*Household Words*, 1853, p. 590).

front, the cottage was an agreeable bachelor pad which d'Orsay turned into an exquisite gem of a house – not that he spent much time in it. He was in effect the man of Gore House: host, master of ceremonies, decorator, artist in residence as well as Lady Blessington's eyes and ears about town. That Benjamin Haydon could say Lady Blessington 'has the first news of everything'[14] was in large part due to d'Orsay's energetic socialising. He was at Gore House so often that a door was built joining the gardens of the two properties.

D'Orsay poured his considerable talents as a decorator into Gore House. As ever there was an excess which teetered on the theatrical. Once visitors had negotiated the gates, the 'hall door was flung wide open by a powdered footman in a gorgeous livery of green and gold, and the name passed on to another servitor that looked in every particular his counterpart; both were certainly upwards of six feet in height'.[15] Once past this pair of powdered pantomime flunkeys, visitors were received by Lady Blessington in what was undoubtedly the most impressive room in the house: the library, which had been created from two separate rooms. It was here that the theatricality of d'Orsay's decorative skill paid substantial dividends. Although nominally a library, it was in effect the social fulcrum of the house, a stage set designed to show off Lady Blessington in her role as grande dame of the London literary scene. The impression was one of refined gravitas, and as a piece of impressive, faintly intimidating, yet simultaneously delicate interior design it was highly effective, as the following contemporary description given by a visitor shows:

> I have already called it the library, and since the walls were almost entirely covered with books, it assuredly deserved the name. But the shelves, or at any rate the edges of them, instead of being dark, were of that enamelled white which looks like ivory, small interstices being filled up with looking-glass; the

panels of the doors were also of looking glass, and the handles glass. It was a very large room on the right hand, entering the house, and, from its two fireplaces and supporting columns in the centre had evidently been originally two compartments. It ran through the house from north to south, the southern windows looking out on the lovely garden, with its fine old trees. It was at this end of the room we always sat, though the door from the hall was near the north windows [in other words, on entering visitors had to walk the entire length of the room, almost as if being presented to a monarch in a throne room]. The furniture was delicate apple-green silk damask set in white and gold, with fauteuils in abundance, protected by the finest antimacassars I ever saw – not the abominations of crochet and knitting, but delicate fabrics of muslin and lace. The carpet was of a very minute pattern, a shade darker than the furniture. Summer and winter, Lady Blessington always occupied the same seat, a large easy-chair near the fireplace, with a small table beside her, on which was probably a new book with a paper-knife between the leaves, and a scent-bottle and a fan.[16]

It seems that even the accessories of scent bottle and fan, together with the latest book, so new that its pages were still in the process of being cut, had been arrayed to create the maximum effect. By now d'Orsay and Lady Blessington were becoming adept at scene setting. And it was for the salons at Gore House that she acquired her greatest fame. As an early-Victorian cultural salon, Gore House was the leader, frequently alluded to in the letters, diaries and memoirs of the time.

The combination of d'Orsay's highly sensitive social antennae, lavish and innovative hospitality, the chance of picking up easy hack-work for one or other of Lady Blessington's annuals, the opportunity to network furiously and the likelihood of bumping into visiting international celebrities made Gore House a social magnet. The ambience must have been somewhere between a house-party, a literary gathering and, to judge from some of the more eccentric forms of entertainment, a variety theatre. 'Have you seen the Magnetic boy?' wrote Dickens to Lady Blessington about Alexis Didier, a fashionable medium. 'You heard of him no doubt from Count d'Orsay. If you get him to Gore House, don't, I entreat you, have more than eight people – four is a better number – to see him.'[17]

It is not known whether Alexis Didier did in fact appear at Gore House, though various experiments with the occult are alluded to, with at least one source suggesting that Disraeli was among a group at Gore House who attempted to contact the spirit world. More orthodox entertainment was supplied by Liszt, who played piano here on at least one occasion, at an evening party in May 1840.[18] And among the international visitors was Longfellow, who dropped in with Dickens in October 1842, on his way back to Boston having taken a cure for rheumatism, about which d'Orsay wrote at length to his friend Lord Lichfield, also a sufferer.[19]

The celebrated Danish children's author Hans Christian Andersen captures the spirit of Gore House and its charming setting in a letter of July 1847, written when its social and cultural hegemony was at its height:

A man came into the room, quite like the portrait we have all seen, someone who had come to town for my sake and had written 'I *must* see Andersen!' When he had greeted the company I ran from the writing desk to meet him, we seized both each other's hands, gazed in each other's eyes, laughed and rejoiced. We knew each other so well, though we met for the first time – it was Charles Dickens. He quite answers to the best ideas I had formed of him. Outside the house there is a lovely veranda running the whole breadth of the house, vines and roses hang like a roof over the pillars, here are gaily-coloured birds, and below a green field, green as you only see them in England; out here we stood for a long time talking – talking English, but he understood me, I him.[20]

The charm of Gore House as an oasis and a refuge was easily apprehended by Landor, Lady Blessington's old friend and supporter from Italian days, who put up here to get away from his nagging wife in Bath. Another guest, as we have seen, was Countess Guiccioli, who stayed at Gore House when visiting London and kept up a lively correspondence with Lady Blessington from the continent. Disraeli was also someone who used Gore House as an hotel. At the beginning of 1837 he was in debt and London was in the grip of a virulent influenza epidemic, so he sought refuge from both his creditors and the flu with d'Orsay, while he worked on his latest novel *Venetia*.

'An impenetrable fog has hung over London every day with the exception of this,' he wrote to his sister on 21 January,

w[hi]ch howr. is gloomy eno' – yesterday I did not even come to town but remained at K[ensington] G[ore] where I wrote ten pages. No life can be more easy and agreeable than Mirabels and the adjoining establish[men]t. Everything so perfectly appointed and conducted with such admirable taste and finish in all the details. We dine with Miladi à tête à trois.

Déjeuner a la fourchette at ½ past one; before that tea and admirable pipes and my own room, which has every luxury of writing materials; so you see this is my own life and the second breakfast bell sounds just at the time the lion wishes to feed.

Ld L[yndhurst] is expected to night [*sic*] or tomorrow.

I have taken twice medicated air baths at D'O[rsay's], I find them renovating and if possible will go through half a doz.[21]

He finishes his letter to his sister with a request for a couple of brace of pheasants to be sent to Lady Blessington, adding the breezy assurance, 'my mother will pay for my acct'.[22] Unfortunately no pheasants were to be had, but Disraeli's mother made 'some Cocoa sweetmeat and some chips of orange for D'Or'.[23]

'People die here by dozens,' he reports cheerfully in a letter a couple of days later. 'I have just heard a report that the young Lady Glengall is dead.* D'Orsay and myself however defy the disorder with a first rate cook, a generous diet and medicated vapour baths.'[24] Disraeli stayed at Kensington Gore until early February, working on his novel, taking dinner with Lady Blessington and sharing hot-air baths with d'Orsay. It is interesting to note that even in matters of health d'Orsay was ahead of his time. The custom for hot-air baths is generally thought to have been introduced to England in 1850, and yet d'Orsay was enjoying them as early as the winter of 1836–1837.

Other intimates of the house included Lady Blessington's beautiful niece Louisa Fairlie (her sister's daughter) who helped with editing the annuals. Louisa Fairlie, a tragic figure, had a disabled daughter, Isabella, who though congenitally deaf and dumb was credited with 'extraordinary intellectual powers'.[25] This little girl was a haunting figure, who was often at Gore House, becoming 'more than ever attached to Alfred'.[26] She became a familiar sight to visitors at the house, to whom she was known as the beautiful mute. Disraeli wrote a five-stanza poem dedicated 'To a beautiful mute / the Eldest Child of Mrs Fairlie'.[27] The child died after a protracted illness in January 1843, predeceasing her mother by only a few weeks.

After Louisa Fairlie's death the duty of assisting Lady Blessington fell to two other nieces. The Misses Power, daughters of her brother, had joined her from New Brunswick, whence the rest of the family moved to try their luck in Tasmania. The elder Miss Power, Margaret,

* Disraeli was mistaken; she did not die until 1864.

sometimes called Marguerite, joined the entourage at Gore House in 1839. Ellen, the younger one, arrived in the early 1840s. Certainly the presence of the two young Powers gave another dimension to the attractions of Gore House, as the *Satirist* points out in an item in January 1842: 'The tedium of confinement, Count d'Orsay says, is much reli[e]ved by the friendly visits of Lord Pembroke, who cannot resist the power-full attraction at Kensington Gore.'[28]

Nor was Lord Pembroke the only one who found the young Power girls charming company. Writing in his memoirs at the end of the century, William Archer Shee noted of Margaret, 'I must not, however, omit her [Lady Blessington's] pretty and attractive niece, Miss Power, who adds much to the *agrément* of the society.'[29] Sadleir mentions the affection that Dickens had for the young women. 'The more real intimacy of contemporaries came to exist between Dickens and the Misses Power.'[30] Whether writing to Lady Blessington or d'Orsay, Dickens seldom forgot to pass on his 'regards' or 'best regards' to the Misses Power, except that he preferred to call them the Miss Powers: 'I can't say "the Misses Power", for it looks so like the blue board at the Gate of a Ladies' Seminary'.[31] 'Towards one of them – Marguerite – he showed great kindness after her aunt's death,' says Sadleir, 'accepting her work for his magazines, helping her with her writing, and sending her letters full of an easy affection.'[32] Marguerite Power was also a favourite of d'Orsay's friend and near neighbour Thackeray, who wrote in his diary of a dinner at Gore House: 'The Miss Powers were very kind pleasant witty and *good* as I thought.'[33]

Indeed the arrival of the Misses Power at Gore House was to provide ample fodder and potential puns for the gossip columns. In August 1843, the *Satirist* wrote that 'The handsome Count was parading the Power-full attractions of his family on the banks of the Serpentine on Sunday last; he looked well.'[34] In May 1844, another item was run that testified to the Powers' pulchritude: 'Miss Power, according to the Countess, would be, in point of figure a perfect model for an artist. D'Orsay says she sometimes is!'[35] The *Satirist* of 8 November 1846 carried the item, 'D'Orsay with much truth calls his new manufactuary the "Power-loom".'[36] The next month there was a cryptic piece, 'Gore House, on dit, is about to change its title to the Pavilion Powers-Court. Query, will "great lass" stand this?'[37] The following November the *Satirist* was back to its puns: 'When the Countess of Blessington's carriage contains herself, her nieces, and her nephew, why is it like a person holding a high office? – Because it is Power full (powerful).'[38]

Perhaps because of Lady Blessington's notoriety, of which the *Satirist* wrote, 'Lady Blessington is much visited by the aristocracy of rank and Talent. We never hear, however, that any of them took their wives and sisters to see her',[39] the Power sisters never left Gore House to find husbands, for all their attractiveness. And as the years drew on and the chances for marriage dwindled, along with Lady Blessington's income, they must have been another burden on the budget of Gore House. As the *Satirist* of 5 March 1848 stated, 'The Countess of Blessington says her nieces, by the blessed Powers! Are extremely like damp gunpowther, for they won't go off at all, at all.'[40]

CHAPTER NINETEEN

Track and Stage

WHILE THE LITERARY GIANTS OF THE DAY WERE DRAWN ALONG the southerly side of Hyde Park to Gore House, the sporting elite was attracted to the opposite side of the Park, by one of the more remarkable sporting experiments London had ever witnessed: the Hippodrome, Bayswater, 'a race-course of some two and a half miles in circuit' that had come into existence after 'a Mr. John Whyte had turned his attention to the slopes of Notting Hill, and to the Portobello meadows west of Westbourne Grove, and prepared a course, not for golf, but for horse-racing and steeple-chasing, with the accompaniments of a training-ground and stables for about eighty horses'.[1]

According to the handbill that advertised its inaugural meeting in 1837 on 'Saturday, the 3rd Day of June, being the Saturday in the week after Epsom', the 'Hippodrome is situated about one mile and a half from Hyde Park Corner, on the Uxbridge Road, leading from London, and close to Kensington Gardens'.[2] The gentle 'slopes of Notting Hill' and the fragrant 'meadows west of Westbourne Grove' are now of course buried beneath some of the most fashionable real estate in London. In the 1830s it was open country, but for it to rival Ascot and Epsom, Whyte would have needed to make his new venture fashionable, and to this end he persuaded Count d'Orsay and Lord Chesterfield to act as stewards; their names appeared in bold capitals at the bottom of the first handbill.

Given his experience as a proponent of racing *à l'anglais* in Paris, and his status as London's fashion leader, d'Orsay was a perfect choice. By the late 1830s, his friend the Earl of Chesterfield was making quite a name for himself as a successful racehorse owner, with a string of winners including Industry, winner of the 1838 Oaks at Epsom, and Don John, which won the 1838 St Leger, while others of d'Orsay's friends, including Lord Lichfield, with Corsair and Elis, appeared in the winners' enclosures.

The Hippodrome was a true product of its time. London was prosperous and expanding, but before the speculative building booms of the Victorian age, which threw up Italianate villas and stucco-fronted houses of varying degrees of pretension and shoddy construction, pleasant land still existed sufficiently close to town to accommodate such schemes. Racing was a fitting occupation for the national elite and, even though William IV was not as fanatical about the turf as George IV had been, he kept on his late brother's horses. Gambling was a vice more or less accepted, or at least tolerated, and had yet to become stigmatised as it would in the years of Victoria's reign. The early years of the nineteenth century saw a racing boom.

'It must be a matter of sincere congratulation to every possessor of true British sentiments,' wrote James Christie Whyte in his *History of the British Turf* shortly after the opening of the Hippodrome, 'and consequently every admirer of the field sports so peculiar to our native country, that in spite of all the cant and false religion brought to bear against the amusements of the turf by a numerous class whom in common charity, we will call misled fanatics, racing has still gone on increasing in prosperity and the national favour.'[3]

The statistics Whyte invoked were impressive. According to him, racing had been on the decline in Britain during the late eighteenth century as a result of the 'wars which so entirely engrossed the attention of the British nation at that period'.[4]

'Thus in 1800, we find that annual racing meetings were held at only sixty-six towns in England and Wales, five in Scotland, and four in Ireland. In 1816, after the last great peace, we already find them on the increase, the number in that year being eighty-four in England and Wales, nine in Scotland, and eight in Ireland,' records Whyte, adding with a note of triumph, 'so rapid has been the increase since then, that the number at the present day (1839) is no less than one hundred and thirty-two in England, many of which consist of two, and several, more, annual meetings; nine in Wales, nine in Scotland and three in Ireland'.[5]

The identical surnames of the author of the *History of the British Turf* and the proprietor of the Hippodrome hint that they might be related. This could account for the eulogistic mentions the latter's racecourse receives in the former's book, which talks of the popularity of the meetings here 'and the patronage they met with among our first nobility'.[6] The Hippodrome seems to have opened to an almost unanimously rapturous press. A reporter for the *Sporting Magazine* of 1837 provides a description of the place that is little short of an encomium. 'Making the *cours aristocratique* of Routine (*alias* Rotten) Row, you pass out at Cumberland Gate, and then trot on to Bayswater. Thence you arrive at the Kensington Gravel Pits, and descending where on the left stands the terrace of Notting Hill, find opposite the large wooden gates of a recent structure.'[7] One enthusiastic newspaper report, which dubbed the Hippodrome 'the greatest addition to the recreations of London which has been made during the last hundred years',[8] is even illustrated with a woodcut of the entrance, a structure only marginally less grand than Marble Arch or the arch at Hyde Park Corner. Whether this arch was ever built is open to speculation, since the report appeared at the end of 1836 and no other illustrations seem to feature it.

Having passed through the gates the enthusiastic reporter from the *Sporting Magazine* continued his hymn of praise:

> I was by no means prepared for what opened upon me. Here, without figure of speech, was the most perfect race-course that I had ever seen. Conceive, almost within the bills of mortality, an enclosure some two miles and a half in circuit, commanding from its centre a view as spacious and enchanting as that from Richmond Hill [*sic*], and where almost the only thing that you can *not* see is London. Around this, on the extreme circle, next to the lofty fence by which it is protected, . . . is constructed, or rather laid out – for the leaps are natural fences – the steeple-chase course of two miles and a quarter. Within this, divided by a slight trench, and from the space appropriated to carriages and equestrians by strong and handsome posts all the way round, is the race-course, less probably than a furlong in circuit. Then comes the enclosure for those who ride or drive as aforesaid; and lastly, the middle, occupied by a hill, from which every yard of the running is commanded, besides miles of country on every side beyond it, and exclusively reserved for foot people. I could hardly credit what I saw. Here was, almost at our doors, a racing emporium more extensive and attractive than Ascot or Epsom, with ten times the accommodation of either, and where carriages are charged for admission at three-fourths less.[9]

At this point the reporter is so overcome by the splendour and beauty of his surroundings that he embarks on a panegyric to Mr Whyte that is a publicist's dream. The Hippodrome was to be the epicentre of fashion, a perfect location for training, a safe place for women to practise their equestrian skills 'without the danger or exposure of the parks';[10] it was in fact little short of miraculous that life in London had managed to continue for so long in the absence of such a necessity as a racecourse at Notting Hill.

When Saturday 3 June eventually arrived, d'Orsay and Chesterfield acquitted themselves well as stewards, attracting what one source calls 'as brilliant an assembly as ever met together in London'.[11] 'As a place of fashionable resort,' declared the *Sporting Magazine*, 'it certainly opened under promising auspices, the stewards being Lord Chesterfield and Count d'Orsay. Another year, I cannot doubt, is destined to see it rank among the most favourite and favoured of all the metropolitan rendezvous, both for public and private recreation. Unquestionably, of the varieties of the present season none has put forward such a claim to popularity and patronage as the "Hippodrome".'[12] Doubtless it helped that 'every refreshment was provided at a rate for which those who had been used to the terrible extortions elsewhere would hardly have been prepared'.[13] A particular favourite seems to have been the 'iced champagne, which can hardly be called a mortal beverage'.[14] Among the estimated fifteen to twenty thousand patrons who thronged the Hippodrome on its inaugural day's racing were three dukes – Grafton, Beaufort and Brunswick – as well as Lords Jersey, Anglesea, Uxbridge, Southampton, Macdonald, Poltimore, Kinnaird, Harewood, Clarendon, Forester, Wilton, Paget, Waterford and many other peers. D'Orsay's patronage also helped attract what one newspaper report called 'the distinguished foreigners at present in this country'.[15] These included d'Orsay's friend Count Tolstoy, the Duke d'Ossuna and the Grand Duke of Russia.

The scene must have been exhilarating on that long-distant summer afternoon. It would appear that London emptied to descend upon this quiet rural hamlet. One reporter makes it seem that an entire city was on the move. 'There certainly was a call upon the inhabitants of the metropolis to show what they were made of, to which they unanimously responded, every vehicle that coach, cab, or cart-builder, ever constructed or imagined, was *en route* soon after mid-day: Oxford-road [*sic*] looked like Sutton on the Derby day; every order of man, woman, and child, vehicle and quadruped, showed.'[16] By one o'clock, an hour and half before the start of the first race, the entrances were thronged and Notting Hill was besieged by the sort of crowds it had never seen before. At 2.30 p.m., the bell sounded and there was a mad scramble for places to watch the first race: free-flowing champagne, crowds cheering their favourites on around the course and occupants of both 'saddle or easy-slung barouche'[17] racing alongside to catch the action at the finishing post – it must have been a remarkable afternoon.

'Certainly as far as patronage goes, the projector of the Hippodrome has every reason to be most abundantly satisfied,' ran one newspaper report.[18] The presence of the names of d'Orsay and Chesterfield at the foot of advertisements for the racecourse fulfilled a valuable public-relations function, lending a veneer of metropolitan chic and sporting credibility to Mr Whyte's speculative venture. Given the Frenchman's perpetual requirement for ready money and the bankability of the d'Orsay name, it seems highly likely that some sort of mutually acceptable pecuniary arrangement was reached. And, in addition to any remuneration that he would have received, the scheme was exactly the sort of glamorous, high-profile and decadent enterprise that would have appealed to him.

It amused Count d'Orsay to be a steward of the latest and most fashionable sporting and social venue in town and his function seems to have been more than merely ornamental. One newspaper report of a day at the Hippodrome records that the races 'were appointed to commence at two o'clock; but as two parties had horses engaged in each of the Plates (Aurelius, Ruinous, Lochinvar, &c.), and did not agree which should be run first, nothing could be done till the arrival of Count d'Orsay, at four o'clock'.[19] It is easy to picture d'Orsay's leisurely arrival, no doubt detained by some final adjustments to his appearance, perhaps top-hatted on horseback, looking glamorous like his portrait by Haydon, or in one of his fashionably appointed carriages; and to imagine how, with a few well-chosen and charming words of his accented English, like a social and sporting Solomon he adjudicated on this knotty problem of racing etiquette. This was the d'Orsay of London legend, a creature of mythology: at once the good-humoured social sage and shimmering apparition of sheer glamour. Whatever Mr Whyte was paying, he was surely getting value for money, and as time wore on he would have increasing need of d'Orsay's help.

For all the favourable press comment and carefully orchestrated hype surrounding the opening of the Hippodrome, it was beset by two major problems. The first became apparent at the opening meeting. Whyte had ringed the entire course with a wall of wooden palings, which at its lowest point was seven feet high: having invested a considerable sum in his scheme, he was not about to let the racing be seen for free. However, a public footpath ran across the Hippodrome: it was to prove a massive inconvenience to Whyte and a considerable drain on the profits. It would eventually contribute to the closure of the Hippodrome in 1841. The first meeting saw the wall breached by the 'gigantic efforts of the Kensington right-of-way-ers – down went bolt and barrier; prostrated were hoops and hoarding; the claimants fairly made their way over the course, the proprietor finding it impolitic to oppose such a demonstration of public feeling, consented to the "way" remaining open, and some thousands thus obtained gratuitous admission'.[20]

But Whyte was well connected. After he had failed to silence the right-of-way lobby in the courts, the *Mirror of Parliament* records a debate about a private member's bill to enclose the Notting Hill footpath, in which Whyte's interest was staunchly defended by Lord George Lennox. Public opinion, however, effectively marshalled by the parish authorities, was opposed, arguments about the deleterious effects on the morals of pupils at nearby boarding schools were invoked and satirical pieces appeared in *The Times*. In the autumn of 1838 the bill was dropped.

Whyte's other problems were the standard of racing and of the ground itself: the heavy clay soil made it a course of variable quality. As an article in the *British Racehorse* put it 130 years later, 'the soil was strong clay which made the land useless even as a training ground at many times of the year'.[21] Some reports exhorted Whyte to raise the stakes in the hope of improving the quality of racing. Instead he resorted to using the site for other attractions, such as the ascent of 'The Great Montgolfier Balloon', which burst at the Hippodrome in August 1839.[22] Other diversions were offered, including the chance to shoot tethered pigeons with a bow and arrow.

One particular publicity stunt, in July 1838, seems to have d'Orsay's fingerprints all over it:

Hippodrome – Wednesday

This was the additional day of the seventh meeting, and the public must have been somewhat astonished at the aristocratic names put before those of the nags. It is true that the regular racegoers saw the technical 'na,' and knew that his Grace of Beaufort, Prince Esterhazy, Earls Chesterfield and Wilton, Counts Bathyany, d'Orsay, and Zaradowsky only subscribed five guineas each, and named nothing but second-rate horses; but to the mass it had the effect of a delusion . . . If the noblemen we have named wish to serve Mr Whyte, they must send, not a paltry subscription and a name, but their horses to him; and that they will not do until he has spirit and policy enough to get up good stakes. There are many improvements that we could suggest, but it is an ungracious task. We, however, do hope that the judge will, for the future, prevent a pack of boys climbing up his chair, so as to make it doubtful whether he could see the race at all. At such a meeting, what, more than mockery is it to call d'Orsay and Chesterfield stewards.[23]

After such a stinging broadside in the press and the embarrassment caused to some of his smart friends, the Hippodrome must have seemed a less attractive prospect for d'Orsay. He continued to appear among the list of fashionables who attended race meetings at the Hippodrome, but by 1841 neither he nor Chesterfield was a steward; their duties had been taken on by the Duke of Beaufort and the Hon. Captain Rous.

By this time the Hippodrome had changed considerably. In 1839 Whyte had given up his struggle against the right-of-way protesters, surrendered the eastern half of the ground and altered his racecourse so that it did not infringe upon the footpath. But to the variable quality of soil and the vociferous complaints of the footpath lobby Mr Whyte had to add a third worry. The second meeting at the Hippodrome in the summer of 1837 had to be postponed at short notice due to the death of William IV. Following his death, the sale of the Royal Stud did not augur well for racing in Britain. Victorian values, as they would come to be known, would be incompatible with such highly public, raffish endeavours as the Hippodrome: the character of the racecourse and its surroundings was hardly spotless. 'About this time Pottery Lane* was nicknamed Cut Throat Lane,' runs one account, 'and it was possible, and sometimes advisable, to hide in the ditch beside the track.'[24] Moreover, 'gipsies, prigs (thieves) and hawkers did not neglect the opportunity of mingling with the nobility and the gentry'.[25] And in 1840 'one well-dressed man was carried away on a stretcher, apparently dead',[26] after an incident on the

---

* The chimney of one of the pottery kilns can be seen in the background of a print depicting the last Grand Steeplechase at the Hippodrome in 1841.

way home from a race meeting at the Hippodrome attended by Count d'Orsay and, among others, his old friend from Florence, the Marquis of Normanby.

Press advertisements for the season of 1841 indicate that desperate attempts were being made to clean up the image of the Hippodrome. Renamed the Hippodrome at Victoria Park, doubtless in the hope of finding favour with the young Queen, as well as with the new stewards, it was stated that 'Omnibuses, carts, or waggons will not be admitted' and that refreshments were supplied by 'Mr Careless, of the Epsom and Ascot Grand Stand'.[27] A partnership had been entered into with a bill broker turned property developer called Connop, whereby land to the east would be covered with a 'series of Italian villages, with an elegant church'. But these attempts at gentrification, and indeed the promise of improved stakes, came too late to save the Hippodrome from closure. The last race was run in June 1841. And in May 1845 the *Sunday Times* reported Connop as being 'confined to the Queen's Prison'.[28]

Happily d'Orsay did not have to depend upon the Hippodrome for his amusement; there were the delights of Crockford's, country-house parties, Gore House salons and the theatre, where d'Orsay was as much of a fixture as on the racecourse. At the end of 1836, the year before the Hippodrome opened, he was recorded as having gone to rehearsals of *La Vallière* with its author, his friend and fellow dandy Bulwer.[29] And after the first night of the play on 4 January 1837 d'Orsay and Lady Blessington gave a supper party, albeit 'too rich a supper' for one palate,[30] to celebrate. But Bulwer seemed unhappy with his play and when it was excoriated for its profanity, irreverence and immorality, it was d'Orsay, acting the part of peacemaker, who wrote to the celebrated actor Macready to secure his assent to various changes made by the playwright.

His friendship with the actor seems to have been genuine on both sides. It is interesting to record the priggish footnote in a 1912 edition of Macready's diaries, in which Macready is noted as appearing 'to have entertained an unqualified regard for him, in spite of shortcomings which he would have severely denounced in members of his own fraternity. D'Orsay, in fact, stripped of his social glamour was anything but an estimable character, and it is surprising to find so austere a moralist as Macready a frequent visitor of the tarnished d'Orsay Blessington establishment.'[31] But at the time the crushing morality of the latter half of the nineteenth century had yet to emerge as a dominant force, and prominent figures in the performing arts were evidently glad to seek d'Orsay's advice and valued his opinion.

For d'Orsay this was an avenue that allowed him some form of intellectual activity beyond concocting outlandish costumes with his tailor. The count was a cultivated man as well as a kind and patient nurturer of talent – indeed Bulwer admitted that it was encouragement from d'Orsay that sustained him in his ultimately successful attempts to become a playwright. 'The moment you liked the Lady of Lyons, I was satisfied,' he wrote to Lady Blessington of his second play. 'The wish to prove that your and Alfred's kind belief that I *could* hit off the Dramatic Knack impelled me to the attempt, as much as anything else.'[32]

D'Orsay was also able to help Macready prepare himself for the role of Richelieu in the eponymous play by Bulwer, introducing him to his old schoolfriend Alfred de Vigny, author of *Cinq Mars*, in which various of Richelieu's character traits had been delineated. Vigny was visiting London in early 1839 and on 16 February met Macready at Gore House, where he advised him on the part. And when it was announced that the young queen had expressed a wish to see Richelieu and had sent the Lord Chamberlain's deputy to obtain a copy of the play, d'Orsay too requested a copy.[33] It is as if he wanted to demonstrate that he was more than a mere clotheshorse. However, even in the theatrical world he was unable to escape his reputation as a dandy for long.

In June 1840 Bulwer wrote to Macready, 'I have thought of a comedy . . . My proposed title is "Appearances", the idea a genteel Comedy of the present day – the Moral, a satire on the way appearances of all kinds impose upon the public.'[34] The title of the proposed play and the significance of its subject can hardly have been lost on d'Orsay and Lady Blessington, whose lives were forever to be judged by appearances.

In the event the play was called *Money*, but the theme of deceit through appearances and the ensuing confusion was retained and worked up to produce a light yet entertaining comedy, which was revived at the National Theatre in London at the end of the twentieth century. Given the play's theme, that one of the principal characters was a dandy and that one scene took place in a gambling hell clearly intended to represent Crockford's, it was inevitable that Bulwer would seek d'Orsay's advice. 'Sir John should wear a blue coat with velvet collar, buttoned up – the *King's button*. In the Evening – his order of the Guelph – breeches & silk stockings. Blount must be perfectly dressed – also Smooth,' wrote Bulwer of two characters to Macready, as the writing of the play progressed. He added, 'D'Orsay may be consulted here.'[35] D'Orsay was to be consulted again on 'whether whist & piquet would be *ever* played in the great Drawing-room at Crockford's – or in some other room set apart for the purpose'.[36] And in a diary entry that November Macready wrote, 'D'Orsay called to see what I wanted. I inquired of him his hatter, the mode of keeping accounts at the clubs in play, about servants etc. It was very kind of him.'[37] And d'Orsay's concern for theatrical verisimilitude extended beyond talking Macready through his wardrobe and his social habits. 'Called at Ashmead's for a hat,' noted Macready in his diary a few days later, 'and found d'Orsay had been there to speak about one for me!'[38]

Such a close interest in the details of mounting plays was matched by a desire to introduce new talent to the London stage, be it in the form of thespians or of material. As well as keeping up a friendship with Macready the actor and Bulwer the playwright, d'Orsay felt himself to be on sufficiently good terms with Frederick Henry Yates, proprietor and manager of the Adelphi Theatre, to write the following: 'I have a melodrama in two acts to offer you, written by one of my friends. The story is taken from a work of George Sand – one of the better French writers of our time: it is called *L'Usocco*. The characters would be well suited to the company of excellent actors that you have at the Adelphi; if you think that this might interest you, I shall send you the manuscript.'[39]

But d'Orsay's interest in the performing arts was more than merely cultural; he had risen to fame as a dandy and, however cerebral, sensitive and helpful he might have been, it was as a dandy that he would be viewed by the majority of those who did not take the time to get to know him. Besides, it was an easy role for him to play – he liked the attention and the theatre was a diverting social arena. As well as a place to see, be seen and exchange gossip, for men of fashion it was the place to go and ogle actresses, *danseuses* and *cantatrices*: the dandies of the early nineteenth century would gather in their boxes and appraise the talent on stage much as they might appraise the parade of horseflesh at Tattersall's.

A box might cost around three hundred pounds for a season. An evening's entertainment was often long and varied, and might include an opera and a romantic ballet. A visit to the Haymarket would take up much of the night, and during the 1820s and 1830s it was considered chic for the man of fashion to leave his box and gather with his friends in the aisles between benches of the pit, known colloquially as Fop's Alley, to chat, laugh, gossip and generally annoy those who had actually come out for the evening to appreciate the latest opera or ballet. Although a numerical minority, the dandies dictated the pace and tone of a night at the opera or ballet. There were times when they considered mere words inadequate to convey their opinions. In 1840, d'Orsay's friend the Duke of Beaufort, together with Prince George of Cambridge, led a charge of dandies on to the stage to convince the management of the wisdom of engaging Tamburini, a celebrated tenor. This incident later became known as the Tamburini Riot.

And when not invading the stage, lurking in their private boxes or gathering in Fop's Alley it was seen as fashionable to make an appearance in the omnibus boxes, which flanked the proscenium arch on the same level as the stage and were occupied by the more fashionable and flashy members of White's and Crockford's. Such was their proximity to the stage that occupants were afforded an unparalleled view of the female performers and kept up a commentary, often noisy, on the quality of the evening's entertainment. 'We cannot really forbear noticing', ran a report in the *Satirist* during 1833, 'the annoyance caused by those omnibus tadpoles, Sefton, Tullamore, Allen, Wombwell and others, who, in order to attract the attention of the figurantes, keep up a continual clatter of approbation, which at times reminds us of the unwelcome din of little children in sulky contention with their nurses.'[40]

These men were friends of d'Orsay, and indeed in the same year that the *Satirist* wrote about their behaviour in the box, d'Orsay was suspected of bad behaviour with a pretty young ballet dancer called Fanny Elssler. What is interesting is that this dalliance sheds a little more light on the question of his sexual orientation. That Elssler was the object of his attention was apparently widely known throughout London at the time, and several years later, when she asked a friend to look after her daughter while she danced in America, the friend replied, 'Well, Fanny, send the brat to me. I don't ask you whose child it is, and I don't care, so long as it isn't that fool d'Orsay's.'[41] The prospect of an illegitimate d'Orsay daughter finds no favour with the sour Sadleir, who posited that d'Orsay was impotent, writing that the count 'would not wish, by untimely disapprobation or by admitting his own inability to share their [his friends'] tastes, to weaken his hold on their loyalty. So he would go with Chesterfield to see Elssler in her dressing-room, would accompany Duncombe or Lichfield to the discreet dwellings of the demi-monde. It would not have been difficult at the right time to slip away, untouched in pocket and with his abnormality unbetrayed.'[42] If Sadleir is right, d'Orsay certainly acted the part of ladies' man well enough, as a typical report from the *Satirist* of December 1840 indicates: '"Don't you perceive a strong scent of turtle?" asked Chesterfield of d'Orsay, as they entered Guildhall, on the night of the ball. "No" replied the Count, casting his eyes upon a group of City belles, who were waiting to join the mazy dance, "but I scent the turtle-doves".'[43]

And there is no doubt that, when not ogling City beauties, d'Orsay hung around the stars' dressing rooms. In his diaries Macready writes frequently of welcoming the count and friends, including Bulwer and 'King' Allen, an Irish viscount and West End dandy, backstage. In Mills's thinly veiled *roman à clef*, the eponymous protagonist the Marquis d'Horsay is involved in farcical sexual scenes; in one, Clara, a cameo of the famous *danseuse* Cerito, is seen bundling Chesterlane (Chesterfield) out of her dressing room in order to spend time with d'Horsay (d'Orsay), whose arrival is imminent.

Indeed d'Horsay is frequently caught *in flagrante*. For instance, a member of a hunt clears a fence to find d'Horsay and Clara canoodling on the other side. On another occasion d'Horsay tosses a dozen withered daisies from the omnibus box to remind her of a pleasurable night spent near Windsor:

> when she turned to the omnibus box and saw the little cluster of dried daisies thrown at her feet, Clara could not control her risible muscles, and skipped away with a laugh that was distinctly heard in the first row of the pit.
>
> The companions of the Marquis enjoyed this joke amazingly, and it was some few minutes before any part of speech was mingled with its chorus.[44]

It would seem that the d'Orsay of Mills's telling was an entertaining lover in quite a few ways.

But life was not all *figurantes* and fillies. As he aged, d'Orsay seemed to tire of an existence composed entirely of frivolity. He wanted to be more than a mere dandy. Having conquered the world of fashion, he turned his attention to superpower politics.

CHAPTER TWENTY

Man of Destiny

'ONE OF THE GUESTS AT GORE HOUSE WAS A PERSONAGE WHOM I was destined to see very often afterwards in active life,' recalled an habitué of the house at the end of the nineteenth century.

A short, slight form he had, and not a very graceful way of standing. His complexion was swarthily pale, if I may be allowed to make use of that somewhat paradoxical expression. His hair struck me as being of a dark brown; it was much lighter in after years; and while his cheeks were clean-shaven, the lower part of his face was concealed by a thick moustache and an 'imperial' or chin-tuft. He was gorgeously arrayed in the dandy evening costume of the period – a costume which to some up-to-date critics might seem preposterous; but which others, comprising, I should say, Mr. Oscar Wilde, might deem comely and tasteful and worthy of revival . . . He wore a satin 'stock,' green, if I am not mistaken; and in the centre of that stock was a breast-pin in the image of a gold eagle encircled with diamonds. I am trying to be throughout these pages as strictly accurate as I possibly can, but I am not prepared to declare with certainty whether the eagle in the young gentleman's stock had closed or outspread wings. They should properly have been closed; since the bird of Jove with outspread wings is the cognisance of Prussia, of Russia, and of the United States; whereas the eagle with the closed wings was borrowed from the Roman standards to be the emblem of Imperial France; and the young gentleman with the satin stock and the diamond breast-pin was none other than Prince Louis Napoleon Bonaparte, Pretender to the throne of France.[1]

This recollection is of a meeting that took place in the mid- to late 1830s. The short, graceless, swarthily pale young man would later be known as the arbiter of Europe; as Emperor Napoleon III he would rule France for twenty years, presiding over a period of French prestige that would be known as the Deuxième Empire.

D'Orsay and Louis Napoleon had been in Rome at the same time in the late 1820s. And while the count had spent the 1830s establishing himself as the undisputed leader of fashion, the young Louis, son of Hortense and nephew of Napoleon, had found himself the heir to the imperial throne. First his elder brother died, then Napoleon's son the Duke of Reichstadt (and King of Rome), ever frail, succumbed to consumption in 1832. In his will the duke bequeathed Napoleon's favourite sword to Louis.

Some months before Reichstadt's death, the perspicacious statesman Metternich had written to Austria's ambassador in France, suggesting that he alert King Louis-Philippe to 'the character of the man who will succeed the Duke of Reichstadt'. Metternich's ominous appraisal of a man many saw as a harmless, irrelevant scion of the Napoleonic dynasty would have made uncomfortable reading for the King of France. 'The young Louis Bonaparte is a man tied up with the plots of the secret societies. He is not formed as the Duke under the safeguard of the principles of our Emperor. The day of the Duke's death, he will look upon himself as called upon to rule France.'[2]

However, like many people at the time, the portly people's monarch Louis-Philippe dismissed the idea of another Napoleon ruling France as an idiotic fantasȳ – especially as the pretender was by many accounts an uninspiring figure, a bland character, interesting primarily as a contrast to his remarkable uncle. Greville dismissed him as 'a short thickish vulgar-looking man without the slightest resemblance to his Imperial uncle or any intelligence in his countenance'.[3] According to another visitor to Lady Blessington's salons, whose memoirs were published late in the nineteenth century, the emperor-to-be who skulked around Gore House was a 'much-ridiculed knight-errant', who 'looked and talked in those days as if oppressed by a heavy dread of the future, rather than sustained by an unquenchable flame of hope, and gave one the idea of a man whose omens of his after-career were far more gloomy than sanguine. He seldom spoke, except on trivial matters of the day; and of a surety few who met him there had the faith which it is said her ladyship held, that he was destined to be – "Great hereafter."'[4]

'Among the company last night was Prince Louis Napoleon,' recorded William Archer Shee in his diary of an evening at Gore House in May 1839.

He was quiet, silent, and inoffensive, as, to do him justice, he generally is, but he does not impress one with the idea that he had inherited his uncle's talents any more than his fortunes. He went away before the circle quite broke up, leaving, like Sir Peter Teazle, 'his character behind him,' and that few remaining did not spare him, but discussed him in a tone that was far from flattering. D'Orsay, however, who came in later with Lord Pembroke, stood up manfully for his friend, which was pleasant to see.[5]

It was probably out of deference to d'Orsay's loyalty to Louis that Disraeli observed in the prince 'that calm which is rather unusual with foreigners, and which is always pleasing to an English aristocrat'.[6] Perhaps that was just another way of dubbing Louis as dull.

During the early 1830s, Louis Napoleon made a couple of visits to London, but his base was at his mother's castle at Arenberg in German-speaking Switzerland on the southern shore of Lake Constance, where he was beginning to position himself as a leader-in-exile. In 1834 news reached him of insurrection in Lyons against Louis-Philippe. He voiced his support and raced to Geneva, naively intending to cross the border and lead the revolt, even though the insurrectionists had not declared themselves as Bonapartists. By the time he reached Geneva the revolt had been crushed. Undeterred, two years later he tried again. Assisted by his friend and ardent supporter, a former revolutionary and journalist turned devout Bonapartist, the Comte de Persigny, Louis attempted a coup that would resemble Napoleon's Hundred Days. It was supposed to start with seizure of the garrison at Strasbourg. This too failed, and, tired of the young pretender's attempts to take over France, the government of Louis-Philippe refrained from making a martyr of him but packed him off to America.

He returned to Switzerland in time to see his mother die. Later, under pressure from the French government, he left Switzerland for Britain, arriving at Fenton's Hotel on St James's Street in October 1838. He soon moved into a smart house in Carlton House Terrace and then to another in Carlton Gardens. He had been left a considerable fortune by his mother and made something of a splash with a coach decorated with the imperial eagle and so on. His household was controlled by the Comte de Persigny.

In his biography of Napoleon III, Fenton Bresler makes the following analysis of the relationship between Persigny and Louis: 'The two men took an instant liking to each other: the dreamer had met his man of action, the man of action had met the living embodiment of his dream. Over the next few years, Persigny had so great an influence over Louis and their relationship was so intense that now it would be fashionable to question if there was a homosexual link between them.'[7] The same seems to have been true of the relationship between d'Orsay and Louis Napoleon: d'Orsay the glamorous man of action, whose Napoleonic enthusiasm had been reignited by the young pretender, and the quixotic Louis Napoleon enjoying the protection of the older, more assured and more securely established, not to mention much taller and more handsome, count. The two men were certainly very close. 'There is not the slightest doubt that very intimate relations existed between d'Orsay and Louis Napoleon during his days of exile in England,' is the opinion of the count's 1911 biographer Teignmouth Shore.[8]

Just how close the two men were would become apparent early in 1840. That January, the Comte Léon, an illegitimate son of Napoleon who, though a larger man than his father, bore a striking resemblance to the emperor, arrived in London. He had recently been released from prison in France where he had been held for debt. One source says that he had come to London to see Joseph Bonaparte, the former king of Spain now living in exile in London, in the hope of claiming various dispositions made in his favour by Napoleon I's uncle Cardinal Fesch.[9] Another view is that Léon was in England as an *agent provocateur* on the payroll of the French government.

Whatever his motives for coming to London, the legitimate scions of the Bonaparte dynasty were not prepared to meet with the product of a union between the great emperor and a woman identified by one source as Eléonore Denvelle, a lady-in-waiting. First Joseph refused to see Léon, who was then snubbed by Jérôme and finally by Louis. The last insult was too much for Léon, who launched into a bilious and contemptuous letter addressing Louis as 'mon petit-cousin', accusing him of 'une impolitesse bien basse' and swearing by the ashes of the emperor that Louis' shabby treatment of him would be punished.[10] Louis sent Colonel Parquin, an old co-conspirator from Strasbourg, to explain why the imperial family would have nothing to do with Léon. Enraged, Léon fired off another poisonous letter, to which Louis did not bother to reply, after which a duel was proposed. Louis did not hesitate, nominating as his seconds the doughty Parquin and the glamorous d'Orsay.

Once again d'Orsay found himself involved in a high-profile duel and, although by 1840 duelling was beginning to fade away as the favoured method of resolving disputes, d'Orsay still seemed to be the man of fashion's second of choice. Thus it was that early in the morning of 3 March, while it was still dark, the combatants set off from town to a location Colonel Parquin charmingly identified in a letter as 'Wimbleton Commons'.[11] The small but distinguished group met on rural ground, suitably distant from the metropolis and its police force, at seven o'clock. Given the early start perhaps d'Orsay had travelled there straight after a night at Crockford's.

Straight away, the Comte de Léon began to behave most oddly. Having filled his letters to Louis with all sorts of invective and taunts couched in preposterously heroic language and having subsequently issued a challenge to a duel, he now baulked at Louis' choice of weapon, the epée. Having been shown a pair of foils by Parquin, Léon announced that he preferred to use a pistol. This was a serious breach of etiquette and a long argument ensued, with Parquin not bothering to disguise his view of Léon. It is easy to imagine d'Orsay, languidly elegant, stifling a yawn and trying to keep his eyes open as this affair of honour descended into farce. To bring about a result, and presumably to enable him to retire swiftly to bed, d'Orsay suggested that lots be drawn to to decide which weapon was to be used. Léon's second thanked the opposition for their indulgence, but Léon remained obdurate and in the end, after further discussion, Louis acquiesced in the employment of pistols. These were just about to be loaded when proceedings were abruptly halted by the arrival of the police, who arrested the combatants for an attempted breach of the peace and their seconds in their capacity as aiders and abettors. They were bound over to keep the peace at the Bow Street police court, with the Hon. Francis Baring standing surety for d'Orsay. The theory that Léon was in the pay of the French government, and intent on embarrassing Louis, is given some weight if one considers that the police may have been tipped off. It is possible that by disputing the choice of weapons he was merely playing for time, waiting for the arrival of the constabulary.

This (non-)event certainly brought Louis and d'Orsay closer together, and they were often together at Gore House in the early part of 1840. Indeed at this time Louis Napoleon was seen less about London and appeared to have withdrawn himself from fashionable Society, preferring instead the company of his cronies in exile and d'Orsay. The reason for this became apparent in August that year.

'News arrived this morning of Louis Napoleon having landed yesterday morning at Boulogne with fifty followers,' wrote Lord Malmesbury, a friend of d'Orsay and a frequent visitor to Gore House, in his diary on 7 August. 'None of the soldiers, however, having joined him, the attempt totally failed, and he and most of those who accompanied him were taken. This explains an expression he used to me two evenings ago. He was standing on the steps of Lady Blessington's house after a party, wrapped up in a cloak, with Persigny by him, and I observed to them, "You look like two conspirators," upon which he answered, "You may be nearer right than you think."'[12] There is something almost childlike about the way in which Louis Napoleon dropped hints. It would seem that his attempt to seize power in France was an open secret at the house, with dinner guests trying to make sense of gnomic utterances. At least one group of visitors to Gore House in July came away scratching their heads in bemusement at the behaviour of their fellow guest and wondering,

'What could Louis Napoleon mean by asking us to dine with him this day twelvemonths at the Tuileries?'[13]

But what might have seemed like a good idea strolling round the gardens of Gore House on a summer evening, smoking a post-prandial cigar with the loyal and glamorous d'Orsay, quickly fell apart once it was put into action. Louis had rented a pleasure steamer called the *Edinburgh Castle* to travel to Vimereux near Boulogne. Here with the force of his personality – which from the accounts above would seem to be at best a dubious weapon – the help of a small band of followers (a motley group of servants, disillusioned Frenchmen and assorted Eurotrash who found the idea of toppling the French government appealing), some fake uniforms, five dozen rifles and twenty thousand pounds (close to a million pounds today) in cash and bullion, he attempted to invade France. The invasion was delayed because the French authorities had kept his house under observation, and Louis had to travel round London for five hours before he could shake off the spies. But his invading force was not unduly perturbed; the delay allowed time to stop at Gravesend and shop for cigars and a live eagle, which was purchased for a pound and strapped to a mast as mascot.

The Boulogne expedition was as much of a fiasco as the attempted insurrection at Strasbourg – except that this time the French government did not feel as leniently disposed to the rogue Bonaparte as before. Having been pulled from the sea, where he was clinging to a buoy after the lifeboat in which he had attempted to escape had capsized, he was tried and on 6 October the court sentenced him to perpetual imprisonment at the Château de Ham, in north-eastern France.

So close were d'Orsay and Louis Napoleon that, once the latter had disappeared on his second ill-fated attempt to inspire the French populace to rise up against their king, Lady Blessington was moved to write a letter in defence of the count to Edward Bulwer's diplomat brother Henry, who was at the time chargé d'affaires in Paris. 'Alfred is at Doncaster,' she wrote in September 1840, but he charges me to authorize you, to contradict, in the most positive terms, the reports about his having participated in, or even known of the intentions of the Prince Louis. Indeed, had he suspected them, he would have used every effort in his power to dissuade him from putting them into execution. Alfred, as well as I, entertain the sincerest regard for the Prince, with whom for fourteen years we have been on terms of intimacy; but of his plans we knew no more than you did. Alfred by no means wishes to conceal his attachment to the Prince, and still less that any exculpation of himself should in any way reflect on him.[14]

In spite of Lady Blessington's strangely worded letter, professing d'Orsay's and her ignorance of Louis' plans while reaffirming their warmth of feeling for him, the count was still in touch with the imprisoned leader of the attempted coup, as a letter written by Louis Napoleon to Lady Blessington in January 1841 shows. 'I have received from Gore House only one letter, from Count d'Orsay, which I hastened to answer when I was at the Conciergerie. I bitterly regret that my letter was intercepted, for in it I expressed all the gratitude at the interest he took in my misfortunes,' he wrote from his damp chilly cell the year following his abortive putsch. Incarcerated in the Somme in the middle of winter, his mind turned to happier times at Gore House. 'My thoughts often wander to the place where you live, and I recall with pleasure the time I have passed in your amiable society, which the Count d'Orsay still brightens with his frank and spiritual gaiety.'[15]

However, in May 1846 Louis Napoleon was back in London eating dinner at Gore House, telling d'Orsay and the others around the table how he had disguised himself as a builder and managed to slip out of Ham while some construction work was being carried out. 'Before or since,' wrote d'Orsay to his old friend Walter Savage Landor, 'I have never seen his face as it was then; for he had shaved his moustaches as part of his disguise, and his lower, and least pleasing, features were completely exposed under the straggling stubble of hair beginning again to show itself.'[16]

Before long Louis was back to his old London self, his bank balance restored by the death of his father – the ostensible reason for his jailbreak was an uncharacteristic burst of filial grief at his father's failing health. From time to time the not noticeably grief-stricken orphan would be out and about in the Park with d'Orsay to ensure that he did not miss out on the changes in fashion that had taken place during his incarceration. 'In those days', recalled journalist and novelist Edmund Yates, son of Frederick Henry Yates, actor and manager at the Adelphi, 'the fashionable drive and promenade were along the north side of the Serpentine – just previously they had been from the Marble Arch to Apsley House.' Yates continued:

> There in a hooded cabriolet, the fashionable vehicle for men-about-town, with an enormous champing horse, and the trimmest of tiny grooms – 'tigers' . . . – half standing on the footboard behind, half swinging in the air, clinging on to the straps, would be Count d'Orsay, with clear-cut features and raven hair, the king of the dandies, the cynosure of all eyes, the greatest 'swell' of the day . . . By his side was occasionally seen Prince Louis Napoleon, an exile too, after his escape from Ham, residing in lodgings in King Street, St James's.[17]

It seems that d'Orsay's assistance to Louis Napoleon extended beyond taking him out in his carriage and inviting him to dinner at Gore House. He did what he could for the prince's profile in the press: as a propagandist d'Orsay had the immediate, easy charm that it would seem his protégé lacked. During 1846, he saw and wrote to John Forster, who was then editor of the *Daily News*. One of these letters ventures to correct an unfavourable impression of Louis given in an article. 'The best contradiction to the paragraph about Prince

Napoleon, will be this extract of the will of his father. Will you have the kindness to have it inserted?'[18] Another acknowledges a little puff placed on behalf of the escapee from Ham. 'Many thanks, dear Forster; the little article is perfect, and will give great pleasure to Prince Louis.'[19]

And it was through d'Orsay and Lady Blessington that Louis encountered Miss Howard, the woman who would become his mistress. They met in June 1846 shortly after his escape from Ham, when she was the mistress of Francis Mountjoy Martyn, a major in the Life Guards and a cousin of the late Lord Blessington. William Archer Shee seems not to have been wholly correct when he wrote that 'with the exception of Lady Charlotte Bury, the Countess of Guiccioli, and her own sisters, Lady Canterbury and Madame San Marseau, one never meets any ladies at Gore House'.[20] According to Napoleon III's biographer Fenton Bresler it was at Gore House that pretty Lizzie Howard met the future emperor of the French. Hardly a woman of spotless character – as well as living as Major Martyn's 'hostess', she had borne him a son and accepted his generous protection – nonetheless it took her a year to decide to leave her Life Guard to set up home with Louis Napoleon. When she did, she devoted herself to her new man and effectively bankrolled his final, ultimately successful attempt to become emperor.

CHAPTER TWENTY-ONE

Debt

D'ORSAY MUST HAVE ENVIED HIS FRIEND LOUIS HIS LAVISH LOVER. While Louis had been imprisoned in Ham, d'Orsay too had become a *de facto* prisoner at Gore House. 'Your friend Alfred charges me with his kindest regards to you,' wrote Lady Blessington to Byron's erstwhile mistress Teresa Guiccioli in August 1839. 'He is now an inmate of Gore House having sold his own residence, and this is not only a great protection but a great addition to my comfort.'[1]

This almost casual aside marks a new period in d'Orsay's life. Following his legal separation from Harriet in February 1838 any pretence at maintaining the façade of a 'proper' relationship with Lady Blessington was gone. It was more convenient for d'Orsay to give up his cottage orné and more cost-effective to move into Gore House. Moreover, with its high walls, barred gates and tall footmen, it offered greater protection from his numerous creditors who could have had him arrested. Debtors' prison was still an uncomfortable reality of life for those who could not pay what they owed. The decade-long spending spree that had characterised d'Orsay's life following the death of Lord Blessington was coming to an end. And by the early 1840s his financial difficulties had become intrusive, as Dickens noted in a letter to a friend in the summer of 1842: 'D'Orsay is confined at home by bailiffs, but is not an atom the worse in temper, health, looks, or spirits.'[2]

His financial difficulties began as far back as the early 1830s. It would seem that he was arrested shortly after his arrival in England for a debt outstanding to his Paris bootmaker, a man called McHenry. The amount of the debt, three hundred pounds, was not immense. But, as it was not in d'Orsay's character to be particularly conscientious about debts to tradesmen, it is reasonable to assume that McHenry the belligerent bootmaker was one of a pack of tailors, hatters, glovers, coachbuilders, wine merchants and so on to whom the Frenchman owed the odd hundred here and there. As it was, on the occasion of the arrest on behalf of McHenry he was saved from imprisonment by the bootmaker's indulgent acceptance of bail.

It seems that the pulling power of d'Orsay's patronage was worth the outstanding debt. In the course of compiling his life of Lady Blessington, Madden contacted McHenry who informed him 'that he had allowed that debt to remain unsettled for many years, and had consented to accept the security finally offered to him, on account of the very large obligations he felt under to the Count; for the mere fact of its being known in Paris, that Count d'Orsay's boots were made by McHenry, had procured for him the custom of all the tip-top exquisites of Paris'.[3]

Sadleir estimates that during the 1830s d'Orsay had been receiving an annual income of somewhere between £1600 and £2400. On 14 July 1834, it seems that pending final disposition of the estate of Lord Blessington and the claims upon it by d'Orsay, Harriet and Charles Gardiner the illegitimate son, the Court of Chancery awarded d'Orsay a further £500 per annum and £450 to his wife.[4] Thus for the latter half of the 1830s his annual income can be estimated at somewhere between £2100 and £2900 (between £94,000 and £130,000 in today's values), which was nowhere near sufficient for the rate at which he was spending. He got ready money by gambling and by raising funds against his expectations from Lord Blessington's Irish estates. However, by the early 1840s his situation was precarious and the outlook bleak. In an uncharacteristic moment of realistic behaviour in 1845 he drew up a schedule of his debts, which came to around £107,000 (almost five million pounds today). Even so, 'these claims did not comprise many debts to private friends, which were not likely to be pressed, or which could not be enforced, probably amounting to about £13,000 more'.[5]

It might seem remarkable that d'Orsay was allowed to run up such considerable debts. But, when compared to the achievements of truly epic fraudsters, they are not so astonishing. Besides, it does not appear that d'Orsay was engaged in anything as remotely organised as systematic fraud – the notion that he might actually be distressing others by non-payment of his bills did not appear to enter his head. It was his 'frank naïveté' that seems to have accounted for an ingenuous expectation that the money to pay for his baubles and toys would somehow be found.

It could not last, nor did it. His belief in the talismanic powers of the Blessington estates as a financial panacea of limitless capacity would seem to have been shaken at around the time of his legal separation from Harriet. And certainly by 1841 the proposed liquidation of those estates was no longer a secret. 'My dear Count d'Orsay,' wrote his artist friend Landseer from the Albion Hotel in Ramsgate in April that year,

> I venture to write to you about what does not concern me to serve an old friend, so you must forgive the liberty. *Lord Charleville* tells my 'fat friend' that there is a chance of *your employing* some *Land agent* for the disposal of the Irish

property – now my old acquaintance is a man of great reputation in that line and has considerable knowledge of landed – *property in Ireland* – where he is well known and has been *trusted* with the sales of estates of great value – You must have seen in the news papers; W. W. Simpsons name – almost as often as your – own – I have known his *character* ever since I was 9 years old and have much to thank him for which you will readily believe as I under-take to *bore* my friends on his account. In sober truth W. W. is a man to *trust* and to *recommend* with great safety – employ him if *feasible.*[6]

If Landseer could write blithely from a seaside holiday saying that he had heard d'Orsay was thinking of unloading his estates and wanted to put forward a friend for the job, it is safe to assume that the dozens of tradesmen and particularly the moneylenders to whom d'Orsay owed money had heard about it too. It was hardly the sort of news to inspire confidence in a creditor.

Once again, as she had over Louis Napoleon's bungled invasion, Lady Blessington performed an act of damage limitation, writing to Henry Bulwer in Paris in December 1841 that 'Alfred's embarrass-ments have been greatly exaggerated, and when the sale of the northern estate in Ireland is effected – which must be within a year, as Lady H. and her brother are now in Ireland for the purpose of urging it forward – he will be relieved from all his difficulties.'[7] Earlier in the year, Bulwer had received another letter from Gore House, this time from d'Orsay. Dated 2 May, it offers a remarkable insight into the count's state of mind at the time:

When I arrived in this country I hoped that my business affairs would be soon settled. My lawyers made me hope so, and I went from month to month in hope retarded, borrowing money from Jews, supposing I was only waiting, and that consequently the

sacrifices I was making in the way of interest were only momentary. I gambled, I won, I paid for hundreds of renewals right and
left. I was not aware of it, for all that would go back into the fluc-
tuations of play was as much saved from the common enemy
Crockford as from paying the Jews with the fleeting coin of my
pocket. My credit was immense. They vied in lending me, to
have the pleasure of receiving renewals with so good grace.

All this time the laggards of lawyers did not advance my
business. All those interested in the Irish properties pulled in
different ways, and the years rolled by without result.

I ceased being lucky at play, I prudently stopped, I sold my
house and my hunters, and limited my expenditures. That
determination, which should have done me honour, began to
frighten the Jews and produced a contrary effect. They grew
tenacious of being paid their principal. I did it by borrowing
with my right hand to pay with my left, and maintained equi-
librium. But now that I am reduced, and in consequence more
embarrassed, and see that the Shylocks want their pound of
flesh cost what it may, I begin to reflect more seriously upon the
position. I have made my calculations, and I can pay all, and
have a good surplus.

But if I consent to continue to pay forty per cent I shall not
be able to pay on all sides, and I shall find myself signing paper
I can't honour – which I am determined to resist.

Typically d'Orsay would not think of blaming himself for his
predicament, it simply did not occur to him that his current status had
anything to do with his lavish expenditure (nor, of course, would he
have stopped to consider the blatantly anti-semitic tone of his letter). It
was the fault of lazy lawyers and unscrupulous usurers. Having
explained, one might say explained away, his situation, adding his own
efforts at economy at prudence as evidence of his good faith in the face

of bad luck, he switches his tone, embarking upon a self-indulgent and self-righteous orgy of self-justification.

Here then is the preface to my position. It is now well stocked with prestige. I do good on every hand. I have for ten years helped all Frenchmen in distress, whatever their class, and it has become proverbial that I am morally the true Ambassador of the French. It would be a pity to see such a position collapse, and I can only avoid such a catastrophe by resisting exaggerated pretensions of my usurers. I am tormented only by them, for all my tradesmen cherish me, seeing that I make their fortune.

My friends my consulting lawyers advise me to go to a foreign country, and [say] that in six months the Israelites will be only too happy to enter into negotiations that I dictate. I reply that if I do such a thing I shall be called a *bolteur* in society, and classed amongst the Levanters. I don't approve of that advice.

Others urge me to stay home, not to show myself, and thus avoid arrest. That would be feasible, but would give rise to a report that I was locked up in the King's Bench [Prison] – which I approve still less.

Others advise me to become an attaché of the French Embassy. Then I could play a perfect Jesuit and take time to settle my affairs. To that I reply I am not well with the present government of France, that on account of my family I even pass for a Legitimist,* and even more Bonapartist than Philippist. Between ourselves, in spite of what may be said, I engage very little one way or the other, and my natural tendency in 1830 was wholly for the Revolution of July, as was known to all who saw

* That is, the followers of the Bourbon family whose last king was Charles X, as opposed to the Orleanists, whose head Louis-Philippe occupied the throne of France.

me in Paris during that Revolution. If in my social position I at my age attached myself as follower of an embassy the reason I had done so would be trumpeted all over Europe.

Here then are the objections from all points of view. They reply to me by saying that after all the services I have rendered the French, that with this title, if asked of the King, I should have a sort of appointment which would guarantee my being attached to the Embassy, and that I ought to have my position explained to him by you, and by my friend Brougham* as soon as he revisited Paris. I should send him a retaining fee as advocate, and finally I should thus avoid all the above difficulties.

Now my dear Henry, reflect upon what I have told you, and give me your candid opinion on this business. I count as well upon your discretion as upon your friendship. That says all.[8]

Perhaps he might have altered the last sentence to read 'that says too much'. This letter was *de trop* and must have been read with mounting incredulity. It is impossible to say whether d'Orsay really believed that he was a victim of circumstance and whether he genuinely considered that his life had been a model of parsimony and fiscal continence. Maybe Lady Blessington in her complex role as mother–lover hugged him to her increasingly ample bosom, comforted him and stroked his curly hair.

---

* Lord Chancellor and legal reformer; Lord Brougham was exactly the sort of person who would have appreciated a character like d'Orsay. As well as being a righter of wrongs, an anti-slaver and educationalist, he was a bon vivant and francophile, who could be said to have 'invented' the French Riviera. He 'discovered' Cannes in 1834 when, on his way to Italy, an outbreak of cholera further up the coast forced him to make an unscheduled stop in what was then little more than a sleepy fishing village. He liked it so much that he stayed and built himself a splendid Italianate villa. He had soon persuaded his friends to do the same.

With 'friends' like those who suggested that he might become an attaché at the French Embassy in London d'Orsay had little need of enemies. In fact it is doubtful that any friend of his would have been so half witted as to suggest that he try for a diplomatic post representing abroad the nation whose government he had tacitly helped Louis Napoleon to try to overthrow. In truth these 'friends' were probably the sort that people faced with embarrassment invent in the hope of deflecting shame or blame. But the uninhibited way in which d'Orsay refers to his prestige, his good works and so on would indicate a stunning self-regard that Lady Blessington and those close to him did little to deflate. He was by now deluded about himself, he had lived his fantastic life completely without thought for the consequences it would have for himself and indeed for Lady Blessington. That he was not 'an atom the worse in temper, health, looks, or spirits' suggested that he was no nearer realising what he had done.

Doubtless it was with Lady Blessington's high regard for d'Orsay in mind that Henry Bulwer wrote to her in December 1841, agreeing that the count was 'a man whom the Government would do well to employ' and 'that he has acted most honourably, delicately, and in a way which ought to have served him'. With some delicacy he points out the blindingly obvious fact that 'The French Ambassador did not, I think, wish for the nomination. M. Guizot, I imagine, is at this moment afraid of anything that might excite discussion and opposition, and it is idle to disguise from you that d'Orsay, both in England and here, has many enemies.' However, he advises d'Orsay not to 'lose courage' and cites the example of one French nobleman who waited ten years for a diplomatic appointment and also recalls that he himself waited a while to get into Parliament. 'Alfred has all the qualities for success in anything, but he must give the same trouble and pains to the pursuit he now engages in that he has given to other pursuits previously.'[9] This was hardly the sort of thing that d'Orsay wanted to hear.

It might have been with a notional nod towards the 'trouble and pains' recommended by Henry Bulwer that, in a gesture pregnant with irony, d'Orsay founded the Société de Bienfaisance, a charitable organisation to help French people suffering hardship in Britain. In February 1842 he had himself elected president, and, no doubt to protect himself from arrest and curry favour with the French government, he had the French ambassador join him on stage at the charity's inaugural meeting.

But it was not in d'Orsay's nature to be patient. Moreover, he seems to have become slightly 'stir crazy' as the 1840s progressed and he found himself cooped up at Gore House, still full of vigour though now himself in his forties. His movements were not entirely circumscribed; he could go out at night and on Sundays, which was a source of considerable drollery at the offices of the *Satirist*. 'The handsome Count has repudiated Sunday as a day of rest; it is to him a day of pleasure, on that day he invariably dines out!' is typical of the scandal sheet's barbs.[10] Another ran thus:

> D'Orsay has become quite religious, and secludes himself all the week that he may come out with a better grace on the Sunday. The gallant Count makes it a point, now, to visit Crockford's only on that day, and then but for the purpose of exhorting his old associates to 'give up St. Evremont, and read St. Paul,' by following his example of abonding the follies, the vanities, the wickedness of the world! We do most sincerely congratulate the Count on his reformation, and the prospect before him of a full and complete 'remission of sin!'[11]

And one habitué of the club recalled that after midnight on Saturday d'Orsay would leave Gore House and 'be seen at Crockford's, always gay and smiling, as if he had no anxiety or fears', returning again on Sunday evening but never staying later than 11.30 p.m., 'so as to reach

Gore House before the Cinderella hour of twelve . . . safe until the last stroke'.[12]

Nevertheless, his appearances at Crockford's were made in a spirit of bravado. As he wandered among those playing for great sums, all around him knew perfectly well that he was experiencing severe money troubles. He cannot have been unaffected by his predicament, and as a proud and sensitive man he would have felt the diminution in his standing most keenly – even if he still denied to himself and others that his own extravagance was to blame. In his letters to his friend Lord Lichfield, who was avoiding his own creditors in Naples, he comes across as a man obsessed by debt. He appears to have been handling some of Lichfield's outstanding obligations and actually began one of his letters on the premises of Margaret Edmunds, a woman identified as the 'keeper of a gambling "hell" at 14 St James's Place'[13] writing the letter in front of her so as to be able to repeat exactly what she has to say. He then launched into a description of a fiendishly complicated web of interconnected debt, ending with the sentence, 'Tout ceci est comme vous voyez un Veritable Labyrinthe, j'espère pourtant que nous en trouverons le fil pour sortir.'[14] It was of course equally true that d'Orsay himself was lost in a maze of debt, with little chance of either slaying the Minotaur or finding the thread to guide him out.

At times he wrote to Lichfield with a sort of grim amusement at the apocalyptic decimation of an entire generation by debt. It was with satisfaction that he described how one mutual friend had outpaced a bailiff in a carriage chase that led many miles outside London and ended in a dramatic fashion, with the bailiff's horse dropping dead and the bailiff attempting to continue the pursuit on foot but collapsing out of breath. It was with regret that he recounted how another mutual friend had sold off his horses and his stud in order to take a prolonged tour of the continent; and how a third had come to sympathise with him about being ruined before shutting up one house, selling another and moving to Italy. This is typical of d'Orsay again, wallowing in the details, but not attempting any sensible solution. In one letter he even admits that he would have liked to flee to Italy, 'mais j'ai pensé que je surveillerois mieux mes affaires sur les lieux; ma Garnison est bonne, et très forte, si Les Israelites osoient tourner ma position ils seroient devorés par mes Bloodhounds, et j'en massacrerois au moins deux, ainsi Gore House seroit montré dans les temps futurs, comme le lieu d'un Terrible Carnage'.[15]

The military language and the imagined slaughter of his creditors were not as far-fetched as they sounded. Visitors to Gore House had to present identification before being allowed to enter, and one of them recalled being 'cautiously admitted to the grounds and safely piloted between two enormous mastiffs to the door of the house'.[16] Another visitor recorded in his diary, 'There are two large deer-hounds in the courtyard, which T. Duncombe told me were unchained at night to scare off creditors.'[17]

D'Orsay was immune from arrest after sunset and on Sundays, but the time seems to have weighed heavily on him and had a deleterious effect on his mental balance. He clutched at every passing notion that might extricate him from his difficulties. In June 1844, the ever vigilant *Satirist* noted that d'Orsay had skipped town. 'Lady Blesington had much satisfaction in communicating to her friend Baroness Cab-umbrella the pleasing intelligence that the "handsome Count" had arrived safe in France, having travelled to Dover on Sunday, adding, he had received the greatest kindness from his numerous lady acquaintances and private friends in Paris.'[18] His father had died, so d'Orsay had slipped over to Paris to pursue a case for compensation against the French government for works of art seized from the Hôtel d'Orsay during the French Revolution. He returned within a fortnight, his arrival in London recorded once again in the *Satirist*: 'The handsome Count, who shipped out one Sunday to Paris, has been irresistibly drawn back again by the powerful attractions at Gore

House.'[19] Unfortunately, if unsurprisingly, the French courts did not think much of a case relating to the events of the late eighteenth century.

At one time he toyed with the idea of availing himself of what he euphemistically called the 'benefit of the act' and declare himself bankrupt. As Barbara Weiss explains in *The Hell of the English*, a study of bankruptcy and the Victorian novel, 'Theoretically the bankrupt possessed several advantages over the insolvent debtor; since modern bankruptcy laws entitled him to a certificate of discharge, the bankrupt could be freed from future liability for his debts, and was more likely to avoid the ignominy of imprisonment than the insolvent debtor.' The problem in d'Orsay's case was that 'bankruptcy law was restricted to those involved in trade, although the definition of trade proved somewhat troublesome'.[20] As Madden points out with characteristic understatement, 'there were difficulties in the way of identifying him with some legitimate commercial or agricultural pursuit'.[21] However vague one's definition of trade, it is difficult to imagine any of d'Orsay's activities falling under that heading, unless one counts rough trade such as the match-seller.

If the ambassadorial role necessary to deliver him from his predicament was unlikely to materialise, there was little he could do about it. If the French government was not going to compensate him for the ravages of the French Revolution upon his inheritance, he could do even less. However, if English law could not benefit him, the law clearly had to be changed. At the time there was much debate about the laws surrounding debt, insolvency and bankruptcy; a commission inquiring into bankruptcy had been set up in 1840 and one of the commissioners was a friend of d'Orsay's. Lord Brougham, *the* authority on bankruptcy law, was a friend too, and d'Orsay's old crony the radical MP Tommy Duncombe, warmly encouraged by the count, was campaigning hard for legal change.

'My Dear Tommy,' wrote d'Orsay in April 1842, 'I see by the

papers that Lord Campbell and Mr T. S. Duncombe received a petition against the *Imprisonment for Debt!* It is the moment to immortalise
yourself, and also the *sweetest* revenge against all our gang of Jews, if
you succeed in carrying this petition through. I have taken proper
means to keep this proposal alive in the Press. Will you come and dine
with us? – Yours affectionately, d'Orsay'.[22] 'Vous serez très amusé
aussi d'apprendre que je suis la cause du Bill intitulé Debtors et
Creditors Insolvent Bill,' he wrote to Lichfield three months later.[23]
D'Orsay had mentioned to his commissioner friend that there was no
distinction in law between the fraudster and the 'honest' debtor, and
he suggested that provision be made to enable the latter to put his
property and his debts into the hands of a commissioner and claim
legitimate protection against arrest from his creditors. By 1845, he
was said to have expressed 'extraordinary glee at his present "licence"
out of doors'.[24]

However, his situation was at best precarious; he was forever looking over his shoulder, as a seasonal anecdote published in the *Satirist* in
December 1845 indicated. '[The wit Henry] Luttrell remarked to
d'Orsay that the weather was remarkably unpleasant, for the season, it
was often so frightfully foggy. "De London fog!" ejaculated the sensitive Count, "is the finest thing in the world, you shall not see de dun!
and de dun shall not see you." Lutty was silenced.'[25]

In his desperation he turned to increasingly bizarre schemes that
he hoped would yield rapid and limitless wealth. A letter dated 9 May
1845 shows that he was consumed by the notion of 'the contemplated
project of a rail-road between Lisbon and Madrid'.[26] The following
month his attention switched from railway speculation to railway
safety. In a letter to Forster he announced that he had been thinking
for a long time that it would be an important addition to public safety
on the railways if a guard in the final coach could communicate via a
wire with the engine and ring a bell to indicate 'qu'il y a quelque
chose *out of order*'.[27]

Living in a state of near siege in Gore House, d'Orsay's connection with reality was becoming increasingly tenuous; indeed for the rest of the summer and much of the autumn of 1845, it seemed to him that his fortune was to be saved by his communication cord. That summer witnessed carnage on the British railway network: during one week in August there were seventeen accidents, some fatal, on nine different railways. This was admittedly an unusually high weekly total: there had been a mere nine accidents the preceding week and, after the peak of seventeen, the number of weekly mishaps dropped to eight, just over one a day. Once the British rail user was locked into his or her carriage, there was no chance of communication between carriages, and his or her chances of suffering an accident was a staggering fifteen times greater than on the German network.

Unsurprisingly d'Orsay was not the only person working on plans to assist the British rail traveller. *Punch* came up with a travel essential called 'The Railway Pocket Companion, containing a small bottle of water, a tumbler, a complete set of surgical instruments, a packet of lint, and directions for making a will'.[28] D'Orsay, however, took the nationwide game of railway roulette perfectly seriously. Letter after letter poured out of Gore House, suggesting refinements that could be added to his system. Proposed additions of lights and trumpets, gongs and hammers, were interspersed with colourful imagery directed against the greedy railway directors showing how the count intended to rub not just salt, but Cayenne pepper into the wound that these accidents had caused. As further reports of death and destruction on the railways reached him daily in Gore House, he went into ever more detail rebutting various suggested complications and overcoming technical problems. Like his clothes, his involvement in the theatre and his 'work' as a steward at the Hippodrome, the railway project dominated his life, and for a time held his interest.

But, despite his absorption in the project, d'Orsay was not destined to profit from the need for increased safety on the railway. The following year he turned his attention from railway accidents to shoe polish. In January 1846 the *Satirist* ran a couple of references to a blacking that he had patented, but while it afforded the satirical press the opportunity of puns on the count being a polished man and prompted the suggestion that a patented whitewash might have been a more useful invention, the effect on his bank balance seems to have been negligible.

Yet if the notions of the dandy turning into a railway safety officer or shoe-polish magnate seem far-fetched, they appear entirely sensible when compared to his most preposterous scheme. 'One of the most remarkable illusions', recalls Madden,

> which took possession of his mind, was the hope of making a vast and rapid fortune, by succeeding in the attempt of the alchemists of old, of converting the baser metals into gold! Some foreign schemers and impostors had persuaded the Count they had discovered the great arcana of alchemy, and all that was wanted was the necessary funds to set to work. The poor Count lived to see the folly of this speculation; like that of many other schemes suddenly adopted in his difficulties, they began brilliantly, and ended in a bubble.[29]

It is testimony to d'Orsay's almost unassailable self-belief that during the 1840s, with his finances in collapse, his movements restricted, his sporting activities limited to shooting sparrows in the gardens of Gore House and his brand of dandyism looking decidedly dated, he managed to keep his spirits up. In one of his letters to Lichfield, he says how much he would like to come and see him 'but I've embarked on so many schemes – which I'm keeping a tight rein on – that if I were to go away some of them would be bound to collapse, so I must wait for them to run their course'.[30] It seems that he really believed that salvation was about to come from one or other of his increasingly insane schemes and he wanted to be on hand to benefit.

This was Micawberism on a grand scale, with every bell, whistle, gong and noisy railway-safety device attached. Throughout this time d'Orsay seems to have believed not merely that something would turn up, but that this something would be appropriate and fitting to his self-ascribed status and imagined eminence. In this, however, he was deluding only himself. The truth about his severely straitened, almost pathetic circumstances was becomingly increasingly evident, as this poignant report, which ran under the headline 'Economy and Fashion' in the *Satirist* in April 1846, makes clear:

D'Orsay still manages to sport a cab, almost the last relic of former greatness. It is a faded affair, but, therefore, the Count thinks, only in keeping with his own looks! For a fallen fashionable, however, the very smallest medium of sympathy will suffice; there is nothing in d'Orsay's case to make the world less selfish than usual. His history is an illustration of the axiom, that the end is generally worthy of the means.[31]

CHAPTER TWENTY-TWO

Society's Favourite Artist

COUNT D'ORSAY'S NEED FOR MONEY HAD ONE USEFUL SIDE effect: it prompted him to develop his talent for dashing off portrait sketches into a talent that paid. Although the few guineas he charged for a sitting made only a limited impact on his financial status, the 1840s saw him emerge as a fashionable artist with a large, loyal and vocal following, which bolstered his self-esteem.

Much in the way that he kept the company of leading writers, he also enjoyed spending time with artists, and by the late 1830s he was on sufficiently intimate terms with the acclaimed artists of the day to be able to drop in to their studios and offer them advice. 'D'Orsay called, and pointed out several things to correct in the horse,' recalled Benjamin Haydon of a visit by the count during July 1839. At the time the notoriously touchy Haydon was working on an equestrian portrait of the Duke of Wellington and he remembered how d'Orsay 'took my brush in his dandy gloves, which made my heart ache, and lowered his [the horse's] hindquarters by bringing over a bit of the sky. Such a dress! white great-coat, blue satin cravat, hair oiled and curling, hat of the primest curve and purest water, gloves . . . primrose in tint, skin in tightness. In this prime of dandyism he took up a nasty, oily, dirty hog-tool, and immortalised Copenhagen [the duke's favourite charger] by touching the sky. I thought after he was gone, this won't do – a Frenchman touch Copenhagen! So I rubbed out all he had touched and modified his hints myself.'[1]

A letter written by Edwin Landseer to d'Orsay in the spring of 1841 offers another snapshot of the period when the count was transforming himself from a dandy into an artist:

Dear Count d'Orsay

If you would like to go to the private view at the Royal Academy, and can take the trouble to send to my house for a Ticket – I shall delight in being the means of indulging *the world* there to be assembled with the opportunity – *you will offend* them, in testing the 'god-like beauty' that is annually attempted in many painted subjects, by young artists – who think they know heaven by heart, there may be a little mischief in showing *the Original* – during the Exhibitions of the *ideal* – I shall expect the thanks of the College – for sending a subject so well conceived and fairly executed – well dressed, and particularly addressed, to the gentle sex. My Picture will need no title, let *truth* speak for it self – Let the *connoisseurs* see the *foundation* of the *new* English School! and faultless *costume*!

I shall expect a line from you – on the subject of my letter written yesterday – If you take my Card – for the R. A. you must write the name of whoever makes use of it and sign my name (for me). Believe me

sincerely yrs

Elandseer[2]

That d'Orsay wanted to attend the private view indicates a serious interest in contemporary art. Landseer's tone implies that the image of the dashing dandy of the 1830s still had a currency in fashionable London circles and that d'Orsay would be an exotic specimen at such an august, culturally oriented gathering. In truth the Frenchman's emergence as a prolific and high-profile portrait artist and sculptor was less of a surprise, but rather a shift in emphasis. Perhaps on entering his forties, d'Orsay felt that the calling of artist rather than dandy was more dignified and more suited to the life of a semi-reclusive debtor living in fear of arrest. Certainly within a couple of years of letting him into the RA private view on his ticket, Landseer was able to write to his friend, 'I have heard your Pictures honestly admired by many, ditto the *Statues* – they really deserve all we can say.'[3]

By 1843, d'Orsay's pictures were exhibited at the Royal Academy. The following year the exhibition was not without its dramas, as the following exchange of letters indicates:

My dear d'Orsay

I will do *all* I can but you must *remember* that my voice is not *law* in the R. Academy, if the Pictures received are *placed* they cannot *disarrange* (they would not have time) the whole Room – to extract yours – this is, I know, exactly the answer my applications would receive. – You may rely on my doing my best in obedience to your wishes. and will communicate to you the result as soon as they reply

Ever yours truly
EL[4]

Sunday Evg

My dear d'Orsay

I have just received your note — *sleep* before you *positively command* me to *withdraw all* your works I see the justice of your indignation and am as — much distressed as you (without seeing the parties) can be — but *unheard* I would not put my Foot on the hangmen — if by *tomorrow* you are still in the same mind I will yield to your request I have made various attempts to see neigh-bour Leslie* — he is from Mog till night at the R. A. and was away from home to day. Ever and always

yours EL[5]

Thursday Mor

My dear d'Orsay

I enclose you Stanfields Letters which will give you some idea of the extreme difficulty the executioners at the R. A. have to meet and become responsible for — I regret the mortification (may I say we) have suffered — as much on Lord Chesterfields account as yours. if you could induce his Lordship to lend himself for one hour — as Jack *Ketch*† to the Royal Academy — his *sympathies* would rather belong to the sufferings of the hangmen — than their *victims*. The same generous nature that rouses his Lordships indig-nation in *your* cause — will I am sure convince him that no *shade* of disrespect towards him — was ever contemplated — on the contrary they all attach a just importance to his taste as an admirer and patron of the 'fine arts'. Pray make him understand that I have nothing whatever to do with the business or *arrangements* of this

---

* Probably Charles Robert Leslie, professor of painting at the Royal Academy.
† Hangman and executioner, d. 1686.

year. – I am sorry to say my application (or rather yours) for Ld.
B. (after begging them to withdraw the Picture) came to [*sic*] late!

The first hour I have to myself you will see me at G. house.

Believe me sincerely yours

ELandseer

and be D — to them.[6]

My dear Landseer

The want of sufficient room is the cause 'and no other' of the rejection of the Count's pictures and had we kept them, we should have done great injustice to others who certainly have superior claims on the Academy, and whose works we have been compelled to send out for the reason above stated. His portrait of Lady Blessington which in my opinion is *far away* his best and is really a beautiful thing does good service in the great room and can not be removed. You may be sure that placed as I am on the ever to be cursed hanging committee I am as much annoyed and vexed as you can possibly can be and could the withdrawal of my own pictures in any way have benefited the Count's cause I would have gladly done it to have escaped the unpleasant predicament I am in. Leslie out of three pictures all small sends out one Phillips, Pick, Knight Grant must all have pictures sent back. I have only two – one of which I withdraw to be sure my other a whopper, now knowing as you do 'to your cost' the great and insurmountable difficulties we have to contend with I hope you will help us out of this confounded business and assure Count d'Orsay we have only been actuated by the stern necessity of the case.

Ever dear Landseer

thine most truly

C Stanfield

alias

Jack Ketch the unhappy

Royal Academy
April 24th
in haste, haste, haste[7]

Beneath the polished, urbane and now decidedly middle-aged exterior, d'Orsay was still the touchy young man, unable to deal with criticism, whether real or imagined. There is something in this incident of that disagreement with Mathews all those years ago, when he felt that his position in the affections of Lord and Lady Blessington was being usurped. As ever when threatened by circumstances and when not in control of a situation, he would revert to impetuous and infantile gestures, whether a challenge to a duel or a threat to recall an artwork. D'Orsay was oblivious to the idea that his tantrums might be seen as childish; he probably saw in them only grandeur and nobility. The patience of others in dealing with his moods and coaxing him round to a more reasonable way of behaviour testifies to the impression that his more likeable characteristics made upon his friends.

Eventually d'Orsay seems to have been sufficiently mollified to allow the portrait to which Stanfield refers to remain on show. In May 1844, the *Satirist* ran a report pregnant with *double entendre*. 'When Landseer at the exhibition of the Royal Academy observed to Grant, "I perceive d'Orsay has done Lady Blessington." "Yes," replied Frank, "and I can tell you it is not the first time!"'[8]

D'Orsay's sketches were as much a part of his persona as his clothes and carriages. He was an accomplished amateur draughtsman, and it is easy to imagine him delighting friends and visitors to Gore House with a quick after-dinner sketch. He had of course sketched various characters he had encountered on his tour with Lord and Lady Blessington, and it was a pastime he had continued on his arrival in London.

A portrait by the count became something of a fashion accessory during the 1830s and 1840s. The young Disraeli is almost indecently exultant at having his likeness captured by him. From his evident pleasure, it seems to have been a rite of passage, an exclusive club, and, to judge from the tone of his letters about it, something of a peak that any social climber keen to arrive in London Society had to scale. 'D'Orsay has taken my portrait,' wrote Disraeli triumphantly to Sarah Disraeli on 4 November 1834.[9] So excited is he that he repeats the information again in a letter to her of 29 November and he is still besotted with his portrait in February of the following year. 'My portrait engraved by Lane from d'Orsay's drawing is finished and everybody who has seen it admires it. I cannot send it you save in a portfolio; and I hope to bring it myself in a few days.'[10] The same day he writes to Sara Austen in a similar vein:

> Dearest Lady
>
> Any day, after tomorrow, if your coachman will turn his horses' head to Mitchell's Circulating Lib[rary] Old Bond St. Mr. M. will give you a portrait of your correspondent engraved by Lane from a drawing by Count d'Orsay, and which I hope you will deem a good likeness. If you even think it worth a frame, let Cribb make one of maple wood according to a pattern which I gave him some time back for a portrait of the Duke of Devon[shir]e for Mrs Norton.[11]

A further bulletin on his portrait was supplied by the smug Disraeli to Sarah Disraeli on 21 March 1835: 'Robt. Smith met d'Orsay who took his portrait at Willey Park* and failed, and thus addressed him "So you have been making a fine portrait of Disraeli; I see you can make likenesses of those you like!" Very huffy indeed, and horribly jealous.'[12]

If Disraeli felt honoured to have sat for one portrait, Dickens had twice as much cause to feel pleased with himself, as d'Orsay created

---

* The Shropshire estate of Lord Forester, Smith's father-in-law.

two pictures of the most famous nineteenth-century novelist in 1841 and 1842. 'I have set my heart', explained the count to Dickens, 'on giving the representation of a head, the inside of which, has furnished delight to countless Thousands.'[13] The two images can be seen hanging on the wall between the windows of Dickens's bedroom in his house on Doughty Street in London, and of the second, better portrait Dickens wrote, 'Mrs Dickens thinks the portrait, "capital", and so do divers other domestic authorities who have seen it – though some protest that the lower part of the face is susceptible of improvement.'[14]

As Dickens's letter indicates, the portraits themselves, often the left profile of the sitter's head, the features silhouetted against a plain background, are not bad in their way but are hardly about to bring on a fit of Stendhalism. They are instead the sort of thing one would be pleased to be able to dash off in a moment for the amusement of one's friends and as such said much about d'Orsay, who for most of his life seems to have trivialised what might have been nurtured into a considerable accomplishment; it is almost as if, torn in so many directions by his abilities and talents, he managed to squander them all or at least not develop them to their full potential.

The quality of his drawings improved as time passed, although one of Thackeray's daughters said to her father of a sketch d'Orsay had made of him in 1848, 'I think it's uglier than you are.'[15] However, sitting for the count was as much the point of the exercise as its result, and it seems that smart London frequented his studio partly out of curiosity to see inside the fortress of Gore House and partly to support d'Orsay. There was no shortage of fashionable and aristocratic sitters for him, and a good collection of his portrait sketches are still to be seen on the walls of the famous bay-windowed room of White's.

He also received some favourable press notices. Although it mocked him, the *Satirist* seems to have felt sufficiently proprietorial or at least mildly indulgent towards d'Orsay to run a series of small puffs about his new line of work during the summer and autumn of

1843. On 7 May it announced, 'The handsome Count is devoting himself with laudable industry to portrait painting in which he has of late made great advances in a bolder flight of art than mere profile. The proverbial good taste of the count will obtain him an abundance of sitters and there is no reason why his improved artistic skill should not gain him celebrity, if not fame.' On 4 June there was this jesting aside: 'D'Orsay, for a handsome artist, has more ugly customers than any other portrait painter living!' And on 2 July:

> The handsome Count has been dubbed by his fair sitters, the drawing-room artist, this is to distinguish him from others, we presume, who confine their 'drawings', exclusively to the boudoir.
>
> D'Orsay says, face-painting is after all but a species of sign painting, for no man sits for his portrait that he does not exhibit some 'sign' of vanity or folly – perhaps both!

The puffs kept on coming. 'D'Orsay in his portrait of Mrs. Anson has thrown so strong a light on the prominent feature of the face as to lead to the conclusion that imagination was more at work from truth' (3 September). 'The handsome Count's artistic skill is most extolled for his mode of treating the ladies. It is in general remarked that a lady who once sits to him, has never the least objection to sit to him a second time!' (22 October). 'It was asked by a club friend if the handsome Count put his name to his drawings. "O dear, yes," exclaimed our George, "I have seen his name to a multitude of drawings – some of them of great reputed value – indeed, his name," concluded the wit, "constituted their sole worth"' (19 November). 'D'Orsay says making a handsome picture of an ordinary woman is telling a lie on canvas. The Count will be called upon to lie through thick and thin for some sitters, if he do not mind' (10 December).[16]

Once again the tone of some of these snippets and asides indicates that d'Orsay's fashionable status worked for and against him: ensuring that he would have a stream of curious fashion-conscious sitters but that his work would forever be dismissed as that of a dilettante. Even so, the *Satirist* continued to be commendably supportive of his attempt to earn a living as an artist. His more important commissions were frequently mentioned and often the poorest pun was a pretext to remind its readers that the fashionable and faintly scandalous d'Orsay was working as a portrait painter. A mention on 30 March 1845 is typical: 'The Countess, the other day, put d'Orsay a leetle out. He threw down his brush in a pet, saying, "Who de deuce can paint in dis temper?" "In distemper?" playfully replied my lady, "why, you can, and very well, too." The Count chuckled, and resumed his work.'[17]

D'Orsay seems to have applied himself to his métier. Certainly Landseer took him seriously enough as an artist, writing to him in the summer of 1848 that 'We (the members) assemble at the Ral Academy on Saturday next when I will write you a true report touching your works.'[18] He also liked to begin his letters to d'Orsay with affectionately artistic greetings, for instance 'My dear Michael Angelo or Sir Joshua!'[19] or 'My dear Brother Brush'.[20] And, reservations about his lower jaw aside, Dickens too was warm in his enthusiasm for his friend's work. 'I think Maclise's profile, *most excellent*,' he wrote to d'Orsay. 'I should have recognized it instantly, though I had seen it pasted on the wooden leg of a Greenwich Pensioner, or in any other equally unexpected place.'[21] Though he eagerly anticipated a glittering debut for a more ambitious work by the count — 'J'espère que je verrai votre grand tableau de la reine, à l'exposition de l'Académie Royale'[22] — the picture of the queen on a 'superb grey charger in rapid motion'[23] went on show at the Amateur Artists' Gallery in Pall Mall.

As ever Lady Blessington was busy on d'Orsay's behalf, eliciting support for him and attempting to influence key opinion-formers. She seems to have written about d'Orsay's picture of the queen on the grey charger to the Duke of Wellington, from whom she was in the habit of seeking favours, not always with success. Wellington judiciously distanced himself from backing a plan to issue an engraving of this work. 'I shall be delighted to see a good engraving of Count d'Orsay's picture of the Queen on horseback. But I should prefer not to take any steps to attain that object till it is seen what the Queen and the Prince themselves do as to the object of your wishes. Unless it should be decidedly disadvantageous to the Count to wait a little longer, I would recommend him to do so,' came the Iron Duke's non-committal response.[24]

Indeed favours were called in from all around the world. Nathaniel Parker Willis, the American journalist who had been a guest at Seamore Place, was roped in to help influence opinion in America. No sooner had he been introduced to a potentially useful contact than he was at work on behalf of d'Orsay. 'Dear Sir,' wrote Willis to Baron de Trobriand,

It is rather early in an acquaintance to call on you for a service, the first moment after the pleasure of an introduction to you, but, as I expect immediately to be called upon to act in the matter in which your aid may be very essential I venture upon it thus à l'improvista, trusting to your kindness to excuse it.

The letter I enclose you from d'Orsay explains, (with the printed circular) what his expectations & wishes are, touching his picture, & I have a long letter from Lady Blessington, urging attention to it as a matter very important to him. I wrote to Capt Payne, & find that he has exhibited it *six weeks* in Boston – probably no one there believing that it was a genuine picture! I have seen no mention of it in the Boston papers, & heard nothing of it, & it must have been wretchedly managed. What I think wisest now, is to remove the picture here, and say as much as possible about it before its appearance, & the Courrier des

Etats Unis having great influence, its favor would be very important. The aid of your brilliant pen would be a charming thing to
mention to d'Orsay in my letter to him, & as I have not the
pleasure of M. Gaillardet's acquaintance, it would essentially
serve d'Orsay if you could speak of the picture in that able
paper.[25]

Finding critical and moderate financial success as a working artist
inspired him to branch out into different media. He fancied sculpture
and started taking instruction from William Behnes, who by 1840 had
gained a fashionable reputation for portrait busts. Sometimes
Behnes's sitters would be rewarded by sight of d'Orsay. 'Went to
Behnes,' recorded the actor Macready in his diary. 'Sat to him.
D'Orsay came in and stayed about three quarters of an hour. What
a delightful man he is! He took great interest in the bust.'[26] The result
of his 'great interest' in Macready's and other busts was evident by
the mid-1840s. Having informed its readers that 'the accomplished
Count seems disposed to show the world of how much he is really
capable', the *New Monthly Magazine* of 1845 eulogised his talents
quite shamelessly. 'His croquis de société had long charmed his
friends, and his great skill in modelling was bruited abroad, when the
world began to ask, Is it true, that in the man of fashion exists the
genius of the sculptor and the painter? Evidence was soon given that
such surmises were true. Count d'Orsay's statuettes of Napoleon
and the Duke of Wellington, and his portraits of Dwarkanauth
Tagore and Lord Lyndhurst, exhibited capabilities of the first order,
and satisfied every inquiry.'[27]

Well, perhaps not every inquiry was satisfied. At first, in the early
spring, the *Satirist* seemed pleased enough to puff d'Orsay's work and
take the opportunity to make none too subtle allusions to his debt-
inspired absence from the fashionable round. The count's sculpture of
Wellington on horseback 'has attracted many visitors, who have

admired the taste and skill of its execution,' ran a piece in March 1845. 'During its progress the handsome Count confined himself entirely to Gore-house, allowing himself only Sunday for recreation. The Countess feared lest other pressing engagements should have distracted his attention from this "labour of love".'[28]

However, by the end of June the *Satirist* was obliged to moderate its praise. 'D'Orsay does not appear likely to add to his artistic laurels by his statuette of the Duke of Wellington, which even the Post scruples to praise while the Times is almost contemptuous in its critical notice. The French critics were not quite agreed about his Napoleon or his horse either; but clever and admirable as are most of the Count's productions, gentlemen artists who "sit at home" and model at their ease must not be tried by the canons of rigid criticism.'[29] It was also suggested that in his efforts at sculpture he was assisted in the modelling of the faces by Behnes. But whatever *The Times* and the *Post* had to say about the matter, the Duke of Wellington himself was delighted.

This was as much due to his skilful courting by the indefatigable Lady Blessington as to the innate quality of d'Orsay's work. In the autumn of 1844, by way of a teaser she sent the duke a little gift and mentioned in passing a new work which d'Orsay had completed. The duke replied, 'I should be delighted to see the new work of art just finished by Count d'Orsay: would you be so kind as to tell me where I could see it?'[30] By February of the following year, Wellington had visited Gore House and, although sorry that he 'had not the pleasure of finding your Ladyship at home', he was rewarded with a private view of d'Orsay's 'beautiful sketches'.[31] And by the summer of that year the old boy was hooked. Writing to Lady Blessington to assure her that he would call upon her 'at the very first moment I can', Wellington declared, 'Count d'Orsay will really spoil me, and make me vain in my old age! By sending me down to posterity by the exercise of every description of talent with which he is endowed!'[32]

Wellington clearly had a soft spot for d'Orsay. Perhaps he remembered the precocious youth from that meet of the Royal Staghounds in the Bois de Boulogne all those years before, or maybe the charisma and freshness of character that had bewitched Byron had once again worked its magic. It might also have been that in his studio d'Orsay felt less need to pretend to be the puffed-up glass of fashion. Whatever the reason, Madden records that Wellington 'had so great a regard for him that it was sufficient to mention Count d'Orsay's name to ensure his attention and interest even when otherwise occupied'.[33] Certainly the duke's exclamation on completion of a portrait by d'Orsay – 'At last I have been painted like a gentleman! I'll never sit to anyone else'[34] – is frequently repeated. One example of d'Orsay's view of Wellington hangs in the Coffee Room at White's, albeit incorrectly attributed to Count d'Oranier. The Traveller's Club has a version too, another hangs in the British Embassy in Paris, another is at the National Portrait Gallery, while yet another was sold by Sotheby's in May 2000 when it auctioned the contents of Benacre Hall in Suffolk. They are certainly glamorous and imposing paintings – perhaps not the most avant-garde works of art ever produced, but flattering, in a craggy sort of way, to a national hero.

The subject's feeling of warmth for the artist was reciprocated, and from time to time d'Orsay would send examples of his work along the Park from Gore House to Apsley House. 'Mon Cher Duc, J'ai le plaisir de vous offrir la statuette de l'Empereur de Russie,' wrote d'Orsay to Wellington in May 1846, adding that he was particularly pleased with the result 'car les Russes ont une idée très exaltée de leur Empereur'.[35] But on d'Orsay's part the friendship was not entirely altruistic; there was an ulterior motive. He hoped to profit from his grand friendship. 'You must have seen by the newspapers that I have completed a great work,' he wrote to Madden, which creates a revolution in the Duke of Wellington's own mind, and that of his family. It is a statuette on horseback of himself, in the costume and at the ag [*sic*] of the Peninsular war. They say that it will be a fortune for me, as every regiment in the service will have one, as the Duke says publicly, that it is the only work by which he desires to be known, physically, by portraits. They say that he is very popular in Portugal and Spain. I thought possibly that you could sell for me the copyright at Lisbon, to some speculator, to whom I would send the mould. What do you think of it? Enquire.[36]

D'Orsay was once again in pursuit of the chimera of vast and rapid wealth. And Madden was not the only person he pestered about selling the rights to his work.

Henry Cole, who would later serve on the management committees of the London Exhibitions of the 1850s and 1860s, acquire a knighthood and have a wing of the Victoria & Albert Museum named after him, received a letter from d'Orsay inviting him to Gore House. Having passed through the house's elaborate security arrangements, he was ushered in to see the count, who was wearing a characteristically flamboyant dressing gown. D'Orsay lost no time getting down to business. 'You are a friend of Mr Minton's! I can make his fortune for him!' He then turned to his servant. 'François, go to my studio and in the corner you will find a bust. Cover it over with your handkerchief and bring it carefully here.' The servant returned cradling the object and placed it gently on a table. With a flourish d'Orsay whisked off the handkerchief and gazed at it with evident admiration. 'What do you think of that?'

'It's a close likeness,' replied Cole warily.

'Likeness! indeed it is a likeness!' boomed d'Orsay. 'Why, Douro when he saw it exclaimed: "D'Orsay, you quite appal me with the likeness to my father!"'

D'Orsay went on to impress upon Cole how much he was favoured by the victor of Waterloo. He told him how Wellington had given him four sittings but had refused Landseer a single one, and how he had marched up to the finished bust and exclaimed, 'By God, d'Orsay, you have done what those damned busters never could do.' However, as the count confided to Cole, 'the old Duke will not live for ever, he must die one of these days. Now, what I want you to do is to advise your friend Minton to make ten thousand copies of that bust, to pack them up in his warehouse and on the day of the Duke's death to flood the country with them, and heigh presto! His fortune is made!'[37]

D'Orsay gave Cole to understand that the rights to this infallible get-rich-quick scheme could be Minton's for a trifling ten thousand pounds (a sum approaching half a million pounds today). Unsurprisingly Minton preferred to offer a royalty for every copy sold, an arrangement that did not meet d'Orsay's need for ready cash. Indignantly, the count called the deal off.

Increasingly petulant if he could not get his own way, d'Orsay would often throw a tantrum. He was desperate for cash but doubtless felt guilty at having to stoop to such a scheme to restore his fortunes, a guilt that was exacerbated when he was turned down. It seems that at times the pressures of life and his own waning star could affect his once perpetually sunny mood and destroy his sang-froid. Nevertheless, some of his work was commercially reproduced, but without the staggering financial reward for which he had hoped. A large series of around 150 portraits, 14 inches by 10 ½ inches, of celebrities of the day, engraved by the lithographer Lane and sold by Bond Street stationer Mitchell, fetched the more modest sum of five shillings a piece.

He persisted with sculpture and in the latter half of 1848 he produced a bust of the recently deceased Tory MP, gambler and student of the turf Lord George Bentinck. As well as having had the honour of employing Ude as his cook, Bentinck, the second surviving son of the fourth Duke of Portland, had done much to promote the career of Benjamin Disraeli. This tall, good-looking aristocratic playboy, who would sometimes wander into the House of Commons with a white greatcoat draped over his hunting pink or stop by for a post-prandial snooze on the back benches after supper at White's, had introduced Disraeli to the nobility and squirearchy, members of which had been prejudiced against the young Jew. He saw in Disraeli a man who lacked the many advantages he enjoyed, but was intellectually dextrous where he was barely educated, and articulate where he had a shrill voice and long-winded manner. Bentinck and his brother had lent Disraeli the vast sum of twenty-five thousand pounds, with which he had purchased his country estate, and more importantly they had given him the patronage which propelled him into the Tory leadership. They had bonded in 1846 over the issue of the repeal of the Corn Laws, becoming leading figures in the Protectionist lobby, and in effect in the Tory party. Ironically Bentinck's death opened even greater opportunities for Disraeli, so it must have been with mixed feelings that he wrote to d'Orsay in October 1848:

My dear d'Orsay

I came in a spirit of severe, & even savage, criticism, despairing of seeing that countenance of blended blended [*sic*] energy & beauty reproduced to my eye & heart by the pencil of even as felicitous an artist as yourself.

I beheld again my beloved friend; & after gazing on the bust with an eye wh: wd glance at nothing else in your studio, I left your room with the consolation, that the magic finger of art had afforded the only solace wh: his bereaved & devoted friends, can now welcome – the living resemblance of George Bentinck.

Ever yours
D[38]

This was a poignant moment in so many ways. With the death of Bentinck, another figure was missing from the cast of rakish characters – already decimated by debt and death – that had dominated London social life during the d'Orsay years. While for the count this was a sadness and another indicator of the end of an era, for Disraeli it was the moment that his social and political career really took off. His opportunistic espousal of the Protectionist cause had made his name and with the death of Bentinck he was to achieve a prominence that would eventually lead to his premiership twenty years later. Already Disraeli was shedding his past life; he had married a rich widow and, now in his forties, he had discarded his violent, colourful and d'Orsay-inspired dress of the 1830s in favour of a black frock coat.

But the death of Bentinck and the arrival of the recently radical Disraeli in the upper echelons of the party of the landed aristocracy were far from being the only events of moment during 1848.

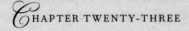

CHAPTER TWENTY-THREE

Revolution Abroad, Collapse at Home

THE LATE 1840S HAD NOT BEEN GOOD YEARS FOR FRANCE AND its monarch Louis-Philippe. Like Britain, France had enjoyed a railway boom, which had lasted from 1844 until 1846, after which the bubble had burst and investors had suffered. If the middle classes had lost their investments, a bad harvest during 1846 and the potato blight of the mid-1840s hit the poor at a time of rising unemployment during an economic slump. Unlike Britain, an industrial powerhouse where the emerging factories soaked up labour from the land, and unlike Germany, the industrialisation of France was painfully slow.

Moreover, corruption and sleaze were seen as endemic among the French ruling elite. Many of the new railway lines had been built to bolster the interests of local politicians rather than the economy. A widely publicised trial during 1847 exposed a cash-for-industrial-concessions scandal involving the ministries of War and Public Works, while the Duke de Praslin seemed to embody the morals of the ruling caste when he battered his wife to death so that he could pursue an affair with an English governess – though he did have the good grace to commit suicide after being brought to trial.

To add to the troubles of Louis-Philippe, the bourgeoisie was in revolt and in the summer of 1847 the political opposition, headed by d'Orsay's old dinner guest Thiers, inaugurated a series of banquets at which speakers denounced the government and called for reform. There were approximately seventy of these banquets, which became a focus for discontent, and a Monster Reform Banquet was planned for Paris on 22 February 1848. Eventually the aged and increasingly inflexible king was unable to ignore these protest dinners any longer. The Monster Reform Banquet was banned.

This was a serious misjudgement. The vocal but largely middle-class opposition, which despite being committed to reform was still in favour of the monarchy, suddenly found itself on the streets, literally, with the working class, the disfranchised and the republicans. On the evening of the cancelled banquet there were sporadic disturbances and clashes with soldiers. Warm and cosy in the Tuileries the plump and jowly Louis-Philippe was complacent. His view was that the 'Parisians will not make a revolution in winter.'[1] He was wrong.

Dawn on 23 February brought bigger crowds on to the streets. The king called out the National Guard, some of whom sided with the demonstrators. Rattled, he dismissed his prime minister François Guizot, which was perhaps his second mistake as Guizot had been a loyal and intelligent supporter. Later that day, in a disturbance outside Guizot's house, sixteen people were killed (either shot or trampled to death). This was the spark that ignited the revolution.

The corpses of these martyrs were loaded on to a wagon and rolled through the streets. That night, gunsmiths were looted, barricades went up, and by morning the mob was in control. By 1 p.m. on the 24th the king had abdicated in favour of his grandson the ten-year-old Comte de Paris, child of his eldest son (and Harriet d'Orsay's lover) the late Duke d'Orléans, and fled under armed guard. Two hours later the mob stormed the Chamber of Deputies, interrupting the proclamation of the child king. By three o'clock that afternoon, France was no longer a monarchy. And on 3 March the former king and queen landed at Newhaven, Louis-Philippe sporting a peajacket, a red and white neckerchief and a week's growth of beard.

The ramifications of the toppling of France's citizen king reached well beyond the borders of France. March saw popular demonstrations in Berlin, the abdication of the King of Bavaria, and riots and bloodshed in Vienna, whence Metternich likewise fled to England. Two months later the Emperor of Austria also fled Vienna, abdicating at the end of the year in favour of Franz Joseph. Revolt was afoot almost everywhere in Europe: Hungary wanted independence from Austria; Lombardy and Venice rose in revolution against Austria, with disturbances rippling through the Italian statelets as far as the Papal States, causing Pope Pius IX to flee in disguise; even the Bohemian Czechs wanted an assembly of their own. Britain became a safe haven for kings and their ministers from all over Europe, with *Punch* composing a satirical poem that captured the spirit of the times:

> Come, all ye kings kick'd out of doors
> By foreign insurrection.
> Oh! Come to Britain's peaceful shores
> For safety and protection.[2]

Although this continent-wide revolution eventually fizzled out amid grave debate, the granting of token reform and brutal military action, with most monarchs or their heirs reclaiming their thrones, 1848 would come to be regarded as a crucial year in the evolution of liberal democracy in Europe. As historian Norman Davies writes, 'The reactionary regimes had triumphed, but only at such heavy cost that they could not bear a repeat performance.'[3]

England escaped largely unscathed. There were just two potential flashpoints. On 6 March, Trafalgar Square was the scene of a riot following the cancellation of a rally to protest against income tax, with clashes between police and rioters and the destruction of the wooden fence surrounding the unfinished Nelson's Column. The second and potentially more serious event was a Chartist rally, which took place in London on 10 April. Troops were stationed in government offices and the Bank of England, but kept out of sight so as not to exacerbate matters. Instead an army of some 170,000 special constables, issued with wrist-badges and armed with truncheons and cudgels, assisted police. With the exception of minor disturbances and a few arrests, the rally passed off peacefully enough.

Among these special constables was Count d'Orsay, who took a characteristic delight in the rigmarole of his new duties. 'Dorsay [*sic*] always frank & pleasant,' wrote his neighbour Thackeray to a friend, 'showed us his special constables wrist-badge and truncheon: and took us in custody in the way the police manage it – You must go under this singular grip Lord Strangford & I were walked around the room like a pair of babies.'[4]

Also present at this demonstration of police skills was d'Orsay's fellow special constable Louis Napoleon. The moment he had heard about the toppling of Louis-Philippe he scurried over to Paris to place himself at the service of the provisional government, a senior figure in which was Alphonse de Lamartine, with whom d'Orsay and the Blessingtons had become friendly in Italy during the 1820s. It was to Lamartine that Louis Napoleon wrote on his arrival on the evening of 28 February. Lamartine, however, did not share d'Orsay's enthusiasm for the great Napoleon's nephew. He wrote back saying that in light of the unstable situation it might be better if Louis were to return to England until things became calmer. Given his previous farcical attempts to take over France, Louis Napoleon wisely chose to return to London to bide his time and so found himself instead a special constable.

He was soon once more at the centre of French politics when in June supporters entered him as a candidate for the Constituent Assembly and he found himself elected deputy in a number of départements, among them Paris. The symbolism of this was not wasted on Lamartine, who announced that an 1832 law banning Louis Napoleon from French soil was still in force. The elected but illegal exile stayed cool and wrote a letter saying that as his arrival might occasion disorder he felt it prudent to avoid taking his place in the Assembly.

He was wise to wait. In June the working classes rose up in an attempt to topple the middle-class government they felt had betrayed them. Anarchy and class war loomed. A frightened Assembly handed over power to the army, which under the ruthless General Cavaignac brought the situation under control in a matter of days, killing thousands and rounding up thousands more and confining them in packed dungeons before their eventual deportation to Algeria. 'That man', said Louis of Cavaignac while at dinner one evening at Gore House, 'is clearing the way for me.'[5]

After this, the Assembly limped on under the protection of the army. Further elections in September again gave Louis Napoleon a place in the Assembly, which this time he took up, returning to France to campaign for the presidency, an office which, as a result of the new constitution approved on 4 November, could be held for only a single term of four years.

D'Orsay was brimming with excitement and premonitory enthusiasm. Lane, the engraver of his drawings, would later recall how 'on the morning of the day of the first election of the President, he came to my house before church time, and diverted me from graver duties, to listen to his confident anticipations of the result of that memorable day'. Doubtless with a touch of melodrama in his voice, d'Orsay said, 'I have seen where is the wind, and I tell you, that on Paris is what they will call the sun of Austerlitz. To-morrow you shall hear that, while we are now talking, they vote for him with almost one mind, and that he has the absolute majority.'[6]

On 10 December Louis Napoleon duly achieved a landslide victory, capturing 5,434,226 votes. His nearest rival General Cavaignac polled 1,448,107. The other three candidates only managed 424,949 votes between them, with Lamartine garnering a woeful 17,910. Ten months after being told to leave the country by Lamartine, Louis Napoleon had been elected President of France.

His victory was greeted with ecstasy at Gore House. By the late 1840s life there was becoming increasingly difficult, with economies cutting into the house's famously lavish hospitality: on one occasion guests were obliged to accompany their dinner not with the finest wines but instead with a filthy concoction of honey and whisky called Balmoral Brose.

D'Orsay, while still ostensibly high spirited, was the butt of jokes about his weight, which started to increase towards the end of the decade as he approached his half-century. On their second meeting in the spring of 1845 Mrs Carlyle noted the count's 'slightly enlarged figure and slightly worn complexion'.[7] 'I was disappointed in the physique of Count d'Orsay, who is a fleshy animal-looking creature, instead of the *spirituel* person I expected to see,' wrote one who encountered him at a breakfast in the summer of 1846, adding, however, that the Frenchman 'certainly dresses *à merveille*, and is besides a clever fellow'.[8] And by the late summer of 1848 the *Satirist* was openly referring to him as 'the fat Count'.[9] Although he was brave about it, d'Orsay was pained to be losing the looks that had for so many years been his fortune.

Lady Blessington was in an even worse predicament. As well as inclining to corpulence, and herself getting on for sixty, she was increasingly described as subdued and reserved. It would appear that she was suffering from depression, which in view of the many pressures on her is hardly surprising. Effectively imprisoned in Gore

House, the life of a hostess for which she had struggled so long had become a burden, and the relentless cycle was taking its toll. While having d'Orsay living under the same roof may have been a comfort, it was also an additional burden: fear of his creditors forced him to remain at home where he was a constant reminder to her both of happier days and of her own, largely self-imposed obligation to look after him. D'Orsay, whether in his almost perpetual good humour or descending occasionally into one of his fits of pique, was of scant help to her, his pictures bringing only a few guineas and his fanciful get-rich-quick schemes coming to nothing – he was little better than a child. Those who remembered her in earlier times were struck by her deterioration. Madden plots Lady Blessington's downward emotional graph from its high point in Naples:

> Any person acquainted with Lady Blessington, when residing at the Villa Belvidere [*sic*] at Naples, the Palazzo Negrone [*sic*], her delightful residence at Seamore Place in London; and her latest English place of abode, in Gore House, must have observed the remarkable changes that had come over her mind at the different epochs of her career in intellectual society and in fashionable life, from 1823 to 1849.
>
> In Naples, the charm of Lady Blessington's conversation and society was indescribably effective. The genial air, the beautiful scenery of the place, and all the 'influences of the sweet south,' seemed to have delighted, soothed, and spiritualized her feelings. A strong tendency to fastidiousness of taste, to weariness of mind in the enjoyment of any long continued entertainment or amusement, to sudden impulses of hastiness of temper (as distinguished from habitual ill-humour), had been subdued and softened by those changes of scenery and 'skiey [*sic*] influences;' and above all, there was observable in her animal spirits a flow of hilarity, a natural vivacity, such as those

who knew her in early life, were well aware had belonged to her childhood, and which having been restrained and checked to some extent, had resumed in the south of Italy, its original character of out-bursting *gaité du coeur* [*sic*]. The ringing laugh of joyous girl-hood, which Mrs. Jordan used to act to such perfection, was a reality with Lady Blessington, in those merry moods of hers in Naples, which were then indeed neither 'few nor far between.'

In society Lady Blessington was then supremely attractive; she was natural and sprightly, and *spirituelle* in proportion to her naturalness, and utter absence of all appearance of an effort to be effective in conversation.

Three years would pass until Madden next met Lady Blessington at Rome, when he noticed 'that vivacity to which I have referred, seemed to me to have been considerably impaired.' However Madden ascribed her change in mood to the gravitas of age and increasing eru-dition: 'She has become more of a learned lady, a queen regant in literary circles, expected to speak with authority on subjects of art and literature, and less of the agreeable woman, eminently graceful, and full of gaiety, whom I had parted with in Naples in 1824.' She was, in short, more of a woman of the world, yet soignée and charming: 'But she was at all times attractive and triumphant in her efforts to reign in the society she moved in; and she was, moreover, at all times kindly disposed and faithful in her friendships.' It was only on her return to London that she began to appear careworn and downcast.

After an interval of nearly five years, I renewed my acquain-tance with Lady Blessington in Seamore Place. It was evident that another 'great change had come over the spirit of her dream' of life since I had last seen her. Cares and troubles, and trials of various kinds had befallen her, and left, if not visible external traces, at least perceptible internal evidence of their effects.

After a lapse of two or three years, my acquaintance with Lady Blessington was renewed at Gore House. The new establishment was on a scale of magnificence exceeding even that of Seamore Place.

The brilliant society by which she was surrounded, did not seem to have contributed much to her felicity. There was no happiness in the circles of Gore House, comparable to that of the Palazzo Belvidere [*sic*] in Naples. There was manifestly a great intellectual effort made to keep up the charm of that society, and no less manifest was it that a great pecuniary effort was making to meet the large expenditure of the establishment, that was essential for it. That society was felt by her to be a necessity in England. It had been a luxury in Italy, and had been enjoyed there without anxiety for cost, or any experience of the wear and tear of life that is connected with arduous exertions to maintain a position in London *haut ton* society, acquired with difficulty, and often supported under continually increasing embarrassments.[10]

Madden was not the only one to detect these changes and nor was his judgement of her declining state of mind based upon retrospective observation, as Disraeli demonstrates as early as the spring of 1842:

I have agreed to dine at Gore House to day, Lady B[lessington] having asked me every day. But I dislike going there, d'Orsay being in high spirits, quite unchanged, but Lady B. very altered – silent, subdued & broken. She told me another year wd. kill her, & complained bitterly that after having fought against so much prejudice, & made a sort of position, with her two nieces about her and not owing a shilling in the world, she is perhaps to see it all shattered & scattered to the winds. I think it is horrid. But perhaps it may end better than she anticipates.[11]

Now, in December 1848, at last it seemed as though it would end better than anyone could have anticipated. Louis Napoleon, for so long an intimate of Gore House, was the democratically elected President of France. A man who at the beginning of the year had been hanging around Gore House watching d'Orsay practise his special policeman's armlock was now running a bona-fide superpower. It had been a long time coming, but Lady Blessington could at last relax from her gruelling regime and d'Orsay could indulge himself with dreams of diplomatic posts galore and perhaps even political office in the fledgling Republic of France.

The count had every reason to expect that it was payback time and for once he was not the only one to think so. But by Christmas he still had not received the call from Louis Napoleon, even though Gore House was regarded as the place to pick up news and intelligence about the state of affairs in France. On 27 December, the journalist and essayist Abraham Hayward 'went to drink tea at Lady Blessington's, to learn the French news. D'Orsay has got nothing yet, and does not stir.'[12] By the end of January 1849 the situation was the same with Dickens describing d'Orsay in a letter to a friend in America as still 'looking, as I take it, towards France'.[13] It began to seem that it would be some time before d'Orsay would receive a presidential summons to Paris.

In the meantime life continued at Gore House as best it could. One Saturday afternoon at the end of March, a man delivered a tray of cakes to the kitchen at Gore House. There was nothing unusual in this as there was to be a dinner that night. However, instead of leaving after he had made his delivery, the man showed his badge as a sheriff's officer. The creditors had finally penetrated the defences of Gore House.

There are conflicting stories as to what happened next. One version of events has it that the sheriff's man entered d'Orsay's dressing room to present the writ. Exhibiting the coolness he had so often shown at Crockford's, d'Orsay kept the sheriff's man waiting and spent an hour and a half in front of the cheval glass, completing his appearance. All the time he watched the sun sinking, and, when it was safely below the horizon, he bowed to his visitor and announced that as it was after sunset the writ no longer ran. This was the law and the sheriff's man was escorted out. This version is picturesque, very d'Orsay, and would make a wonderful scene in a film. However, the sequence of events as they seem to have unfolded is rather more poignant and ironic. It was Lady Blessington, and not d'Orsay, who was the object of the writ.

Howell & James on Lower Regent Street was the most fashionable shop of its type in London during the mid-nineteenth century: it sold jewellery, furnishings and wine, and supplied Queen Victoria with silk for dresses. While the carriage trade stopped and perused the wares, their coachmen would go into the basement and enjoy complimentary beer, bread and cheese. Anyone with pretensions to fashion would have passed through the impressive and palatial showrooms of Howell & James. Lady Blessington was an excellent customer; much of the sumptuous decoration of Gore House had been achieved using goods bought there on account. However her line of credit had been running for thirteen years and Messrs Howell & James felt that this was long enough. No longer as fashionable as she had been and surrounded by rumours of impending financial collapse – even the annuals that she edited had ceased to sell – Lady Blessington was no longer a good risk, nor the sort of client that Howell & James needed to pander to any longer. Thus a draper finally put an end to the majestic artifice that was the London career of Count d'Orsay and Lady Blessington.

Retail historian Alison Adburgham describes their decision as initiating a domino effect. 'It was Howell & James who in 1849 precipitated the collapse of Lady Blessington's glittering but equivocal ménage at Gore House. This they did by putting in an execution for a debt of some thousands of pounds that Lady Blessington had incurred when furnishing Gore House thirteen years earlier, thereby firing the starting gun for all her other creditors to foreclose.'[14]

The panic in Gore House that evening must have been dreadful. Although the impending collapse cannot have been unexpected, the quarter from which it came must have been a surprise and the swiftness with which the end would follow was positively brutal. There is something truly pathetic in the image of the bloated former beauty being informed of the presence of a sheriff's officer in the house and the shock that must have registered as she realised that it was for her and not d'Orsay that he had come. Nevertheless she kept her head and sent a servant to the count's room.

Even at this time, she thought first of her beloved boy's safety, although at nearly fifty the stout count was a boy only in her eyes. She wanted him to know that he had to leave the country immediately; with the word out that Howell & James had put in an execution for their debt, he would no longer be safe from his own creditors. 'The count was at first incredulous,' records Madden; '– *bah!* after *bah!* followed each sentence of the account given him of the entrance of the sheriff's officer. At length, after seeing Lady Blessington, the necessity for his immediate departure became apparent. The following morning, with a single portmanteau, attended by his valet, he set out for Paris, and thus ended the London life of Count d'Orsay.'[15]

D'Orsay had arrived in England a beautiful epicene creature in a blaze of publicity; he fled at three o'clock in the morning under cover of darkness, a corpulent middle-aged man. Madden's account of his departure omits a few details. As well as his portmanteau d'Orsay took with him a jewelled umbrella and he was accompanied by a friend, the poet and politician Richard Monckton Milnes, later Lord Houghton, an interesting character who was rumoured to be bisexual, collected erotica and later proposed to Florence Nightingale. In his papers, Milnes makes d'Orsay's flight from debt seem like a little seasonal holiday. 'I went to Paris at Easter with Count d'Orsay, who is now a sort of Chamberlain to the President,' he recalled, delicately avoiding the pecuniary problems that had precipitated his departure.[16] D'Orsay, however, felt no need to euphemise. 'Mon Bon Quin,' he wrote to his friend the homeopathic doctor from Paris, shortly after his arrival. 'I've made an unexpected departure but happily I am safe on this shore. I had to take the decision to leave at three in the morning, so as to make good use of Sunday.'[17] It had been a close-run thing, but he had once more eluded his creditors.

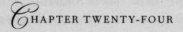

CHAPTER TWENTY-FOUR

An Auction in London and a Death in Paris

THE AUCTION CATALOGUE PREPARED BY MR PHILLIPS OF 73 NEW
Bond Street is a poignant document, lising page after page of 'the
property of the Rt. Honble the Countess of Blessington retiring to the
continent'. At least there was one consolation: even in its liquidation
Gore House was at the height of fashion. On 4 March 1807, Mr
Phillips had sold 'the property of a Man of Fashion', a man known as
Beau Brummell; on 9 February 1822 he had sold the effects of the late
Queen Caroline; in August 1836 his was the first and only auction
house to hold a sale at Buckingham Palace when, the year before her
coronation, Victoria had undertaken a clear-out.

Now in the spring of 1849 Phillips would stage the sale of, if not
the century, then certainly the decade, as all the costly and elegant
effects assembled in the course of three lifetimes of pathological shopping would go under the hammer. Catalogues were printed and sold
for three shillings, allowing admission to the sale for two. Barely a
fortnight after d'Orsay had fled to France, posters advertising the
sale were put up. 'I passed Gore House to day,' noted Dickens grimly

on 18 April, 'and saw the bills up for a Sale (in the East Wind) with a very doleful eye.'[1]

Lasting twelve days, the sale would see such icons as the Lawrence portrait of Lady Blessington knocked down to Lord Hertford for the surprisingly modest sum of 320 guineas – the picture is now at the Wallace Collection. There were also numerous busts and images of Lady Blessington, d'Orsay and his hero Napoleon. Saddest of all were the numerous high-ticket trinkets and historical gewgaws that were such a part of the Gore House scene: an antique jug formerly owned by the Empress Josephine; Sèvres vases once the property of Marie Antoinette; a pair of scissors once owned by Mary Queen of Scots; a tankard that had belonged to Queen Anne; marble paper-weights from Napoleon's desk; a ring given to Lady Blessington by Lord Byron (perhaps this was the ring of lava that Byron had sent to d'Orsay) and bracelets presented to her by the King of Naples; and a Landseer drawing of Montaigne, d'Orsay's favourite poodle and the principal figure in Landseer's picture, *Laying Down the Law*.

During the five days that the sale was on view, it was estimated that the number of visitors was in excess of twenty thousand.[2] It was a huge attraction, pulling in crowds of visitors who often dressed up for the occasion, curious to see the inside of a much discussed establishment before its contents were dispersed. Madden was on hand to give an account of the disposal of the Gore House collection.

On the 10th of May, 1849, I visited Gore House for the last time. The auction was going on. There was a large assemblage of people of fashion. Every room was thronged; the well-known library saloon, in which the conversaziones took place, was crowded, but not with guests. The arm-chair in which the lady of the mansion was wont to sit, was occupied by a stout coarse gentleman of the Jewish persuasion, busily engaged in examining a marble hand extended on a book – the fingers of which were modelled from a cast of those of the absent mistress of the establishment.

People as they passed through the room poked the furniture, pulled about the precious objects of art, and ornaments of various kinds, that lay on the table. And some made jests and ribald jokes on the scene they witnessed.

It was a relief to leave that room: I went into another, the dining room, where I had frequently enjoyed 'in goodly company,' the elegant hospitality of one who was indeed a 'most kind hostess.' I saw an individual among the crowd of gazers there, who looked thoughtful and even sad. I remembered his features. I had dined with the gentleman more than once in that room. He was a humourist, a facetious man – one of the editors of 'Punch,'* but he had a heart, with all his customary drollery and penchant for fun and raillery. I accosted him, and said, 'We have met here under different circumstances.' Some observations were made by the gentleman, which shewed he felt how very different indeed they were.[3]

Madden was not the only one to find the situation upsetting. Thackeray was described by one observer as having tears in his eyes as he left Gore House for the last time. 'I have just come away from a dismal sight – Gore House full of snobs looking at the furniture – foul Jews; odious bombazine women who drove up in mysterious flies wh. they had hired, the wretches, to be fine so as to come in state to a fashionable lounge – Brutes keeping their hats on in the kind old drawing-rooms – I longed to knock some of 'em off: and say Sir, be civil in a lady's room,' he wrote to a friend. 'There was one of the servants there not a powdered one but a butler a whatdoyoucallit – My heart melted towards him & I gave him a pound – Ah it was a strange

* Mr Albert Smith.

sad picture of Wanaty Fair. My mind is all boiling up with it. Indeed it is in a queer state.'[4] Thackeray seems to have been genuinely affected by the break-up of Gore House, which was just around the corner from his own house on Young Street. It was of Thackeray that Lady Blessington's valet Avillon, perhaps the one into whose hand he pressed a pound, wrote to his mistress, 'C'est peut etre la seule personne que j'ai vu réellement affecté en votre depart.'[5]

Lady Blessington chose not to stay to watch the dispersal of her property. On 14 April together with her nieces she set out for Paris, where she checked into the Hôtel de la Ville l'Evêque, where she would remain until 3 June. She was to start a new life, her sole income the jointure from her late husband's estates, plus whatever residue there may have been from the Gore House sale. Nevertheless, after the long-impending collapse of Gore House and the strain on her nerves she seems to have reacted well, better than might have been feared, to the change of scene. The crisis actually made her feel more alive – it is almost as if she experienced feelings of relief. At last the burden of maintaining the costly salon had been lifted and with it the necessity of keeping up the complex charade of appearing not to mind being an important hostess to whom her many hypocritical male guests felt it unsuitable to introduce their wives.

She got up earlier in the morning than had been her wont and even started to take exercise. At times she was short of breath – it was after all a considerable change to her routine of nineteen years of the salons in London. But a doctor diagnosed her breathing difficulties as in part a nervous reaction (perhaps fits of hyperventilation occasioned by panic attacks) or a symptom of the bronchitis that was prevalent in Paris at the time. Whatever their source the doctor prescribed a remedy, after which 'the attacks diminished perceptibly in violence' and the medic 'entertained no serious alarm'.[6]

She was welcomed by Byron's former mistress the Countess Guiccioli, now married to the Marquis de Boissy, who placed a carriage at her disposal, and when she went to visit her friend she must have been comforted to find a portrait of Byron above the fireplace – the marquis, far from being jealous of his wife's involvement with Byron, revelled in it. Another old friend, Lord Normanby, was also in Paris, as British ambassador, while d'Orsay's sister and her husband, who had now succeeded to the title of Duke and Duchess de Grammont, were pleased to be able to recreate the social circle of earlier years.

On 6 May, Henry Bulwer, who had been the recipient of letters pressing for d'Orsay's ambassadorial appointment, wrote to Lady Blessington evidently pleased that she was finding life agreeable. 'I was very glad to get your letter. I never had a doubt (I judged by myself) that your friends would remain always your friends, and I was sure that many who were not Alfred's, when he was away, would become so, when he was present. It would be a great ingratitude if Prince Louis forgot former kindnesses and services, and I must say, that I do not think him capable of this.'[7]

But it seemed that Bulwer was mistaken in his appraisal of Louis Napoleon's character. Monckton Milnes's assertion that d'Orsay was working as a sort of chamberlain was somewhat optimistic. It appears that the newly elected President of France was cordial enough towards his old supporters, to whom indeed he owed much – it is mooted that d'Orsay even helped his election campaign by turning such influential figures as the opinion-forming journalist Girardin to his support. They met, and in one of her letters from Paris Lady Blessington mentions an invitation to dinner. However, much as d'Orsay may have expected and, from the point of view of friendship, deserved an appointment, no sinecure was forthcoming.

'It was affirmed that he had been ungrateful to Lady Blessington and Count d'Orsay, who "believed in him" when few others did,' wrote one observer much later in the century; 'but ingratitude was not one of the Emperor's vices. It is certain that both expected too much;

that after the events of 1848 her ladyship demanded from the Prince-President social recognition and admission to his private parties, the inevitable consequence of granting which must have been that from receptions where Lady Blessington was present, Lady Cowley, the wife of the English Ambassador, would have been absent.'[8] This is all very well as far as it goes, but as an apology for Louis Napoleon's ingratitude it simply does not work. Cowley took up the post of ambassador in Paris only in 1852; as has already been stated, the ambassador in 1848 was Lord Normanby, a friend of the Blessingtons since the 1820s in Italy.

Yet the general thrust of this argument is correct. Whether by nature Louis Napoleon was ungrateful or not, he was primarily an ambitious, democratically elected politician who wanted to become an emperor or, to put it plainly, a dictator, and he was prepared to sacrifice any of his old friends to this end. He was to get rid of his lover, who had met his expenses and supported him in exile, when he thought it wise to acquire a wife: so what chance had d'Orsay? Louis had only recently been installed as president, against a backdrop of bloodshed and electoral confusion, so these were uncertain times for him. Europe was still putting itself back together after the turmoil of 1848, and as France had oscillated between monarchy and anarchy in the preceding months, his first concern was to shore up his position. It was d'Orsay's very romanticism and his carefree manner towards authority, attitudes that had helped Louis Napoleon in exile, which militated against a government position.

And it must not be forgotten that d'Orsay was effectively on the run, a fugitive from English law; he had a controversial reputation as a bisexual dilettante artist and in the eyes of many he was nothing more than a disgraced, ageing dandy who had not lived in France for almost twenty years. Had such opinions been put to him, d'Orsay would have found them profoundly shocking and diametrically opposed to his own self-image as a politician manqué and kingmaker.

However, in a country still reeling from the allegations of sleaze that had dogged the final administration of Louis-Philippe's reign, it would have been inviting criticism and opprobrium to install d'Orsay as an official in the new regime. It is suggested by Greville in his memoirs that Louis Napoleon did attempt to find an ambassadorial role for d'Orsay in Hanover, but the proposed appointment was blocked by his ministers.

Whatever Louis Napoleon's personal feeling about Lady Blessington and Count d'Orsay might have been, it is undeniable that he was keeping his distance from them officially. It is perhaps this ambivalence and uncertainty that accounts for a story, probably apocryphal, of an exchange that took place between the President of France and Lady Blessington. Shortly after her arrival she was out for a drive in heavy traffic, and the wheels of her carriage locked with those of none other than Louis Napoleon. Louis lifted his hat graciously. 'Vous restez longtemps à Paris, Lady Blessington?' he asked. 'Je ne sais pas, monsieur,' she replied. 'Et vous?'[9]

Whatever Lady Blessington said on that occasion, she was intending to stay in Paris. On 3 June 1849, after seven weeks in her hotel, she and the Misses Power moved to an apartment in the Rue du Cerq. Although nothing like as splendid as the Hôtel Ney it was a pleasant enough address, near the Champs-Elysées. By way of a housewarming celebration, they dined 'en famille with the Duc and Duchesse de Guiche (Count d'Orsay's nephew)'.[10] It is perhaps this same dinner that is referred to in a letter written by the Duke de Grammont:

> My dear Lady Blessington
>
> My Aunt the Duchesse de Polignac desires me to tell you that unwilling to have recourse to the formality of a letter between you and her to request you to dine with her on Sunday next, she called this day upon you to make her herself the invitation, not having had the pleasure to find you at home, she

hopes that yourself, your amiable nieces and Alfred will not forget that you had agreed upon accepting that réunion de famille.

I received a letter from L^y Tank^lle [Lady Tankerville] quite enchanted with the prosperous sale of your furniture at Gore House but lamenting upon the cause of it. I cannot agree with her in that respect for a little egotism is allowable on such circumstance and we gain to [*sic*] much by it.

Your ever most attached and devoted
Grammont[11]

It was a delightful family gathering, which took place on a balmy early-summer evening. Perhaps it even brought to mind memories of another *dîner en famille* that had taken place in Paris on a similar June evening, in happier circumstances, twenty-one years earlier when the scent of orange trees had wafted in from the Tuileries. Perhaps it was to drink in the fragrance of a summer evening in Paris that, after dinner, Lady Blessington decided to walk home. When they arrived, Marguerite Power helped her aunt to undress. It was a little after midnight. By noon the following morning Lady Blessington would be dead.

The attacks started early in the morning, and at six o'clock she heaved herself out of bed and into a chair in the hope that her breath would come more easily. She called for d'Orsay, and soon the whole house was around her. The doctor was summoned and meanwhile 'the remedies he had ordered – sitting upright, rubbing the chest and upper stomach with ether, administering ether internally, &c. – were all resorted to without effect'.[12] In fact her situation deteriorated visibly, her chest shuddering and heaving with every agonised breath. Her face began to swell and turn purple, her pupils dilated, her limbs became cold, speech became impossible and the only noise she made was a loud whooping with every intake of breath. And then just as the symptoms seemed at their worst there came a respite; she even managed to say, 'The violence is over, I can breathe freer.'[13] But it was only a temporary reprieve, after which she declined even more rapidly; from purple, her face, then her hands and feet, turned black. The doctor, who had been detained by another patient, arrived but could do nothing for her and at about ten o'clock in the morning she died in d'Orsay's arms. Her last minutes were mercifully peaceful – 'she expired so easily, so tranquilly, that it was impossible to perceive the moment when her spirit passed away'.[14]

It seems that Lady Blessington had suffered a heart attack. Two days later an autopsy took place during which it was discovered 'that enlargement of the heart to nearly double the natural size, which enlargement must have been progressing for a period of at least twenty-five years, was the cause of dissolution, though incipient disease of the stomach and liver had complicated the symptoms'.[15] She was a few weeks short of her sixtieth birthday.

'Count d'Orsay would himself have answered your letter, but had not the nerve or the heart to do so,' wrote Miss Power on behalf of d'Orsay almost six weeks later; 'although the subject occupies his mind night and day, he cannot speak of it but to those who have been his fellow-sufferers; it is like an image ever floating before his eyes, which he has got, as it were, used to look upon, but which he cannot yet bear to grasp and feel that it is real: much as she was to us, we cannot but feel that to him she was all; the centre of his existence, round which his recollections, thoughts, hopes, and plans turned.'[16]

After Lady Blessington's death d'Orsay and the Misses Power moved out to Chambourcy near Saint-Germain-en-Laye to stay with his sister on her husband's country estate. Although today Chambourcy is a virtual suburb of Paris, accessible by subway to Saint-Germain-en-Laye and then by bus, it is still a quiet little community with all the appurtenances of a small village in rural France:

church, small *mairie*, a square with plane trees and so on. In the mid-nineteenth century it must have been even more of a sleepy backwater, a world away from the bustle of Paris and London.

Here d'Orsay pursued a reclusive, almost monastic existence. 'Of d'Orsay I hear very little,' wrote Forster to Bulwer Lytton* at the end of July. 'He writes to no one, not even his most intimate former associates here, and I believe it to be quite the truth that poor Lady Blessington's death has been a frightful blow to him. They are all living at Chambourcy and d'Orsay's whole employment is to mow hay and devise a monument for Lady Blessington.'[17]

The summer passed and d'Orsay remained grief-stricken. Thackeray, who was in France, went to visit him on 12 September and described him in a letter as 'the poor old faded and unhappy Dorsay'.[18] He was wretched. Through the rest of 1849, his chief occupation continued to be the design and construction of a mausoleum for Lady Blessington's remains. He had chosen the spot and sold one of his pictures to cover the cost of constructing a striking yet minimalist pyramidal monument of his own design.

Work continued rapidly, and Lady Blessington's embalmed body, which had initially been deposited at La Madeleine, was moved into its final resting place before Christmas 1849. It must have been a miserable scene in the chilly winter. The completion of the mausoleum combined with the interment of Lady Blessington renewed d'Orsay's grief to an almost unbearable pitch. Madden describes a man on the brink of mental collapse. 'On d'Orsay's first visit to the tomb where the remains of Lady Blessington had been deposited his anguish is said to have been most poignant and heart-rending. He seemed almost frenzied at times, bewildered and stupefied; and then, as if awakened suddenly to a full consciousness of the great calamity that had taken

* The one-time scandalous novelist, who had been plain Edward Bulwer, was an increasingly important public figure and had collected a baronetcy in 1838.

place, he would lament the loss he had sustained as if it had occurred only the day before.'[19]

After Lady Blessington's remains had been put into the mausoleum, d'Orsay composed himself sufficiently to return to Paris. It was a severe winter and the early days of 1850 saw him back on the Rue de la Ville l'Evêque with the Misses Power. Gradually and painfully he began to reimmerse himself in art, politics and social life.

In January he wrote to Hayward to thank him for sending an article which Hayward evidently intended him to show Louis Napoleon. The letter indicates that d'Orsay was trying to pick up the pieces of what he saw as his political career. It is obvious from its tone that he regarded himself as something of a player in the plot-riven viper's nest of mid-nineteenth-century French politics; his capacity for self-deception was still with him, but at least the notion that he had a future in public life gave him something to cling to in his grief. In this letter he complained how amour propre makes everyone a revolutionary – not thinking for a minute that he himself suffered from amour propre – and he railed against the duplicity of those in political life, claiming that 'il n'y a pas dix hommes de bonne foi dans ce beau pays'; he tells how Thiers is busily engaged in conspiracy; how the coming elections will show which way the wind blows; how in the Midi the government supports legitimist candidates rather than allow 'des extrêmes rouges' to triumph; and yet he still rather touchingly believes that 'Napoleon a le plus grand désir to run straight'.[20]

As the harsh winter mellowed into spring, the Misses Power returned to London and d'Orsay took rooms on the Rue Lord Byron. He got out and about more, renewing friendships with, among others, Emile Girardin, whose journal La Presse had been extremely supportive of Louis Napoleon. But it was uncertain, in the ever-shifting landscape of political alliances at the time, how much longer Girardin would continue to back the President. The political complexion of a dinner he held with d'Orsay, Victor Hugo and Lamartine towards the end of April was variegated. Hugo, a bestselling author who delighted his public with historical blockbusters, had been elevated to the aristocracy by Louis-Philippe and was a deputy in the Legislative Assembly;* while Lamartine had been a key member of the provisional government that had succeeded the citizen king, and had stood unsuccessfully against Louis Napoleon, who had been supported by both d'Orsay and Girardin. Like d'Orsay, Lamartine was on a downward slope. Pompous and vain, his political career over, he put himself about Paris as something of an elder statesman and kept himself busy churning out turgid histories, sentimental novels and excruciating verse. He and d'Orsay seemed to have got on well, perhaps reminiscing of their time together in Italy.

D'Orsay too was becoming something of a curiosity and a tourist attraction in Paris. English visitors to Paris looked him up much in the way that he and the Blessingtons had courted the older cicerones in Naples during the 1820s. During May, Hayward came to Paris and met up with the septuagenarian legislator Lord Brougham, who was also staying in the city. Writing to his sisters Hayward recalled how 'on Tuesday I dined with him, d'Orsay, Alexandre Dumas (the celebrated writer), Lord Dufferin, and Stuart of the Embassy. I went to an evening party at the Duchess of Grammont's, and saw the Duke de Guiche. Paris was very full.'[21]

In his letter Hayward does not do justice to the dinner between the venerable British peer and Dumas, a meeting orchestrated by d'Orsay, who seemed to have rediscovered his flair as a host. The cheerful

---

* According to Alfred Cobban's *A History of Modern France* (vol II, p. 153) 'The Constituent Assembly had no real justification for its existence now that the Constitution had been made and put into effect, but it hung on as long as it could, in a moribund condition. Finally it had to dissolve and in May 1849 elections were held for a Legislative Assembly.'

spirit of a pleasantly boozy evening at Philippe's in Rue Mont Orgueuil is captured in a report that ran in the *Quarterly Review* a number of years later. 'Brougham was punctual to the hour, and they were formally introduced by Count d'Orsay, who, observing some slight symptoms of stiffness, exclaimed, "*Comment, diable, vous, les deux grands hommes, embrassez-vous donc, embrassez-vous.*"' They fraternised accordingly *à la française*, Brougham looking very much during the operation as if he were in the gripe of a bear.' Dumas was a vast man with leonine hair, Brougham almost skeletally thin, 'though nobody could look more cordial and satisfied than Dumas. The dinner was excellent. Some first-rate *Clos de Vougeot*, of which Dumas had an accurate foreknowledge, sustained the hilarity of the company; the conversation was varied and animated; each of the distinguished guests took his fair share, and no more than his fair share; and it was bordering on midnight when the party separated.'[22]

Another month, another set of distinguished dinner guests: during June, two of d'Orsay's London friends, Dickens and Maclise, were in town. In July the count wrote to Henry Bulwer, to introduce a relative by marriage of his nephew the Duke de Guiche, and to say that he had just seen Henry's brother Edward – 'j'ai vu Edward dernièrement ici, cela m'a fait du bien de revoir une de mes bonnes associations!!'[23]

As well as catching up with friends visiting from England, arranging jolly dinners and discussing politics, d'Orsay was getting his life back to normal in other ways too. He was becoming short of money again, and, with neither Lady Blessington nor his reputation as a young man of fashion around to protect him, he was in danger of becoming homeless. Happily Théodore Gudin, an artist with a reputation for important state commissions, was able to help and offered him an empty atelier at his house on Rue de la Ville l'Evêque. This kindness allowed d'Orsay to create another fine interior. The result was a triumph, especially when one considers his limited resources; visitors flocked to see what he had created – part bedroom, part tented salon, part museum, part studio. There were hammocks and couches, ottomans and mirrors.

A centre of attention and established in sumptuous surroundings, he became more like his old self. In October Henry Fox, now the fourth Lord Holland, was travelling through Paris with his family, in a vast yellow coach likened to a mayoral conveyance, en route to southern Italy. They stopped for three weeks, renting an apartment on the Boulevard de la Madeleine, where d'Orsay was a frequent visitor.

The two men had effected a rapprochement in London before d'Orsay's departure and were now on sufficiently good terms for the count to have given Dumas a letter of introduction to Holland when the author had attended the funeral of King Louis-Philippe in August. Neither man was young any longer – Holland was suffering from an eye complaint, and the former dandy d'Orsay was surviving on the charity of friends; they must have had a nostalgic time reminiscing about the good old days in southern Europe in the 1820s. It is interesting to note the impression d'Orsay was still able to make on those who were meeting him for the first time. Among those travelling in the giant yellow coach with Lord Holland was his physician Dr Chempell, who was introduced to d'Orsay. 'He was a man of striking appearance, with a head of Jove and Apollo combined, tall and grace-ful, elaborately dressed, and full of wit and humour; speaking faultless English, with just enough French accent in it to remind one of his actual nationality. He was said to be bitterly disappointed in failing to obtain a post in connection with the "Beaux Arts", which he had fully expected.'[24]

Political preferment still evaded him, and it grated. However, he was at work again on other projects, most significantly a portrait bust of the old windbag Lamartine, which was finished in time to be exhib-ited at the Salon in November. It was greeted with ecstasy by *La Presse*, which on 10 November published a fulsome account of d'Orsay's talent and his miraculous bust of the man of letters and former statesman; given Girardin's friendship with d'Orsay and his involvement with the journal, *La Presse*'s enthusiasm is hardly a surprise. Lamartine too was delighted and dashed off eight eulogistic stanzas about the work.

Thackeray, however, visiting Paris in January 1851, was less impressed and his view is something of a counterpoint to the rapture with which the bust had been received:

> Today I went to see Dorsay who has made a bust of Lamartine who too is mad with vanity. He has written some verses on his bust – he asks who is this? is it a warrior, is it a hero, is it a priest, is it a sage, is it a tribune of the people, is it an Adonis? – meaning that he is all these things – verses so fatuous & crazy I never saw. Well, Dorsay says they are the finest verses that ever were written & imparts to me a translation wh. Miss Power has made of them: and Dorsay believes in his mad rubbish of a statue wh. he *didn't* make – believes in it in the mad way that madmen do, that it is divine and that he made it: – only as you look in his eyes you see that he doesn't quite believe, and when pressed hesitates & turns away with a howl of rage. Dorsay has fitted himself up a charming atelier with arms and trophies pictures and looking glasses – the tomb of Blessington the sword & star of Napoleon and a crucifix over his bed: and here he dwells without any doubts or remorses, admiring himself in the most horrible pictures wh. he has painted and the statues wh. he gets done for him.[25]

It is interesting that Dickens, visiting Paris a month afterwards, seems to have found none of the incipient lunacy that so struck the author of *Vanity Fair*. 'We had d'Orsay to dinner yesterday,' wrote Dickens to his wife from the Hôtel Wagram, 'and I am hurried to dress now, in order to pay a promised visit to his "atelier." He was very happy with us, and is much improved both in spirits and looks.'[26]

But there is no disguising d'Orsay's increasing annoyance with Louis Napoleon's failure to reward him with a suitably august role in his administration. Nor did the count's absence from office go unheeded by his friends; in March of 1852, Dickens wrote to a friend saying, 'I don't see, Mon ami, that D'Orsay has a place yet.'[27]

Although with the benefit of hindsight – he was to remain as ruler of France until 1870 – it may seem that Louis Napoleon was merely settling into his role and that there would be time enough to dish out sinecures to his cronies, for most of 1851 he was still ostensibly the elected head of state in France, occupying the post for a fixed term. After that time, his successor might have been someone over whom d'Orsay would have no claims of previous friendship. Moreover, the count was an impatient man, who preferred not to have to wait to get his way. He was weary of being passed over, as a letter written to Lord Holland at the end of March 1851 demonstrates. 'I am tired, aggrieved, afflicted, by this system of reaction, by this incorrigible imbecility, which makes one man deprive himself of three million votes of those who have put him where he is. I have not the constitution to swallow all that with an official and officious grin, and when I have seen nominations like those of M. de La Valette,* a species of adventurer, I have written to L N that he only had audacity for his enemies and sluggishness of heart for his friends.'[28]

As earlier in his life, when he did not get his way d'Orsay became vicious and vindictive, although nowadays there was little he could do: to propose a duel would be ridiculous. He could only torture himself with watching the preferment of others and worsen his own prospects by sending sour letters that Louis Napoleon would dismiss as the bilious rants of a poor loser.

Disappointed, d'Orsay busied himself in his studio. Perhaps hoping to recreate a similar, and potentially advantageous, relationship

---

* De La Valette would eventually serve as minister of the interior.

to the one he had enjoyed with the Duke of Wellington, he re-established his friendship with Louis Napoleon's uncle Jérôme, governor of Les Invalides, who had been married to his relative the late Princess of Württemberg. He also got to know Jérôme's son 'Plon Plon', or Prince Napoleon Joseph Bonaparte. He was commissioned to produce a bust of him, and he also received a commission for a much more important public sculpture of Jérôme to be placed at Versailles.

But mere artistic commissions were not going to satisfy him for long. The lure of politics, together with his desire to cast himself as a political fixer and man of influence, meant that he still meddled when and where he could in affairs of state, whipping up the press, targeting opinion formers and lobbying political figures at home and abroad. He believed that his life in London had somehow qualified him to emerge as a statesman. Once again the issue of d'Orsay's self-deception, or at least the gulf in perception that existed between the way he saw himself and the way others did, is brought into focus. Where he saw a dignified and wise man putting himself at the disposal of his country, others saw a broken and discredited dandy, almost an embarrassment from a previous age.

On 19 May 1851 he began a vigorous and voluminous correspondence with the Marquis of Londonderry that would continue until the end of the year and involve over two dozen letters; the ostensible subject was the incarceration of Abd-el-Kader. Following an attack on Algiers in 1830 and the subsequent conquest of other cities in the next few years, French influence in North Africa had grown stronger. In 1839 the Arab chief Abd-el-Kader had decided to fight the invaders. A brutal war had ensued, with atrocities on both sides. But in 1847 Abd-el-Kader was defeated and captured. D'Orsay's idealism and his innate sympathy for the underdog led him to believe that the continued imprisonment of the defeated Arab leader was a stain on the honour of France. Typical of the letters to Londonderry was one written on 26 May 1851:

Thanks My Dear Marquis for Dorling's Card, which is a capital joke. I saw Brougham last night, and spoke to him strongly about our friend Abdil Kader he is quite ready to embark with us in that question. I dine with him to day at Holland, and we will canvass again the subject. The reason why I wanted to have the Chronicle in our side, is, that in Paris it has more influence, as the Morning Post is only looked at, as a Journal of Fashion. I had seen the paragraph[s?] you sent me as I receive regularly the Post. – you may count entirely on me, I will follow you, dans cette grande Croisade – we have all those with any intelligence in this country on our side. Only the slow coaches want to keep him prisoner. Let me assure you, my dear Marquis, that as you intend our best plan of action is to publish the letters of which the public know nothing, and to then immediately appeal to the President, who does not dare to exercise the power that he has, which he is very angry about. We must go on pecking at that, it's our only chance. The nation will finally see sense when I reprint in *La Presse* the correspondence of Lamoricière* and the Duke of Aumale. We must stress that a proud Arab is only prisoner because he was arrested with his handsome steed. He has done nothing. I am amazed that you haven't received the paper that I sent you. I am going to try to locate the paragraph about the visit to the castle at Chenonceaux. Everyone was in good form, and I took great care to ensure their feelings remained amenable towards the Emir's position. Yesterday I dined with Victor Hugo, Girardin and others who sympathise with our demands.

I know we don't need anyone to convince the public, but we

* General Christophe Léon Juchault de Lamoricière (1806–65). Served in Algeria 1833–47, and through his energy chiefly the war was brought to an end by the capture of Abd-el-Kader in 1847.

shall be more successful with the *Chronicle* in our court. If you like I shall send you Haywood, on whom I can count. Adieu for now my dear Marquis,

Votre très affectionné

d'Orsay[29]

Whatever d'Orsay's feelings about the imprisoned North African leader, and there is no reason to think he was not genuinely concerned about his fate and his wellbeing, there is little doubt that any other cause would have done as well. Much as the idea of making his fortune on the back of the railway boom of the 1840s had obsessed him when he was in debt at Gore House, so Abd-el-Kader preoccupied him in Paris for the latter half of 1851. D'Orsay the polymath was not content to be merely an artist, he wanted to be an influence-pedlar too – and this issue was a perfect hobby-horse for him. Abd-el-Kader was a project that allowed him an outlet for his talents and his interests: whether it was organising a lunch for English journalists who, he wrote with his amour propre of old, were enchanted with a letter he had penned; recounting an argument that he had at the house of one of Garibaldi's followers; or suggesting that Lord Londonderry apply a compress of arnica to a bruised knee, an avant-garde remedy that Dr Quin would be happy to prescribe. Moreover it kept him in contact with his smart friends in England.

He would also complain about his lack of position. For instance on 6 October 1851, he wrote 'You know that I have established a Charitable Society in London, and that I have been of invaluable help to all my fellow countrymen, from cooks to claimants. At the moment amongst my letters I have one from Napoleon, in which he writes: "You are the guardian angel of influential and ordinary Frenchmen". So I felt I should tap on the shoulder of my homeland to remind them that they owe me.'[30]

As Louis Napoleon's term of office reached its end, d'Orsay

began to sense the possibility that he might choose to prolong his ascendancy by illegal and unconstitutional means. In a letter dated 7 October he says that Louis Napoleon 'a si peu de temps (*legalement*) à vivre, comme President' (italics added).[31]

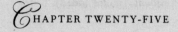

CHAPTER TWENTY-FIVE

Coup d'Etat

AS PARIS HEADED TOWARDS THE CHRISTMAS SEASON THERE WAS
a sense of political uneasiness, although d'Orsay himself seems to
have continued to believe in Louis Napoleon's fundamental honesty.
On 1 December 1851 he wrote to Londonderry:

> One can only wonder at the debate on his inconsistency and
> immorality, coming from these so-called 'men of the state', who
> are all rogues. Napoleon simply disarms them by being an hon-
> ourable man – they are so unused to having to deal with a nature
> of this kind that they can't begin to understand it. The situation
> will be much clearer in a fortnight – it is like a game of chess and
> he must manoeuvre his pawns very cautiously and slowly. If
> you read our papers you would be amazed at the trivialities they
> discuss in the face of a vital issue. The reign of the gossips twit-
> ters away, Thiers, Derryier and co. hardly listen any more;
> we've become very matter of fact.
>
> Paris doesn't seem much fun, political preoccupations

abound: the Dauphine's devils for the Legitimists, the king of Hanover for the English. All this gives the city a glum air at the beginning of the season – the theatres are the only places thriving, there is an abundance of new plays.[1]

Through various petitions, some legislative manipulation and an attempt to change the constitution, Louis Napoleon had sought to extend his mandate beyond the expiry date of his term as president. However, although the vote in July 1851 to overturn the status quo had gone in his favour, it had not achieved the two-thirds majority required to effect constitutional change. Although more than a single term as president was forbidden, Louis Napoleon's popularity was considerable. Big business backed him, fearing a return to anarchy when he stepped down. Meanwhile the army had been sown with high-ranking officers sympathetic to the president. A republican general had been dismissed early in 1851 and in the postscript of his letter of 1 December d'Orsay notes that 'on vient de changer le General Command & la Garde Nationale, c'est le Gl Loinestine ancien aide camp de Sebastiani qui est nommé'.[2]

On the very day that d'Orsay was completing this letter, Louis Napoleon was putting the finishing touches to a plot that would show him to be a ruthless Machiavel. Once again France was to descend into one of its periodic bouts of blood-letting as the president, frustrated in his desire to extend his presidency by legal means, decided to get his way by staging a coup.

Learning from his embarrassing record of attempted armed insurrection, Louis Napoleon was leaving nothing to chance this time. Early in the morning of 2 December, the anniversary of the Battle of Austerlitz, newspaper offices and various strategic points including the Palais Bourbon, were occupied. Even bell towers were taken over, and the drums in the barracks of the National Guard were broken so that there could be no call to arms. At the same time

Louis Napoleon had proclamations put up around Paris claiming that he had uncovered a conspiracy against him planned by members of the Assembly, and potential conspirators including sixteen deputies and seventy or eighty other prominent figures were arrested, among them Thiers and the merciless General Cavaignac. Louis also promised that within a couple of weeks he would hold a plebiscite to decide whether he should be allowed to continue as president. By daybreak, Paris was in the hands of around fifty thousand troops loyal to Louis Napoleon.

Initially resistance was negligible. But the following day various intellectuals, organised by Victor Hugo, coalesced into some form of opposition and barricades began to be erected. In the Faubourg Saint-Antoine a radical deputy was shot, but still there was little popular support for an uprising, since the urban proletariat broadly favoured the prince–president and felt little empathy with Hugo and other members of the bourgeoisie. However, by 4 December there were a few more barricades; more republicans, who cared that Louis Napoleon had broken his word, took to the streets; and it was then that the tens of thousands of heavily armed troops turned their rifles, bayonets and even their artillery against their countrymen. It was a massacre, and there is little doubt that Napoleon III, as he would shortly become, wanted a decisive show of brutal and overwhelming force. 'In the twinkling of an eye', recorded Victor Hugo, 'there was butchery on the boulevard a quarter of a league long. Eleven pieces of cannon wrecked the Sallandrouze carpet warehouse. The shot tore completely through twenty-eight houses. The baths of Jouvence were riddled. There was a massacre at Tortoni's. A whole quarter of Paris was filled with an immense flying mass, and with a terrible cry.' Victor Hugo's account is far from neutral, as he was one of the prime agitators against the coup. Nevertheless it provides a chilling picture of the human scale of the misery and the horrific, wanton acts carried out by the military.

New Year's Day was not far off, some shops were full of New Year's gifts. In the Passage du Saumon, a child of thirteen, flying before the platoon-firing, hid himself in one of these shops, beneath a heap of toys. He was captured and killed. Those who killed him laughingly widened his wounds with their swords. A woman told me, 'The cries of the poor little fellow could be heard all through the passage.' Four men were shot before the same shop. The officer said to them, 'This will teach you to loaf about.' A fifth, named Mailleret, who was left for dead, was carried the next day with eleven wounds to the Charité. There he died.

They fired into the cellars by the air-holes.

A workman, a currier, named Moulins, who had taken refuge in one of these shot-riddled cellars, saw through the cellar air-hole a passer-by, who had been wounded in the thigh by a bullet, sit down on the pavement with the death rattle in his throat, and lean against a shop. Some soldiers who heard this rattle ran up and finished off the wounded man with bayonet thrusts.

One brigade killed the passers-by from the Madeleine to the Opéra, another from the Opéra to the Gymnase; another from the Boulevard Bonne Nouvelle to the Porte Saint-Denis; the 75th of the Line having carried the barricade of the Porte Saint-Denis, it was no longer a fight, it was a slaughter. The massacre radiated – a word horribly true – from the boulevard into all the streets. It was a devil-fish stretching out its feelers. Flight? Why? Concealment? To what purpose? Death ran after you quicker than you could fly. In the Rue Pagevin a soldier said to a passer-by, 'What are you doing here?' 'I am going home.' The soldier kills the passer-by. In the Rue des Marais they kill four young men in their own courtyard. Colonel Espinasse exclaimed, 'After the bayonet, cannon!' Colonel Rochefort exclaimed, 'Thrust, bleed, slash!' and he added, 'It is an economy of powder and noise.' Before Barbedienne's establishment an officer was showing his gun, an arm of considerable precision, admiringly to his comrades, and he said, 'With this gun I can score magnificent shots between the eyes.' Having said this, he aimed at random at someone, and succeeded. The carnage was frenzied.

At the corner of the Rue du Sentier, an officer of Spahis, with his sword raised, cried out, 'This is not the sort of thing! You do not understand at all. Fire on the women.' A woman was flying, she was with child, she falls, they deliver her by the means of the buttends of their muskets. Another, perfectly distracted, was turning the corner of a street. She was carrying a child. Two soldiers aimed at her. One said, 'At the woman!' And he brought down the woman. The child rolled on the pavement. The other soldier said, 'At the child!' And he killed the child.

In the Rue Mandar, there was, stated an eye-witness, 'a rosary of corpses', reaching as far as the Rue Neuve Saint-Eustache. Before the house of Odier twenty-six corpses, thirty before the Hôtel Montmorency. Fifty-two before the Variétés, of whom eleven were women. In the Rue Grange-Batelière there were three naked corpses. No. 19, Faubourg Montmartre, was full of dead and wounded.[3]

The horror aside, for d'Orsay the significance of the *coup d'état* of 2 December was that it was an anti-liberal, anti-intellectual movement and he found himself divided by it. On one hand he had been a long-standing and staunchly loyal supporter of Napoleon III; on the other as an artist himself, and by personal inclination, he was drawn to the writers, artists and journalists who opposed the coup.

The ambivalence of his position was made clear in a note sent to Hayward on 5 or 6 December, enclosing a letter written by his friend, the ex-king Jérôme addressing his nephew in the name of Napoleon I, declaring his horror of civil war and urging him to restore universal male suffrage to complete his material victory with a moral one. Obviously d'Orsay had been contacted by Jérôme and had been asked to have the letter published in England 'in some other paper than the Chronicle, which is prohibited in Paris'. The count finished his brief note to Hayward with a melancholy sentence. 'I always think of dear old England, that one must like every day more from what we see everywhere else.'[4] And what he expressed on paper he also uttered in speech. He apparently caused considerable consternation at a smart dinner shortly after the coup when, speaking of recent developments, he said loudly and emphatically, 'It is the greatest political swindle that ever had been practised in the world.'[5] There can be no doubt that he took Louis Napoleon's actions as an almost personal betrayal.

Weeks later similar disillusionment and weariness were discernible in a letter that he wrote to Lord Londonderry, ostensibly concerning the fate of their favourite political prisoner. The letter is dated 31 December 1851, the day that the results of the election Louis had promised in his proclamation were announced. It was a landslide: 7,145,000 votes were cast in his favour, a mere 592,000 against.

Mon Cher Marquis —
I would have replied to you a long time ago, but as I opened my letters I felt I must deprive myself of the pleasure of writing to you. — There is no doubt that if Napoleon keeps his word this time Abdul Kader will be released. To me that would be some consolation for the coup d'état that has given him these extraordinary powers, if he could settle all questions of clemency personally. When one calculates it, seven and a half million votes, without those of the Legitimists, is more than at the last election, when there were five and a half million. My politics have always been Napoleonic — since my childhood this movement has been almost a religion to me, but I confess to you

that I regret this coup. Napoleon hasn't kept his word and therefore has lost some prestige, however I must admit that the rest of the world will absolve him, if there is the possibility of him being absolved in such a case. My impression is that he would have made it without a coup: the French aren't a Republican nation, even less are they adherents of the Legitimists, the Bourbons were chased out of France four times by the people and we don't want to have to do so a fifth time, and the Orleanists fell in the 1848 revolution. So you see the field is open for Napoleon and with a little more patience he could have got universal suffrage and a revision to the constitution legally.

Anyway I have the impression that everything's functioning in the Empire, and we are just putting the eagle back on the flag. – De Guiche has left for Hesse Cassel. Myself, I am making no move, I don't want to be the first. But I am too English in my outlook to agree with everything, unlike my put-upon countrymen.

Adieu for the moment my dear Marquis. I said yesterday that the first thing I'd demand from Napoleon would be the safe release of Abdel Kader.

Votre affectionné

d'Orsay[6]

The coup was one of the cruellest agents of disillusionment for d'Orsay. Since childhood he had been a Bonapartist, and had ascribed only noble motives to the Napoleonic cause. He had been blind to the less palatable aspects of the emperor's rule. Now as a man on the threshold of old age this cause, which had been a basic tenet of his life, in which he had hoped to find employment and satisfaction, had been stolen from him.

A couple of days later he elaborated further on these feelings in a long letter to Hayward, which he sent via the British Embassy so that he could express himself frankly; it seems that even d'Orsay had reason to worry about being too outspoken in his criticism of the new regime. 'I was, and I am, furious about the coup d'état,' he wrote, adding that 'Napoleon has lost a lot of respect in my eyes. I thought he was a man who would never break his word.' His personal feelings of betrayal aside, he went on to say that he was sure that Louis Napoleon would have achieved the necessary revision to the constitution to allow him to continue. He also said that for forty years he had been known as 'the biggest and most sincere Napoleonist there was. But I wished he had got to where he is by another route, the one that Proudhon, Girardin and I traced for him. But no! In spite of his success, I don't wish to go to see him, his Uncle Jerome has just come to find me to pressure me to but I refused and I think of my dignity when I say, let him come to me.'[7]. His characteristic petulance is commensurate with the mounting sense of bitterness he felt. He described in excoriating terms how those in public life were nothing but sycophants and servants and how the whole country was heading towards empire: 'You see the eagles leaving their nests and the contents decorating the flags flying in the Jardin de Plantes, now one must call his cousins "Your Highness", and he is paving the way to the Tuileries.'[8] All these symbols that had been so potent for d'Orsay when he was a boy growing up in the imperial Paris of Napoleon I seemed now as empty baubles, a sick joke, a sham. He ended his letter with a familiar refrain: 'Ah! Si j'étais riche, je serais bien vite à Londres. Je suis exilé ici.'[9]

No matter how exiled d'Orsay felt in Paris, he could at least have counted himself lucky that he was not expelled from France as were two of his friends, Eugène Sue and Victor Hugo, neither of whom found favour with the new regime.

Coming as it did after the spectacular collapse of his own fortunes and the death of Lady Blessington, the coup had a terrible effect on d'Orsay. If anything the fiction that he had enjoyed some influence over Louis Napoleon had sustained his self-esteem. Now this was gone and, facing another winter in Paris, d'Orsay succumbed to a bout of what he thought was lumbago. It laid him out for much of the latter half of February and March 1852.

Although in considerable pain, he did not forget his friends in London. 'My dearest D'Is,' he wrote to his old friend Disraeli on 7 April to mark his appointment as Chancellor of the Exchequer, 'I wanted to write to you all this time but I have been ill I may say for the first time of my life. Fancy me on a sofa with an atrocious lumbago for the last six weeks and obliged to write with a pencil. I cannot resist longer to congratulate you, and myself, on your present position. I say myself because for many years I said there was no power which could prevent you to arrive at the Ministry and at the head of the House of Commons.'[10]

And although it would never match the easy warmth with which he addressed Disraeli, his old friend and fellow roisterer from the good old Crockford's days, there are signs that his relationship with Louis Napoleon was improving. Doubtless through the intercession of Jérôme Bonaparte, he was talked of in connection with three appointments, including that of Directeur Générale des Beaux Arts, which he would eventually be awarded. There is other, less obvious evidence that he and Louis Napoleon were enjoying a rapprochement. Among the people with whom d'Orsay had struck up an acquaintance since arriving in Paris in 1849 was the writer George Sand. The two knew of each other: d'Orsay had praised her work in London years earlier, they had many friends and acquaintances in common and it seems likely that they would have come into contact with each other through the sculptor Clesinger, with whom d'Orsay collaborated and with whose wife Sand was friendly. But after the coup of 2 December, to which Sand like so many other liberal bohemians was opposed, they became much closer. During 1852 she bombarded d'Orsay with letters begging him to intercede with the regime on behalf of herself and her liberal friends who had fallen foul of the crackdown with the arrests and deportations of potential opponents of the regime.

One of her earlier notes to d'Orsay, dated 2 February 1852, begins in tentatively quasi-conspiratorial fashion. 'Cher comte, lisez la letter ci-jointe dont je n'ai pas le temps de prendre copie pour vous l'envoyer à part et si vous ne désapprouvez rien, soyez assez bon pour la faire parvenir où sera le prince [Jérôme's son Plon Plon]. C'est vous aussi qui êtes bon et que j'aime de tout mon coeur.'[11] It would seem that she had asked d'Orsay to pass on an invitation to a clandestine meeting with Jérôme's son – after all it was Jérôme who had issued the letter urging Louis Napoleon's restraint. The result was swift, as Sand wrote to d'Orsay the following day: 'Oui cher comte, vous avez admirable-ment réussi. Le prince est venu tout à l'heure déjeuner avec les couverts d'étain de l'atelier. Il avait déjà agi. Il est excellent. Et vous aussi et je vous aime de tout mon coeur.'[12]

For a soi-disant bohemian, Sand seems to have been overly impressed that Prince Napoleon condescended to dine off pewter in artisanal surroundings, but the real source of her wonder seems to have been d'Orsay's efficacy as a conduit between those she wanted to spare from the retribution of Louis Napoleon's repressive edicts and ruthless police, and those in the imperial family who were able to do something to help her. Her postscript to a letter dated 14 April demonstrates her feelings: 'Ne m'oubliez pas auprès de votre aimable prince Jérôme quand vous le verrez. Vous n'avez pas idée comme il a été bon pour mes amis . . . Dites-moi donc. Je fais un roman. On vous en a dédié mille mais jamais de meilleur coeur. Voulez-vous m'autoriser à vous dédier celui-là? S'il est mauvais, tant pis. Vous êtes bien sûr que je ne l'aurai pas fait exprès!'[13]

It might have seemed like old times for d'Orsay, putting in a good word here and there with the ruling elite, having a fashionable author promise to dedicate a book to him – except that he was dying. His lumbago was no lumbago, but rather kidney disease. By the summer it was evident that he would soon be dead. Madden went to see him in his studio and was shocked by the broken shadow of the man he had known since those carefree days in Naples in the 1820s:

I visited my poor friend a few weeks before his death, and found him evidently sinking, in the last stage of disease of the kidneys, complicated with spinal complaint. The wreck only of the *beau* d'Orsay was there.

He was able to sit up and to walk, though with difficulty and evidently with pain, about his room, which was at once his studio, reception room, and sleeping apartment. He burst out crying when I entered the room, and continued for a length of time so much affected that he could hardly speak to me. Gradually he became composed, and talked about Lady Blessington's death, but all the time with tears pouring down his pale wan face, for even then his features were death-stricken.

He said with marked emphasis, *'In losing her I lost every thing in this world – she was to me a mother! a dear, dear mother! a true loving mother to me!'* While he uttered these words he sobbed and cried like a child. And referring to them, he again said, '*You understand me, Madden.*' I understood him to be speaking what he felt, and there was nothing in his accents, in his position, or his expressions, (for his words sounded in my ears like those of a dying man,) which led me to believe he was seeking to deceive himself or me.

I turned his attention to the subject I thought most important to him. I said, among the many objects which caught my attention in the room, I was very glad to see a crucifix placed over the head of his bed; men living in the world, as he had done, were so much in the habit of forgetting all early religious feelings.

D'Orsay seemed hurt at the observation. I then plainly said to him, 'The fact is, I imagined, or rather supposed, you had followed Lady Blessington's example, if not in giving up your own religion, in seeming to conform to another more in vogue in England.' D'Orsay rose up with considerable energy, and stood erect and firm with obvious exertion for a few seconds, looking like himself again, and pointing to the head of the bed, he said, 'Do you see those two swords?' pointing to two small swords (which were hung over the crucifix crosswise); 'do you see that sword to the right? With that sword I fought in defence of my religion.'

He then told Madden of the duel he had fought over an oath during his brief career in the Garde Royale, before adding that 'Lady Blessington never ceased "in her heart" to be a Catholic, although she occasionally attended the church of another persuasion; and that while she was in Paris, she went every Sunday to the Madeleine, in company with some member of his family'.[14]

There was an attempt to improve his health by sending him to convalesce at Dieppe, where he was nursed by the Misses Power. His condition worsened and by the middle of July he contracted a pulmonary illness. By the end of the month it became apparent that he had only days to live and he returned to Paris. News of his impending end quickly reached England. 'I have exceedingly bad accounts of d'Orsay,' wrote Lord Brougham in a letter, 'and that he is come back to Paris. It is said there is a message every day from the Elysée.'[15] It seems that at long last Louis Napoleon had an attack of conscience.

During the last three days of his life, d'Orsay received the Archbishop of Paris, a new friend but one who was quickly charmed by the dying dandy. 'J'ai pour vous plus que de l'amitié, j'ai de l'affection,' the cleric is reported to have said to d'Orsay as he left.[16]

He was also visited by the curé of Chambourcy, for whom he had restored many paintings in the village church.

Between three and four o'clock on the morning of 5 August at the age of fifty-two, he died and yet, even at the moment of his death, there is some dispute about the way in which he left this life. The more prosaic account has him dying in bed attended by his doctor. But there is a rather more colourful, romantic and altogether more appropriate version. Half a century later an elderly woman offered the following account of his death. 'Count d'Orsay became, during the last months of his life, very fond of waltz music, and one of his—' she paused '—nieces would play to him when he was exhausted or in pain. One August evening he was sitting in his chair, listening to the piano. "Play it faster," he said suddenly. And again: "Play it faster, play it faster!"'[17] By the time the tune was finished, continued the woman, the count was dead. She knew of this, she said, because it was she who had been playing the piano.

Whether this old woman was one of the Misses Power and whether the story is true is almost immaterial, since it is exactly the sort of way in which d'Orsay would have liked to die.

CHAPTER TWENTY-SIX

Burial and Obituaries

THE DEATH OF D'ORSAY WAS A MAJOR INTERNATIONAL NEWS event. Lengthy and largely eulogistic obituaries appeared in most fashionable newspapers. The *Globe* (reprinted in *The Times*) declared, 'Unquestionably one of the celebrities of our day, the deceased man of fashion, claims more than the usual curt obituary.'[1] The *Annual Register* said generously, 'Few men in his position have shown greater accomplishments,'[2] and the *Gentleman's Magazine* enumerated some of them: 'His literary compositions were lively and imaginative. His profile portraits of his friends . . . are felicitous and characteristic, and his statuettes are not only graceful, but possess greater originality of conception than evinced by the majority of professional artists.'[3] There was even belated recognition from Louis Napoleon; the *Bulletin de Paris* reported, 'When the news of the death of Count d'Orsay was communicated to the Prince President he exclaimed that he had lost "his best friend".'[4] Emile Girardin wrote in *La Presse*, 'the pain and the void left by his death will be deeply felt by all his friends, whom he had in profusion in France and England in all classes of society and under every colour of the political world.'[5]

Nor was any fashionable diary, memoir or indeed any letter of the time complete without a reference to the passing of d'Orsay. Typical was Dickens's observation: 'Poor d'Orsay! It is a tremendous consideration that friends should fall around us in such awful numbers as we attain middle life. What a field of battle it is.'[6] And the ripples caused by this event even reached across the Atlantic where, on 7 August 1852, Macready wrote in his diary,

To my grief perceived the notice of the death of dear Count d'Orsay. No one who knew him and had affections could help loving him. Where he liked he was most fascinating and captivating. It was impossible to be insensible to his graceful, frank, and most affectionate manner. I have reason to believe that he liked me, perhaps much, and I certainly entertained the most affectionate regard for him. He was the most brilliant, graceful, endearing man I ever saw – humorous, witty, and clear-headed. But the name of d'Orsay alone had a charm; even in the most distant of cities of the United States all inquired with an interest about him.[7]

D'Orsay's funeral was a low-key affair, reported with uncharacteristic restraint by the *Age* on 14 August:

The funeral ceremony for the late Count d'Orsay took place on Friday at Chambourcy, near Saint Germain. Among the persons assembled to perform the last rites for the deceased were Prince Napoleon Bonaparte, Count Bouffet de Montauban, Count de Latour du Pin, the Marquis du Prat, M. Emile de Girardin, M. Clesinger, the sculptor, M. Charles Laffitte, M. Bixio, M. Alexandre Dumas, jun, Mr Hughes Ball, and several other English gentlemen. The Duke de Grammont, brother-in-law of the Count d'Orsay, being confined to his bed by illness,

Count Alfred de Grammont and the Duke de Lasparre, nephews of the deceased, were the chief mourners. On leaving the church, the body was conveyed to a tomb in the form of a pyramid, built under the direction of the count himself, and in which he had signified his desire that his remains should be placed. No funeral oration was pronounced over the body, but the emotion of the persons present was great, and the sadness of the scene was increased by the appearance of the Duchess de Grammont, sister of the deceased, kneeling at his tomb, every effort to induce her to abstain from being present having been made in vain.[8]

The sobriety of the *Age*'s report evinces the hypocritical respectability of the second half of the nineteenth century; it even omits to state that the tomb was already occupied by the remains of the Countess of Blessington. Things had changed immensely in the twenty-odd years that the *Age* had taunted Lady Blessington about her ménage with the dashing Count d'Orsay.

On the whole the latter half of the nineteenth century was kind to those who survived d'Orsay. Napoleon III ruled France, presiding over a period of prosperity until his defeat by Bismarck at the Battle of Sedan in 1870. While Paris descended into the anarchy and bloodletting of the Commune, Louis slipped off to Britain, dying in exile in 1873. Dickens became the most celebrated novelist in the English language and achieved monumental status. Thackeray did almost as well. Edward Bulwer Lytton re-entered Parliament in 1852, became Colonial Secretary and was elevated to the peerage, dying in 1873. Disraeli became Prime Minister of Great Britain on two occasions, and as a close friend of Queen Victoria he urged her to assume the title of Empress of India; from a scurrilous novelist and social-climbing debtor he became one of the chief architects of the British Empire.

In 1870, Disraeli, who had by then resigned as Prime Minister, found time to reissue a set of his novels. Among them was the 1837 love story *Henrietta Temple*, which he had dedicated to d'Orsay and in which he appeared thinly disguised as glamorous Count Alcibiades de Mirabel. In a new preface to the novel, Disraeli described d'Orsay thus: 'the inimitable d'Orsay, the most accomplished and the most engaging character that has figured in this country, who, with the form and universal genius of an Alcibiades, combined a brilliant wit and a heart of quick affection, and who, placed in a public position, would have displayed a courage, a judgement, and a commanding intelligence, which would have ranked him with the leaders of mankind'. Although rather late with public acknowledgement of his friend, Disraeli deserves greater credit than George Sand, who, following the count's death, did not bother to dedicate a novel to him as she had promised.

Rampant respectability and the rapid change of the nineteenth century would, within a few years, eradicate much of the world that d'Orsay knew and loved. At around the time of the 1851 Great Exhibition Gore House was turned into a cluster of restaurants super-intended by Soyer, former chef of the Reform Club. The effect was one of a kitsch gastronomic theme park: *table d'hôte à la française* in the 'Blessington Temple of the Muses' for six shillings and sixpence (waiters included); 'Dinners Anglo-Français' for three shillings and sixpence in the 'Baronial Hall'; cold dinner for two shillings in the 'Encampment of All Nations, where, also, M. Soyer's Magic Stove will be in operation for cooking Chops, Steaks, &c'; ales, stouts, wines, ices sandwiches and cigars could be had at the 'Gipsey and Pic-Nic Tents'; while the 'Washington Refreshment Lounge' was the place for 'transatlantic beverages in endless variety'. The enterprise was not a success. The house was then purchased by the commissioners of the Exhibition, turned into an art school and subsequently was demolished to make way for the Albert Hall.

The Hippodrome fared little better: 'Part of the course, with a few hedges, was kept open for horse-exercise as late as 1852, and was well patronized',[9] but all that remains today to commemorate what was once London's fashionable racecourse are the addresses Hippodrome Mews and Hippodrome Place, both in London W11.

Howell & James, the emporium that precipitated the collapse of Gore House, continued to trade until it was acquired by Debenham & Freebody in 1900.

The early twentieth century saw a resurgence of interest in the life of Count d'Orsay. In the autumn of 1901 the celebrated actor–manager Herbert Beerbohm Tree appeared in what seems to have been a truly atrocious play called *The Last of the Dandies*. One critic wrote, 'there was little to arouse eager interest, there was absolutely nothing that gave birth to excitement. To put the matter briefly, *The Last of the Dandies* was picturesque, but dull; a fine study in costume, but hardly worthy of the name of play.' The best he could say of it was that 'the performance which on the first night was unwisely protracted until midnight, has since been brought within more reasonable limits'.

D'Orsay's name was invoked with rather more commercial success by a French perfumer, which registered the trademark Parfumerie d'Orsay in Berne in 1911 and by the 1920s had shops across Europe and in New York. Noted artists were called in to design packaging and promotional materials: René Lalique made bottles for the Parfumerie d'Orsay, and after the Second World War Jean Cocteau created a poster.

In the mid-1990s there came news that would have pleased d'Orsay. After its closure in the 1840s Crockford's was used variously as a restaurant called the Wellington, as the Devonshire Club and as the Jamaican High Commission; then in 1996 London Clubs International purchased the freehold of 50 St James's and restored London's first purpose-built casino to its original use.

In Chambourcy, now an affluent dormitory town with its own golf club and commuter villas, Lady Blessington and Count d'Orsay have even achieved a modicum of respectability, with streets named after them. Their tomb, once neglected, is now well maintained and visited occasionally. Recently it was graced with a gaudy bouquet of plastic flowers and a note that read, 'In memory of Lady Blessington and Count d'Orsay From the International Byron Society'.

NOTES

CHAPTER 1: *A Child of Empire*

1 Madden, vol. I, p. 319.
2 Connely, p. 12.
3 Disraeli to Sarah Disraeli, 5 February 1836, 'I dined with d'Orsay yesterday to keep his birthday.' See also 4 February 1839. Gunn (ed.), *Benjamin Disraeli letters*, vol. II, p. 147 and vol. III, p. 134.
4 Quoted in Cronin, p. 319.
5 Dupuy, *De Vigny: Ses Amitiés*, vol. I, pp. 37–8.
6 Ibid., p. 38.
7 Vigny quoted in Rolle, pp. 22–3.
8 Ilchester (ed.), *Fox Journal*, p. 72.
9 Cronin, p. 291.
10 Davies, p. 728.

CHAPTER 2: *The Precocious Parisian*

1 Gronow, *Days of the Dandies*, vol. II, p. 51.
2 *Idler in France*, vol. I, p. 167.
3 Ibid., p. 286.
4 Ibid., p. 288.
5 McLynn, p. 157.
6 Cobban, vol. I, p. 251.
7 Service Historique de l'Armée de Terre, Etat signalétique et des services du général Jean-François-Louis Marie-Albert d'Orsay (7 Yd 1016).
8 Blessington, *Idler in France*, vol. I, pp. 238–9 (hereafter *Idler in France*).

9   Lennox, vol. I, p. 158.

10 Ibid.

11 Ibid.

12 Ibid., pp. 161–2.

13 Ibid., p. 162.

14 Ibid., p. 176.

15 Ibid., p. 179.

16 D'Aurevilly, pp. 48–9.

17 Ibid., p. 56.

18 Ibid., p. 56.

19 Raymond, *Reminiscences of Gronow*, p. 56.

20 Engraving reproduced in Chenoune, pp. 32–3.

21 Raymond, *Reminiscences of Gronow*, p. 56.

22 Ibid., p. 57.

23 Gronow, *Days of the Dandies*, vol. I, p. 278.

24 Ibid.

25 Thomas Creevey, *The Creevey Papers*, 1905, pp. 236–7, quoted in Hibbert, p. 185.

26 Stanhope, p. 89.

27 Ibid., p. 89.

28 Ibid., p. 89.

29 The *Age*, 30 August 1829.

30 Raymond, *Reminiscences of Gronow*, p. 108.

31 Ibid., p. 109.

32 Ibid., p. 76.

33 Hibbert, p. 86.

34 Raymond, *Reminiscences of Gronow*, p. 81.

35 *Idler in France*, vol. I, pp. 355–6.

CHAPTER 3: *A Frenchman in London*

1   Patmore, p. 218.

2   Landor to Miss Rose Poynter, 16 July 1842, Wheeler (ed.), *Landor Letters* p. 107.

3   Boulenger, *Sous Louis-Philippe*, p. 48.

4   Sheppard, p. 113.

5   Carey (ed.), *The London Journal of Flora Tristan*, tr. Jean Hawkes, Virago, 1982, quoted in *The Faber Book of Reportage*, pp. 310–11.

6 Raymond, *Reminiscences of Gronow*, p. 43.
7 Margetson, p. 28.
8 Chateaubriand, *Mémoires d'Outre-Tombe*, quoted in Boulenger, *Sous Louis-Philippe*, p. 78.
9 Byron, quoted in an essay on Lady Holland included in Quennell (ed.), *Genius in the Drawing Room*, p. 40.
10 Ibid.
11 Ibid.
12 Hewlett (ed.), *Chorley: Autobiography, Memoirs and Letters*, vol. I, pp. 179–80.

CHAPTER 4: *The 'Divine Bit of Blue'*

1 Madden, vol. I, p. 23.
2 Ibid., p. 20.
3 Ibid., p. 23.
4 Ibid., p. 22.
5 Ibid., pp. 35–6.
6 Ibid., p. 24.
7 Unpublished letters of Lady Bulwer Lytton to A. E. Chalon, p. 124.
8 Ibid., p. 126.
9 Sadleir, p. 14.
10 Joseph Jekyll, quoted in Teignmouth Shore, p. 33.

CHAPTER 5: *Her Comical Earl*

1 Molloy, p. 33.
2 County Tyrone web page.
3 Madden, vol. 1, p. 52.
4 Teignmouth Shore, p. 29.
5 Madden, vol. 1, p. 51.
6 Molloy, p. 31.
7 Madden, vol. I, p. 52.
8 Ibid., p. 64.
9 Sadleir, p. 18.
10 Molloy, p. 44.
11 Madden, vol. I, pp. 55–6.
12 Ibid., p. 56.

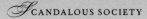

13 Ibid., p. 57.

14 Ibid., p. 68.

15 Ibid., p. 58.

16 Contemporary quotation taken from Weinreb and Hibbert (eds), *London Encyclopaedia*, p. 446.

17 *Morning Herald*, 28 October 1817.

18 Joseph Jekyll, quoted in Sadleir, p. 28.

19 Murray, p. 29.

20 Patmore, vol. I, p. 13.

21 Teignmouth Shore, p. 37.

22 Raymond, *Reminiscences of Gronow*, p. 196.

CHAPTER 6: *Ménage à Trois*

1 *Dictionnaire Georges Six*, vol. II, p. 272.

2 Blessington, *Idler in Italy*, vol. I, p. 170.

3 Madden, vol. I, p. 353.

4 Ibid., p. 319.

5 Ibid., p. 320.

6 Ibid.

7 Ibid., vol. III, pp. 232–3.

8 Sadleir, p. 37.

9 Madden, vol. III, p. 235.

10 *Idler in Italy*, vol. I, p. 1.

11 Ibid., p. 31.

12 Connely, p. 23.

13 *Idler in Italy*, vol. I, p. 21.

14 Ibid., pp. 24–5.

15 Ibid., p. 33.

16 Madden, vol. I, p. 66.

17 Ibid., p. 69.

18 Ilchester (ed.), *Fox Journal*, p. 158.

19 *Idler in Italy*, vol. I, p. 27.

20 Sadleir, p. 58.

21 *Idler in Italy*, vol. I, p. 42.

22 Ibid., p. 43.

23 Ibid., p. 171.

24 Ibid., p. 170.

25 Ibid., p. 172.
26 Ibid., p. 240.
27 Ibid., p. 259.
28 Ibid.
29 Ibid., p. 265.
30 Ibid., pp. 265–6.
31 Ibid., p. 329.
32 Dickens to d'Orsay, 18 March 1845, House and Storey (eds), *Dickens Letters*, vol. IV, p. 282.
33 Ilchester (ed.), *Fox Journal* puts the date at 23 March 1823, and according to the *Idler in Italy* the Blessingtons set out for Mentone on 22 March.
34 Ilchester (ed.), *Fox Journal*, pp. 158–9.
35 *Idler in Italy*, vol. I, p. 373.

CHAPTER 7: *Byron and Genoa*

1 *Idler in Italy*, vol. I, p. 393.
2 Nicolson, p. 15.
3 Eisler, p. 718.
4 Ilchester (ed.), *Fox Journal*, p. 160.
5 Lovell (ed.), *Lady Blessington's Conversations*, p. 40.
6 Molloy, p. 98.
7 Ibid., p. 72.
8 Nicolson, p. 67.
9 Madden, vol. I, pp. 81–2.
10 *Idler in Italy*, vol. I, p. 397.
11 Lovell (ed.), *Lady Blessington's Conversations*, p. 39.
12 A memoir of Countess Blessington, Introduction, *Lady Blessington's Conversations*, p. 25.
13 *Idler in Italy*, vol. I, p. 396.
14 Ibid., p. 398.
15 Ilchester (ed.), *Fox Journal*, p. 161.
16 *Idler in Italy*, vol. II, p. 19.
17 Carey (ed.), *Faber Book of Reportage*, p. 302.
18 Ibid., p. 303.
19 Lovell (ed.), *Lady Blessington's Conversations*, p. 168.
20 Quennell (ed.), *Byron*, p. 720.

21 Lovell (ed.), *Lady Blessington's Conversations*, p. 47.
22 Ibid., p. 46.
23 Quennell (ed.), *Byron*, pp. 721–2.
24 Ibid., pp. 724–5.
25 See Lord Byron to Lord Blessington, 24 May 1823: 'My Dear Lord: I find that I was elected a Member of the Greek Committee in March, but did not receive the Chairman's notice until yesterday, and this by mere chance, and through a private hand'.
26 Madden, vol. I, p. 323.
27 Ibid.
28 Connely, p. 71.
29 Lovell (ed.), *Lady Blessington's Conversations*, pp. 152–3.
30 Ibid., p. 47.
31 Origo, p. 400.
32 Lovell (ed.), *Lady Blessington's Conversations*, p. 131.
33 Ibid., p. 82.
34 *Idler in Italy*, vol. II, pp. 93, 94.
35 Nicolson, p. 17.
36 Madden, vol. I, p. 89.
37 Ibid., pp. 120–1.
38 *Idler in Italy*, vol. II, p. 180.
39 Dickens (ed.), *Life of Mathews*, vol. I, p. 98.
40 Ibid., p. 99.

CHAPTER 8: Dolce Far Niente

1 *Idler in Italy*, vol. II, pp. 179–80.
2 Ibid., p. 97.
3 Ibid., p. 191.
4 Ibid., pp. 191–2.
5 Acton, p. 666.
6 Ibid., p. 667.
7 Ibid.
8 *Idler in Italy*, vol. II, p. 229.
9 Introduction by Sir Harold Acton to Clay, p. 3.
10 *Idler in Italy*, vol. II, p. 194.
11 Ibid., p. 194.
12 Ibid., pp. 203–5.

13 Ibid., p. 205.

14 Ibid., pp. 203, 205.

15 Ibid., pp. 219–20.

16 Molloy, Grolier Society edn, p. 330.

17 Edward Bulwer to Lord Durham, quoted in Teignmouth Shore, p. 159.

18 *Idler in Italy*, vol. II, p. 386.

19 Ibid., p. 221.

20 Dickens (ed.), *Life of Mathews*, vol. I, p. 95.

21 *Idler in Italy*, vol. II, pp. 287–8.

22 Dickens (ed.), *Life of Mathews*, vol. I, p. 63.

23 Ibid., p. 93.

24 Ibid., pp. 93–4.

25 Ibid., p. 107.

26 Ibid.

27 Ibid.

CHAPTER 9: *A Duel Narrowly Averted*

1 Dickens (ed.), *Life of Mathews*, vol. I, p. 95.

2 Joseph Jekyll, quoted in Teignmouth Shore, p. 54.

3 *Idler in Italy*, vol. II, pp. 242–3.

4 Dickens (ed.), *Life of Mathews*, vol. I, p. 96.

5 Ibid., p. 129.

6 Ibid., pp. 124–5.

7 Ibid., p. 129.

8 Ibid., p. 109.

9 Madden, vol. II, p. 433.

10 Ibid.

11 Dickens (ed.), *Life of Mathews*, vol. I, p. 109.

12 Ibid. pp. 109–10.

13 Ibid., Appendix I.

14 Ibid., Appendix II.

15 Ibid., p. 111.

16 Ibid., Appendix III.

17 Ibid., p. 113.

18 Ibid., pp. 113–14.

19 Ibid., pp. 115–17.

20 Ibid., Appendix IV.

21 Ibid., pp. 119–20.
22 Ibid., p. 120.
23 Ibid., Appendix V.
24 Madden, vol. II, p. 449.
25 Ibid.
26 Ibid.
27 Madden, vol. I, p. 327.
28 Ibid., p. 352.

CHAPTER 10: *A Change of Scene*

1 *Idler in Italy*, vol. II, p. 413.
2 Ilchester (ed.), *Fox Journal*, p. 215.
3 Ibid.
4 Ibid., p. 216.
5 Lord Holland to Mrs E. Fazakerly 31 October 1825, BL Mss Add. 61937.
6 Ibid.
7 Ibid., 15 November 1825.
8 Ilchester (ed.), *Fox Journal*, p. 216.
9 BL Mss Add. 61937, 15 November 1825.
10 Ibid., *Fox Journal*, 22 November 1825, p. 216.
11 Ilchester (ed.), *Fox Journal*, pp. 216–17.
12 Ibid., p. 217.
13 Ibid., p. 218.
14 Madden, vol. II, p. 429.
15 *Idler in Italy*, vol. II, p. 511.
16 Ibid., p. 501.
17 Ibid., pp. 501–2.
18 Ibid., pp. 483–4.
19 Ibid., p. 484.
20 Ibid., pp. 476–7.

CHAPTER 11: *Marriage à la Mode d'Orsay*

1 At the end of a d'Orsay letter to an anonymous count, 24 January 1827, MA3521, Pierpont Morgan Library.
2 Ibid.

3 Lady Blessington to C. J. Mathews, 7 August 1827, Madden Collection, NY Public Library.

4 Sadleir, p. 114.

5 Ilchester (ed.), *Fox Journal*, pp. 235–6.

6 Letter dated 16 August 1831, Ilchester (ed.), *Lady Holland to her Son*, p. 112.

7 Molloy, vol. I, pp. 162–4.

8 Ilchester (ed.), *Fox Journal*, pp. 241–2.

9 Ibid., p. 243.

10 Madden, vol. I, p. 125.

11 Molloy, vol. I, p. 164.

12 Ilchester (ed.), *Fox Journal*, pp. 250–1.

13 Madden, vol. I, p. 126.

14 Ilchester (ed.), *Fox Journal*, p. 281.

15 Letter from Lady Charleville, 20 August 1831, Department of Manuscripts and Special Collections, University of Nottingham, My 1972.

16 Sadleir, p. 87.

17 Ibid., pp. 175–6.

18 *Idler in Italy*, vol. II, p. 528.

19 Ilchester (ed.), *Fox Journal*, p. 288.

20 *Idler in Italy*, vol. II, pp. 550–1.

21 Ibid., p. 558.

22 Ibid., p. 559.

23 Ibid., pp. 560–1.

24 Bresler, p. 52.

25 *Idler in Italy*, vol. II, p. 540.

26 Bresler, p. 82.

27 Letter from Joseph Severn, quoted in Birkenhead, p. 72.

28 Ibid., p. 88.

29 Ilchester (ed.), *Fox Journal*, p. 266.

30 Ibid., pp. 266–7.

31 Ibid., p. 268.

32 Ibid., pp. 279–80.

33 Ibid., p. 282.

34 Ibid., p. 286.

35 Ibid., p. 287.

36 Ibid.

37 Ibid., p. 289.

38 Ibid.

39 Ibid., p. 290.

40 Ibid., pp. 290–1.

41 Ibid., p. 293.

42 Birkenhead, p. 93.

43 Ibid.

44 Letter dated 25 April 1828, Ilchester (ed.), *Lady Holland to her Son*, p. 81.

45 Ibid., p. 84.

CHAPTER 12: *Paris Fashion*

1 *Idler in France*, vol. I, pp. 60–1.

2 Ibid., p. 83.

3 Ibid., p. 77.

4 Ibid., p. 112.

5 Ibid., p. 97.

6 Ibid., p. 98.

7 McLynn, p. 532.

8 *Idler in France*, vol. I, pp. 104–5.

9 Ibid., p. 109.

10 Ibid., p. 117.

11 Ibid., pp. 119–21.

12 Ibid., p. 122.

13 Harris, p. 46.

14 Poirson, p. 34.

15 Yriarte, p. 16.

16 Chenoune, p. 60.

17 The *Age*, 23 August 1824 (269).

18 The *Age*, 18 October 1829 (331).

19 Ibid.

20 Boulenger, *Sous Louis-Philippe*, p. 66.

21 A receipt for this prize, signed by d'Orsay appears as an appendix in ibid.

22 Letter dated 5 January 1829, Ilchester (ed.), *Lady Holland to her Son*, p. 93.

23 *Idler in France*, vol. II, p. 5.

24 Hibbert, p. 269.

25 Mme de Flahault, quoted in Ilchester (ed.), *Chronicles of Holland House*, pp. 91–2.

26 *Idler in France*, vol. II, pp. 64–5.

27 Ibid., p. 11.
28 Ibid., p. 76.
29 Ibid., p. 77.
30 Madden, vol. I, pp. 140–1.
31 *Idler in France*, vol. II, p. 96.
32 Ibid., p. 97.

CHAPTER 13: *Blackmail and Revolution*

1   The *Age*, 23 August 1829 (269).
2   The *Age*, 27 September 1829 (309).
3   The *Age*, 11 October 1829 (325).
4   The *Age*, 7 March 1829 (75).
5   The *Age*, 23 August 1829 (269).
6   Vitzetelly, vol. I, p. 172.
7   Ibid.
8   Adburgham, *Silver Fork Society*, p. 54.
9   Vitzetelly, vol. I, p. 172.
10 Ibid.
11 Ibid.
12 Thomas Creevey, quoted in Adburgham, *Silver Fork Society*, p. 42.
13 Countess Cowper, quoted in ibid., p. 43.
14 Ibid., p. 54.
15 Vitzetelly, vol. I, p. 172.
16 Ibid., pp. 173–4.
17 *Idler in France*, vol. II, p. 98.
18 Ibid., pp. 139–40.
19 Ibid., p. 130.
20 Ibid., pp. 132–3.
21 Ibid., pp. 134–5.
22 Ibid., pp. 135–6.
23 Ibid., p. 135.
24 Ibid., p. 113.
25 Ibid., p. 114.
26 Ibid., p. 108.
27 Gronow, *Days of the Dandies*, vol. II, p. 63.
28 G. de Berthier de Sauvigny, *The Bourbon Restoration*, quoted in Randell, pp. 30–1.

29 Cobban, vol. II, p. 90.

30 *Idler in France*, vol. II, p. 149.

31 Ibid., pp. 148–9.

32 Voltaire, quoted in ibid., p. 164.

33 Ibid., p. 174.

34 Ibid., pp. 154–6.

35 Ibid., p. 161.

36 Ibid., pp. 166–7.

37 Ibid., p. 184.

38 Ibid., p. 182.

39 Ibid., pp. 184–5.

40 Ibid., p. 198.

41 Cobban, vol. II, p. 90.

42 *Idler in France*, vol. II, p. 209.

43 Ibid., p. 220.

44 Ibid., pp. 223–5.

45 Yates, vol. I, p. 148.

46 Lord Lamington, quoted in Vincent, pp. 64–5.

47 Hewlett (ed.), *Chorley: Autobiography, Memoir and Letters*, vol. I, p. 180.

48 *Fraser's Magazine for Town and Country*, vol. X, no. LX, 1834.

49 *Idler in France*, vol. I, p. 326.

50 Harris, p. 46.

51 Gower (ed.), *Letters of Countess Granville*, p. 291.

52 Sala, pp. 108–9.

53 *Idler in France*, vol. II, pp. 248–9.

54 Ibid., p. 250.

CHAPTER 14: *Return to London*

1 Carey (ed.), *Faber Book of Reportage*, pp. 303–4.

2 Leslie, pp. 165–6.

3 Raymond, *Reminiscences of Gronow*, p. 203.

4 *Concise Dictionary of National Biography*, vol. III, p. 3225.

5 Madden, vol. I, p. 168.

6 Ibid.

7 Adburgham, *Silver Fork Society*, p. 30.

8 Lady Morgan, quoted in ibid., p. 31.

9 Beaconsfield, *Henrietta Temple*, Longmans edn, p. 212.

10 Ibid., p. 213.

11 Sadleir, pp. 149–50.

12 Ibid., p. 154.

13 Joseph Jekyll, quoted in Teignmouth Shore, p. 102.

14 Molloy, p. 197.

15 Sadleir, p. 154.

16 N. P. Willis, *Pencillings by the Way*, 1834, quoted in *Lady Blessington's Conversations*, p. 16.

17 Molloy, Grolier Society edn, p. 197.

18 Joseph Jekyll, quoted in Teignmouth Shore, p. 102.

19 N. P. Willis, *Pencillings by the Way*, 1834, quoted in the 1859 William Veazie reprint of Lady Blessington's *Conversations with Lord Byron*, pp. 6–7.

20 Ibid., p. 10.

21 Ibid., pp. 12–13.

22 Ibid., pp. 14–15.

23 Ibid., p. 18.

CHAPTER 15: *Break-up of a Marriage*

1 Joseph Jekyll, quoted in Teignmouth Shore, p. 102.

2 Ibid.

3 Department of Manuscripts and Special Collections, University of Nottingham, My 1973.

4 Department of Manuscripts and Special Collections, University of Nottingham, My 1955.

5 Sadleir, p. 177.

6 Ilchester (ed.), *Lady Holland to her Son*, p. 112.

7 Lady Charleville, quoted in Sadleir, pp. 168–9.

8 Department of Manuscripts and Special Collections, University of Nottingham, My 1972.

9 Ibid.

10 Ibid.

11 Department of Manuscripts and Special Collections, University of Nottingham, My 1973.

12 Ibid.

13 Harriet d'Orsay to Lord Tullamore, T3069/F/1, Public Record Office of Northern Ireland.

14 D'Orsay to Lord Tullamore, 14 October 1834, T3069/F/2 PRONi.

15 D'Orsay to Lord Charleville, 11 June 1838, T3069/F/3 PRONi.

16 Countess d'Orsay, *Clouded Happiness*, pp. 6–7.

17 Ibid., p. 186.

18 Department of Manuscripts and Special Collections, University of Nottingham, My 1983.

19 Marlay papers, University of Nottingham library, MY 1983.

CHAPTER 16: *The Glass of Fashion*

1 Mills, pp. 1–2.

2 Ainsworth, vol. I, p. 265.

3 Gunn (ed.), *Disraeli Letters*, vol. I, p. 246.

4 Ibid., p. 265.

5 Mills, pp. 3–4.

6 Bernal Osborne's poem about the Hyde Park Achilles, quoted in Teignmouth Shore, p. 149.

7 Richard Walker, *Saville Row Story*, pp. 31–2.

8 Benjamin Haydon, quoted in Sadleir, p. 307.

9 Raymond, *Reminiscences of Gronow*, p. 198.

10 Byrne, vol. I, p. 117.

11 *A Parliamentary Sketch*, *Sketches by Boz*, Second Series, quoted in House and Storey (eds), *Dickens Letters*, vol. II, p. 538n.

12 Byrne, vol. I, p. 117.

13 D'Orsay to Lord Lichfield, 12 May 1842, Staffordshire Record Office, D615/P(S)/6/13/3.

14 Byrne, vol. I, p. 118.

15 The Domestic and Artistic Life of John Singleton Copley, p. 367.

16 Raymond, *Reminiscences of Gronow*, p. 198.

17 Dickens (ed.), *Life of Mathews*, vol. I, pp. 93–4.

18 Thomas Carlyle, quoted in Sadleir, pp. 307–8.

19 Jane Welsh Carlyle, quoted in Wilson, p. 133.

20 George Eliot, quoted in the Introduction to the World's Classics edition of Carlyle, *Sartor Resartus*, pp. vii–viii.

21 'Critical Observations on Gentlemen's Fashion', quoted in Walker, p. 35.

22 Mills, p. 10.

23 Walker, p. 28.

24 Ibid.

25 Byrne, vol. I, p. 119.
26 Chenoune, p. 65.
27 Teignmouth Shore, p. 120.

CHAPTER 17: *Man about Town and Country, Man of Letters*

1   Dated July 25 1846; original MSS held at Reform Club.
2   Raymond, *Reminiscences of Gronow*, p. 57.
3   Hayward, *Art of Dining*, pp. 70–1.
4   Buckle, p. 113.
5   Gunn (ed.), *Disraeli Letters*, vol. I, letter no. 339, p. 421.
6   Ude, p. xiii, quoted in Hayward, *Art of Dining*, p. 70.
7   *Literary Chronicle and Weekly Review*, 15 December 1827.
8   Blyth, p. 79.
9   Ibid.
10 Raymond, *Reminiscences of Gronow*, p. 256.
11 Graves, p. 45.
12 Raymond, p. 45.
13 Graves, p. 160.
14 Raymond, p. 258.
15 Ibid.
16 Connely, p. 263.
17 Mills, pp. 102–3.
18 McCausland, p. 28.
19 Raymond, *Reminiscences of Gronow*, pp. 196–7.
20 McCausland, p. 27.
21 Ibid., p. 85.
22 Watney, p. 63.
23 Patmore, vol. I, p. 226.
24 Ibid., p. 229.
25 Sidney, quoted in Teignmouth Shore, pp. 118–19.
26 Carlisle (ed.), *Hayward Correspondence*, vol. I, p. 63.
27 Buckle, p. 126.
28 Creevey, quoted in Connely, p. 224.
29 Edwin Landseer to d'Orsay, 1841–42, letter dated 28 1842, Harvard University Library, Houghton Library, MS 1272 (6–10).
30 Edwin Landseer to d'Orsay, 1848, (n.d.), Harvard University Library, Houghton Library, MS 1272 (31–35).

31 'In 1839, Count d'Orsay took away a gun, No 1847, for which he did not pay, costing Purdey £57 19s 6d' (Beaumont).

32 Memoirs of the Life and Correspondence of Henry Reeve, by John Knox Laughton, vol. I, p. 101.

33 Letter, no. 858 to Mary Anne Lewis, 27 December 1838, Gunn (ed.), *Disraeli Letters*, vol. III, p. 121, Letter no. 855 to Mary Anne Lewis, December 1838, ibid., p. 118, and Letter no. 1010 to Sarah Disraeli, 3 December 1839, ibid., p. 232.

34 National Library of Scotland, MS 3219 f. 169.

35 *New Sporting Magazine*, vol. xiv, p. 174, quoted in Sadleir, pp. 301–2.

36 Letter no. 1013 to Sarah Disraeli, 9 December(?) 1839, Gunn (ed.), *Disraeli Letters*, vol. III, p. 237.

37 Ainsworth, vol. I, p. 262.

38 Byrne, vol. I, p. 118.

39 D'Orsay to Edward Bulwer, Knebworth Collection, D/EK C9/64.

40 Wilson, p. 81.

41 *The Times*, quoted in Gunn (ed.), *Disraeli Letters*, letter no. 396, vol. II, p. 33, n. 2.

42 Ibid.

43 Letter no. 396 to Morgan O'Connell, 5 May 1835, ibid., p. 33.

44 Letter no. 399 to Sarah Disraeli, 6 May 1835, ibid., p. 38.

45 Ibid.

46 Letter no. 402 to Sarah Disraeli, 9 May 1835, ibid., p. 40.

47 Sir Robert Peel to Lord Chesterfield, 26 December 1834, BL Mss Add. 40407 f.268.

48 Lady Holland, quoted in Adburgham, *Silver Fork Society*, p. 143.

49 D'Orsay to Edward Bulwer, Knebworth Collection, D/EK C9/66.

50 Thomas Creevey, quoted in Connely p. 224.

51 Gunn (ed.), *Disraeli Letters*, letter no. 357, vol. I, p. 437.

52 Ilchester (ed.), *Lady Holland to her Son*, 2 December 1836, p. 163.

53 Gunn (ed.), *Disraeli Letters*, letter no. 178, vol. I, p. 265.

54 Ainsworth, p. 267.

55 Gunn (ed.), *Disraeli Letters*, letter no. 342, vol. I, p. 424.

56 Ibid., letter no. 354, p. 435.

57 D'Orsay to Edward Bulwer, Knebworth Collection, D/EK C9/72.

58 Ibid., D/EK C9/78 and 79.

CHAPTER 18: *Gore House*

1 Madden, vol. I, p. 181.
2 Sadleir, p. 254.
3 Edward Bulwer to Lord Durham, quoted in Teignmouth Shore, p. 158.
4 Madden, vol. I, p. 183.
5 *Survey of London*, vol. XXXVIII, p. 12.
6 Ibid., p. 53.
7 William Wilberforce, quoted in Dickens (ed.), *Household Words*, 1853, F753, p. 590.
8 Chancellor, p. 197.
9 William Wilberforce, quoted in *Household Words*, 1853, F753, p. 590.
10 Chancellor, p. 198.
11 Teignmouth Shore, p. 158.
12 Chancellor, p. 69. Chancellor says that this terrace of smaller houses extended to the west of Gore House, while *The Survey of London* says it was to the east.
13 *Survey of London*, vol. XXXVIII, p. 12.
14 Chancellor, p. 202.
15 Mrs Crosland, quoted in Chancellor, p. 205.
16 Ibid.
17 Dickens to Lady Blessington, April 1840, House and Storey (eds), *Dickens Letters*, vol. II, p. 291.
18 Toynbee (ed.), *Diaries of Macready*, vol. II, p. 64.
19 D'Orsay to Lord Lichfield, Gore House, 12 October 1842, Staffordshire Record Office, D615/P(S)/6/13/5.
20 Letter to Henriette Wulff, quoted in Wullschlager, p. 304.
21 Letter no. 559 to Sarah Disraeli, 21 January 1837, Gunn (ed.), *Disraeli Letters*, vol. II, pp. 214–15.
22 Ibid., p. 215.
23 Letter from Sarah Disraeli, 27 January 1837, quoted in ibid., letter no. 564, p. 230.
24 Letter no. 560 to Sarah Disraeli, 23 January 1837, ibid., p. 215.
25 Madden, vol. I, p. 383.
26 Lady Blessington to Disraeli, 27 March 1837, quoted in Gunn (ed.), *Disraeli Letters*, vol. II, letter no. 588, p. 243n.
27 Ibid., p. 383.
28 *Satirist*, 30 January 1842.

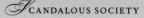

29 Shee, p. 97.

30 Sadleir, p. 263.

31 Dickens to d'Orsay, 26 December 1842, House and Storey (eds), *Dickens Letters*, vol. III, p. 402.

32 Sadleir, p. 263.

33 Diary entry for 13 March 1848, Ray (ed.), *Thackeray Letters*, vol. II, p. 362.

34 *Satirist*, 13 August 1843.

35 *Satirist*, 26 May 1844.

36 *Satirist*, 8 November 1846.

37 *Satirist*, 13 December 1846.

38 *Satirist*, 14 November 1847.

39 *Satirist*, 20 December 1846.

40 *Satirist*, 5 March 1848.

CHAPTER 19: *Track and Stage*

1 798.4 Hip/A K 1.2260/B.

2 Handbill, Kensington Public Libraries, 293–6 (5) 798.4 HIP/D (1837).

3 *Whyte's History of the British Turf*, vol. I, p. 187.

4 Ibid.

5 Ibid.

6 Ibid., p. 274.

7 *Sporting Magazine*, 1837, quoted in *Old and New London*, Kensington Public Libraries, private collection of Miss F. M. Gladstone.

8 Newspaper cuttings, 25 December 1836, Kensington Public Libraries, 293–6(2) 798.4 HIP/A.

9 *Sporting Magazine*, 1837, quoted in *Old and New London*, private collection of Lesley du Cane.

10 Ibid.

11 *Old and New London*.

12 *Sporting Magazine*, 1837, quoted in *Old and New London*, ibid.

13 *Old and New London*.

14 Ibid.

15 Newspaper cutting, 1838, Kensington Public Libraries, 293–6 (3) 798.4 HIP(A).

16 Unidentified newspaper cutting, June 1837, from collection of the *Daily Chronicle*.

17 Kensington Public Libraries, DC, 294B 798.4.HIP/D [1837].

18 Unidentified newspaper cutting, June 1837, from collection of DC.

19 Kensington Public Libraries, 295e 798.4 HIP/D [1837].

20 Unidentified newspaper cutting, June 1837, from collection of 'DC'.

21 *The British Racehorse*, December 1966, K67 314 798.4 HIP/A.

22 Newspaper cutting, 293–6(1) 798.4 HIP/A

23 293–6 (1) 798.4 HIP/A.

24 Gladstone and Barker, p. 84.

25 Warwick Wroth, *Cremorne and Later Gardens*, 1907, quoted in *Notting Hill in Bygone Days*, pp. 84–5.

26 *The Era*, 14 June 1840.

27 *John Bull*, 1841, 293–6 (3) 798.4 HIP(A).

28 *Sunday Times* 10 May 1845, Kensington Public Libraries, K68/232 798.4 HIP/A.

29 Toynbee (ed.), *The Diaries of Macready*, vol. I, p. 366.

30 Ibid., p. 370.

31 Ibid., p. 366n.

32 Edward Bulwer to Lady Blessington, [n.d.] letter no. 78, Shattrick, p. 72.

33 John Forster to Edward Bulwer, 7 March 1839, letter no. 140, Richard Renton, *John Forster and his Friendships*, London: 1912, pp. 101–2, quoted in Edward Bulwer to William Macready, 27 June 1826, ibid. p. 124.

34 Ibid., letter no. 186, pp. 151–2.

35 Edward Bulwer to William Macready, 26 September 1840, ibid., letter 201, p. 162.

36 Edward Bulwer to William Macready, 3 November 1840, ibid., letter 210, p. 170.

37 Toynbee (ed.), *Diaries of Macready*, 28 May 1837, vol. II, p. 96.

38 Ibid., p. 98.

39 Yates, vol. I, pp. 21–2.

40 *Satirist*, 14 July 1833, quoted in Guest, pp. 14–15.

41 Fanny Kemble, *Records of a Later Life*, 1882, quoted in ibid., p. 38.

42 Sadleir, p. 316.

43 *Satirist*, 6 December 1840.

44 Mills, p. 224.

CHAPTER 20: *Man of Destiny*

1 Sala, p. 434.

2 Metternich, quoted in Bresler, p. 101.

3   Greville, quoted in Guedalla, p. 104.

4   Hall, vol. II, p. 110.

5   Shee, pp. 74–5.

6   Guedalla, p. 104.

7   Bresler, p. 113.

8   Teignmouth Shore, p. 197.

9   Lebey, p. 232n.

10 Ibid.

11 Ibid., p. 233.

12 Harris, pp. 120–1.

13 Teignmouth Shore, p. 202.

14 Madden, vol. III, pp. 68–9.

15 Louis Napoleon to Lady Blessington, 13 January 1841, in Molloy, p. 373.

16 D'Orsay to W. S. Landor, 27 May 1846, in Molloy, p. 420.

17 Yates, vol. I, pp. 147–8.

18 Madden, vol. II, p. 418.

19 Ibid., . p. 419.

20 Shee, p. 97.

CHAPTER 21: *Debt*

1   Lady Blessington to Contessa de Guiccioli, 16 August 1839, NY Public Library, Madden Collection, 52Bo.

2   Dickens to T.J. Thompson, 13 July 1842, *Dickens Letters*, vol. III, p. 270.

3   Madden, vol. I, pp. 196–7n.

4   Ibid., p. 150.

5   Ibid., vol. II, p. 456n.

6   Edwin Landseer to d'Orsay, 28 April 1841, Harvard University Library MS 1272 (6–10), 6.

7   Lady Blessington to Henry Bulwer, 14 December 1841, quoted in Sadleir, p. 320.

8   D'Orsay to Henry Bulwer, 2 May 1841, quoted in part in Sadleir and in full in Connely, pp. 341–3.

9   Henry Bulwer to Lady Blessington, quoted in Connely, pp. 354–5.

10 *Satirist*, 20 November 1842.

11 *Satirist*, 20 February 1842.

12 Lamington, pp. 28 and 35, quoted in House and Storey (eds), *Dickens Letters*, vol. II, p. 291n.

13 Handwritten note to letter from d'Orsay to Lord Lichfield 13 November 1841, Staffordshire Record Office, D615/P(S)/6/13/1.

14 D'Orsay to Lord Lichfield, 6 and 11 March 1842, Staffordshire Record Office, D615/P(S)/6/13/2.

15 D'Orsay to Lord Lichfield, 18 August 1842, Staffordshire Record Office, exD615/P(S)/6/13/4.

16 Teignmouth Shore, p. 231.

17 Broughton, Dorchester (ed.) vol. VI, p. 104.

18 *Satirist*, 30 June 1844.

19 *Satirist*, 14 July 1844.

20 Weiss, p. 36.

21 Madden, vol. II, p. 456n.

22 D'Orsay to T. S. Duncombe, 6 April 1842, quoted in Teignmouth Shore, p. 251.

23 D'Orsay to Lord Lichfield, 18 August 1842, Staffordshire Record Office, ex D615/P(5)/6/13/4.

24 *Satirist*, 7 September 1845.

25 *Satirist*, 28 December 1845.

26 Letter to R. R. Madden, quoted in Madden, vol. II, p. 455.

27 Letter to John Forster, 18 June 1845, quoted in ibid., p. 414.

28 *Punch*, quoted in Dodds, p. 217.

29 Madden, vol. II, p. 456n.

30 D'Orsay to Lord Lichfield, 12 October 1842, Staffordshire Record Office, exD615/P(S)/6/13/5.

31 *Satirist*, 5 April 1846.

CHAPTER 22: *Society's Favourite Artist*

1 Benjamin Haydon diary, 19 July 1839, quoted in Teignmouth Shore, p. 159.

2 Edwin Landseer to d'Orsay, 1841–2, 29 April 1841, Harvard University Library, Houghton Library, MS 1272 (6–10) 7.

3 Edwin Landseer to d'Orsay, 12 May 1848, Harvard University Library Houghton Library, MS 1272 (16–20) 19.

4 Edwin Landseer to d'Orsay, n.d. [c. April 1844], Harvard University Library, Houghton Library, MS 1272 (41–45) 43.

5 Edwin Landseer to d'Orsay, n.d. [c. April 1844], Harvard University Library, Houghton Library, MS 1272 (41–45) 42.

6   Edwin Landseer to d'Orsay, 1844–7, [c. April 1844], Harvard University Library, Houghton Library, MS 1272 (21–25) 22.

7   Clarkson Stanfield to Edwin Landseer, 24 April [1844], Harvard University Library, Houghton Library, MS 1272 (55).

8   *Satirist*, 19 May 1844.

9   Disraeli to Sarah Disraeli, 4 November 1834, Gunn (ed.), *Disraeli Letters*, letter no. 352, vol. I, p. 432.

10 Disraeli to Sarah Disraeli, 12 February 1835, ibid., letter no. 374, vol. II, p. 14.

11 Disraeli to Sara Austen, 12 February 1835, ibid., letter no. 375, p. 15.

12 Disraeli to Sarah Disraeli, 21 March 1835, ibid., letter no. 384, p. 24.

13 Paragraph on Dickens's bedroom in *Guide to Dickens's House*.

14 Dickens to d'Orsay, 2 January 1843, House and Storey (eds), *Dickens Letters*, vol. III, p. 419.

15 Thackeray to Mrs Procter, June 1848, Ray (ed.), *Thackeray Letters*, vol. II p. 387.

16 *Satirist*.

17 *Satirist*, 30 March 1845.

18 Edwin Landseer to d'Orsay, 1848, dated 19 August, Harvard University Library, Houghton Library, MS 1272 (26–30) 28.

19 Edwin Landseer to d'Orsay, n.d. [1839?], Harvard University Library, Houghton Library, MS 1272 (51–54) 51.

20 Edwin Landseer to d'Orsay, 1848, Harvard University Library, Houghton Library, MS 1272 (31–35) 35.

21 Dickens to d'Orsay, 27 December 1842, House and Storey (eds), *Dickens Letters*, vol. III, pp. 401–2.

22 Dickens to d'Orsay, 5 April 1847, ibid., vol. V, p. 53.

23 *Examiner*, 29 May 1847 quoted in note to letter of 5 April, ibid.

24 Wellington to Lady Blessington, 19 June 1847, quoted in Madden, vol. III, p. 24.

25 N.P. Willis to Baron de Trobriand, University of Iowa MsL W735d, dated 1847 in later hand on letter.

26 Toynbee (ed.), *Diaries of Macready*, 23 July 1843, vol. II, p. 215.

27 *New Monthly Magazine*, August 1845, quoted in Madden, vol. I, p. 343.

28 *Satirist*, 23 March 1845.

29 *Satirist*, 29 June 1845.

30 Duke of Wellington to Lady Blessington, 22 November 1844, Madden, vol. III, p. 22.

31 Duke of Wellington to Lady Blessington, 21 February 1845, ibid.

32 Duke of Wellington to Lady Blessington, 19 June 1845, ibid.

33 Ibid., vol. I, p. 335.

34 Ibid.

35 D'Orsay to Duke of Wellington, 6 May 1846, letter held at Stratfield Saye House and quoted by kind permission of the Duke of Wellington KG.

36 D'Orsay to R.R. Madden, Madden, vol. II, p. 455.

37 Dialogue taken from Teignmouth Shore, pp. 231-2.

38 Disraeli to d'Orsay, 7 October 1848, BL Mss Add. 36677 f2, British Library (purchased at Sotheby's White sale, 21 April to 2 May 1902).

CHAPTER 23: *Revolution Abroad, Collapse at Home*

1 Louis-Philippe, quoted in Bresler, p. 209.

2 *Punch*, quoted in Dodds, p. 325n.

3 Davies, p. 10.

4 Ray (ed.), *Thackeray Letters*, vol. II, p. 362.

5 Quoted in Bresler, p. 217.

6 R.J. Lane, quoted in Madden, vol. II, p. 470.

7 Mrs Carlyle, April 1845, Wilson, p. 280.

8 Richard Cobden, 13 June 1846, Morley, vol. I, p. 386.

9 *Satirist*, 2 September 1848.

10 Madden, vol. I, pp. 182-4.

11 Disraeli to Mary Anne Disraeli, 13 March 1842, Letter no. 1231, Gunn (ed.), *Disraeli Letters*, vol. IV, p. 35.

12 Hayward to Lady Charleville, 28 December 1848, Carlisle (ed.), *Hayward Correspondence*, vol. I, p. 137.

13 Dickens to H.G. Adams, 30 January 1849, House and Storey (eds), *Dickens Letters*, vol. V, p. 482.

14 Adburgham, *Shopping in Style*, p. 115.

15 Madden, vol. I, p. 201n.

16 Reid (ed.), *Life of Lord Houghton*, vol. I, p. 432.

17 D'Orsay to Dr Quin, April 1849, Madden, vol. II, pp. 453-4.

CHAPTER 24: *An Auction in London and a Death in Paris*

1 Postscript to letter from Dickens to John Leech, 18 April 1849, House and Storey (eds), *Dickens Letters*, vol. V, p. 530.

2   Letter from F. Avillon, valet to Lady Blessington, Madden, vol. I, p. 206.

3   Ibid., pp. 203-4.

4   Thackeray to Mrs Brookfield, 4 May 1849, Ray (ed.), *Thackeray Letters*, vol. II, p. 532.

5   F. Avillon to Lady Blessington, Gore House, 8 May 1849, Madden, vol. I, p. 207.

6   Letter from Miss Power, 18 February 1850, ibid., p. 217.

7   Henry Bulwer to Lady Blessington, 6 May 1849, ibid., vol. III, p. 73.

8   Hall, vol. II, p. 110.

9   Quoted in Sadleir, p. 349.

10 Letter from Miss Power, 18 February 1850, Madden, vol. I, p. 217.

11 Duke de Grammont to Lady Blessington, [n.d.] La.II.422/17 Edinburgh, University Library.

12 Letter from Miss Power, 18 February 1850, Madden, vol. I, p. 218.

13 Ibid.

14 John Forster to Edward Bulwer Lytton, 11 June 1849, quoted in Sadleir, p. 325.

15 Ibid.

16 Letter from Miss Power, 12 July 1849, quoted in Madden, vol. I, p. 224.

17 Letter from John Forster to Edward Bulwer Lytton, 31 July 1849, quoted in Sadleir, p. 355.

18 Thackeray to Mrs Brookfield, 13 September 1849, Ray (ed.), *Thackeray Letters*, vol. II, p. 593.

19 Madden, vol. I, p. 224.

20 D'Orsay to Hayward, 38, Rue de la Ville l'Evêque, Paris, 17 January 1850, Carlisle (ed.), *Hayward Correspondence*, vol. I, pp. 142-3 .

21 Hayward to his sisters, 4 May 1850, ibid., p. 148.

22 *Quarterly Review*, January 1869, no. 251, pp. 57-8, ibid.

23 D'Orsay to Henry Bulwer, Paris, July 1850, Norfolk Record Office, BUL 1/87/29.

24 Ilchester, *Chronicles of Holland House*, p. 381.

25 Ray (ed.), *Thackeray Letters*, Thackeray to Mrs Brookfield, 13-16 January 1851, vol. II, pp. 733-4.

26 Dickens to Mrs Charles Dickens, Hôtel Wagram, Paris, 12 February 1851 (apparently Dickens was mistaken, or superstitious; the date was 13 February), House and Storey (eds), *Dickens Letters*, vol. VI, pp. 289-90.

27 Dickens to Hon. Spencer Lyttelton, March 1852, ibid., p. 633.

28 D'Orsay to Lord Holland, 29 March 1851, quoted in Connely, p. 536.

29 D'Orsay to Lord Londonderry, 26 May 1851, D/Lo/C74 (5) Durham Record Office.

30 D'Orsay to Lord Londonderry, 6 October 1851, D/Lo/C74 (16) Durham Record Office.

31 D'Orsay to Lord Londonderry, 7 October 1851, D/Lo/C74 (17) Durham Record Office.

CHAPTER 25: Coup d'Etat

1   D'Orsay to Lord Londonderry, 1 December 1851, D/Lo/C74 (2) Durham Record Office.

2   Ibid.

3   Victor Hugo in Carey (ed.), *Faber Book of Reportage*, pp. 328–31.

4   D'Orsay to Hayward, 5 or 6 December 1851, vol. I, p. 159.

5   Madden, vol. I, p. 359.

6   D'Orsay to Lord Londonderry, 31 December 1851, D/Lo/C74 (25) Durham Record Office.

7   D'Orsay to Hayward, 2 January 1852, Carlisle (ed.), *Hayward Correspondence*, vol. I, pp. 160–2.

8   Ibid., p. 162.

9   Ibid.

10 W.F. Monypenny and G.E. Buckle, *Life of Disraeli*, 1910–20, quoted in Blake, p. 315.

11 Letters from George Sand in the collection of Count Armand-Ghislain de Maigret. (All quotations are based on transcriptions printed in *La Revue de Paris*, May 1969.)

12 Ibid.

13 Ibid.

14 Madden, vol. I, pp. 352–3.

15 Lord Brougham to Hayward, 3 August 1852, Carlisle (ed.), *Hayward Correspondence*, vol. I, p. 170.

16 Teignmouth Shore, p. 302.

17 Sadleir, p. 365.

CHAPTER 26: *Burial and Obituaries*

1   *The Times*, 6 August 1852, p. 3.

2   Madden, vol. I, p. 345.

3   *Gentleman's Magazine*, September 1852, pp. 308–10.

4   *Bulletin de Paris*, quoted in ibid.

5   Madden, vol. I, p. 355.

6   Dickens to John Forster, House and Storey (eds), *Dickens Letters*, vol. VI, p. 736.

7   Pollock (ed.), *Macready's Reminiscences*, p. 407.

8   The *Age*, 14 August 1852.

9   *Home Counties Magazine*, vol. 14, p. 17, 1912, Kensington Public Libraries, K63/1024 798.4 HIP/A.

ℬIBLIOGRAPHY

Published Correspondence and Memoirs

Anglesley, Marquess of. *One-leg: The Life and Letters of Henry William Paget*. London: Jonathan Cape, 1961

Armstrong, Margaret (ed.). *Trelawny, a man's life*. London: Robert Hale Ltd, 1949

Ballantine, Sergeant. *Some Experiences of a Barrister's Life*. 2 vols. 6th edn. London: Richard Bentley & Son, 1882

Beaconsfield, Lord. *Home Letters. Written by Lord Beaconsfield, 1830–1852*. London: Cassell & Co., 1928

Benjamin, L. S. (ed.). *The Wellesley Papers: The Life and Correspondence of Richard Colley Wellesley. Marquess Wellesley, 1760–1842*. 2 vols. London: Herbert Jenkins, 1914

Berkeley, Hon. George Charles Grantley Fitzhardinge. *My Life and Recollections*. 4 vols. London: Hurst & Blackett, 1865

Bouffé, H. M. D. *Mes souvenirs 1800–1880*. Paris: Librairie de la Société des Gens de Lettres, 1880

Brougham, Henry, Lord. *The Life and Times of Henry Lord Brougham*. 3 vols. Edinburgh and London: William Blackwood & Sons, 1871

Bulwer, Edward George. *Letters of the Late Edward Bulwer, Lord Lytton, to his Wife*. London: W. Swan Sonnenschein & Co., 1884

Byrne, J. C. *Gossip of the Century, Personal and Traditional Memories. Social, Literary & Artistic &C. By the Author of 'Flemish Interiors'*. London: Ward & Donney, 1893

Carey, John (ed.). *The Faber Book of Reportage*. London: Faber & Faber, 1987

Carlisle, H. E. (ed.) *A selection from the Correspondence of Abraham Hayward, 1834–1884*. 2 vols. London: John Murray, 1886

Chateaubriand, François René de, Viscount. *Memoirs of Chateaubriand*. Selected, translated and with an introduction by Robert Baldick. London: Hamish Hamilton, 1961

Clay, Edith (ed.). *Lady Blessington at Naples*. London: Hamish Hamilton, 1979

Craufurd, Rev. A. H. *General Craufurd and his Light Division*. London and Sydney: Griffith, Farran, Okeden & Welsh, 1891

Delacroix, Eugène. *Journal of Eugène Delacroix*. Translated by Walter Pach. New York: Grove Press, 1961

Dorchester, Lady (ed.). *Lord Broughton, Recollections of a Long Life – With additional extracts from his [John Cam Hobhouse] private diaries*. 6 vols. London: John Murray, 1911

Dufort, Jean-Nicholas. *Mémoires du Cte Dufort de Cheverny*. 2nd edn., 2 vols, Paris: Plon-Nourrit & Cie, 1909

Duncombe, T. H. (ed.). *The Life and Correspondence of Thomas Slingsby Duncombe*. 2 vols, London: 1868

Ellis, S. M. (introduction and noted by). *Unpublished Letters of Lady Bulwer Lytton to A. E. Chalon, R. A.* London: Eveleigh Nash, 1914

Fagan, L. *The Life of Sir Anthony Panizzi*. 2nd edn, 2 vols. London: Remington & Co., 1880

Galt, John. *The Autobiography of John Galt*. London: Cochrane & McCrone, 1883

Girardin, Mme Emile de. *Lettres Parisiennes*, Paris: Charpentier, 1843

Gower, the Hon. F. Lever (ed.). *Letters of Harriet Countess Granville*. 2 vols. London: Longmans & Co., 1894

Gunn, J. A. W. (ed.). *Benjamin Disraeli Letters 1815–1834*. 4 vols. Toronto: University of Toronto Press, 1982.

Hale Shackford, Martha (ed.). *Letters from Elizabeth Barrett to B. R. Haydon*. New York: Oxford University Press, 1939

Hall, C. S. *Retrospect of a Long Life from 1815–1883*. London: Richard Bentley & Son, 1883

Hamilton, Edward. *A Memoir of Frederick Hervey Foster Quin*, London: Messrs Barraud & Lenard, 1879

Hare, Augustus. *The Story of my Life*. 6 vols. London: George Allen, 1896

Harris, James Howard, Third Earl of Malmesbury. *Memoirs of an Ex-Minister. An Autobiography*. 2 vols. London: Longmans & Co., 1884

Hennessy, James Pope. *Monckton Milnes. The Years of Promise 1809–1851*. London: Constable, 1949

Hewlett, Henry G. (ed.). *Henry Fothergill Chorley: Autobiography, Memoir and Letters.* 2 vols. London: R. Bentley & Son, 1873

House, M. and Storey, G. (eds.). *The Letters of Charles Dickens.* 12 vols. Pilgrim Edition. Oxford: Clarendon Press, 1965–1998.

Ilchester, the Earl of (ed.). *Elizabeth, Lady Holland, to her Son, 1821–1845.* London: John Murray, 1946

Ilchester, the Earl of (ed.). *John Baron Hervey and his Friends, 1726–38. Based on Letters from Holland House, Melbury, and Ickworth.* London: John Murray, 1950

Ilchester, the Earl of (ed.). *The Journal of Elizabeth Lady Holland (1791–1811).* London: Longmans & Co., 1908

Ilchester, the Earl of (ed.). *Journal of the Hon. Henry Edward Fox, 1818–1830.* London: Thornton Butterworth, 1923

Jerdan, W. *The Autobiography of William Jerdan.* 4 vols. London: Virtue & Co., 1852

Jerdan, W. *Men I Have Known,* London: George Routledge & Sons, 1866

Kemble, Frances Anne. *Records of a Later Life.* 3 vols. London: Richard Bentley & Son, 1882

Knepler, Henry (translated and ed.). *Man about Paris: The Confessions of Houssaye.* London: Gollancz, 1972

Lang, Cecil Y. (ed.). *The Swinburne Letters.* 6 vols. New Haven: Yale University Press, 1959–62

Laughton, John Knox. *Memoirs of the Life and Correspondence of Henry Reeve.* 2 vols, London: Longmans Green & Co., 1898

Lemaître, Frédérick. *Souvenirs de Frédérick Lemaître.* Paris: Paul Ollendorf, 1880

Lennox, Lord William Pitt. *Fifty Years Biographical Reminiscences.* London: Hurst & Blackett, 1863

Lytton, Edward Robert Bulwer. *The Life, Letters and Literary Remains of Edward Bulwer, Lord Lytton.* 2 vols. London: Kegan, Paul & Co., 1883

Madden, R. R. *The Literary Life and Correspondence of the Countess of Blessington.* 3 vols. London: T. C. Newby, 1855

Mathews, Mrs. *Memoirs of Charles Mathews, Comedian.* 4 vols. London: Richard Bentley, 1839

Morley, John. *The Life of Richard Cobden.* 8 vols., London: Chapman & Hall, 1881

de Musset, Alfred. *Confessions d'un Enfant du Siècle,* Paris: Librairie Garnier Frères, 1968

O'Driscoll, W. J. *A Memoir of Daniel Maclise*, R. A. London: 1871

Origo, Iris. *The Last Attachment: The Story of Byron and Teresa Guiccioli as Told in their Unpublished Letters and Other Family Papers*. London: Collins, 1962

Patmore, P. G. *My Friends and Acquaintances*. 3 vols. London: Saunders & Otley, 1854

Perkins, Jane Gray. *The Life of Mrs Norton*. London: John Murray, 1909

Persigny, Duc de. *Mémoires*, Paris: Librairie Plon, 1896

Pollock, Sir Frederick (ed.). *Macready's Reminiscences, and a Selection from his Diaries*. London: Macmillan & Co., 1875

Quennell, Peter (ed.). *Byron: A Self Portrait, Letters and Diaries, 1798–1824*. 2 vols. London: John Murray, 1950

Raikes, Thomas. *A Portion of the Journal by Thomas Raikes Esq., from 1831–1847*. London: Longmans, 1894

Ray, Gordon N. (ed.). *The Letters and Private Papers of William Makepeace Thackeray*. Cambridge, Massachusetts: Harvard University Press, 1946.

Raymond, John. *Reminiscences and Recollections of Captain Gronow*, London: Bodley Head, 1964

Redding, C. *Fifty Years' Recollections, Literary and Personal*. 2 vols. London: Charles J. Sheet Publishers, 1858

Reid, T. Wemyss (ed.). *The Life, Letters, and Friendships of Richard Monckton Milnes First Lord Houghton*. London: Cassell & Co., 1890

Rose, Hinda and Beauwin, Polly (compiled by). *Autograph Letters and Historical Documents Catalogue 1275*. London: Maggs Bros., 1999

Sadler, Thomas. (ed.). *Diary, Reminiscences and Correspondence of Henry Crab Robinson*. 3 vols. London: Macmillan & Co., 1869

Sala, George Augustus. *The Life and Adventures of George Augustus Sala*. 2nd edn. 2 vols. London: Cassell & Co., 1896

Sala, George Augustus. *Twice Round the Clock, or the Hours of the Day and Night in London*. London: John and Robert Maxwell, 1859

Sand, George. *Correspondence*. Vol. X, Paris: Editions Garnier Frères, n.d.

Seymour, Lady (ed.). *The 'Pope' of Holland House: Selections from the Correspondence of John Whishaw and his Friends, 1813–1840*. London: T. Fisher Unwin, 1906

Shee, William Archer. *My Contemporaries*. London: Hurst & Blackett, 1893.

Stanhope, Philip Henry, Earl. *Notes of Conversations with the Duke of Wellington, 1831–1851*. London: Prion, 1998

Strachey, Lytton & Fulford, Roger (eds.). *The Greville Memoirs, 1814–1860*. 8 vols. London: Macmillan & Co., 1938.

H. T. 'Memoir of Macready', in *Tallis's Acting Edition of Shakespeare*. London: John Tallis & Co., 1851

Thomson, Mrs. *Recollections of Literary Characters and Celebrated Places*. 2 vols. London: Richard Bentley, 1854

Thornbury, W. *The Life of J. M. W. Turner: Founded on Letters and Papers Furnished by his Friends and Fellow Academicians*. London: Ward Lock, 1970

Toynbee, William (ed.). *The Diaries of William Charles Macready*. London: Chapman & Hall, 1912

Trewin, J. C. (ed.). *The Journal of William Charles Macready 1832–1851*. London: Longmans, 1967

Vizetelly, Henry. *Glances Back Through Seventy Years: Autobiographical and Other Reminiscences*. 2 vols. London: Kegan Paul & Co., 1893

Wellington, Duke of (ed.). *A Selection from the Private Correspondence of the 1st Duke of Wellington*. London: Dropmore Press, 1952

Wellington, 7th Duke (ed.). *Arthur Wellesley, Duke of Wellington. Letters. Wellington and his Friends*. London: Macmillan & Co., 1965

Wheeler, Stephen (ed.). *Letters and Other Unpublished Writings of Walter Savage Landor*. London: Richard Bentley & Son, 1897

Willis, Nathaniel Parker. *Pencillings by the Way*. London: T. Werner Laurie, 1942

Yates, Edmund. *Edmund Yates: His Recollections and Experiences*. 2 vols. London: Richard Bentley & Son, 1884

Yriarte, Charles. *Cercles de Paris, 1828–1864*. Paris: Librairie Parisienne, 1864

Secondary Literature

D'Orsay and his Acquaintances

Ackroyd, Peter. 'Victorian London'. In a programme for the National Theatre Ensemble's performance of *Money* by Edward Bulwer Lytton in 1999

Acton, Harold. *The Bourbons of Naples*. London: Prion, 1998

Adams, James Eli. *Dandies and Desert Saints*. New York: Cornell University Press, 1995

Ellis, Stewart Marsh. *William Harrison Ainsworth and His Friends*. 2 vols. London, New York: John Lane, 1911

Amory, Martha. *The Domestic and Artistic Life of John Singleton Copley*. Boston: Houghton, Miffin & Co, 1882

Anonymous. *Philips 1796–1996*. London, Philips Auctioneers, n.d.

Armour, Richard Willlard. *Barry Cornwall. A Biography of Bryan Walker Procter*. Boston: Meador, 1935

Armstrong, Margaret. *Trelawny. A Man's Life*. London: Robert Hale Ltd, 1941

d'Aurevilly, Jules Barbey (tr. Douglas Ainslie). *Dandyism*. New York: PAJ Publications, 1988

d'Auvergne, Edmund B. *Envoys Extraordinary*. London: George G. Harrap, 1937

Baudelaire, Charles (tr. Jonathan Mayne). *The Painter of Modern Life and Other Essays*. London: Phaidon Press, 1995

Bennett, D. *Roller Coaster*. London: Aurum Press, 1999

Berechet, Jean-Claude (ed.). *Mémoires de la Comtesse de Boigné*, Paris: Mercure de France, 1971

Birkenhead, Sheila. *Illustrious Friends*. London: Hamish Hamilton, 1965

Blackstone, William. *Commentaries on the Laws of England*. London: 1778

Blake, Robert. *Disraeli*. London: Prion, 1988

Boger, Alnod J. *The story of General Bacon*, London: Methuen & Co., 1903

Boulenger, Jacques. *Le Boulevard*. Paris: Editions Balzac, 1933

Boulenger, Jacques. *Sous Louis-Philippe. Les Dandys*. Paris: Librairies Paul Ollendorff, n.d.

Bredsdorff, Elias. *Hans Christian Andersen – The Story of his Life and Work 1805–75*. London: Phaidon, 1975

Bresler, Fenton. *Napoleon III*. London: HarperCollins, 1999

Breton, Paul. *Mémoires du Marquis de Boissy*, Paris: Libraire E. Dentu, 1870

Breward, Christopher. *The Hidden Consumer*. Manchester: Manchester University Press, 1999

Buckle, Richard (ed.). *The Prettiest Girl in England*. London: John Murray, 1958

Camp, W. D. *Marriage and the Family in France Since the Revolution*. New York: Bookman Associates, 1961

Carlyle, Thomas. *Sartor Resartus*. World's Classics edn. Oxford: Oxford University Press, 1987

Cartmell, Robert. *The Incredible Scream Machine*. Amusement Park Books, Inc., 1987

Census Reports of Great Britain 1801–1931. London: HMSO, 1951

Chambers, L. *Married Women and Property Law in Victorian Ontario*. Toronto: Toronto University Press, 1997

Chancellor, E. Beresford. *Life in Regency and Early Victorian Times: An Account of Brummel and D'Orsay 1800–1850*. London: B.T. Batsford, 1933

de la Cheyne-Desbois and Badier. *Dictionnaire de la Noblesse*. 3rd edn. Nendeln, Lichtenstein: Kraus Reprint, 1969

Cobban, Alfred. *A History of Modern France*. 2 vols. London: Penguin, 1990–91

Cohen, J. M. (ed.). *Letters of Edward Fitzgerald*. London: Centaur Press, 1960

Connely, Willard. *Count D'Orsay*. London: Cassell & Co., 1952

de Contades, Comte Gerard. *Le Comte D'Orsay, Physiologie d'un Roi de la Mode*. Paris: Maison Quantin, 1890

Cronin, Vincent. *Napoleon*. London: Collins, 1971

Davies, Norman. *Europe – A History*. London: Pimlico, 1997

Dickens, Charles (ed.). *The Life of Charles James Mathews*, 2 vols. London: Macmillan & Co., 1879

Disraeli, Benjamin. *Henrietta Temple*. London: Peter Davies, 1927

Dodds, John W. *The Age of Paradox*. London: Victor Gollancz, 1953

Dupuy, Ernest. *Alfred de Vigny. La vie et l'oeuvre*. Paris: 1913

Dupuy, Ernest. *Alfred de Vigny: Ses Amitiés, son rôle littéraire*. 2 vols. Paris: Société Française d'Imprimerie et de librairie, 1910

Eisler, Benita. *Byron*. London: Hamish Hamilton, 1999

Favardin, Patrick & Brouëxière, Laurent. *Le Dandysme*. Lyon: La Manufacture, 1988

Fields, James, *Old Acquaintances. Barry Cornwall and Some of his Friends*, Boston: James R. Osgood and Company, 1876

Floud, R., Wachter, K. W. and Gregory, A. *Height, Health and History: Nutritional Status in the United Kingdom 1750–1980*. Cambridge: Cambridge University Press, 1990

Forster, John (ed.). *The Works and Life of Walter Savage Landor*. 8 vols. London: Chapman & Hall, 1876

Fyvie, John. *Noble Dames and Notable Men of the Georgian Era*. London: Constable & Co., 1910

Garelick, Rhonda K. *Rising Star: Dandyism, Gender and Performance in the Fin de Siècle*. New Jersey: Princeton University Press, 1998

Gash, Norman, *The Life of Sir Robert Peel after 1830*. London: Longman, 1972

Gigoux, J., *Causeries sur les Artistes de mon temps*. Paris: 1885

von Gleichen-Russwurm, Alexander. *Dandies and Don Juans*. New York & London: Alfred A. Knopf, 1928

Glueck Rosenthal, L., *Biographical Memoir of his late Royal Highness the Duke of Sussex*. Brighton: 1846

The Graham Stuart Thomas Rose Book, Oregon: Sagapress/Timber Press, 1994

Graves, Algernon. *Catalogue of the Works of the Late Sir Edwin Landseer*. London: Henry Graves & Co., 1875 de Grenville, Vicomte E. *Histoire du Journal La Mode*. Paris: 1861

Gronow, Captain. *Days of the Dandies*. 2 vols. London: The Grolier Society, n.d.

Guedalla, Philip. *The Second Empire. Bonapartism, the Prince, the President, the Emperor*. London: Constable & Co., 1922

Guest, Ivor. *Fanny Cerrito. The Life of a Ballerina*, London: Phoenix House, 1956

Guest, Ivor. 'Dandies and Dancers', in *Dance Perspectives*, No. 37, Spring, 1969

Hall F. S. A., Thornton. *Love Romances of the Aristocracy*. London: T. Werner Laurie, n.d.

Hayward, A., *The Art of Dining*. London: John Murray, 1883

Hibbert, Christopher. *Wellington*. London: HarperCollins, 1998

Hill, Anne. *Trelawny's Strange Relations*. Stanford: The Mill House Press, 1956

Hylton, Lord (ed.). *The Paget Brothers, 1790–1840*. London: John Murray, 1918

Lamington, Lord. *In the Days of the Dandies*. Edinburgh and London: William Blackwood & Sons, 1890

de Langlade, Jacques. *Lady Blessington et le Comte d'Orsay*. Paris: Editions Tallandier, 1987

Lebey, André. *Les Trois Coups d'Etat de Louis-Napoléon Bonaparte*. Paris: 1906

Lecomte, Maurice. *Le Prince des Dandys*. Paris: Librairie Alphonse Lemurre, 1928

Lennie, C. *Landseer – The Victorian Paragon*. London: Hamilton, 1976

Leslie, Doris. *Notorious Lady: The Life and Times of the Countess of Blessington*. London: William Heinemann, 1976

Lytton, The Right Honourable Lord. *Pelham or Adventures of a Gentleman*. New York: George Routledge & Sons, 1873

de Marcellus, Comte. *Chateaubriand et son temps*. Paris: Libraires Michel Lévy Frères, 1859

Markham Lester, V. *Victorian Insolvency*. Oxford: Clarendon Press, 1995

Maude, Mrs Raymond. *The Life of Jenny Lind*. London: Cassell & Co., 1926

Maurois, André (trans. S. C. Roberts). *Aspects of Biography*. Cambridge University Press, 1929

McLynn, Frank. *Napoleon*. London: Pimlico, 1998

du Mensil, Robert. *Notice historique sur Orsay*. Paris, 1888

Mills, John. *D'Horsay, or the Follies of the Day by a man of Fashion (John Mills); with an introductory sketch of Count D'Orsay's famous career*. London: Downey & Co., 1902

Moers, Ellen. *The Dandy*. London: Secker & Warburg, 1960

Molloy, Joseph, F. *The Most Gorgeous Lady Blessington*. London: The Grolier Society, n.d.

Monsarrat, Ann. *An Uneasy Victorian – Thackeray the Man*. London: Cassell & Co., 1980

Mottram, R. H. *Old England*. London and New York: The Studio, 1937

Murray, Venetia. *High Society in the Regency Period 1788–1830*. London: Penguin, 1999

Musée du Louvre, Cabinet des Dessins, *Les Collections du comte d'Orsay – dessins du Musée du Louvre LXXVIIIe exposition du Cabinet des Dessins, Musée du Louvre, 24 février–30 mai 1983*. Paris: Editions de la Réunion des Musées Nationaux, 1983

Nicoll, Sir William Robertson and Wise, Thomas James (eds.). *Literary Anecdotes of the Nineteenth Century. Contributions Towards a Literary History of the Period*. 2 vols. London: Hodder & Stoughton, 1895

Nicolson, Harold. *Byron*. London: Prion, 1999

Nisbet Bain, R., *Hans Christian Andersen, A Biography*. London, Lawrence & Bullen, 1895

Office municipal pour les loisirs et la culture. *Orsay. D'un Village d'Antan . . . aux Techniques de Demain*. France: Maury, 1986

Ormond, R. (ed.). *Sir Edwin Landseer*. London: Tate, 1982

Paris, Marcellus Comte de. *Châteaubriand et Son Temps*. Paris: Librairies Michel Lévy Frères, 1859

Pine, Richard. *The Dandy and the Herald: Manners, Mind and Morals from Brummell to Durrel*. Basingstoke: Macmillan, 1988

Poirson, Philippe. *Walewski, fils de Napoléon*. Paris: Editions Balzac, 1943

Pressnell, L. S. *Country Banking in the Industrial Revolution*. Oxford: Clarendon Press, 1956

de Puy, Henry Walter. *Louis Napoleon and his Times: with notices of his writings; a memoir of the Bonaparte family; and a sketch of French history*. Buffalo: Phinney & Co., 1852.

Quennell, Marjorie and C. H. B. *A History of Everyday Things in England*. Vol III. London: B. T. Batsford, 1961

Quennell, Peter (ed.). *Genius in the Drawing Room*. London: Weidenfeld & Nicolson, 1980

Randell, Keith. *France: Monarchy, Republic and Empire, 1814–70*. London: Hodder & Stoughton, 1991

Ridley, Jane. *The Young Disraeli*. London: Sinclair-Stevenson, 1995

Ritter, Raymond. *La Maison de Gramont 1040–1967*. 2 vols. Lourdes: Les Amis du Musée Pyrénéen, 1962

Rolle, Serge-Fortis. *Le Beau d'Orsay*. Paris: Juillard, 1978

Sadleir, Michael. *A Biography of Marguerite, Countess of Blessington and D'Orsay. A Masquerade*. London: Constable & Co., 1933

Seilière, E., *George Sand, Mystique de la Passion*. Paris: 1920

de Sereville, E. and de Saint Simon, F., *Dictionnaire de la Noblesse Française*, Paris: Editions Contrepoint, 1977

Shattuck, C. H. (ed.). *Bulwer and Macready. A Chronicle of the Early Victorian Theatre*. Urbana: University of Illinois Press, 1958

Six, Georges. *Dictionnaire Biographique des Généraux et Amiraux Français de la Révolution et de l'Empire 1792–1814*. 2 vols. Paris: G. Saffroy, 1934

Staël von Holstein, Baron. *Fürst Paul Lieven als Landmarschall von Livland*. Riga: 1906

Stanton, D. C. *The Aristocrat as Art: a study of the honnete homme and the dandy in 17th century and 19th century literature*. New York: Columbia University Press, 1980

Stephen, Sir Leslie and Lee, Sir Sidney (eds.). *Dictionary of National Biography*. Oxford: Oxford University Press, 1975

Stigler, Stephen M. *The History of Statistics – The Measurement of Uncertainty before 1900*. Cambridge, Massachussets: Harvard University Press, 1986

Stirling, Monica, *The Wild Swan – The Life and Times of Hans Christian Andersen*. London: Collins, 1965

Teignmouth Shore, W. *D'Orsay or The Complete Dandy*. London: John Long, 1911

Tinterow, Gary and Conisbee, Philip (eds.). *Portraits by Ingrès*. New York: Metropolitan Museum of Modern Art, 1999

Vincent, Leon Henry. *Dandies and Men of Letters*. London and Cambridge, Massachusetts: Duckworth & Co., 1914

Warnock, Mary. 'The Morality of Money'. In a programme for the National Theatre Ensemble's performance of *Money* by Edward Bulwer Lytton in 1999

Wheen, Francis. *Karl Marx*. London: Fourth Estate, 2000

Wilson, David Alec. *Carlyle on Cromwell and Others (1837–48)*. London: 1925

Wullschlager, Jackie. *Hans Christian Andersen*. London: Allen Lane, Penguin Press, 2000

Books by Count d'Orsay, Countess d'Orsay and Lady Blessington

Blessington, The Countess of. *Conversations with Lord Byron*. Boston: William Veazie, 1859

Bibliography

Blessington, The Countess of. *The Idler in France.* 2 vols. London: Henry Colburn, 1841

Blessington, The Countess of. *The Idler in Italy.* 3 vols. London: Henry Colburn, 1839, 1840

Blessington, The Countess of. *Victims of Society.* Philadelphia: Carey, Lea & Blanchard, 1837

Gardiner, Marguerite, Countess of Blessington. *Country Quarters. A Novel. With a Memoir by her Niece, Miss Power.* 3 vols. London: 1850

d'Orsay, Alfred G. *Reminiscences of the Opera.* London: Hurst & Blacket, 1864

d'Orsay, Alfred (or Charles W. Day). *Etiquette; or, a guide to The Usages of Society. With a glance at Bad Habits.* New York: Wilson & Co., 1843

d'Orsay, The Countess. *Clouded Happiness, A Novel.* Translated from the French. London: James & Henry Vizetelly, 1852

Holland House

Hudson, Derek. *Holland House in Kensington.* London: Peter Davies, 1967

Kimber, Thomas. *Students' casual papers. Holland House.* London, Blackheath: 1857

London County Council. *Miscellaneous Publications, Holland House, Holland Park.* 3rd edition, London: 1959

Strangways, Giles Stephen Holland Fox, Earl of Ilchester. *Chronicles of Holland House,* 1820–1900. London: John Murray, 1937

London; London Clubs; Racing; Tailors; Style and Fashion

Adburgham, Alison. *Shopping in Style.* London: Thames & Hudson, 1979

Adburgham, Alison. *Silver Fork Society. Fashionable Life and Literature.* London: Constable, 1983

Bennett-England, Rodney. *Dress Optional.* London: Peter Owen, 1967

Blyth, Henry. *Hell & Hazard.* London: Weidenfeld & Nicolson, 1969

Chancellor, E. Beresford. *Knightsbridge and Belgravia. Their History, Topography and Famous Inhabitants.* London: Sir Isaac Pitman & Sons, 1909

Chenoune, Farid (trans. Deke Flammarion). *A History of Men's Fashion.* Paris: Dusinberre, 1993

Cowell, F. R. *The Athenaeum Club and Social Life in London, 1824–1974.* London: Heinemann, 1975

Cunnington, C. Willett. *The Art of English Costume,* London: Collins, 1948

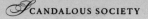

Denny, B. and Starren, C. *Kensington Past*. London: Historical Publications, 1998

Escott, T. H. S. *Club Makers and Club Members*. London: T. Fisher Unwin, 1914

Ford, John. *Ackermann 1783–1983, The Business of Art*. London: Ackermann, 1983

Fox, Celina (ed.). *London: World City 1800–1840*. New Haven and London: Yale University Press, 1992

Gladstone, Florence and Barker, Ashley. *Notting Hill in Bygone Days*. London: Ann Bingley, 1969

Graves, Charles. *Leather Armchairs*. London: Cassell, 1963

Harling, Robert. *The London Miscellany. A Nineteenth Century Scrapbook*. London: William Heinemann, 1937

Humphreys, A. L. *Crockford's*. London: Hutchinson, 1953

Jesse, J. H. *Literary and Historical Memorials of London*. London, 1847

Jesse, J. H. *London: its Celebrated Characters and Remarkable Places*. London: Richard Bentley & Son, 1871

LeJeune, Anthony. *The Gentlemen's Clubs of London*. London: Parkgate Books, 1984

Luttrell, Henry. *Crockford House, a Rhapsody*. London: John Murray, 1827

MacCausland, Hugh. *The English Carriage*. London: the Batchworth Press, 1948

Margetson, Stella. *Leisure and Pleasure in the Nineteenth Century*. Newton Abbot: the Victorian (& Modern History) Book Club, 1971

Montizambert, E. *Unnoticed London*. London: J. M. Dent & Sons, 1922

Nevill, R. *Light Come, Light Go*. London: Macmillan & Co., 1909

Nevill, R. *London Clubs. Their History and Treasures*. London: Chatto & Windus, 1911

O'London, John. *London Stories*, Part 9 and 13. London, n.d.

Orchard, Vincent. *Tattersalls: Two Hundred Years of Sporting History*. London: Hutchinson, 1953

Porter, Roy. *London*. London: Penguin, 1996

Sheppard, Francis. *London 1808–1870: the Infernal Wen*. London: Secker & Warburg, 1971

Sheppard. F. H. W. (ed.). *Survey of London*. Vol. XXXVIII. London: The Athlone Press, 1975

Smith, J. T. *The Antiquarian Ramble in the Streets of London*. Vol. I. 2nd edn. London: 1846

Walford, Edward. *Old and New London*. 6 vols. London: Cassell & Co., 1880

Bibliography

Walker, Annabel with Jackson, Peter. *Kensington and Chelsea*. London: Murray, 1987

Walker, Richard. *The Savile Row Story: An Illustrated History*. London: Prion, 1988

Watney, Marylian. *The Elegant Carriage*. London: J. A. Allen & Co., 1961

Waugh, Nora. *The Cut of Men's Clothes*. London: Faber & Faber, 1964

Weinreb, Ben & Hibbert, Christopher (ed.). *London Encyclopaedia*. London: Macmillan, 1995

Weiss, Barbara. *The Hell of the English: Bankruptcy and the Victorian Novel*. New Jersey and London: Associated University Presses, 1986

Wroth, Warwick. *Cremorne and the Later London Gardens*. London: Elliot Stock, 1907

Guns

Beaumont, Richard. *Purdey's: The Guns and the Family*. London: David & Charles, 1991

Billett, Michael. *A History of English Country Sports*. London: Robert Hale, 1994

Greener, W. W. *The Gun and Its Development*. 9th edition. London: Arms and Armour, 1972

Lugs, Jaroslav. *Firearms Past and Present*, London: Grenville Publishing, 1975

Wilkenson-Latham, R. *Antique Guns in Colour to 1865*. Poole: Blandford Press, 1977

Wilkinson, F. *Sporting Guns. An Illustrated Reference Guide*. London: Arms and Armour, 1984

Journals

Athenaeum

The *Age*

Annual Register

Fraser's Magazine for Town and Country, vol. X, no. LX, 'Gallery of Literary Characters'.

Gentleman's Magazine, September 1852, 'Obituaries', pp. 308–10

Household Words. A Weekly Journal. Conducted by Charles Dickens, vol. II, No. 176, August, 1853

Metropolitan Magazine

Newsletter of the Disraeli Project, Queens University Ontario, Canada, 1976, vol. 1, 2; 1977, vol. 2, 2; 1978, vol. 3, 1; 1979, vol. 4, 2; 1980, vol. 5, 1 and 2

Quarterly Review

Revue de Paris, November 1968, 'Dickens and d'Orsay'; May 1969, 'George Sand and d'Orsay'; November 1969, 'Disraeli and d'Orsay'

The *Satirist* (all issues published)

The Times

Poems in Books

Browning, Robert. *The Poetical Works of Robert Browning*. London: Smith, Elder & Co., 1888–1894

Dobson, Henry Austin. *Collected Poems*. London: Kegan Paul, Trench, Trübner & Co., 1913

Gaultier, Bon (ed.). *The Book of Ballads*. London: William S. Orr & Co., 1849

Gilbert, W.S. *The Bab Ballads*, New York: Routledge & Sons, 1898

Hunt, Thornton (ed.). *The Poetical Work of Leigh Hunt*. New York: Routledge, 1860

Ingoldsby, Thomas. *The Ingoldsby Lyrics*. London: Richard Bentley, 1881

Ingoldsby, Thomas. *The Ingoldsby Legends or Mirth and Marvels*. London: Richard Bentley, 1840

McGann, Jerome J. *Lord Byron, Selected Poetry*. Oxford: Oxford University Press, 1998

Unpublished Manuscripts and Sources

Bibliothèque Thiers
Documents relating to the Grimod d'Orsay family

The British Library
The Peel Papers, Lord Holland to Mrs Fazakerley, letters from Lady Blessington and d'Orsay
Centre Historique des Archives Nationales, Paris
Documents relating to d'Orsay

Durham Record Office
D'Orsay's correspondence with Lord Londonderry

Bibliography

The Harrowby Manuscript Trust
Letters to and from d'Orsay

Henry E. Huntingdon Library
Letters to and from Lady Blessington, Harriet, Countess d'Orsay and d'Orsay

Kensington & Chelsea Public Libraries
Collection of Miss F. M. Gladstone. Material Relating to the Bayswater Hippodrome

Lambton Park
Letters from d'Orsay

Mulgrave Castle Archives
Lady Blessington's correspondence with Lord Normanby

The National Archives of Ireland
Leases, deeds 9686 & 9688

The National Art Library
Letters by d'Orsay

National Library of Scotland
Letters from d'Orsay

New York Public Library
The R. H. Madden Collection

Norfolk Record Office
Heydon and Knebworth papers

Pierpont Morgan Library, New York
Letters to and from Lady Blessington and d'Orsay

Private Collection of His Grace the Duke of Beaufort
Letters from d'Orsay

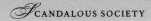

Public Record Office, Kew
Letters from d'Orsay

Public Record Office of Northern Ireland
Howard Bury/Lord Tullamore papers

The Science Museum
Ledgers of Barker and Company, Coachbuilders, Reel B35

Trinity College Library
Letters to and from Lady Blessington and d'Orsay

University of Edinburgh Library
Letters to Lady Blessington

University of Harvard Library
Houghton MS 1272 – Landseer d'Orsay correspondence

University of Iowa Library
Letter by Nathaniel Willis Parker and one by Barry Cornwall to Lady
    Blessington

University of Nottingham Library
Marlay Papers

Index

AD: Alfred d'Orsay
Lady B: Lady Blessington

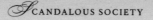

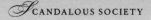

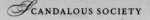

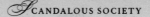